HISTORICAL PROBLEMS OF IMPERIAL AFRICA

Problems in African History

VOLUME I
The Precolonial Centuries
edited by
Robert O. Collins and Ruth Iyob

VOLUME II
Historical Problems of Imperial Africa
edited by
James M. Burns and Robert O. Collins

VOLUME III
Problems in the History of Modern Africa
edited by
Robert O. Collins, James McDonald Burns,
Erik Kristofer Ching, and Kathleen S. Hasselblad

Historical Problems of Imperial Africa

UPDATED AND REVISED EDITION

Edited by
JAMES M. BURNS
and
ROBERT O. COLLINS

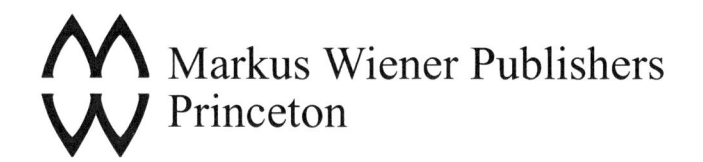

Markus Wiener Publishers
Princeton

Copyright © 2014 by Markus Wiener Publishers for the updated and revised edition

Copyright © 1994 and 2007 by Robert O. Collins

All rights reserved. No part of this book may be reproduced or transmitted in any form or by any means, whether electronic or mechanical—including photocopying or recording—or through any information storage or retrieval system, without permission of the copyright owners.

For information write to:
Markus Wiener Publishers, Inc.
231 Nassau St., Princeton, New Jersey 08542
www.markuswiener.com

Cover illustration: Henry Morton Stanley exploring the Congo. With King Leopold II of Belgium, he largely invented the country known as the Belgian Congo. (Detail of an image by C. L. Doughty.)

Map design: The maps were drawn by Jason Simpson and Michele Aurand under the leadership of Professor David Lanter of the Department of Geography at the University of California, Santa Barbara, and the Director of the Digital Cartography Laboratory at UCSB

Library of Congress Cataloguing-in-Publication Data

ISBN 978-1-55876-584-9 (alk. paper)

Markus Wiener Publishers books are printed in the United States of America on acid-free paper and meet the guidelines for permanence and durability of the Committee on Production Guidelines for Book Longevity of the Council on Library Resources.

Dedication

To Bob Collins, a scholar, teacher, and friend

Contents

Introduction to the Updated and Revised Edition ix
By James M. Burns

Maps
Europe in Africa on the Eve of Partition: 1884 xiii
Missionaries and Explorers in Africa Prior to the Partition xiv
African States on the Eve of Partition: 1884 xv
Africa in 1914 264

Problem I. The Partition of Africa 1
Robinson and Gallagher: Egypt and the Partition of Africa 4
Cain and Hopkins: Britain and the Partition of Africa 9
Darwin: Imperialism and the Victorians 17
Headrick: Malaria, Quinine, and the Penetration of Africa 23
Adas: Africa: Primitive Tools and the Savage Mind 30
Suggested Readings 39

Problem II. Colonial Rule in Africa 41
Lugard: Principles of Native Administration 45
Collins: Indirect Rule Sudan Style 57
Deschamps: Association and Indirect Rule 64
Berry: Hegemony on a Shoestring 75
Mamdani: Indirect Rule 84
Gordon: Colonial Chiefs in the Borderlands of Northern
    Rhodesia and the Belgian Congo 91
Suggested Readings 99

Problem III. Colonial Rule and Ethnic Identity 101
Southall: The Illusion of Tribe 104
Vail: Ethnicity in Southern African History 120
Ranger: The Invention of Tradition 131
Peel: The Making of the Yoruba 145
Hamilton: Shaka Zulu and the Limits of Historical Intervention 151
Suggested Readings 157

Problem IV. Colonialism and the African Environment 159
Beinart: African History and Environmental History 162
Vail: Ecology and History: The Example of Eastern Zambia 171
Fairhead and Leach: Misreading the African Landscape 182
McGregor: Conservation, Control, and Ecological Change 190
Tilley: Africa as a Living Laboratory 202
Suggested Readings 215

Problem V. African Nationalism 217
Fanon: National Consciousness 220
Ranger: Early Nationalism in East and Central Africa 229
Kilson: Nationalism in Sierra Leone 239
Berman: Nationalism and Mau Mau 247
Davidson: The Black Man's Burden 257
Suggested Readings 263

Problem VI. Exploitation or Development? 265
Gann and Duignan: The Burden of Empire 268
Fieldhouse: The Myth of Economic Exploitation 277
Crowder: The Economic Impact of Colonial Rule in West Africa 285
Rodney: How Europe Underdeveloped Africa 292
Boahen: The Colonial Impact 302
Austin: African Economic Development and Colonial Legacies 310
Suggested Readings 323

Acknowledgments 325

Introduction to the
Updated and Revised Edition

This volume was first published as *Problems in the History of Colonial Africa* by Robert O. Collins in 1970. In 1994, it was my privilege as a graduate student to help Bob revise the text for the first time in a quarter century. With Bob's passing in 2008, I'm honored to once again revise and update the collection. The original idea for the series emerged naturally from Bob's approach to teaching African history. He was fascinated by the historiographical debates that energized our field and sought to share them with students beyond his classroom. The initial two volumes focused on the pre-colonial and the colonial, as in 1970 there was barely a post-colonial to consider. But today some African countries have been independent almost as long as they were colonies, and thus the series has been expanded to three volumes.

Calling these books the "Problems" series will be seen by some readers as somewhat problematic. The West's vision of Africa is that of a continent in a state of constant crisis, and such a title threatens to subtly reinforce such a perspective. If the series were beginning today, instead of the late 1960s, perhaps another title—"Debates in African History," for example—would have been preferred. But the books have been known by students and teachers alike as the "Problems" series for more than forty years, and thus, as a tribute to Bob's original concept, it remains.

As ideas about Africa have changed, so too have the pressing historical problems. Several of the topics of the original edition have been replaced here by newer historiographical debates, while others have been updated to reflect recent scholarship. Such revisions reflect the dynamism of the field of African history.

This updated volume, like the original published four decades ago, begins, in Problem I, by exploring the debate surrounding the European conquest of Africa in the late nineteenth century. The "scramble for Africa" was one of the great diplomatic puzzles of the century. Before 1881, Europe's relationship with Africa had been characterized by what one scholar has termed "the Empire of Free Trade." For centuries, Europeans had extracted what they desired from Africa without risking the hazards and expense of conquest and colonization. Then suddenly, between 1878 and 1900, the major powers of Europe embarked on a frenzied partition of the continent. Why, after centuries of equilibrium, had the balance between Europe and Africa shifted so rapidly? It was a subject of great debate at the time, and is a question that has continued to fascinate historians. Forty years ago most scholars focused their attention on the specific goals and motivations of the various colonial powers. But a generation later the debate has shifted, and the readings focus on the broader impulses that made imperialism suddenly attractive to these powers. These essays explore the roles of diplomacy, technology, finance, and African actors in the process. The "problem" of the partition is no longer one of personal motives, but rather a question as to which particular trends in global history sparked such aggressive colonial policies.

Once conquered, African colonies presented European authorities with an enormous administrative challenge. Western politicians had promised their publics that colonies in Africa would be economic as well as strategic assets, making it difficult to justify large expenditures on the new colonies. This forced new African administrations to pay for themselves, encouraging a policy of empire "on the cheap." Because of the high costs of attracting Europeans to live and work in the tropics, colonial administrations would always be staffed by a remarkably small number of Europeans. Faced with the enormous task of ruling millions of new subjects in some of the earth's most challenging and remote environments, the great powers recruited Africans leaders to serve as their intermediaries with the masses. The British popularized an administrative philosophy they dubbed "indirect rule," which aspired to shelter African communities from disruptive and harmful aspects of Western influence by allowing them to be ruled by their traditional leaders. On the one hand, indirect rule implied the concept of trusteeship, a sense of global responsibility to vulnerable peoples that would be popularized thereafter through the creation of the League of Nations, and later the United Nations. On the other, indirect rule was regarded as an expedient approach to imperial administration that acted as a brake on cultural and economic progress.

Indirect rule was predicated on the assumption that there were fundamental differences between Africans and Europeans that necessitated that they be ruled separately, an idea which became manifest most apparently in the Apartheid state of South Africa. On the other hand, the policy of "Assimilation," as articulated by the French and Portuguese, sought to rule African communities directly, rather than through traditional authorities. This appeared to discount, or at least downplay, the innate differences between Europeans and Africans, and had the potential to integrate Africans into European political and cultural life. The idea of "a hundred million Frenchmen" in Africa struck a chord in the French tradition that originated among the philosophers of the eighteenth century. But assimilation's critics regarded it as a demeaning policy which threatened to eradicate African cultures.

These approaches were fine in theory, but how did they actually function on the ground? Did indirect rule recruit "traditional" African leaders, or invent leadership to suit its administrative purposes? Did assimilation actually create

Africans who were French in outlook? Or did French administrators succumb to the same logistical challenges facing their British rivals, and resort to their own version of "indirect rule?" And what is the legacy of these colonial administrations for post-colonial African nations? Do the challenges of modern African politics flow directly from the administrative policies of the colonial era? These are questions that politicians, civil servants, and academics have been exploring for nearly a century. Problem II provides a representative sample of the contributions to this debate.

All colonial officials took it as an article of faith that their new charges lived in tribal communities. Indeed, this assumption was the building block of indirect rule, as the legitimacy of the "traditional" ruler was rooted in their tribal identity. Problem III explores the historical debate surrounding the use of this term in the colonial era. Did Africans see themselves as living in distinct, immutable, "tribal" communities at the time of the conquest? Did indirect rule tap into pre-existing forms of tribal identity in administering its subjects? Or was the idea of "tribe" a construct by pragmatic colonial officials? If tribes were created, imagined, or invented, then by whom, and to what end? Problem III looks at the robust debate about tribal identity and the colonial state. It demonstrates that, while there is a strong consensus among contemporary scholars that tribal identities only gained currency during the colonial era, there is a wide degree of disagreement as to how this came to be.

Problem IV explores the impact of colonial rule on the African environment. Since the original *Problems* volume was published four decades ago, historians have become increasingly aware of the ways in which the relationship between human communities and nature has shaped global history. In this chapter, several scholars—all writing relatively recently—explore the influence and legacy of colonial policies on nature. Did colonialism significantly restructure the ecology of Africa? Or are the profound transformations in the African environment the results of deeper historical processes? The excerpts in this chapter provide several different views of these questions.

It could be argued that nationalism was the most baleful inheritance bequeathed by Europe to Africa. In the name of the nation-state, colonies, whose boundaries had been arbitrarily drawn without relevance to the ethnic or geographical realities of Africa, became independent countries. It was the African *elite* who rose after independence to defend these new borders and the political order left by their former rulers. A generation has passed since the plethora of states emerged from the ruins of imperial Africa. They remain virtually unchanged in their configuration to this day. Over the past half century, the national interest has been invoked to justify the suppression of civil liberties and the exploitation and persecution of ethnic minorities. Problem V looks at the debates about African nationalism that emerged in the wake of the Second World War. Before the war, the ambition of most politically aware Africans was to earn social and legal equality within colonial society. But after 1945, educated Africans became increasingly clamorous for independence from Europe altogether. They articulated their demands for democracy, free speech, and political autonomy in the language used by European nationalists of the eighteenth and nineteenth centuries. In the brief span of a quarter century, the independence of African colonies had gone from unimaginable to inevitable. This dramatic and abrupt process has posed to scholars several important questions. Which social groups gave these movements their influence? What were the goals of these groups? How did the process of making the African nation compare to similar movements in Europe? Did such movements reflect authentic expressions of African mass politics? Or the manipulations of a handful of elites? Or are they best understood as the byproduct of a confused and hurried process that saw colonizer and colonized alike stumbling towards an unlikely and unexpected destination? The scholars excerpted in this chapter emphasize different aspects of the process.

The history of imperial Africa is characterized by its brevity. Compared to the millennia of the pre-colonial African past, the age of the imperialists is but a historical fragment in time. Some territories, like the pre-colonial kingdom of Benin, were part of an empire for barely six decades. Nevertheless, Europeans brought profound economic changes to their African colonies. Problem VI provides an overview of scholarly evaluations of the economic impact of colonial rule in Africa. One of the most scathing denunciations of imperialism has been the accusation that Europeans exploited the continent for their own benefit. This perception remains deeply rooted among many Africans today, and has been shared widely by European liberals, socialists, Marxists, and humanitarians. The imperialists were outraged at these charges. What critics regarded as exploitation, they argued, was in fact the introduction of civilization in Africa through the development of its human and material resources symbolized by schools, hospitals, railroads, roads, bridges, buildings, dams, and agricultural schemes, all for the purpose of bringing the African subsistence economy into the international market economy. This chapter contains selections from scholars who bitterly condemn colonial economic policies, from others who defend them vehemently, and from still others who find a middle ground between these opposing interpretations.

Taken together, these problems introduce the reader to some of the most vibrant and contentious debates in African studies. They are "problems" in that they are important questions, whose solutions promise to shed light on the contemporary experience of African peoples. But they are also intellectual debates that reflect the dynamism and vigor of the field of African studies, and indeed, of the historical profession.

James M. Burns
Clemson, South Carolina

Europe in Africa on the Eve of Partition: 1884

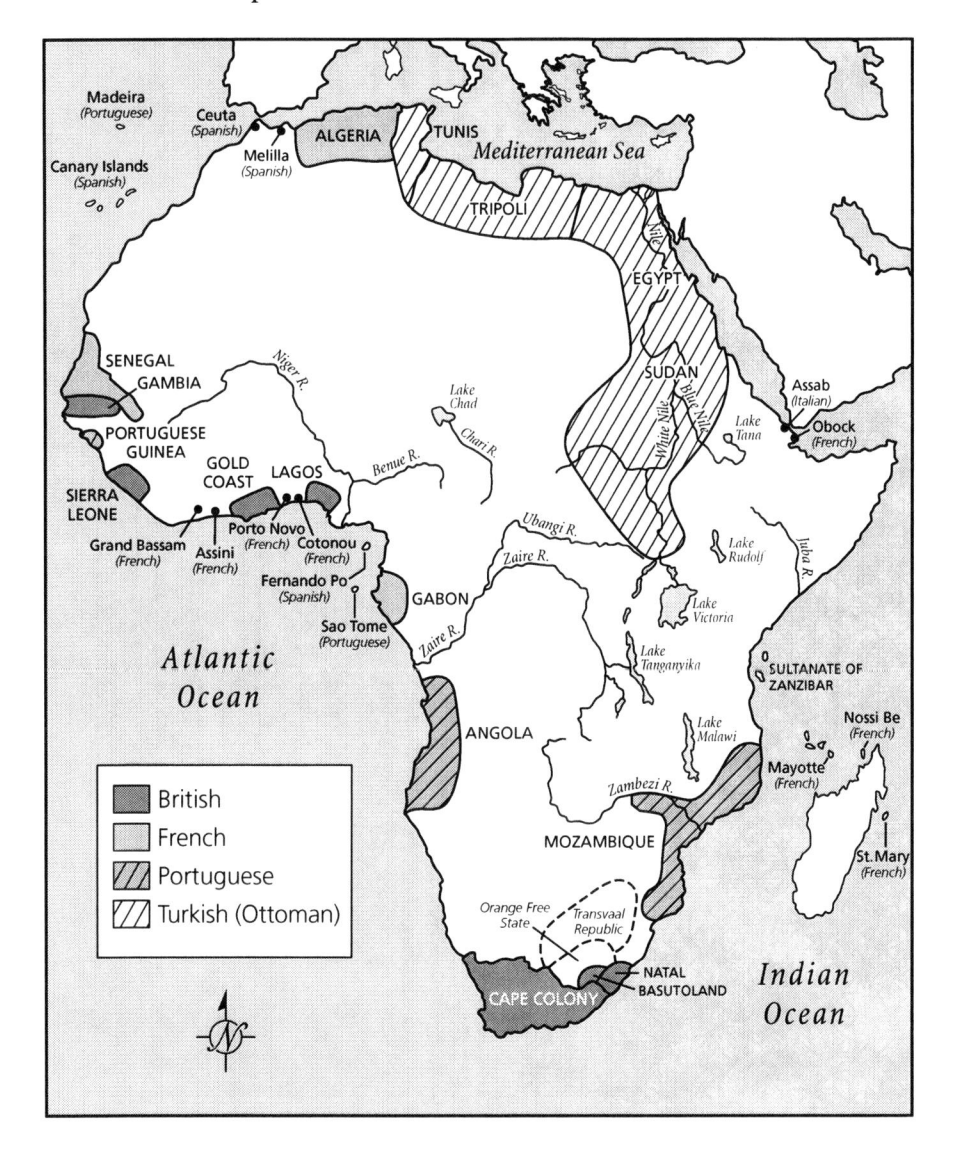

Missionaries and Explorers in Africa Prior to the Partition

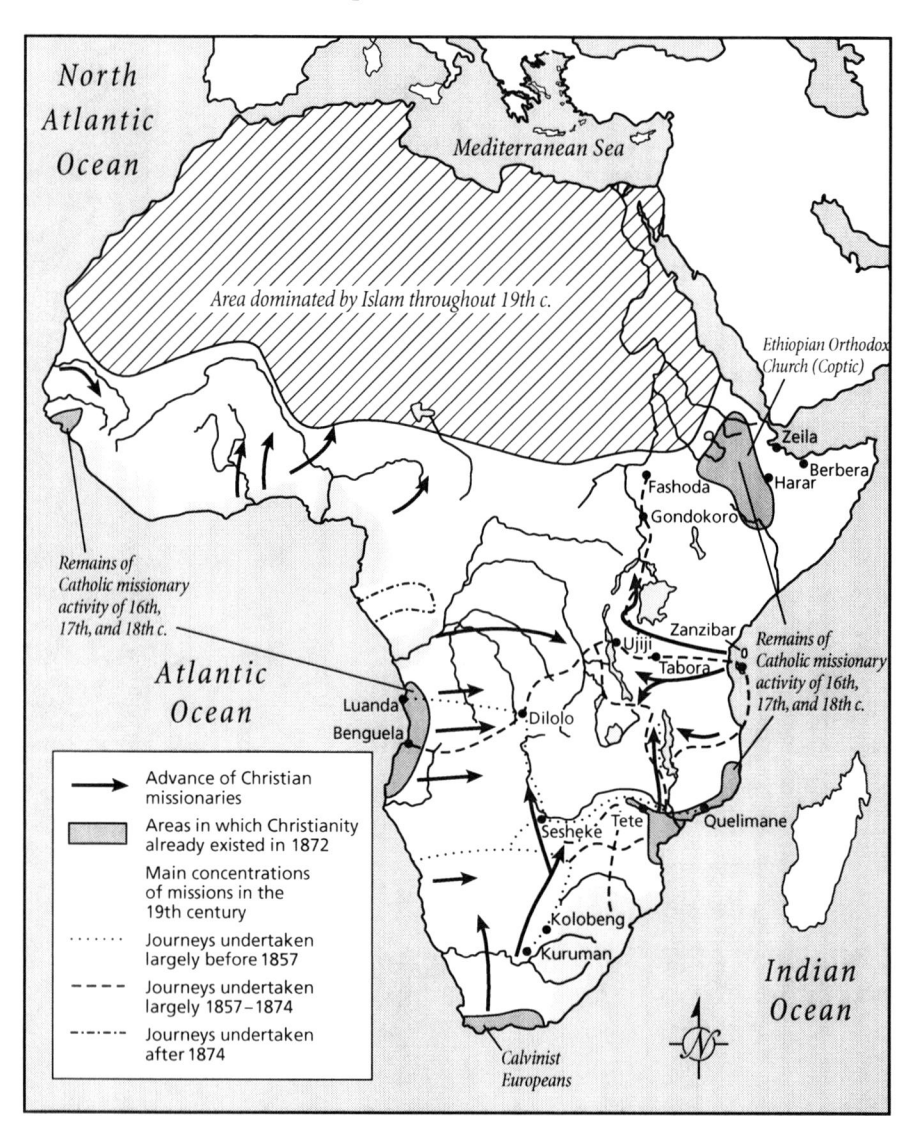

African States on the Eve of Partition: 1884

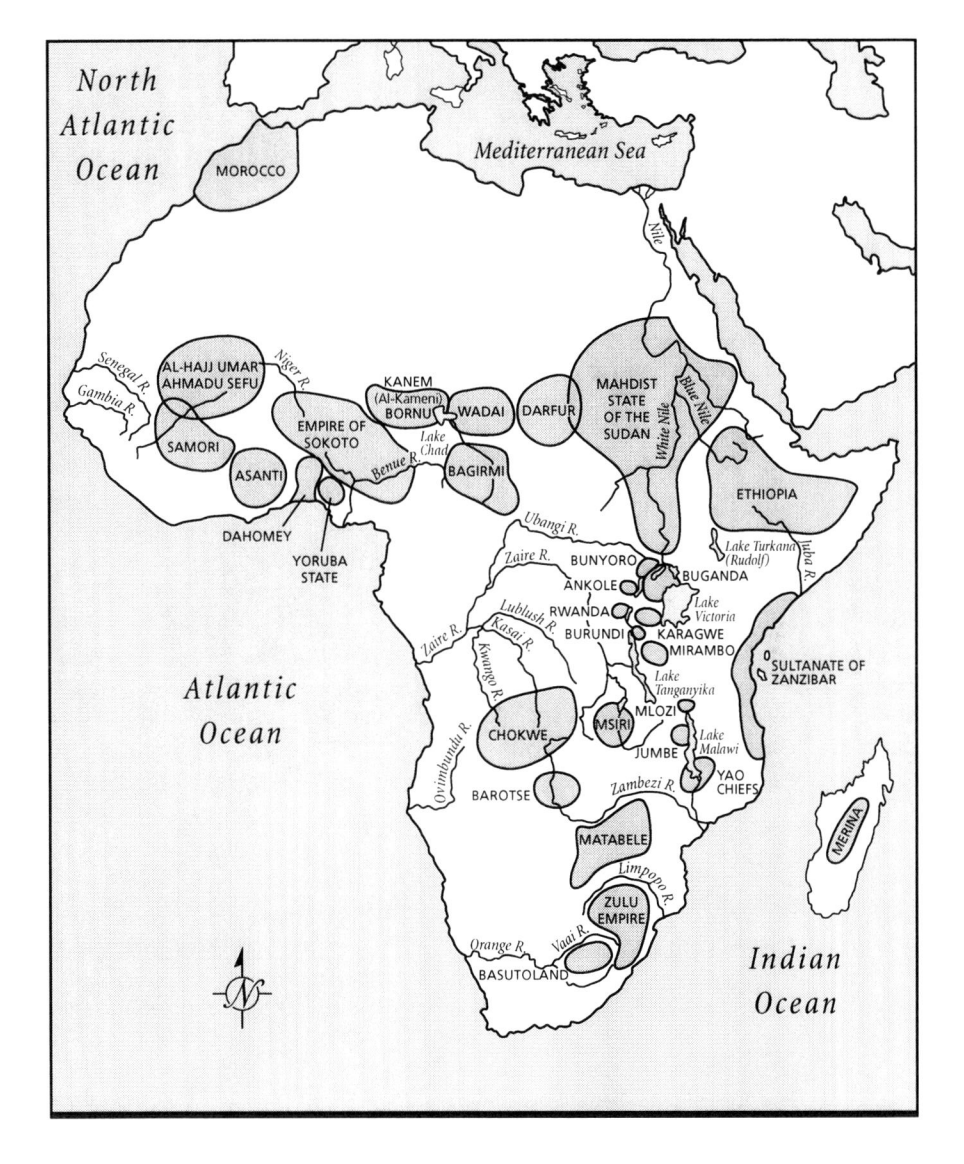

PROBLEM I

THE PARTITION OF AFRICA

During four centuries of commerce with Africa, the European powers had been content to restrict their activities to scattered coastal trading stations, which passed from one state to another as the balance of power shifted. In the nineteenth century, European explorers journeyed into the interior and opened the enormous hinterland of Africa; yet no European government rushed to follow in their footsteps. Missionaries began to venture into the interior from the coastal enclaves, but they rarely regarded themselves as agents of their imperial governments. Merchants expanded their trade, but they remained focused on profit rather than conquest or occupation. By 1870, the presence of missionaries, merchants, and explorers had cleared the way for the expansion of Europe in Africa. But nothing in history is inevitable until it occurs, and despite this growing relationship with Africa, European rulers expressed little interest in African colonies as the century entered its final decades. Then suddenly, beginning after 1880, within less than twenty years, the continent was conquered and divided amidst rising national feeling at home and increasing belligerency abroad. Why? To scholar and student alike, this is the problem of the partition of Africa. As with many historiographical questions, this is a debate not about events, but about emphasis.

What had triggered this sudden rush for colonies? Historians Ronald Robinson and John Gallagher find the answer in the strategic diplomacy of the great powers. Britain's expansion into Africa was a defensive response to perceived threats to its link with its valuable colony of India. Before 1881, the governments of Britain and France had agreed not to permit the quarrels of their traders and officials along the coasts of Africa to justify imperial expansion. The British occupation of Egypt in 1882 destroyed this Anglo-French collaboration and strengthened the elements in French political and military circles who wanted to conquer African colonies, which could be used to put pressure on the British presence in Cairo. Soon, on the Niger and the Congo, French officials and explorers were active, and British attempts to enlist the Portuguese and the Belgian King Leopold in order to check the French soon proved abortive. Moreover, Britain's occupation of Egypt provided the German Chancellor Bismarck with the opportunity to exacerbate Anglo-French differences while carving out an African empire for Germany. From every European capital the Egyptian affair had seemed to precipitate the scramble for Africa.

In emphasizing the strategic imperative of British imperialism, Robinson and Gallagher broke with an older school of scholarship that had ascribed African imperialism to the Industrial Revolution, which sent Europe's newly capitalist powers in search of raw materials and captive markets. Robinson and Gallagher studied the "official mind"—that is, the correspondence of the policy-makers who supervised the diplomatic partition of Africa—to determine their true motivations. In these documents, Robinson and Gallagher found that statesmen were primarily concerned with the defense of British India. In 1881, when a nationalist revolt in Egypt threatened the security of the newly opened Suez Canal, the government acted to quell the rebellion and support the pliable Egyptian Khedive. Worried by Britain's sudden occupation of Egypt, French authorities turned to African annexations with an eye towards forcing Britain to abandon Egypt. This set off a chain reaction, as other great powers began seizing African territories, in large part to forestall the claims of their rivals.

Since its initial publication in 1961, *Africa and the Victorians* has shaped subsequent discussions of African imperialism. The most influential response to their argument was published by P.J. Cain and A.G. Hopkins, economic historians who produced a sweeping history of the British empire in 1993. Cain and Hopkins, speaking of the assertion that it was a crisis in Egypt that drew Britain (and subsequently, much of Europe) into Africa, asserted, "To claim that imperialism was the result of crises on the periphery is to report the symptoms, not diagnose the cause." To Cain and Hopkins, the "official mind" of imperialism disguises the close, unspoken relationship between the British civil servants and politicians who pulled the levers of conquest, and the financial interests of the London banking and services industry. It was the interests of this "gentlemanly capitalism," as they termed it, which guided the conquest of territories all over the world and influenced British "informal empire" in many others.

But Robinson and Gallagher's argument for the significance of strategic motives continues to have its defenders. Imperial historian John Darwin argues that their thesis has a greater explanatory value in understanding the scramble than Cain and Hopkins' "Gentlemanly Capitalism." Like Robinson and Gallagher, Darwin views British statesmen such as Lord Salisbury, not the forces of finance, as the driving force behind imperial conquests. But to Darwin, the "official mind" did not follow a clear and consistent policy, but rather "continually relapsed into its habitual schizophrenia" forced upon it by the diverse interests making demands upon it. These included both strategic imperatives and the interests of British finance. But they also involved political lobbies that forced politicians and civil servants to take an interest in new acquisitions throughout the globe. Ultimately, Darwin asserts that over-arching theories of African imperialism must permit for nuance and local variations. As he says of *Africa and the Victorians*, "For all its attractions, the influential model in which a platonic official mind reluctantly licenses defensive annexations when the national interest is threatened by local crisis on the periphery needs modification if it is to explain the global pattern of Victorian expansion." But nor does he accept the Cain and Hopkins alternative: "But it is doubtful whether its defects can be remedied by locating the whole impetus for expansion in the metropole or in the single-minded promotion of a particular interest, however powerful, by a like-minded oligarchy of gentlemen capitalists."

The final two authors represented here are less interested in the imperial motives than the context that permitted European conquest. Daniel Headrick demonstrates that technological innovations and medical discoveries after 1870 made the expansion of European empire less expensive and less dangerous worldwide. Writing here about Africa, Headrick asserts that disease had been one of the principal factors confining Europeans to the continent's shores before 1875. Malaria, in particular, had given West Africa the nickname "the White Man's Graveyard." The discovery of new drugs that could stave off or mitigate the symptoms of malaria opened a new chapter in Europe's relationship with Africa. Neither Robinson and Gallagher's "official mind" or Cain and Hopkins' "Gentlemanly Capitalism" could have sparked an imperial rush until Europeans had developed strategies for dealing with these dangerous diseases.

In a similar vein, Michael Adas shows how the growing technological disparity between the West and Africa that developed during the nineteenth century encouraged Europeans to think about Africans in a way that made imperialism justifiable. As the Industrial Revolution produced increasingly sophisticated technologies, Europeans became more inclined to view Africans as primitive and savage. Adas doesn't discuss per se the motives or process of imperial conquest. But he identifies the changing mind-set that made the conquest of Africa acceptable in the eyes of Western observers. Thus, advances in Western technology didn't simply make colonial conquest easier—they appeared to justify imperialism as a crusade to lift technologically primitive peoples into the modern world.

Egypt and the Partition of Africa

RONALD ROBINSON AND JOHN GALLAGHER[1]

Without the occupation of Egypt, there is no reason to suppose that any international scrambles for Africa, either west or east, would have begun when they did. There seem to have been no fresh social or economic impulses for imperial expansion that would explain why the partition of tropical Africa should have begun in the early 1880s. Gladstone's second administration was totally devoid of imperial ambitions in west Africa. Granville was unimpressed by the dingy annals of the west coast. Kimberley, at the Colonial Office, was eager to give sleeping dogs every chance of lying. The pessimistic Derby, who succeeded him in 1882, was temperamentally opposed to any suggestion, however modest, for expansion on the west coast. Finally there was Gladstone, himself, who knew little and cared little about the problem. In so far as these men possessed any coherent view of the situation in tropical Africa, it was the view sometimes of Cobden, sometimes of Palmerston and the mid-Victorian imperialism of free trade. As in Gladstone's first ministry, they still concurred in looking on tropical Africa as a third-rate adjunct of the British economy, which might be worth the exertion of coastal influence, but did not justify the effort of administration inland. There was none of them likely to plant the flag in the middle of the African bush in a fit of absence of mind.

For decades, all the European governments concerned with the coast of Africa both east and west had tacitly agreed not to allow the petty quarrels of their traders and officials to become occasions for empire. The ministries in London and Paris wanted nothing more than to continue their gentleman's agreement, although each faintly suspected the other of wanting to break it.

It was the British invasion of Egypt that shattered this system, because it shattered the general Anglo-French collaboration. When France came out in open opposition to the new regime in Egypt toward the end of 1882, she began

---

[1] This excerpt is taken from *Africa and the Victorians: The Official Mind of Imperialism* (London: Macmillan, 1961), by Ronald Robinson and John Gallagher, pp. 163, 166, 168-74. John Gallagher was a Fellow of Balliol College, Oxford, and Trinity College, Cambridge. Ronald Robinson was a Fellow of Balliol College, Oxford, and the Beit Professor of the History of the British Commonwealth.

to cast around for ways of putting pressure on London. There was plenty of scope for a policy of pinpricks in west Africa, and these now began in earnest. Two French firms were on the lower Niger, trading not only at the coast, but pushing into the interior. The alarming feature of this activity was that the French consular agent in the river was now hard at work making treaties as far upstream as the kingdom of Nupe and along the Benue. In Paris they had no illusions about their chances on the lower Niger, for the British position seemed too strong. But the Minister of Marine and Colonies had high hopes for the Benue. At the same time, another British sphere looked like it was slipping away. Trade in the delta of the Congo was dominated by British firms; in the interior, Lieutenant Cameron had made a set of treaties in the seventies which gave the United Kingdom an option on the inner basin of the river. Then Her Majesty's Government had rejected it. Now French and Belgian private enterprises were ready to take the Congo seriously. There was a vast river behind the mouths of the Congo, as Stanley had shown; and it had become possible to break into the hinterland, as Brazza had found. King Leopold II of the Belgians, who had floated an International Association to explore central Africa at the end of the seventies, launched Stanley on another mission to open communications between the navigable Congo and Stanley Pool in the interior. At the same time, Brazza too went back, acting in the name of the French section of the International Association. Here was a scramble, but only at the personal level of two explorers racing each other to the interior, each with the skimpiest of credentials. Stanley was little more than the personal agent of a petty monarch, for the International Association was a piece of mummery, and the Belgian Parliament would have nothing to do with its king's speculations. The status of Brazza was no less peculiar. He too was nominally the agent of the International Association. Although his expedition was given a tiny grant by the French government, the chief inspiration of his mission came from his own pleadings. Paris had little desire to be involved in his adventures. Brazza, however, had heard that Leopold intended to seize all the interior basin of the Congo, and this which would cut off the French colony of Gabon from its hinterland and cast it into bankruptcy. To avoid the ruin of their colony, the French government in 1879 authorized Brazza to make a treaty at Stanley Pool. Just as the Foreign Office in the eighteen-fifties had worked to open the Niger hinterland, so the French government in the eighteen-seventies worked to open the Congo basin. They were far from wanting to extend their political control into the interior; their aim was simply to block the political extensions of others. Brazza's treaty was meant to "reserve our rights, without engaging the future."

Between 1880 and 1888, Stanley and Brazza played out their game in the Congo. This raised awkward questions for the British government. Leopold was a puny rival, and his association could be pushed into the wings if the need arose. But after Brazza had made his treaty at Stanley Pool, the Foreign Office had to rely on the French disinclination to move in central Africa. In April 1882 the British ambassador in Paris asked the Quai d'Orsay whether the Congo mission had an official character. The discussion that followed showed that in the opinion of the Ministry of Marine and Colonies, Brazza had no right to have made a treaty at all. But on the Congo, as on the Niger, all this was to change. After the Egyptian affair had reached its climax, Paris did not feel the old need to pay deference to British susceptibilities; on 10 October the Foreign Minister overrode the protest of the Marine and announced that he intended to ask the Chamber to approve the treaty. Ratification followed on 30 November. On 15 December the Foreign Office countered by recognizing Portugal's claims to the Congo and its hinterlands—claims which Britain had steadily rejected for the past forty years. In return, Britain was to enjoy most favored nation treatment in the trade of the Congo, a maximum tariff rate, and the setting up of an Anglo-Portuguese commission to supervise the traffic on the river. The treaty took fifteen months to complete, because the Portuguese went on hoping to get better terms from France than from the United Kingdom; but its purpose was always painfully clear. When it had at last been signed, the French ambassador in London caustically defined it as:

> A security taken by Britain to prevent either France or an international syndicate directed by France from setting foot in the Congo Delta. . . . The British Government . . . would rather parcel it out with Portugal, whom it can influence at will, than leave France with an open door.

That was true enough. During 1883 and 1884, the Gladstone Cabinet hoped to use the Portuguese as a sort of holding company which would decently veil the preeminence of British interests. Lisbon would do the governing, London would do the trade. In fact, British optimism went further than that. It was rumored in the Foreign Office that King Leopold's own organization might become ". . . as I hear is not unlikely, an English company." Both these sanguine hopes are very revealing. As a direct result of the Egyptian occupation, British interests in the Congo were now threatened by Leopold and the French. If their sphere were to be saved, then ministers could no longer rely on the old gentleman's agreement; from now on, official acts of policy would be needed. This they understood. Yet they refused to meet the new situation by any territorial extension of their own. Instead, they fell back on a variant of their technique of informal empire. Others could administer on paper, while they enjoyed the trade. With the King of Portugal as their caretaker on the coast and the King of the Belgians as their manager in the hinterland, all might still be saved, thanks to these regal subordinates.

In fact, the British plans went astray both in the Niger and in the Congo. Ministers had their doubts already over the Anglo-Portuguese Treaty. They were to end by thoroughly repenting of it. Although the treaty had been designed to guarantee the interests of British traders, they were loud in opposition to it because of the nominal Portuguese control and the actual Portuguese tariff. Their protests were joined by the ancestral voices of the Anti-Slavery Society and the Baptist Union. Behind all this agitation there may have lain, as Granville suspected, the fine hand of King Leopold. The complaints of these pressure groups, however, were not enough to stop the treaty. That it failed was another of the consequences of the Egyptian crisis. After the occupation of Cairo, it seemed to French observers that Britain was driving for an African empire. French diplomacy attacked the Anglo-Portuguese arrangement as a way of both keeping the Congo open and putting pressure on the British in Egypt. The treaty was signed on 26 February 1884, and during March the Quai d'Orsay was actively inciting opposition in Belgium, Holland, and the United States, the powers with trading interests in the Congo. But in his search for supporters, Ferry hooked a bigger fish than these. On 31 March he tried to get the Germans to join the resistance. This overture was to begin the partition of West Africa.

Bismarck too had his grievances against British policy. To his rooted dislike of Gladstone as a man fit only to chop down trees and make up speeches, he could now add a splenetic indignation at Granville's dawdling. In February 1888 he had enquired whether Britain would be ready to protect the German settlement at Angra Pequena; in December he repeated the enquiry. But for a further six and a half months the only reply he could get from London was a series of vague observations about British claims in that region. In part the muddle was caused by the objections of the Cape, in part by the British feeling that the colonial politicians had to be listened to, if South Africa was one day to be united around that province. But it was an important muddle. The occupation of Egypt gave Bismarck the chance to deepen the rift between Britain and France and to enter the African game. In March and April of 1884, the Germans took steps to assert their own protectorate over Angra Pequena, but the ambiguity of their statements and the imperceptiveness of Gladstone's ministers (one of whom as late as June did not know where Angra Pequena was) left the British as naively ignorant as ever about where their attitude was taking them. It was beginning to take them a long way. On 5 May Bismarck hinted at this in two messages to London, in which German colonial claims and the question of the Congo were ominously linked. By another in this chain of muddles the messages were not delivered. Thereafter Bismarck swung the weight of Germany behind the Congo revisionists and then against the whole British position in West Africa. On 7 June he let the Foreign Office know that Germany refused to recognize the Anglo-Portuguese Treaty and wanted a conference to settle the Congo question. Granville was too discouraged to press on with ratification, and that was the end of the Treaty. But the retreat did not stop there. On 4 August the Germans suggested to the French that they should cooperate over West African questions generally at the impending conference, and at the end of the month the French persuaded their new collaborators to join in an onslaught against the least expendable of the British spheres, the Niger.

It seems then that any attempt to analyze British policy in terms of some one decisive factor breaks down before the facts. There is nothing for it but to approach the problem from another direction. Instead of postulating a single, necessary, and sufficient cause of these events, it is well to be less pretentious and to define them as the result of an interplay between nonrecurrent factors in the early eighteen-eighties. Government policy in West Africa seems to have evolved as a by-product of three major crises—one in Egypt, another in Europe, a third in the domestic politics of Great Britain—and a minor crisis on the west coast itself. The Egyptian affair had started off the "scramble." It had ended the standstill arrangement in Africa. It had run British policy into a noose held by Bismarck. When Germany's policy swung towards France, the two of them squeezed hard on the British position in West Africa. That position was already susceptible to change, as the bases of tribal societies and economies were eroded by the gradual commercial penetration of the interior. So long as other things stayed equal, Gladstone's cabinet thought it could cope with the results of this erosion by making only small adjustments in its traditional policy. But things did not stay equal, and the Egyptian aftermath shifted the European balance, blowing these calculations sky-high.

It would seem that the claiming of the Niger in 1884 was motivated neither by increased enthusiasm for enlarging the empire nor by more pressing economic need to exploit the region. The incentive to advance here was no stronger than of old. It sprang from a passing concatenation of minor trade rivalries in West Africa with major changes of front by the powers in Europe and the Mediterranean, mainly provoked by British blunders and difficulties in Egypt. The Liberals claimed the Lower Niger merely to prevent an existing field of British trade from disappearing behind French tariff walls, and they limited their new commitment to this negative purpose. They had not decided to found an ambitious West African empire. All they had done in the face of French hostility was to make a technical change in the international status of the Lower Niger. Henceforward the powers recognized this country as a British sphere, but the government still had no serious intention of administering, developing, or extending it.

Britain and the Partition of Africa

P. J. CAIN AND A. G. HOPKINS[2]

Nowhere does the weight of historiography press so insistently upon the study of imperialism as in the case of the partition of Africa. So much has been written on this theme on behalf of so many competing theories that few interpretations, even of points of detail, can resist the absorptive-power of the existing literature. Given that the quality of this research is as impressive as its weight, it might be thought that the subject now requires fine-tuning rather than thorough reappraisal. However, the growth of knowledge has had the perplexing result of making it easier to say what is wrong with current interpretations than what is right. Historians who wish to move beyond this point appear to face a choice between retreating to the high ground of deductive certainty and taking shelter in the empirical undergrowth. Yet, as we shall try to show, the anomalies in the literature can be resolved once the assumptions underlying existing interpretations are removed.

Marxist and Marxisant interpretations have performed particularly badly, despite some excellent research on specific subjects, largely because of their failure to relate partition to the realities of capitalist development in the late nineteenth century. Because the trail taken by the agents of advanced industrial capitalism bypassed much of Africa, the hounds seem to have lost the scent. Aside from tentative attempts to treat partition as being an expression of feeble capitalist influences and atavistic social forces (a view that brings Marx uncomfortably close to Schumpeter), most work in the Marxist tradition has fallen back upon very broad generalisations associating capitalism with imperialism. There is at present no study of partition from a Marxist perspective that combines recognition of the analytical weaknesses of parts of the theory of capitalist imperialism with detailed knowledge of the empirical literature.

Liberal interpretations, by contrast, have flourished on the diversity revealed

---

[2] This selection was taken from P. J. Cain and A. G. Hopkins, *British Imperialism, 1688-2000* (2nd edition), pp. 303-41. Peter Cain is professor of history emeritus at Sheffield Hallum University. A. G. Hopkins is the Walter Prescott Webb Chair of History at the University of Texas at Austin.

by recent research, both on Africa and on policy-making in Europe. This evidence has been used to underline the inadequacies of standard Marxist accounts and to construct various alternatives, the most coherent, and certainly the most celebrated, being that advanced by Robinson and Gallagher. However, this interpretation has now become a casualty of the work it has inspired. It commands unanimous respect among specialists but only their qualified support. To claim that imperialism was the result of crises on the periphery is to report the symptoms, not to diagnose the cause; to attribute British intervention to the actions of European rivals is to assign to others impulses that might properly be looked for at home. Indeed, were it not for the fact that metropolitan-based explanations of imperialism have been discredited by the poor performance of Marxist theories, it is unlikely that interpretations of British policy would have come to rest quite so heavily on decisions taken by other countries. However, Robinson and Gallagher's critics have in turn become victims of their own success, for they have provided explanations for every episode and often for every event, with the result that the repertoire of possibilities has become so extensive that it is almost impossible to comprehend the subject as a whole.

Disarray may well be a faithful representation of historical reality; and it also accords with a view of history that denies that there is a whole to be grasped. Nevertheless, an awareness of diversity is consistent with an explanation of partition which seeks to reconstruct the context within which numerous individual actions took place; and in our view, it is also compatible with the historian's obligation to try to advance beyond accounts which rely on "the interplay of the contingent and the unforeseen or make a virtue of surrendering in the face of the infinite complexity of events." The problem, as defined here, is to explain how Britain's changing interest in Africa influenced her presence there in the second half of the nineteenth century with the result that she moved from being a power on the coast to being a power in the land and, more than this, the most important of the continent's colonial powers. Our suggested solution will be presented in two parts. We shall begin by showing how Africa as a whole was touched by Britain's plan for harmonious world development in the nineteenth century, and how this programme was recharged and also reshaped by the extension of finance and services to Africa after 1850. . . .

Britain's First Development Plan for Africa

The decision taken in 1807 to outlaw the slave trade initiated a new era in Britain's long-standing relationship with Africa. Thereafter, there began a campaign to "regenerate" the continent by promoting the "civilising" values of commerce and Christianity.

The demise of the external slave trade was complemented by a new impulse: the extension to Africa of Britain's burgeoning financial and service sector. Investment in a few promising parts of the continent, principally Egypt and South Africa, grew rapidly, and soon drew in modern banking facilities as well. The beginning of regular steamship services in the 1850s increased the capacity and cut the cost of ocean transport; and the appearance, particularly from the 1880s, of "mega merchants" and investment groups introduced forms of commercial organisation which were designed to be more successful than their predecessors in penetrating the interior. In the British case, the "large firm" emerged in the transactions sector much earlier than it did in manufacturing. The impetus for this development, as we have seen in other parts of the world, came from Britain's unique role and continuing dynamism in international commerce. Steamship, mining, and trading companies all had to become larger in the late nineteenth century if they were to be successful, especially on the frontiers of empire. Small firms lacked the resources to buy and run steamships, to finance and manage complex mining operations, and to act as quasi-bankers, advancing credit, often over long periods, to indigenous traders and producers. Moreover, large firms operating in frontier conditions readily acquired political connections and often official functions too, both of which were helpful in reducing risk and suppressing competitors. Steamship companies secured subsidies in return for services to imperial communications; large commercial firms were sometimes awarded royal charters for acting as proxies for officialdom, and particularly for meeting protection costs which the Treasury was unwilling to bear.

The men who created these firms were adventurers as well as entrepreneurs. They were rarely gentlemen by birth, and their willingness to cut corners on the frontiers of empire was often frowned on in London. But, being on the make, they were also gentlemen in the making. As such, they took readily to the imperial mission and helped to rejuvenate it in the second half of the nineteenth century. Imperialism, however, was much more than a cover for new business interests: it gave private ambitions a wider purpose and enhanced their standing. The most successful of the entrepreneurs who descended on Africa carried the gentlemanly code with them. They saw themselves as being Christian knights engaged in a civilising mission and performing a patriotic duty, which in turn expressed their loyalty to the crown—and hence their acceptance of the social order it represented. At the highest levels, business success and social advancement required connections in London, principally within the City and parliament. Thus, Goldie made use of first a Baron (Aberdare) and then an Earl (Scarborough) as chairmen of the Royal Niger Company, and Mackinnon mobilised the Duke of Sutherland to promote the Imperial British East Africa Company. As might be expected, Rhodes went a step further: he acquired a brace of Dukes (Abercorn and Fyfe), and cultivated good relations with Lord Rothschild. Currie, the shipping magnate whose steamers dominated the routes to South Africa, enjoyed Gladstone's friendship and also took a direct path to influence by becoming a Liberal MP in 1880. In return came a good deal of local authority in Africa, a sprinkling of knighthoods, and some recycling of wealth into estates, usually in the south of England.

If Africa's colonial entrepreneurs were proto-gentlemen, their associates, the explorers and the representatives of the Church Missionary Society, tended to be drawn from established gentry families and from the professional classes of southern England. They, too, helped to revitalise the development drive in the second half of the century. A society that had given up protection for free trade took readily to the need to open new frontiers and gave explorers considerable status; one that had committed itself to creating "like-mindedness" (where it could not readily be found) was also likely to inspire missionary activity. Not surprisingly, reports from both sources were cast in the image of metropolitan society, and were accompanied by renewed optimism about Africa's potential and Britain's ability to push the frontiers of economic growth inland, especially by means of the railway and the telegraph—"the keys to the continent," as Rhodes called them. Societies that showed signs of gentility were marked out as being ready for development by settlement or assimilation; those that did not were deemed to require developing by others. This more assertive attitude was endorsed by the Church Missionary Society, whose vision of spiritual egalitarianism retreated before the advance of militant evangelical influences in the late nineteenth century, and by the new academic disciplines of anthropology and phrenology, which lent scientific credence to the congenial view that the service class of the Home Counties was destined to dominate the world. These ideas, and others linking racism to patriotism, were translated by the new popular press in a manner which encouraged statesmen to give increasing consideration to the use imperial issues might serve in an era of semi-democratic politics. This argument is not to be read as disparaging the part played by manufacturers, who undoubtedly showed a keen awareness of the need to open markets for old staple exports outside Europe and the United States, particularly in the last quarter of the century. But to an extent that has been underestimated, the manufacturing interest rode on the back of the new expansionist wave rather than created it. By the late nineteenth century, the manufacture of cotton goods, the principal export to Africa, had ceased to be characterised by striking productivity gains, and further growth had come to depend increasingly on improvements in the transactions sector, especially transport and finance. Expansion also required political influence, in Africa and in London, and here too manufacturers relied to a considerable degree on the representations and actions of financial and commercial houses, while also, of course, making use of their own trade organisations and members of parliament.

The combination of capital and commercial innovation undoubtedly made inroads into Africa during the second half of the nineteenth century, though the poor quality of the data does not allow the results to be traced with any degree of precision. Some approximate orders of magnitude are provided by Austen's calculations, which show that Africa's share of British exports (excluding trade with Egypt) rose from less than 3 percent in the middle of the century to 4.3 percent in 1890 and to 8.3 percent in 1906. The proportions were indeed small, and the striking gains came after partition rather than before. But these are not reasons for dismissing the importance of Britain's trade with Africa on the eve of partition. The fact that the proportion was rising shows that Africa was a growth area for Britain's exports. Such areas were in short supply in the late nineteenth century. Moreover, since Britain's total exports were expanding globally, the increasing share taken by Africa represents a considerable gain in absolute terms. However, the real significance of the data lies in their regional basis. In the 1880s, three-quarters of Britain's direct trade with Africa (imports and exports amounting to about £30m. a year) was conducted with Cape Colony, Natal, and Egypt. This figure (£22.5m.) was larger than Britain's trade with the whole of China (including Hong Kong) during this period and slightly more than half the value of her trade with Latin America. When it is remembered that these were also the areas of Africa that attracted British investment after 1850, the significance of a regional approach to partition became apparent. This was certainly the perspective adopted by contemporary business opinion in London, which had no doubt that South Africa and Egypt were the parts of the continent that really mattered.

The pace of commercial expansion during the second half of the century had profound effects on the African side of the frontier, though these are still imperfectly understood. However, research now available suggests that the various "crises on the periphery" which have attracted the attention of historians of partition derived from structural changes to societies which were adapting to the demands of the new international economic order, and that these adjustment problems were greatly magnified by the renewed development push after 1850. The evidence also indicates that African polities produced a cluster of hybrid and often assertive responses to external forces and were not simply "undermined" by them to the extent that "law and order" had to be reimposed. Slave-raiders in West Africa achieved some success in adjusting to the palm oil trade and to competition from new small producers; hunters in East Africa momentarily held back the clock of history by making windfall gains during the ivory boom. Ismail in Egypt and Kruger in the Transvaal actively sought to use external influences to reinforce their independence. The problem was not that societies in Africa were unresponsive, but that Britain's presence was marked by increasing demands and diminishing tolerance in the second half of the century. From that point onwards, the machinery of adjustment became vulnerable to short-term fluctuations in international trade, transmitted mainly by falling export prices and credit restrictions, and to random influences on the domestic economy, such as the size of the harvest and the incidence of disease. When these struck, as they did in different parts of Africa during the last quarter of the century, local crises were easily precipitated. In these circumstances, it was virtually impossible for African states to pass Palmerston's test: those which ran into difficulties failed because they were no longer "well-kept," while those which turned Cobden's international principles to national advantage failed because they had ceased to be "always accessible."

This assessment suggests the need to question the conventional view that Britain's policy towards frontier disputes was essentially restrained and reactive. This characterisation undoubtedly represents the ideal of a low-cost, harmonious international order which inspired in the official mind a degree of coherence and a sense of purpose that it might otherwise have lacked. But in the real world, the rules had long been bent where they had not been broken, despite Britain's aversion to territorial acquisition and desire for economy in public expenditure. . . .

For the same reasons, it is also necessary to pause before assigning the responsibility for Britain's actions to foreign rivals. This exercise is partly flawed by its circularity: British historians tend to blame the French; but French historians tend to accuse Germany or Belgium; and German and Belgian historians are inclined to attribute responsibility to Britain and France. This line of argument also suffers from empirical difficulties. It has to be remembered that Africa's most important commercial, financial, and diplomatic ties in the period up to partition were with Britain, not France (still less with Germany, Belgium, or Portugal). The enemy of foreign rivals was undoubtedly a complication for British policy. But France and Germany had more influence in tropical Africa, at the margins of Britain's interests, than in Egypt and South Africa, which were central to her position in the continent. Britain had her own reasons for safeguarding her position in Africa. Appearances did not deceive; the tail did not wag the dog. . . .

The Occupation of Egypt

The first, decisive advance inland on the route which Rhodes was later to envisage joining the Cape to Cairo took place in 1882, when British troops occupied Egypt. This event sparked a lively debate among contemporaries and it has made a distinctive contribution to theories of imperialism from that time to the present day. As far as modern scholarship is concerned, the Egyptian case is best known for the central role assigned to it by Robinson and Gallagher in *Africa and the Victorians*. In their view, the occupation of Egypt was the product of a crisis on the periphery prompted by a proto-nationalist revolt.

Britain was reluctant to intervene, but did so because the breakdown of law and order posed a threat to her strategic interest in the Suez Canal, which guarded the route to India. This decision had far-reaching consequences: it destroyed the informal understandings which had governed the major powers in their dealings with Africa, drove the French to seek compensation in West Africa, and pushed the British up the Nile and into East Africa in pursuit of strategic security. Southern Africa was too remote to become the final domino in this particular "great game," but British policy towards the Boer republics nevertheless exemplifies the paramountcy of "excentric" and strategic considerations in understanding the essentially defensive imperialism of the late Victorians.

Robinson and Gallagher's view of events is indeed very close to the official interpretation put forward at the time. The question, however, is whether the authorised version also provides an acceptable explanation of the problem under review. The evidence now available suggests that it does not. . . .

The Suez Canal was not at risk in 1882; nor was it thought to be the cause of intervention by Gladstone or his Foreign Secretary, Granville, or by the Admiralty (which in any case based its strategy on the Cape route until the 1890s), or by the mercantile shipping lobby. The Canal did not become an issue in the public mind until two weeks before the bombardment of Alexandria, and it was only after this event that the possibility of retaliatory action in the region of Suez arose. As for the French, it is now evident that they were indeed worried about safeguarding their interests between 1875 and 1880, when their investments were in a highly exposed position. After 1880, however, French policy towards Egypt was marked by restraint. The Law of Liquidation took care of the worries of French investors. Some sold their holdings and departed. Those who remained were quite happy to have their protection provided by the world's largest security organization—Great Britain. Moreover, after 1881, France was preoccupied by the invasion of Tunisia. The French did not lead Britain into the "Egyptian imbroglio." Their fleet was withdrawn from Alexandria precisely because France did not want to be dragged into Egypt by Britain.

If, in its final stages, the crisis on the Egyptian periphery displayed clear signs of stage management, its deeper origins lay in the expansion of European trade and investment after 1838, especially in the growth of public sector borrowing from the 1860s. British policy was assertive, not because policy-makers were in the pockets of the bondholders, but because they recognised the need to defend Britain's substantial economic interests in Egypt and because they thought that these could be secured by a quick and inexpensive strike that would also produce political benefits at home. The outcome was what Milner called a "veiled protectorate," which enabled Britain to retain control over the budget in much the same way as the Ottoman Public Debt Administration (with rather less power) managed the finances of the Sublime Porte. The other major consequence of the occupation of Egypt was to draw Britain into the Sudan. This further extension of British influence cannot be explored here. But it is worth noting that Britain's involvement in the Sudan stemmed much more from Egypt's indebtedness than it did from a concern with the need to protect the Suez route to India. The collapse of Ismail's regime in 1879 weakened Egypt's hold over the Sudan and opened an opportunity for a coalition of slave traders and taxpayers to unite against the reforms which Britain had tried to impose through Cairo's authority. It is understandable that the Mahdists opposed foreign influence and aimed at creating an independent Muslim state with its own fiscal system; it is not surprising either that the British decided that they could not allow "disorder" to persist in the Sudan when it endangered the settlement they had just imposed on Egypt.

Imperialism and the Victorians

JOHN DARWIN[3]

Imperialism may be defined as the sustained effort to assimilate a country or region to the political, economic, or cultural system of another power. "Formal" imperialism aimed to achieve this object by the explicit transfer of sovereignty and, usually, the imposition of direct administrative control. Its "informal" counterpart relied upon the links created by trade, investment, or diplomacy, often supplemented by unequal treaties and periodic armed intervention, to draw new regions into the world-system of an imperial power. Quite small powers could and did enter this game and it could be played in any geographical setting. But its complex characteristics were most clearly visible in the expansion of strong Western states into the extra-European periphery. No other power developed more varied and far-reaching imperial relationships than Victorian Britain. The futility of trying to make sense of Victorian expansion, in terms of territorial or formal empire alone, has long been recognised. But the central problem of Victorian imperialism remains how to explain why informal imperialism became the vehicle of expansion where it did: why formal empire was extended in some regions but not others, and why only some zones of informal imperialism were later absorbed into the formal empire. In short, how should we explain the peculiar configuration of the world-system bequeathed by the Victorians? Should we treat it as a finished artefact, economically and strategically functional, or as the inchoate, unfinished handiwork of drift and opportunism? Did the strange course of Victorian imperialism derive mainly from the logic of the policy-makers, or was it really the outcome of a decentralized and pluralistic political system only occasionally capable of imposing discipline and direction on its external activity? The best approach to these issues is still to be found in the powerful hypothesis set out by Gallagher and

---

[3] This excerpt is taken from John Darwin, "Imperialism and the Victorians: The Dynamics of Territorial Expansion," published in *The English Historical Review* 112, no. 447 (June 1997), pp. 614-42. John Darwin is the Beit Lecturer in the History of the Commonwealth and a Fellow of Nuffield College, Oxford.

Robinson over forty years ago. The "imperialism of free trade" stressed, above all, the relentless expansionism of Victorian Britain and insisted that the choice of mode was a purely tactical consideration shaped by circumstance. Subsequently, the force of their original insight was widely diffused across the study of Victorian imperialism by a corps of "new believers." As is not unusual, the converts were inclined to embrace some aspects of the new doctrine and to deprecate others, but it is possible to discern in their substantial body of writing the elements of a powerful and seductive model. Radically simplified, this model rests upon five propositions. The first insists that informal empire was the favoured means of mid-Victorian expansion, preferred by governments on grounds of cost and convenience. The second insists that "informality" was typically abandoned for direct intervention or annexation only when "national" (as opposed to private) interests were at stake. The third insists that the occasion for intervention or annexation was usually found in the political consequences of socioeconomic change at the periphery, with a fusillade of "local crises" exploding into a "general crisis" of Europe's relations with Afro-Asia after 1880. The fourth insists that deciding on the scale of political intervention, including the switch from informal to formal empire, was normally the prerogative of the "official mind," an organism largely free from undue external influence and guided by its own memories, traditions, and values. Last, the overall pattern of formal expansion was heavily influenced by the exceptional importance attached to British supremacy on the Indian sub-continent. Implied in the model was the view that the hyperactive formal empire-building after 1880 was reactive or defensive: designed to protect old zones of influence rather than to seek out new ones. It was symptomatic of growing weakness and decline, of a struggle to stabilize Britain's place in the extra-European world against the intrusion of other powers. From that, it was a short step to portray post-Victorian Britain as a status quo power. The dynamic of her expansion had run its course; the highest stage of British imperialism had been reached; decadence lay in wait. For all its appeal, this version has not lacked critics. In recent years, the most formidable assault has been that of Cain and Hopkins. They argued that Robinson and Gallagher and their followers had misunderstood the nature of the "official mind," misdated the decisive phase of Victorian expansion, and mistaken the real causes of the "new imperialism" after 1880. The "official mind" was really the mouthpiece of "gentlemanly capitalism"—an essentially commercial (rather than industrial) ethos infused with the gentlemanly values of a rentier class resident (chiefly) in southern England. There was no conflict between the outlook of Whitehall and that of the City—its counterpart at the other end of the Strand. It was wrong to see late Victorian imperialism as the gloomy epilogue to the mid-Victorian age of confidence; in reality, it was the vehicle of a commercial and financial expansion that continued far into the twentieth century. Nor should the causes of late

Victorian intervention and annexation be sought in the "local crises" of the periphery since these were merely symptomatic of the quickening pulse of British commercial enterprise and the energy of the gentlemen capitalists. This was a bold attempt to replace what might be regarded as the less robust elements of the older model: the uncertain provenance and mysterious workings of the "official mind," the paradox that the profligate expansion of the late nineteenth century was strategically defensive and economically sterile, and the apparent stress laid upon the decisive influence of periphery conditions. Indeed, their insistence upon the commercial vigour of late Victorian Britain and the continued assertiveness of British world power was a welcome corrective to exaggerated rumours of imperial decline. On other fronts, however, this revisionist advance ran into heavy fire, much of it directed at its claims for the political pre-eminence of gentlemanly capitalism. Other critics stressed the diversity of interests behind British expansion and challenged the evidential basis for the primacy Cain and Hopkins had given to financial and commercial considerations in British policy, especially in Egypt and South Africa. In their own account of the partition of tropical Africa (the wind-tunnel in which new models of British imperialism are invariably tested), Cain and Hopkins seemed uncertain how far British intervention was driven by decision-makers at home, by a new breed of "mega-merchants" on the spot, by pressure groups appealing to the "national interest," or by the sub-imperialism of pocket proconsuls like Portal. Nor does their model throw new light on the aspect of Victorian imperialism to which Robinson and Gallagher had given great emphasis: its bifurcation into the formal and informal modes. On that issue, at least, the new historiography followed the old. In fact, Robinson and Gallagher's model of British imperialism rejects explicit reliance on peripheral factors as the prime cause of expansion. In this article, it is argued that it is precisely in the Victorians' choice of expansive techniques that we can find the best clue to the wider character of their imperialism. Any reappraisal ought to be informed by the pluralism of British society (on which recent work has laid such stress), by the diversity of British interests at work in the periphery (on which a large literature now exists), and by careful attention to the international constraints that shaped mid, as well as late, Victorian expansion. On all these grounds, it will be suggested that existing models do insufficient justice to the contingency of Victorian empire-making. But the starting point must be another look at the canny notions riveted into that historiographical dreadnought, the imperialism of free trade. As Gallagher and Robinson rightly insisted, it was the energy of private British interests—settler, commercial, missionary, among others—which supplied much of the dynamic behind Victorian expansion. It was their attempts to "convert" independent regions of the extra-European periphery into an extension of Victorian Britain which constituted "informal empire," a term whose utility has made it indispensable. But was informal imperialism the consistent preference of Victorian governments or merely tacit recognition of the limits of British power? There can be no doubt that Victorian governments sought constantly to exert influence in the extra-European world. This was true of many regions where the possibility—let alone the desirability—of establishing formal empire was remote. . . .

The colonial incorporation of tropical Africa was not so much remarkable as curiously retarded. Nor, if we stand back from the map of Africa and take a more synoptic view of world history, was the much more rapid European penetration of its interior after 1880 an isolated or surprising event. American settlements had taken over two hundred years to crawl westward from the Atlantic seaboard and reach the Mississippi, but less than sixty to cross the plains and close the frontier by 1890. Canadian settlers colonized the Prairies (some 750,000 square miles) in a generation after 1885. European occupation of Australian and New Zealand hinterlands sped up sharply after 1870. In Argentina and Chile, the annihilation of indigenous resistance in the 1880s opened up new tracts to European settlement. Russian colonization rushed headlong into central and north-east Asia after 1890, sending some five million settlers to Siberia by 1914. Almost everywhere, the older bridgeheads of European economic, political, and cultural influence were being enlarged at breakneck speed, drawing on new or expanded supplies of capital and migrants, improved technologies (especially of communications), and better knowledge of alien environments. From this perspective, what was really surprising about late Victorian formal expansion was not so much its gargantuan appetite as its eccentric progression through the available menu. Tropical Africa, where traders were few and settlers almost non-existent, was swallowed while juicier morsels (like Persia or Siam), economically or strategically more desirable, were turned away or their annexation deferred. What lends the partition of Africa its historical fascination, then, is the light which it seems to cast upon the hidden motives and unspoken assumptions of late Victorian imperialism: if formal empire was economically object-less, how else was it to be explained and what function was it meant to serve in the existing ensemble of colonies and semi-colonies? So far, the most powerful hypothesis has been that late Victorian annexationism was a defensive response to new dangers. Further territorial acquisitions were required to protect the gains of mid-Victorian expansion against new enemies, external and internal. British intervention was thus triggered by the onset of a "local crisis" that threatened the informal predominance built up in previous decades, or by the fear that an imperial rival might exclude or subvert British interests. But annexation was, characteristically, not invoked in aid of private enterprise. . . . The imperial competition of France, Germany, Italy, Portugal, and Spain was at best manageable, at worst containable, and only rarely threatened the general crisis of imperial security that any collision with Russia in the Far East was expected to set off. Of the various theatres of

British intervention in Africa after 1880, it is East Africa which has usually been seen as the locus classicus of imperial grand strategy, and the uncluttered playground of the official mind, where its characteristic preoccupations were most vigorously displayed. Here, where commercial impulses were weak or non-existent, strategic necessity was, or became, overwhelming. Uganda and the Sudan, economically worthless, fell under more or less direct British sway because the policy-makers in London were convinced that, without effective occupation of the Upper Nile to its source in Lake Victoria, Britain's control over Egypt and the Suez Canal—the strategic linch-pin of the Anglo-Indian system—would never be safe. It was the discovery of this strategic imperative, once the "temporary occupation" of Egypt in 1882 began hardening into permanency, which explained the timing of British participation in a scramble for East Africa. Above all, it dictated the regions of East Africa which the British government wanted. Formal empire in East Africa was thus the product of high policy, not low sub-imperialist intrigue. Salisbury, the architect of this unwilling experiment in tropical empire, was the cynical grandmaster of the imperial chessboard, ruthlessly sacrificing his pawns and occupying a square here or there not for its intrinsic value, but because it allowed him to protect the vitals of his world-system. . . . Here, as so often elsewhere, Salisbury found himself struggling to regulate the effects of private expansionism, to parry its domestic lobbying, and to balance the weight of British interests on the spot against the wider diplomatic pressures to which London was exposed. That Salisbury carried off so much in 1890 at the cost of Heligoland may say less about his motives than about his virtuosity as a negotiator and the temporary strength of his bargaining position. Like his mid-Victorian predecessors, Salisbury was concerned with stabilizing Britain's foreign commitments. But like them, he often found it impossible to resist the forward pressure of proconsuls and private interests who skilfully fabricated cases for intervention. These two cases suggest that we need to look beyond the conventional hypothesis to explain the pattern of territorial expansion. What is striking is neither the rigour with which the official mind computed "national interest" nor its deployment of strategic insight to calibrate the scale of British intervention. On most occasions the variables at work were less arcane. The real decision the policy-makers had to take was whether the strength of the local "bridgehead" and the force of its domestic lobby outweighed the diplomatic and military hazards of a forward policy. Not infrequently, these variables proved hard to measure and dangerously volatile. The new conditions of world and domestic politics after 1880 exacerbated the difficulty. Buffeted by lobbies from every side, tempted by visions of effortless dominion, disoriented by the instability of late-century geopolitics, the official mind, even under Salisbury, continually relapsed into its habitual schizophrenia. Thus, late Victorian governments did not annex so widely in tropical Africa because this was the only way of maintaining their mid-Victorian interests.

Nor did they espouse pessimistic new doctrines of relative decline. They annexed for the same reasons as mid-Victorian governments: because local British interests pressed them to do so and, in the absence of powerful diplomatic, financial, or military objections, the will to refuse was lacking. If Africa was partitioned before China, Iran, or Turkey, it was not because its strategic, let alone its economic, value was greater. By the 1880s, the modest inputs of local power needed for conquest had been assembled with an adequate lobby to champion the sub-imperialist cause at home. Without the geopolitical constraints which disfavoured annexation elsewhere, the competitive coexistence of rival imperialisms loaded the incentives in favour of peaceful partition. What made the scramble so spectacular was that in Africa these local, domestic, and international pressures converged to create in a sudden burst precisely the conditions in which all Victorian governments, early, middle, or late, found intervention or annexation irresistible. The argument of this paper has been that we need to move beyond the existing historiography to explain the seemingly random course of Victorian imperialism. For all its attractions, the influential model, in which a platonic official mind reluctantly licenses defensive annexations when the national interest is threatened by local crisis on the periphery, needs modification if it is to explain the global pattern of Victorian expansion. But it is doubtful whether its defects can be remedied by locating the whole impetus for expansion in the metropole or in the single-minded promotion of a particular interest, however powerful, by a like-minded oligarchy of gentlemen capitalists. For this task, the open-ended hypotheses framed by Gallagher and Robinson in the "imperialism of free trade" offer a better starting point than the more closed and rigid model derived by later writers from their case-study of the partition. In that original formulation, with its global compass, the part played by government and the policy-makers necessarily bulks less large than in the special conditions of the African scramble. It allows us to see, as much recent work has emphasized, that the engine of British expansion throughout the nineteenth century was the chaotic pluralism of private and sub-imperial interests: religious, commercial, strategic, humanitarian, scientific, speculative, and migrational. The role of government was sometimes to facilitate, sometimes to regulate this multiple expansive momentum. Government had its own purposes: containing its financial and military commitments, avoiding diplomatic embarrassment or worse, and guarding the Anglo-Indian strategic corridor. But it could rarely afford to obstruct powerful expansionist groups or identify itself too closely or for too long with any one of them. Since these interest groups grew collectively larger and more vocal in the later nineteenth century, it was not surprising that governments of all political complexions acceded more readily to their wishes.

Malaria, Quinine, and the Penetration of Africa

DANIEL HEADRICK[4]

By the time Columbus first sighted the Americas, the Portuguese were well acquainted with the west coast of Africa, for they had been exploring it for sixty years. Yet, during the next three and a half centuries, Africa remained in the eyes of Europeans the "dark continent," its interior a blank on their maps, as they chose instead to explore, conquer, and settle parts of the Americas, Asia, and Australia.

How can we explain this paradox? For one thing, there was little motivation for Europeans to penetrate Africa before the nineteenth century. The slave traders—Africans and Europeans alike—who met along the coasts to conduct their business wanted no outsiders with prying eyes disrupting their operations. Furthermore, despite legends of fabulous wealth, there was little concrete evidence that the profits to be derived from the penetration of Africa would even approximate those resulting from the slave trade or from trade with Asia and the Americas. Thus, the penetration of Africa that occurred in the nineteenth century was tied closely to missionary and abolitionist movements reacting against the slave trade.

But even more significantly, the means of penetration were also lacking. Much of Africa is a plateau. Rivers cascade from the highlands to the sea in a series of cataracts. The coasts are lined with mangrove swamps and sandbars. Throughout the tropical regions, pack animals could not survive the nagana or animal trypanosomiasis. Those who wished to enter Africa would have to do so on foot or in dugout canoes.

These deterrents were by no means absolute prohibitions. After all, Europeans had explored the Americas with primitive means of transportation, despite difficult climates and topographies. It was disease that kept Europeans out of the interior of Africa. Although steamboats came to Africa and Asia at

---

[4] This excerpt is taken from Daniel Headrick, *The Tools of Empire: Technology and European Imperialism in the 19th Century* (Oxford. Oxford University Press, 1981), pp. 58-76. Daniel Headrick is professor emeritus of social science and history at Roosevelt University.

the same time, in Asia they wrought a revolution in the power of Europeans, whereas in Africa, their effect was postponed for several decades. Before Europeans could break into the African interior successfully, they required another technological advance, a triumph over disease.

In his novel *War of the Worlds*, H. G. Wells described a group of extraterrestrial creatures who invade the earth in strange futuristic vehicles. As they are about to take over the globe, they are decimated by invisible microbes and are forced to flee. Wells could just as well have been writing about the various European attempts to penetrate Africa before the middle of the nineteenth century. In 1485, the Portuguese captain Diogo Cao sent a party of men to explore the Congo River; within a few days, so many had died that the mission had to be called off. In 1569, Francisco Barreto led an expedition up the Zambezi valley to establish contact with the kingdom of Monomotapa; 120 miles upriver, the horses and cattle fell victim to trypanosomiasis and the men succumbed to malaria. Henceforth until 1835, Portuguese communications with the Zambezi interior were carried on through African or part-African agents.

Similarly, in 1777-79, during William Bolts' expedition at Delagoa Bay, 132 out of 152 Europeans on the journey died. Mungo Park's 1805 venture to the upper Niger resulted in the death of all the Europeans present. In 1816-17, Captain James Tuckey led an exploring party up the Congo River, in which 19 out of 54 Europeans perished.

These setbacks in no way curtailed European attempts to explore Africa. Each generation spawned a fresh crop of adventurers willing to risk their lives to investigate the unknown continent. With the nineteenth century appeared new motives to do so: a revival of the Christian proselytizing spirit, the abolition of the Atlantic slave trade, and a curiosity elevated to the rank of scientific research and funded by a newly wealthy bourgeoisie....

Though very few Europeans ventured into the interior of Africa before the mid-nineteenth century, a substantial number had for centuries been trading along the coasts. After 1807, in an attempt to end the slave trade, the British government stationed a fleet along the West African coast to intercept slaving ships. Small army units were also placed at intervals along the shores to lend weight to the abolition campaign. Here and there the first Christian missions were founded. These various groups of whites were subject to the diseases prevailing in the region.

We know much more about the death rates among British military personnel in West Africa than among their predecessors, the slave traders, for this was the time when the keeping of statistical records became a vital part of Western culture. The Royal African Corps, stationed from the Gambia to the Gold Coast, was composed of military criminals and offenders allowed to exchange their sentences for service in Africa. In most cases, this meant substituting death for prison. In 1840, the *United Service Journal and Naval and Military*

Magazine devoted an article to the health of these troops. It gave the following figures: of the 1,843 European soldiers who served in Sierra Leone between 1819 and 1836, 890, or 48.3 percent, died. The worst year was 1825, in which 447 out of 571 (78.3 percent) succumbed to disease. Despite a constant influx of European arrivals, the size of the garrison declined by over a hundred each year. The Gold Coast was just as deadly: two-thirds of the Europeans who landed there in the years 1823-27 never lived to return home; in the year 1824 alone, 221 out of 224 lost their lives. On the whole, 77 percent of the white soldiers sent to West Africa perished, 21 percent became invalids, and only 2 percent were ultimately found fit for future service. Among West Indian soldiers stationed in the same region, the death rate was only one-tenth that for whites, though still twice that prevailing in their native lands. During the 1825-26 epidemic in the Gambia that killed 276 out of 399 whites, only one out of 40 or 50 West Indians fell victim to the illness. It is likely that the epidemic in question was yellow fever, a disease endemic to the West Indies against which many West Indians had developed a resistance. In 1830, the British government recognized the significance of the death rates and stopped sending white troops to West Africa, except for half a dozen sergeants to command the West Indian soldiers.

The authors of the article, of course, did not understand the exact causes of this horrendous situation. At least they did not blame the men themselves, for they noted that robust, teetotalling English missionaries living on the same coast were as likely to suffer the effects of the disease; of 89 who went to West Africa between 1804 and 1825, 54 died and another 14 returned in bad health. Nor was the climate to blame, for dry and windy stations were as dangerous as those adjoining fetid marshes. The cause of the problem, they concluded, was fevers, either yellow or remittent. A scientific approach was beginning to replace the moralistic judgments of former times.

Philip Curtin, in his writings on the question, gives equally appalling death rates. . . . Among Europeans serving with the African Squadron of the Royal Navy off the coast of West Africa, the death rate in 1825-45 was 65 per thousand; among British troops in West Africa in 1819-36 it was 483 per thousand for enlisted men and 209 for officers. Meanwhile, West African soldiers serving in the British army in the same area suffered a death rate of only 2.5 per thousand. It is for this reason that Africa became known as the "white man's grave."

Though dysentery, yellow fever, typhoid, and other ills contributed to the high death rates, the principal killer of Europeans in Africa was malaria. Throughout history, malaria has probably caused more human deaths than any other disease. It exists in several varieties. Tertian malaria, endemic throughout much of the world, is caused by the protozoan *Plasmodium vivax* and produces intermittent fevers and a general weakening of the body. Another variety, brought on by *Plasmodium falciparum*, is endemic only to tropical Africa and is far deadlier. It is found not only in swamplands and rainforests, but also in the drier savannas. The body's resistance, gained from a successful bout with the disease, is temporary at best, and many Africans suffer repeated low-level attacks throughout their lives. To adult newcomers to Africa, who have not had the opportunity to build up a resistance, the disease is most often fatal. Early nineteenth-century European medical opinion, influenced by the age-old association of malaria with swamps, blamed humid air and putrid smells for the disease; hence the French word *paludisme* (from the Latin word for swamp) and the Italian *malaria*, or bad air. . . .

The dawn of a breakthrough in treating malaria dates from the year 1820, when two French chemists, Pierre Joseph Pelletier and Joseph Bienaimé Caventou, succeeded in extracting the alkaloid of quinine from cinchona bark. Commercial production of quinine began in 1827, and by 1830, the drug was being manufactured in large enough quantities for general use.

From the late 1820s on, doctors in malarial areas conducted experiments with quinine and published the results of their investigations. The first important experiments were carried out in Algeria, following the French invasion of 1830. Serious health problems plagued the French troops stationed there, with typhoid and cholera outbreaks common occurrences. The most severe problem, however, was malaria. Bone, which was surrounded by swamps, had the highest incidence of disease in Algeria, and epidemics broke out every summer. In 1832, of the 2,788 French soldiers stationed in that town, 1,626 were hospitalized. The next year, 4,000 out of 5,500 were similarly affected, and out of every 7 hospitalized soldiers, 2 died. The cause of these deaths was not disease alone, but also the treatment the patients received. French army doctors at the time were influenced by Dr. J. Broussais, head of the army medical school of Val-de-Grilce, who taught that fevers should be treated with purgatives, bleedings, leeches, and a starvation diet. Quinine, he believed, should be administered in tiny doses only after the seventh or eighth attack; among other reasons, the new drug was too expensive, at twenty five francs an ounce, for military use.
. . . H. D. Trotter led 159 Europeans up the Niger to the confluence of the Benue. To avoid the health problems of previous missions, every known precaution was taken. The crew was specially selected from among athletic young men of good breeding, the ships were equipped with fans to dispel bad air, and the expedition raced at top speed through the miasmic delta to reach the drier climate of the upper river as soon as possible. Nonetheless, the first cases of fever appeared within three weeks, forcing the *Wilberforce* and the *Soudan* to return to the Atlantic as floating hospitals. Within two months, forty-eight of the Europeans had died, and by the end of the expedition another seven fell victim to the disease. Africa had regained its terrible reputation among the British.

Despite this disappointment, the Niger expedition of 1841 represents a major step toward a solution to the problem of malaria, for the physician on board one of the ships, Dr. R. H. Thomson, used the opportunity to experiment with various drugs. Some crew members received cinchona bark with wine, others got quinine; Dr. Thomson himself took quinine regularly and stayed healthy. He later wrote his observations on the matter in an article entitled "On the Value of Quinine in African Remittent Fever," which appeared in the British medical journal The Lancet on February 28, 1846. A year later, Dr. Alexander Bryson, an experienced naval physician, published his "Report on the Climate and Principal Diseases of the African Station" (London, 1847), in which he advocated quinine prophylaxis to Europeans in Africa. In 1848, the director-general of the Medical Department of the British Army sent a circular to all British governors in West Africa, recommending quinine prophylaxis.... In the footsteps of the explorers, lesser protagonists of European imperialism penetrated the African interior: missionaries, soldiers, traders, administrators, engineers, planters and their wives and children, and finally tourists. All of them needed their daily quinine. In India and other tropical areas, the influx of Europeans added to the growing demand for the drug.... Scientific cinchona production was an imperial technology par excellence. Without it, European colonialism would have been almost impossible in Africa, and much costlier elsewhere in the tropics. At the same time, the development of this technology, combining the scientific expertise of several botanical gardens, the encouragement of the British and Dutch colonial governments, and the land and labor of the peoples of India and Indonesia, was clearly a consequence as well as a cause of the new imperialism.

River steamers had overcome the obstacle of poor transportation, and quinine that of malaria. Together, they opened much of Africa to colonialism; that is, to the systematic intercourse with Europe on European terms. The scramble for Africa has often been explained as a consequence of French political psychology after the Franco-Prussian War, or of the ambitions of King Leopold II of Belgium, or as a byproduct of the Suez Canal. No doubt. But it was also the result of the combination of steamers, quinine prophylaxis, and, as we shall see, the quick-firing rifle. From among the myriad events of the scramble, let us consider only a few that illustrate the arrival of steamers on the rivers of Africa, their European crews now protected from a certain death by quinine prophylaxis.... What was needed was a double application of steam. One was to be a steamship line between Britain and West Africa, which we shall consider in a later chapter. The other was a regular steamboat service along the Niger in order to bypass the Nigerian middlemen. Laird's first appeals were rejected. After the Pleiad expedition in 1854 had vindicated his faith, however, the Royal Geographical Society convinced the British government to support his projects. In 1857, the Foreign Office agreed to send Dr. Baikie to open relations with the Caliphate of Sokoto on the middle Niger. The Admiralty contracted with Laird to send three steamers up the Niger annually for five years.

The *Dayspring*, the *Rainbow*, and the *Sunbeam* were built by John Laird's Birkenhead shipyard for this service. In the course of their voyages they naturally aroused the resentment of the delta traders whose business they were ruining. In 1859, after traders attacked the *Rainbow* and killed two of her crew members, Laird appealed to the government for a warship to accompany his steamers. Two years later H.M.S. *Espoir* entered the Niger and destroyed the villages that had been responsible for the assault on the *Rainbow*. By the 1870s, several British companies were trading on the Niger with armed steamers, and every year a military expedition steamed up the river to destroy any towns that resisted the British intrusion. By the 1880s, Sir George Goldie's United African Company, uniting all the trading interests in the area, kept a fleet of light gunboats patrolling the river year round. In 1885, the British government declared the Niger delta a protectorate. Despite sporadic resistance, no African town along the rivers and no war-canoe could withstand for long the power of British gunboats.

The Niger River was the scene of the earliest and most active use of steamers by the invading Europeans because it was the easiest to navigate in all of tropical Africa. The other major rivers—the Congo, the Zambezi, the upper Nile, and their tributaries—were broken by cataracts which barred access to them by seagoing steamers. Boats had to be brought in pieces, portaged around the rapids, and reassembled before they could be used to explore the upper reaches of these rivers. To portage the steamers and equipment for an entire expedition required labor, technology, organization, and financing on a scale that the Niger explorers had never faced.

Livingstone used a series of small steamers: the *Ma Roberts*, the first steel steamboat, on which he explored the Zambezi River up to the Kebrabasa Rapids in 1858; the *Pioneer*, in 1861; and the *Lady Nyassa*, which was carried in pieces around the falls to Lake Nyassa. Samuel White Baker had the steamer *Khedive* transported to the upper Nile. To open up the Congo River basin, Henry Stanley had a steamer, the nine-ton *En Avant*, carried in pieces from the Atlantic to Stanley Pool. Shortly thereafter, Savorgnan de Brazza's *Ballay* also appeared on the Congo.

After that, the number of steamers multiplied quickly for exploration, conquest, trade, and missionary work. They were transported to the most remote regions of the continent. In 1895-97, the French lieutenant Gentil conquered the area of the Ubangi and Shari rivers and Lake Chad using the first aluminum steamer, the *Leon Blot*. And in 1898 on his crossAfrica expedition, Commandant Marchand had two steamers and three rowboats carried from the Ubangi to the Nile, on which he then steamed to his celebrated confrontation with Kitchener at Fashoda.

Given the harsh topography of much of Africa, and the lack of pack animals, it is doubtful whether Europeans could have penetrated so fast or dominated so thoroughly if they had had to go on foot. Regions lacking good water transportation—for example, the Central Sudan, the Sahara, Ethiopia, and the Kalahari—were among the last to be colonized. The contrast between the ease of water transport and the difficulty of land transport in nineteenth-century Africa accounts in large part for the European patterns of penetration and control.

Africa: Primitive Tools and the Savage Mind

MICHAEL ADAS[5]

In contrast to the civilizations of India, China, and Islam, which most writers conceded had made significant contributions to scientific inquiry and technological development early in their histories, African cultures were considered by almost all nineteenth-century European observers to be devoid of scientific thinking and all but the most primitive technology. This assessment became more and more central to efforts to demonstrate the validity of the long-standing view of the Africans as backward and inferior peoples. Johann Blumenbach's spirited defense of "Negro" mathematical and scientific aptitudes was forgotten or ignored. Echoing, often unknowingly, an argument that Edward Long had advanced in the 1770s, numerous nineteenth-century authors asserted that the Africans had not been responsible for a single scientific discovery or any mechanical invention. Julien Virey developed this theme at some length. Unlike the Egyptians, he asserted, the Africans had never built great cities or monuments, but were content to live in "primitive" huts. In contrast to the Indians, they were incapable of manufacturing textiles. They had produced no art worth the name and no inventions. In fact, Virey argued, the Africans had never even displayed the sort of ingenuity that the Indians had evinced in devising the game of chess or that the Arabs had revealed in their delightful stories, especially the *One Thousand and One Nights*. The American writer Josiah Nott was equally sweeping in his assertion that in their entire history the Africans had produced no cities, no monumental architecture, no "relic" of science or literature, and not even a "rude" alphabet. Similarly, James Hunt, the first president of the Anthropological Society of London, challenged those who argued for African equality with whites to name one "Negro" who had distinguished himself in any field. In listing careers in which evidence of

---

[5] This excerpt is taken from Michael Adas, *Machines as the Measure of Men: Science, Technology, and Ideologies of Western Dominance* (Ithaca, NY: Cornell University Press, 1989), pp. 153-66. Michael Adas is the Abraham E. Voorhees Professor of History at Rutgers University.

African achievement might be sought (but never found), Hunt ranked "man of science" above all others.

In the view of most nineteenth-century authors of works on Africa, these categorical dismissals of black material achievement appeared to be confirmed by the accounts of European explorers, missionaries, and colonial officials. Though some authors made exceptions for particular peoples, Richard Burton, one of the most wide-ranging and frequently quoted of British explorers, captured the sentiments of the great majority of the on-the-spot observers when he declared that technology in Africa was limited to weaving, cutting canoes, making "rude" weapons, and "practising a rough metallurgy." Less hostile and better informed observers than Burton made distinctions between different African peoples in terms of their level of technological development. In general, there was a strong correspondence between praise for a particular people's tools and weapons and favorable judgments about its society as a whole. The German explorer Karl Peters, for example, had little good to say about most of the peoples whom he encountered during his travels in East Africa. His stereotypes—from the "thieving" and "impudent" Kikuyu to the "proud but savage" Masai—were standard fare for late nineteenth-century readers of explorers' accounts. Relative to his undisguised disdain for most African peoples, however, Peters had high praise for the powerful Ganda, whom he considered extremely skillful builders. Yet he qualified even this rare praise by his supposition that the Ganda's engineering feats had been stimulated by Egyptian and European influences.

As H.A.C. Cairns has shown, the Ganda's skill at road building and their capacity for metalworking were vital in winning very favorable assessments of their level of social development from a number of British travelers and missionaries in this period. The British were particularly impressed by the complexity of Ganda political organization, engineering and architectural skills, and proclivity for experiment and innovation. These were seen as evidence that they shared many of the traits the British considered central to their own superiority. The fact that the Ganda were eager to learn and imitate British techniques, specifically those related to metalworking, only served to reinforce the impression that they were a cut above the rest of the Africans in social development and potential for improvement.

Another of the great experts on colonial affairs of the day, Sir Harry Johnston, distinguished the "Bayansi" from the other "savages" of the Congo as a people who had developed a "decided indigenous civilization of their own." He based the distinction solely on the Bayansi's superior engineering skills, which were evinced in their large houses with swinging doors, sophisticated handicraft industries, and skill in the working of metals. In response to a lecture on Africa delivered some years later by Johnston, a missionary named Milum vehemently rejected Johnston's sweeping assertion that before colonization all

Africans were savages. But in his defense of the Yoruba and claims for the high level of development they had achieved, Milum relied on the standards invoked earlier by Johnston, standards that were overwhelmingly technological:

> What were they [the Yoruba] before they came into contact with Europeans? Certainly not savages. They had smelting furnaces, and they made iron and excellent steel. They were dyers, and to this day their dyes are the envy of European countries. They made their own cloth. They were by no means naked savages, for they dressed in the most decent manner, and I should like to commend the native dress of the Yorubas as the most fit and proper costume, and as being superior to the European style.

Yet, however many travelers or colonial officials may have been impressed with the technical skills of particular peoples, their praise was always qualified by the underlying assumption that a vast gap existed between the capacities of Africans as a whole and those of the Europeans. The French-born explorer Paul Du Chaillu captured this ambivalence in noting that the "cannibal" Fon of the Congo region refused to barter for European or American iron for their knives and arrowheads, preferring metal forged on their own "ingenious bellows." Nevertheless, Du Chaillu saw Fon material culture as woefully primitive: they had not invented, he observed, "a thing so simple as a handle for a hammer."

Perhaps the most striking manifestation of the assumption that the African peoples lacked either technological development or the capacity for invention can be found in works on the riddle of Zimbabwe, which preoccupied so many travelers to southern Africa in this period. The massive and skillfully constructed stone edifices found in what was to become the British colony of Southern Rhodesia appeared to contradict the widespread belief that Africans were utterly lacking in engineering skills and had produced little or no monumental architecture. The ruins of Zimbabwe had to be explained or these assumptions reassessed. The former approach was much more congenial to nineteenth-century authors. The mystery of Zimbabwe's origins was conceded by all who wrote about the impressive ruins, whose impact was considerably enhanced by the paucity of comparable stone buildings in the rest of sub-Saharan Africa. The absence of written records relating to the ruins and the infant state of archeological and anthropological work in the Zimbabwe region left much room for speculation. But one thing was clear to most observers: black Africans were incapable of the architectural, engineering, and stoneworking feats that those who built the great walls and towers of Zimbabwe had obviously possessed.

The British explorer Lionel Decle summarized the general consensus of nineteenth-century writers when he concluded that the construction of buildings as grand as those suggested by the "magnificent ruins" of Zimbabwe was simply beyond the capacity of any African people; the structures in "their extent, their gigantic proportions, and their general plan indicate a loftiness of conception very far superior to the present ability of the Negro race." Decle's contemporary Robert Swan agreed. He cautioned readers of the prestigious journal of the Royal Anthropological Society against assuming that the "Kaffirs" had constructed the edifices simply because Africans then living in the vicinity often built their homes on top of the ruins. Swan declared emphatically that none of the tribes "now living anywhere near Mashonaland" could ever have had "even the small knowledge of geometry and astrology [sic] that was necessary in planning these temples." Frederick Selous, a big-game hunter in the 1890s with strong opinions on all manner of African affairs, was among the tiny minority who believed that the Bantu peoples might have played a role in the construction of Zimbabwe. But his conviction arose from a low opinion of the ruins rather than a maverick respect for African abilities. He called Zimbabwe a "rude structure" and surmised that its architects could have achieved only the low state of development that he associated with Africans.

Though most writers dismissed the Africans as candidates, there was some disagreement over who had in fact built Zimbabwe. The dominant view was advanced by J. T. Bent, who wrote a detailed essay on the origins of the structures in 1893. Drawing on the work of German and Austrian archaeologists in addition to the standard British sources, Bent speculated that the great edifices had been constructed centuries earlier by Arabs who had migrated inland from the Swahili coast. He surmised that if Africans had played any role in the construction, it had been as slave laborers. He found this conclusion inescapable, given "the well-accepted fact that the negroid brain never could be capable of taking the initiative in work of such intricate nature." Until recent years, similar views were espoused by the white settlers who dominated Rhodesia. In official publications and textbooks, the African role in the construction of Zimbabwe was vigorously denied. That the name Zimbabwe was chosen by the new nation which emerged from the struggle for black majority rule in Rhodesia indicates the importance that the discovery of the Bantu origins of the great complex has played in the efforts of Africans to rebut centuries of misinformation about their historic achievements.

Attempts to deny the African contribution to the technological or architectural accomplishments of ancient civilizations had been made, of course, long before European explorers prowled the ruins of Zimbabwe in the late nineteenth century. In the 1850s, the American authors Josiah Nott and George Gliddon, who were widely considered authorities on the "Negro question," had declared that the civilization of Meroe, long noted for the high level of ironworking it had attained, was the product of Egyptian and not "Negro" genius. They also rejected the suggestion that black Africans had played a role in the development of Egyptian civilization and its wondrous architectural feats, other than perhaps the provision of brute labor. Confronted with evidence that the Mandingos and Fulani had historically displayed considerable technical skill and achieved a high level of civilization, Nott and Gliddon countered that these peoples were "less black" ("mahogany") than other Africans and had been highly influenced by Arab migrants and Islamic civilization. A decade later, Frederic Farrar conceded that the Africans had made some contributions to Egyptian civilization but asserted that these had been highly inflated by defenders of the "Negro race." Farrar concluded that the achievements of Egypt were largely the product of Aryan and Asiatic efforts and that black Africans had supplied mainly "strains of cruelty and Fetishism." William Clark, who in the 1850s wrote a highly favorable account of the Yoruba of present-day Nigeria, inexplicably traced the origins of what he regarded as an exceptional people to the Canaanites of ancient Palestine. These claims do much to explain why authors of African descent, from Antenor Firmin in the late nineteenth century to Cheikh Anta Diop in the twentieth, have been so concerned to demonstrate the importance of black African contributions to ancient Egyptian civilization.

Nowhere was the technological gap that grew ever wider between nineteenth-century Europeans and Africans more graphically depicted than in the hundreds of incidents in which travelers, settlers, and missionaries reported the awestruck responses of Africans to even the simplest mechanical devices. Paul Du Chaillu recalled how the "natives" regarded his clock as an "object of wonder" and believed it to be his guardian spirit. On a later journey, Du Chaillu delighted in the Africans' awe (and fear) of his "galvanic battery," magnet, and photographic equipment; even his black-tinted beer bottles were "held in very high estimation by the chiefs." Anna Hinderer, the wife of a missionary in Yoruba country, told of crowds of Africans with "eyes and mouths wide open" gathering around her bungalow to listen to her play the harmonium. A visiting African leader insisted on seeing and attempting to play the instrument. When he could not, he remarked, according to Hinderer, that "only white people can do anything great like make wood and ivory 'speak.'" Lovett Cameron, a British explorer, recorded an even more exuberant response. Having inspected the watches, guns, compasses, and other instruments that Cameron's party carried, the uncle of another African "chief" exclaimed: "Oh, these white men! They make all these wonderful things and know how to use them! Surely men who know so much ought never to die; they must be clever enough to make a medicine to keep them always young and strong, so that they will never die." The old man, Cameron claimed, believed that the Europeans were thousands of years old and able to conjure up these devices from their inner consciousness. The English traveler Richard Freeman "astonished and delighted" his African bearers by allowing them to view the moon through his telescope. Freeman derived even greater pleasure from African wonderment at the flame that engulfed his Christmas pudding (he reported that the "native" onlookers burst into applause) and his use of a fork. The Scottish explorer Henry Drummond, reminding his readers that he was without books or newspapers, reported that he amused himself and was able to "entertain the savages" by lighting matches, buttoning his coat, "snapping" his revolver, or using his mirror to set fire to their clothing.

He added that he found such pleasure in the Africans' awestruck response to these diversions that he sometimes indulged in them three or four times a day. As late as the decade before the Great War, the young Elspeth Huxley described similar African reactions to such commonplace objects as matches, wheels, and oil lamps. She puzzled over the fact that these devices made a much greater impression on the "ignorant" and "backward" peoples of Kenya than did such modern marvels as airplanes and radios.

Perhaps no inventions elicited as much astonishment and respect from Africans as European firearms. As early as the 1820s, G. Mollien, a French traveler with considerable sensitivity to the Africans, reported that when he fired his double-barreled gun, the Bahene people cried out in astonishment, "We are only beasts." Some decades and great advances in firearms manufacture later, Du Chaillu told of the Ashira's praise for his revolver. Even though they had muskets, he wrote, they could not even begin to comprehend the workings of a gun that "fired time after time without stopping." Du Chaillu's contemporary, the French explorer M. E. Mage, noted a similar "avid interest" in his Colt revolver on the part of the ruler Ahmadou. Mage recalled with amusement the obvious amazement of the proud leader, who sought to maintain an air of indifference in all situations. The gun's performance, however, prompted Ahmadou to lose his composure and openly marvel at the "small copper cartridges" that could carry so far. Though the superiority of European firearms to the weapons wielded by Africans was readily apparent, some travelers were not above resorting to ruses to amuse themselves and dazzle the "natives" further. William Devereux recounted how he and his companions told a group of "fine strapping natives" who had boarded his steamship to look it over that the funnel was a large cannon. The visitors were understandably "awe-stricken" by what they believed to be a monstrous gun, but they were even more impressed—Devereux confided—by the white women on board.

Ironically, it was the great missionary-explorer David Livingstone who most accurately and succinctly summarized the advantages for Europeans in Africa of vastly superior firearms: "Without any bullying, fire arms command respect, and lead [African] men to be reasonable who might otherwise feel disposed to be troublesome."

The apparently overwhelming impression that firearms and mechanical devices made on peoples throughout sub-Saharan Africa led many explorers and envoys to the courts of African rulers to recommend guns and machines as gifts for African "chiefs" and kings. In the account of his 1817 mission to the ruler of Ashanti, Edward Bowdich described at great length the king's great interest in British medicines and botanical books and his obvious delight in the many mechanical devices that Bowdich had brought along as presents. Bowdich advised that "ingenious novelties"—including, in this instance, telescopes, pistols, kaleidoscopes, watches, a microscope, a pocket compass, matches, and a camera obscura—had played a critical role in winning the favor of the powerful African ruler. Perhaps acting on Bowdich's instructions, Joseph Dupuis, who led a similar mission to the Ashanti capital at Kumasi three years later, selected "mainly mechanical contrivances" as gifts for the African ruler. Unfortunately, some of the items he had chosen met with a decidedly less favorable reception than Bowdich's presents had enjoyed. The Ashantehene, Dupuis reported, was frightened by a small organ, which had been hauled through the rain forest with great effort, and he was disappointed by a lathe, which Dupuis conceded was "too mechanical for a royal present." Even a watch and a music box failed to win favor. Rather than admit his own failings as a purveyor of royal presents, Dupuis blamed the vast distance separating European and African in technological mastery: "The task of winding up the watch or the musical box required a degree of care foreign to the comprehension of the king; it was requisite, therefore, to put the mechanism in motion each time."

Despite occasional setbacks, mechanical devices were favored as gifts by most travelers and explorers throughout the nineteenth century. In the 1870s, Wilhelm Junker assured his readers that African leaders took "childish delight in the merest mechanical trifles." He recommended knife blades, mirrors, photographs, and even empty candy boxes as presents that were sure to please the "natives." . . .

In addition to the vital role they accorded technological superiority in subduing the peoples of Africa, European writers viewed it as a major determinant of the nature of social and economic interaction between Europeans and colonized Africans. As the builders of railways, seaports, and mine shafts and the suppliers of finance and machine capital, the Europeans thought it fitting that the Africans, whom they regarded as technologically backward, be relegated to the position of laborers. As the following incident related by H. L. Duff demonstrates, most Europeans were also convinced that all but the most truculent Africans accepted this allocation of roles in deference to the Europeans' manifest scientific and technical mastery. Duff, who was Chief Secretary in the British administration in Nyasaland, had decided to take his "boy" back to England with him. As the two were approaching the steamship on which Duff had booked passage to Europe, the servant was dazzled by the lights gleaming in the darkness from the portholes and asked Duff why the flames did not consume the vessel. After patiently explaining the workings of electric lamps and pointing out other technological marvels on the ship, Duff teasingly asked his servant why the Africans had not invented such "wonders." The African protested that his people lacked the white man's magic and that the Europeans were favored by God, who helped them to understand many things that were kept hidden from others. When asked whether God had not made the Africans as well as the Europeans, the African, according to Duff, replied: "Perhaps, but I think he made us to be your tenga-tenga (bearers)."

For many Europeans, the differences between their own highly developed, technologically and scientifically oriented societies and what they perceived to be backward and superstitious African cultures were merely manifestations of the vast gap in evolutionary development that separated "civilized" Europe from "savage" Africa. Richard Freeman's association of the "rude and primitive" tools of the Africans he encountered in his travels with the peoples of the Stone Age was rooted in the widely accepted idea of recapitulation which Stephen Gould has argued was one of "the most influential ideas of late nineteenth-century science." Ethnologists and natural scientists who adhered to the idea of recapitulation believed that primitive cultures represented an ancestral stage in the evolutionary development of more advanced cultures. It followed that contemporary African societies, which were widely held to be primitive or savage, provided living examples of a level of material culture, organization, and thought which European peoples had passed through millennia earlier. Those who lived and worked among African peoples, Harry Johnston observed, felt as if they were going "thousands of years into the past" to ages of savagery and brutishness. That such a journey back in time offered opportunities for the study of the earliest stages of human development was, according to Henry Drummond, one of the most important reasons for African exploration. "Ignorant eyes," he noted, saw only savages, but the informed observer realized that "they are what we were once; possibly they may become what we are now." Drummond confessed that however edifying, the journey back to the dawn of civilization was a profoundly disturbing one: the juxtaposition of civilization as represented by "a steel ship, London-built, steaming six knots ahead" and African savagery in the form of "grass huts, nude natives, and a hippopotamus" was so unsettling that "the ideas refused to assort themselves."

No writer captured better than Joseph Conrad the sense of adventure and unease that late nineteenth-century European explorers and missionaries felt as they traveled into the African interior—and back in time:

> We penetrated deeper and deeper into the heart of darkness. It was very quiet there. At night sometimes the roll of the drums behind the curtain of trees would run up the river and remain sustained faintly, as if hovering in the air high over our heads, till the first break of day. Whether it means war, peace, or prayer we could not

tell. The dawns were heralded by a chill stillness; the wood-cutters slept, their fires burned low; the snapping of a twig would make you start. We were wanderers on a prehistoric planet. We could have fancied ourselves the first men taking possession of an accursed inheritance, to be subdued at the cost of profound anguish and of excessive toil. But suddenly, as we struggled round a bend, there would be a glimpse of rush walls, of peaked grass-roof, a burst of yells, a whirl of black limbs, a mass of hands clapping, of feet stamping, of bodies swaying, of eyes rolling, under the droops of heavy and motionless foliage. The steamer toiled along slowly on the edge of a black and incomprehensible frenzy. The prehistoric man was cursing us, praying to us, welcoming us—who could tell? We were cut off from the comprehension of our surroundings; we glided past like phantoms, wondering and secretly appalled, as sane men would be before an enthusiastic outbreak in a madhouse. We could not understand because we were too far and could not remember because we were travelling in the night of first ages, of those ages that are gone, leaving hardly a sign and no memories.

Suggested Readings

Galbraith, J. S., *Crown and Charter* (Berkeley: University of California Press, 1974).

Harlow, Barbara, and Mia Carter, eds., *Archives of Empire: Volume 2. The Scramble for Africa* (2003).

Hochschild, Adam, *King Leopold's Ghost: A Story of Greed, Terror, and Heroism in Colonial Africa* (1999).

Levering Lewis, David, *The Race to Fashoda: European Colonialism and African Resistance in the Scramble for Africa* (1987).

Nutting, Anthony, *Scramble for Africa: The Great Trek to the Boer War* (Constable, 1994).

Pakenham, Thomas, *The Scramble for Africa* (New York: Random House, 1991).

PROBLEM II

COLONIAL RULE IN AFRICA

Since Africans began their march to independence in the 1950s, scholars have pondered the influence of colonial political structures on their new nations. This question became increasingly acute during the 1960s, as political instability spread throughout virtually the entire continent. Though most African nations began life with democratic elections, many historians have argued that they retained the basic institutions and administrative structures inherited from their former rulers. This continuity has been emphasized in academic texts such as Frederick Cooper's *African History since 1940—the Past in the Present*, and popular works such as Adam Hochchild's bestselling history *King Leopold's Ghost*. This chapter presents an array of scholarly evaluations of the goals and influences of colonial administrations. These works reflect the continuing debate about the nature of the colonial state, and its enduring influence on African societies.

When Europeans conquered new African territories during the late nineteenth century, they did so with little forethought as to how these colonies would be ruled. The two major colonial powers, Britain and France, espoused two opposite administrative philosophies. British "Indirect Rule" sought to exercise power through African authorities. Local leaders—usually identified as "chiefs"—were granted political power and privileged access to resources, so long as they followed the instructions of their British advisors. The French alternative to Indirect Rule was assimilation, an ambitious policy which aspired to rule Africans directly, thereby integrating them eventually into a larger French state. Such a policy had the potential to transform African societies culturally and politically to the point that they might one day constitute "100 million Frenchmen." Other colonial powers adapted aspects of each of these policies as it suited their needs.

The principles of indirect rule were most clearly and eloquently articulated by one of Britain's greatest colonial administrators, Lord Lugard, in his book *The Dual Mandate in Tropical Africa.* Certainly no other book of its time had such a profound influence on the formulation of British colonial policy. To Lugard, the two most important administrative principles to rule subject peoples were "decentralization" and "continuity." In his view, British district officers needed to maintain a balance between supporting the traditional and customary in African societies, while at the same time encouraging the economic and legal innovations that served to support and justify British rule. Such a system required African authorities to be given the latitude to make political decisions based on local historical precedent. The role of the British officers, except in such critical areas as taxation, military forces, and the alienation of land, was to advise, not demand. To Lugard, the key to this system's success was the strong relationships it would engender between British officials and the "native" rulers. Thus, continuity of personnel was critical to its success, as only colonial officials with lengthy experience with "traditional" peoples could be trusted to strike this delicate balance. Executed correctly, Lugard argued, such a system would slowly but surely advance the political maturity and economic prosperity of colonial peoples.

France, the other great colonial power in Africa, initially sought to rule its African empire through a policy known as "assimilation." Its principles and goals are articulated here by Hubert Jules Deschamps, a former governor of the French Ivory Coast, who contrasted French and British approaches to colonial rule in a speech he delivered shortly after the independence of France's colonies in Sub-Saharan Africa. While assimilation ultimately proved untenable for logistical and ideological reasons in many parts of French Africa, Deschamps' speech demonstrates its enduring appeal to administrators right up until the empire's dissolution.

How influential were these ideological approaches in practice? Robert O. Collins demonstrates that the abstract philosophy of indirect rule ran into problems in the culturally and politically diverse environment of the Southern Sudan. Here there were few societies that possessed the kinds of hierarchical, hereditary authority that Lugard had found among the Islamic rulers of Northern Nigeria. The region was characterized by low population densities, pastoral nomads, and included communities such as the Nilotic Dinka and Nuer, who appeared to have no political institutions at all. Here, disputes were settled not by an acknowledged political authority, but by lineage heads who, between them, would arbitrate with the help of ritual specialists. Despite the best efforts of British district commissioners, known as the Bog Barons, to install indirect rule in the swampy southern Sudan, they failed. Tossing *The Dual Mandate* into the swamp, "the Bog Barons devised ingenious and idiosyncratic innovations to meet the needs of their people with few resources that had little relevance to the doctrines of indirect rule."

While Collins demonstrates that indirect rule was ill-suited to the realities of politics in Southern Sudan, other scholars have questioned its broader application among the "traditional" chiefdoms, states, and empires with which it is commonly associated. Historian Sara Berry asserts that Lugard's philosophy was predicated on the misconception that African lived in static, "tribal" communities. By treating them as such, indirect rule served to institutionalize existing conflicts and frictions. In thus arguing, Berry engages with a body of scholarship that has emphasized what Terence Ranger has referred to as "the Invention of Tradition," the manner in which Europeans manipulated, or in some cases manufactured symbols, rituals, institutions, and identities to give indirect rule a gloss of historical legitimacy. To Berry, "the effect of indirect rule was neither to freeze African societies into precolonial molds, nor to restructure them in accordance with British inventions of African traditions, but to generate unresolvable debates over the interpretation of tradition and its meaning for colonial governance and economic activity." Thus, ironically, indirect rule's reliance on "traditional" authorities did not encourage security, but rather "promoted instability in local structures of authority and in conditions of access to productive resources."

Ugandan scholar Mahmood Mandani points out that there were other paths to colonial rule explored in the early colonial period. Throughout the nineteenth century, embryonic colonial states had cultivated indigenous, westernized allies to provide the nucleus of an administration that could have created administrative structures along Western lines. However, after 1900 all colonial administrations gradually abandoned these indigenous intellectuals and elites in favor of the traditional rulers who formed the basis of indirect rule. Thus to Mamdani, "the scarcity of administrative personnel, the key argument in this logical construct, was artificially created; it was not inevitable." This meant that, despite early efforts by French and Portuguese regimes to impose direct forms of political rule, and aggressive efforts at cultural assimilation, eventually all colonial administrations in Africa placed Africans into tribal groups, often invented, and ruled them through "traditional" autocratic leaders. Mamdani describes this triumph of indirect rule as "decentralized despotism," a form of African administration which lay the foundations for the post-colonial ethnic conflicts that continue to plague the continent.

The chapter concludes with an excerpt from David Gordon's comparative study of colonial administrations in British Northern Rhodesia and the Belgian Congo. By studying the colonial experiences of people living on opposite sides of the Lualapa River, which formed the boundary between these two colonies, Gordon finds that an array of economic and political factors shaped the ways in which Africans engaged with the colonial state. On both sides of the river "there was a significant divergence between colonial intentions regarding the spread of state power through chiefs and actual outcomes." Gordon, like

Collins and Berry, highlights the constraints facing colonial states in their effort to establish new, or neo-traditional, state structures. Thus, diverse colonial administrations did not leave identical legacies. Gordon finds that, while administrations on both sides of the river had similar philosophies of how best to rule indigenous peoples, "There was a significant divergence between colonial intentions regarding the spread of state power through chiefs and actual outcomes." These had lasting influences on the chiefdoms that dominated the two sides of the river.

Principles of Native Administration

JOHN FREDERICK LUGARD[1]

The British Empire, as General Smuts has well said, has only one mission—for liberty and self-development on no standardized lines, so that all may feel that their interests and religion are safe under the British flag. Such liberty and self-development can be best secured to the native population by leaving them free to manage their own affairs through their own rulers, proportionately to their degree of advancement, under the guidance of the British staff, and subject to the laws and policy of the administration.

But apart from the administration of native affairs, the local government has to preserve law and order, develop the trade and communications of the country, and protect the interests of the merchants and others who are engaged in the development of its commercial and mineral resources. What, then, are the functions of the British staff, and how can the machinery of government be most efficiently constituted for the discharge of its duties in those countries in Africa which fall under British control?

The staff must necessarily be limited in numbers, for if the best class of men are to be attracted to a service which often involves separation from family and a strain on health, they must be offered adequate salaries and inducements in the way of leave, housing, medical aid, or their equivalents in money, for their maintenance in health and comfort while serving abroad, and this forms a heavy charge on the revenues. Policy and economy alike demand restriction in numbers, but the best that England can supply.

Obviously, a consideration of the machinery of British administration in the tropics involves a review of its relations to the home government on the one hand and of its local constitution and functions on the other. I will take the latter first.

---

[1] This excerpt is taken from John Frederick Lugard, *The Dual Mandate in British Tropical Africa* (London: Frank Cass & Co. Ltd., 1965, by arrangement with William Blackwood and Sons Ltd.), pp. 94-97, 102-5, 199-218. John Frederick Lugard, 1858-1945, was the governor of British Nigeria and one of the great proconsuls of the British Empire.

The government is constituted on the analogy of the British government in England. The governor represents the king but combines the functions of the prime minister as head of the executive. The councils bear a certain resemblance to the Home Cabinet and Parliament, while the detailed work of the administration is carried out by a staff which may be roughly divided into the administrative, the judicial, and the departmental branches.

The administrative branch is concerned with the supervision of the native administration and the general direction of policy; with education, and the collection and control of direct taxes, which involve assessment and close relations with the native population; with legislation and the administration of justice in courts other than the Supreme Court; and with the direct government and welfare of the non-native section of the population. The departmental staff is charged with duties in connection with transport, communications, and buildings (railways, marine, and public works); with the development of natural resources (mines, collieries, forestry, agriculture, and geology) with the auxiliary services of government (medical, secretarial, accounting, posts and telegraphs, surveys, &c.); and the collection of customs duties.

The task of the administrative branch is to foster that sympathy, mutual understanding, and cooperation between the government and the people, without which, as Sir C. Ilbert has observed, no government is really stable and efficient. Its aim is to promote progress in civilization and justice and to create conditions under which individual enterprise may most advantageously develop the natural resources of the country. The task of the departments, on the other hand, is to maintain the government machine in a state of efficiency and to afford direct assistance in material development. Their motto is efficiency and economy. The two branches work together, and their duties overlap and are interdependent in every sphere. The efficient discharge of those duties in combination constitutes the white man's title to control.

There are in my estimation two vital principles which characterize the growth of a wise administration—they are decentralization and continuity. Though, as Lord Morley said of India, "perfectly efficient administration has an inevitable tendency to overcentralization," it is a tendency to be combated. It has indeed been said that the whole art of administration consists in judicious and progressive delegation, and there is much truth in the dictum, provided that delegation of duties be accompanied by public responsibility. This is not applicable to the head of the government alone or in particular, but to every single officer, from the governor to the foreman of a gang of daily laborers. The man who is charged with the accomplishment of any task, and has the ability and discrimination to select the most capable of those who are subordinate to him and trust them with ever-increasing responsibility, up to the limits of their capacity, will be rewarded not only with confidence and loyalty, but will get more work done, and better done, than the man who tries to keep too much in his own hands and is slow to recognize merit, originality, and efficiency in others. . . .

The second of the two principles which I have described as vital in African administration is continuity, and this, like decentralization, is applicable to every department and to every officer, however junior, but above all to those officers who represent the government in its relations with the native population. The annually recurrent absence of leave, which withdraws each officer in West Africa from his post for about a third of his time, the occasional invalidings and deaths, and the constant changes rendered unavoidable of late years by a depleted and inadequate staff have made it extremely difficult to preserve in that part of Africa any continuity whatever. The African is slow to give his confidence. He is suspicious and reticent with a newcomer, eager to resuscitate old land disputes—perhaps of half a century's standing—in the hope that the new officer in his ignorance may reverse the decision of his predecessor. The time of an officer is wasted in picking the tangled threads and informing himself of the conditions of his new post. By the time he has acquired the necessary knowledge, learnt the character of the people he has to deal with, and won their confidence, his leave becomes due, and if on his return he is posted elsewhere, not only is progress arrested but retrogression may result.

It is also essential that each officer should be at pains to keep full and accurate records of all important matters, especially of any conversation with native chiefs in which any pledge or promise, implied or explicit, has been made. It is not enough that official correspondence should be filed—a summary of each subject should be made and decisions recorded and brought up to date, so that a newcomer may be able rapidly to put himself au courant. The higher the post occupied by an officer, the more important does the principle become. It is especially important that the decisions of the governor should be fully recorded in writing, and not merely by an initial of acquiescence or a verbal order. This involves heavy office work, but it is work which cannot be neglected if misunderstandings are to be avoided and continuity preserved. The very detailed instructions regarding the duties of each newly created department, which were issued when the administration of Northern Nigeria was first inaugurated, served a very useful purpose in maintaining continuity of policy, till superseded on amalgamation by briefer general orders.

In the sphere of administration there are obviously many subjects—education, taxation, slavery and labor, native courts, land tenure—in which uniformity and continuity of policy is impossible in so large a country, unless explicit instructions are issued for guidance. By a perusal of the periodical reports of Residents, the governor could inform himself of the difficulties, which presented themselves in the varying circumstances of each province, and think out the best way in which they could be met, or could note where misunderstandings or mistakes had been made. By these means a series of memoranda were compiled and constantly revised as new problems came to light and as progress rendered the earlier instructions obsolete. They formed the reference book and authority of the Resident and his staff.

In a country so vast, which included communities in all stages of development, and differing from each other profoundly in their customs and traditions, it was the declared policy of government that each should develop on its own lines; but this in no way lessens the need for uniformity in the broad principles of policy, or in their application where the conditions are similar. It was the aim of these memoranda to preserve this continuity and uniformity of principle and policy. . . . In Africa we are laying foundations. The superstructure may vary in its details, some of which may perhaps be ill-designed, but the stability of the edifice is unaffected. You may pull down and re-erect cupolas, but you cannot alter the design of the foundations without first destroying all that has been erected upon them.

If continuity and decentralization are, as I have said, the first and most important conditions in maintaining an effective administration, cooperation is the keynote of success in its application—continuous cooperation between every link in the chain, from the head of the administration to its most junior member—cooperation between the government and the commercial community, and, above all, between the provincial staff and the native rulers. Every individual adds his share not only to the accomplishment of the ideal, but to the ideal itself. Its principles are fashioned by his quota of experience, and its results are achieved by his patient and loyal application of these principles, with as little interference as possible with native customs and modes of thought.

Principles do not change, but their mode of application may and should vary with the customs, the traditions, and the prejudices of each unit. The task of the administrative officer is to clothe his principles in the garb of evolution, not of revolution; to make it apparent alike to the educated native, the conservative Moslem, and the primitive pagan, each in his own degree, that the policy of the government is not antagonistic but progressive—sympathetic to his aspirations and the guardian of his natural rights. The governor looks to the administrative staff to keep in touch with native thought and feeling and to report fully to himself, in order that he in turn may be able to support them and recognize their work. Lord Milner's declaration that the British policy is to rule subject races through their own chiefs is generally applauded, but the manner in which the principle should be translated into practice admits of wide differences of opinion and method. Obviously the extent to which native races are capable of controlling their own affairs must vary in proportion to their degree of development and progress in social organization, but this is a question of adaptation and not of principle. Broadly speaking, the divergent opinions in regard to the application of the principle may be found to originate in three different conceptions.

The first is that the ideal of self-government can only be realized by the methods of evolution which have produced the democracies of Europe and America—viz., by representative institutions in which a comparatively small educated class shall be recognized as the natural spokesmen for the many. This method is naturally in favor with the educated African. Whether it is adapted to peoples accustomed by their own institutions to autocracy—albeit modified by a substantial expression of the popular will and circumscribed by custom—is naturally a matter on which opinions differ. The fundamental essential, however, in such a form of government is that the educated few shall at least be representative of the feelings and desires of the many—well-known to them, speaking their language, and versed in their customs and prejudices.

In present conditions in Africa, the numerous separate tribes, speaking different languages and in different stages of evolution, cannot produce representative men of education. Even were they available, the number of communities which could claim separate representation would make any central and really representative council very unwieldy. The authority vested in the representatives would be antagonistic to that of the native rulers and their councils, which are the product of the natural tendencies of tribal evolution, and would run counter to the customs and institutions of the people.

An attempt to adapt these principles of Western representative government to tropical races is now being made in India. Though the powers entrusted to the elected representatives of the people are at first restricted under the dyarchical system (which reserves certain subjects for the central authority), the principle of government by an educated minority, as opposed to government by native rulers, is fully accepted.

The experiment has so far shown much promise of success, but the real test is not merely whether the native councillors show moderation and restraint against extremists of their own class, but whether, when legislation which is unpopular with the illiterate masses and the martial races of India has to be enacted, there may be a reluctance to accept what will be called "Babu-made law," though it would have been accepted without demur as the order of "the Sirkar"—the British Raj. It is, of course, now too late to adopt to any large extent the alternative of gradually transforming the greater part of British India into native states governed by their own hereditary dynasties, whose representatives in many cases still exist, and extending to them the principles which have so successfully guided our relations with the native states in India itself and in Malaya in the past. It is one thing to excite an ignorant peasantry against an alien usurper, but quite another thing to challenge a native ruler.

Such a system does not exclude the educated native from participation in the government of the state to which he belongs, as a councillor to the native ruler, but it substitutes for direct British rule, not an elected oligarchy but a form of government more in accord with racial instincts and inherited traditions.

The second conception is that every advanced community should be given the widest possible powers of self-government under its own ruler, and that these powers should be rapidly increased with the object of complete independence at the earliest possible date in the not distant future. Those who hold this view generally, I think, also consider that attempts to train primitive tribes in any form of self-government are futile, and that the administration must be wholly conducted by British officials. This in the past has been the principle adopted in many dependencies. It recognized no alternative between a status of independence, like the sultans of Malaya or the native princes of India, and the direct rule of the district commissioner.

But the attempt to create such independent states in Africa has been full of anomalies. In the case of Egbaland, where the status has been formally recognized by treaty, the extent to which the crown had jurisdiction was uncertain; yet, as we have seen, international conventions, including even that relating to the protection of wild animals, which was wholly opposed to native customary rights, were applied without the consent of the "independent" state, and powers quite incompatible with independence were exercised by the suzerain.

. . . The danger of going too fast with native races is even more likely to lead to disappointment, if not to disaster, than the danger of not going fast enough. The pace can best be gauged by those who have intimate acquaintance alike with the strong points and the limitations of the native peoples and rulers with whom they have to deal.

The Fulani of Northern Nigeria are, as I have said, more capable of rule than the indigenous races, but in proportion as we consider them an alien race, we are denying self-government to the people over whom they rule, and supporting an alien caste—albeit closer and more akin to the native races than a European can be. Yet, capable as they are, it requires the ceaseless vigilance of the British staff to maintain a high standard of administrative integrity and to prevent oppression of the peasantry. We are dealing with the same generation, and in many cases with the identical rulers, who were responsible for the misrule and tyranny which we found in 1902. The subject races near the capital were then serfs and victims of constant extortion. Those dwelling at a distance were raided for slaves, and could not count their women, their cattle, or their crops their own. Punishments were most barbarous and included impalement, mutilation, and burying alive. Many generations have passed since British rule was established among the more intellectual people of India—the inheritors of centuries of Eastern civilization—yet only today are we tentatively seeking to confer on them a measure of self-government. "Festina lente" ["make haste slowly," ed.] is a motto which the Colonial Office will do well to remember in its dealings with Africa.

The system adopted in Nigeria is therefore only a particular method of the application of these principles—more especially as regards "advanced communities"—and since I am familiar with it I will use it as illustrative of the methods which in my opinion should characterize the dealings of the controlling power with subject races.

The object in view is to make each "emir" or paramount chief, assisted by his judicial council, an effective ruler over his own people. He presides over a "native administration" organized throughout as a unit of local government. The area over which he exercises jurisdiction is divided into districts under the control of "headmen," who collect the taxes in the name of the ruler and pay them into the "native treasury," conducted by a native treasurer and staff under the supervision of the chief at his capital. Here, too, is the prison for native court prisoners, and probably the school, which I shall describe more fully in the chapter on education. Large cities are divided into wards for purposes of control and taxation. The district headman, usually a territorial magnate with local connections, is the chief executive officer in the area under his charge. He controls the village headmen, and is responsible for the assessment of the tax, which he collects through their agency. He must reside in his district and not at the capital. He is not allowed to pose as a chief with a retinue of his own and duplicate officials, and is summoned from time to time to report to his chief. If, as is the case with some of the ancient emirates, the community is a small one but independent of any other native rule, the chief may be his own district headman.

A province under a Resident may contain several separate "native administrations," whether they be Moslem emirates or pagan communities. A "division" under a British district officer may include one or more headman's districts, or more than one small emirate or independent pagan tribe, but as a rule no emirate is partly in one division and partly in another. The Resident acts as sympathetic adviser and counsellor to the native chief, being careful not to interfere so as to lower his prestige or cause him to lose interest in his work. His advice on matters of general policy must be followed, but the native ruler issues his own instructions to his subordinate chiefs and district heads—not as the orders of the Resident but as his own—and he is encouraged to work through them, instead of centralizing everything in himself—a system which in the past had produced such great abuses. The British district officers supervise and assist the native district headmen, through whom they convey any instructions to village heads and make any arrangements necessary for carrying on the work of the government departments, but important orders emanate from the emir, whose messenger usually accompanies and acts as mouthpiece of a district officer.

The tax—which supersedes all former "tribute," irregular imposts, and forced labor—is, in a sense, the basis of the whole system, since it supplies the means to pay the emir and all his officials. The district and village heads are effectively supervised and assisted in its assessment by the British staff,

The native treasury retains the proportion assigned to it (in advanced communities a half), and pays the remainder into colonial revenue. . . .

The authority of the emir over his own people is absolute, and the profession of an alien creed does not absolve a native from the obligation to obey his lawful orders; but aliens—other than natives domiciled in the emirate and accepting the jurisdiction of the native authority and courts—are under the direct control of the British staff. Townships are excluded from the native jurisdiction.

The village is the administrative unit. It is not always easy to define, since the security to life and property which has followed the British administration has caused an exodus from the cities and large villages, and the creation of innumerable hamlets, sometimes only of one or two huts, on the agricultural lands. The peasantry of the advanced communities, though ignorant, yet differs from that of the backward tribes in that they recognize the authority of the emir, and are more ready to listen to the village head and the Council of Elders, on which the Nigerian system is based.

Subject, therefore, to the limitations which I shall presently discuss, the native authority is thus de facto and de jure ruler over his own people. He appoints and dismisses his subordinate chiefs and officials. He exercises the power of allocation of lands, and with the aid of the native courts, of adjudication in land disputes and expropriation for offenses against the community; these are the essential functions upon which, in the opinion of the West African Lands Committee, the prestige of the native authority depends. The lawful orders which he may give are carefully defined by ordinance, and in the last resort are enforced by government.

Since native authority, especially if exercised by alien conquerors, is inevitably weakened by the first impact of civilized rule, it is made clear to the elements of disorder, who regard force as conferring the only right to demand obedience, that government, by the use of force if necessary, intends to support the native chief. To enable him to maintain order he employs a body of unarmed police, and if the occasion demands the display of superior force he looks to the government as, for instance, if a community combines to break the law or shield criminals from justice—a rare event in the advanced communities. The native ruler derives his power from the Suzerain, and is responsible that it is not misused. He is equally with British officers amenable to the law, but his authority does not depend on the caprice of an executive officer. To intrigue against him is an offence punishable, if necessary, in a provincial court. Thus both British and native courts are invoked to uphold his authority.

The essential feature of the system (as I wrote at the time of its inauguration) is that the native chiefs are constituted as an integral part of the machinery of the administration. There are not two sets of rulers—British and native—working either separately or in cooperation, but a single government in which the native chiefs have well-defined duties and an acknowledged status equally with

British officials. Their duties should never conflict, and should overlap as little as possible. They should be complementary to each other, and the chief himself must understand that he has no right to place and power unless he renders his proper services to the state.

The ruling classes are no longer either demi-gods or parasites preying on the community. They must work for the stipends and position they enjoy. They are the trusted delegates of the governor, exercising in the Moslem states the well-understood powers of "wakils" in conformity with their own Islamic system, and recognizing the king's representative as their acknowledged suzerain. . . .

The limitations to independence which are frankly inherent in this conception of native rule—not as temporary restraints to be removed as soon as may be, but as powers which rightly belong to the controlling power as trustee for the welfare of the masses, and as being responsible for the defence of the country and the cost of its central administration—are such as do not involve interference with the authority of the chiefs or the social organization of the people. They have been accepted by the Fulani emirs as natural and proper to the controlling power, and their reservation in the hands of the governor has never interfered with the loyalty of the ruling chiefs, or, so far as I am aware, been resented by them. The limitations are as follows:

> 1. Native rulers are not permitted to raise and control armed forces, or to grant permission to carry arms. To this, in principle, Great Britain stands pledged under the Brussels Act. The evils which result in Africa from an armed population were evident in Uganda before it fell under British control, and are very evident in Abyssinia today. No one with experience will deny the necessity of maintaining the strictest military discipline over armed forces or police in Africa if misuse of power is to be avoided, and they are not to become a menace and a terror to the native population and a danger in case of religious excitement—a discipline which an African ruler is incapable of appreciating or applying. For this reason native levies should never be employed in substitution for or in aid of troops. On the other hand, the government armed police are never quartered in native towns, where their presence would interfere with the authority of the chiefs. Like the regular troops, they are employed as escorts and on duty in the townships. The native administration maintains a police, who wear a uniform but do not carry firearms.
>
> 2. The sole right to impose taxation in any form is reserved to the suzerain power. This fulfills the bilateral understanding that the

peasantry—provided they pay the authorized tax (the adjustment of which to all classes of the population is a responsibility which rests with the central government)—should be free of all other exactions whatsoever (including unpaid labor), while a sufficient proportion of the tax is assigned to the native treasuries to meet the expenditure of the native administration. Special sanction by ordinance—or rule approved by the governor—is therefore required to enable the native authority to levy any special dues, etc.

3. The right to legislate is reserved. That this should remain in the hands of the central government—itself limited by the control of the Colonial Office, as I have described—cannot be questioned. The native authority, however, exercises very considerable power in this regard. A native ruler, and the native courts, are empowered to enforce native law and custom, provided it is not repugnant to humanity, or in opposition to any ordinance. This practically meets all needs, but the native authority may also make rules on any subject, provided they are approved by the governor.

4. The right to appropriate land on equitable terms for public purposes and for commercial requirements is vested in the governor. In the northern provinces of Nigeria (but not in the South), the right of disposing of native lands is reserved to the governor by ordinance. In practice this does not interfere with the power of the native ruler (as the delegate of the governor) to assign lands to the natives under his rule, in accordance with native law and custom, or restrict him or the native courts from adjudicating between natives regarding occupancy rights in land. No rents are levied on lands in occupation by indigenous natives. Leases to aliens are granted by the central government. . . .

The habits of a people are not changed in a decade, and when powerful despots are deprived of the pastime of war and slave-raiding, and when even the weak begin to forget their former sufferings to grow weary of a life without excitement and to resent the petty restrictions which have replaced the cruelties of the old despotism, it must be the aim of government to provide new interests and rivalries in civilized progress, in education, in material prosperity and trade, and even in sport. . . .

Succession is governed by native law and custom, subject in the case of important chiefs to the approval of the governor in order that the most capable claimant may be chosen. It is important to ascertain the customary law and to follow it when possible, for the appointment of a chief who is not the recognized heir, or who is disliked by the people, may give rise to trouble, and in any case the new chief would have much difficulty in asserting his authority, and would fear to check abuses lest he should alienate his supporters. In Moslem countries the law is fairly clearly defined, being a useful combination of the hereditary principle, tempered by selection, and in many cases in Nigeria the ingenious device is maintained of having two rival dynasties, from each of which the successor is selected alternately.

In pagan communities the method varies; but there is no rigid rule, and a margin for selection is allowed. The formal approval of the governor after a short period of probation is a useful precaution, so that if the designated chief proves himself unsuitable, the selection may be revised without difficulty. Minor chiefs are usually selected by popular vote, subject to the approval of the Paramount Chief. It is a rule in Nigeria that no slave may be appointed as a chief or district headman. If one is nominated, he must first be publicly freed.

Small and isolated communities, living within the jurisdiction of a chief, but owing allegiance to the chief of their place of origin—a common source of trouble in Africa—should gradually be absorbed into the territorial jurisdiction. Aliens who have settled in a district for their own purposes would be subject to the local jurisdiction.

There are some who consider that however desirable it may be to rule through the native chiefs of advanced communities, such a policy is misplaced, if not impossible, among the backward tribes. Here, they would say, the Resident and his staff must necessarily be the direct rulers, since among the most primitive peoples there are no recognized chiefs capable of exercising rule. The imposition of a tax is in their view premature, since (they say) the natives derive no corresponding benefit, and learn to regard the district officer merely as a tax collector. Moreover, refusal to pay necessitates coercive expeditions— scarcely distinguishable from the raids of old times. To attempt to adapt such methods—however suitable to the Moslem communities—to the conditions of primitive tribes would be to foist upon them a system foreign to their conceptions. In the criticisms I have read, no via media is indicated between those who are accounted to rank as advanced communities, entitled before long to independence, and direct rule by the British staff. Let us realize that the advanced communities form a very minute proportion of the population of British tropical Africa. The vast majority are in the primitive or early tribal stages of development. To abandon the policy of ruling them through their own chiefs, and to substitute the direct rule of the British officer, is to forgo the high ideal of leading the backward races, by their own efforts and in their own way, to raise themselves to a higher plane of social organization, and tends to perpetuate and stereotype existing conditions.

We must realize also two other important facts. First, that the British staff, exercising direct rule, cannot be otherwise than very small in comparison to the area and population of which they are in charge. That rule cannot generally mean the benevolent autocracy of a particular district officer, well-versed in the language and customs of the people, but rule by a series of different white men, conveying their orders by police and couriers and alien native subordinates, and the quartering of police detachments in native villages. Experience has shown the difficulty in such conditions of detecting and checking cases of abuse of office and of acquisition of land by alien and absentee native landlords. There is a marked tendency to litigation and the entire decay of such tribal authority as may previously have existed.

The changed conditions of African life is the second important fact for consideration. The advent of Europeans cannot fail to have a disintegrating effect on tribal authority and institutions and on the conditions of native life. This is due in part to the unavoidable restrictions imposed on the exercise of their power by the native chiefs. They may no longer inflict barbarous and inhuman punishments on the individual, or take reprisals by force of arms on aggressive neighbors or a disobedient section of the community. The concentration of force in the hands of the suzerain power, and the amenability of the chiefs to that power for acts of oppression and misrule, are evidence to primitive folk that the power of the chiefs has gone. This decay of tribal authority has unfortunately too often been accentuated by the tendency of British officers to deal directly with petty chiefs, and to ignore, and allow their subordinates to ignore, the principal chief. It has been increased in many cases by the influx of alien natives, who, when it suited them, set at naught the native authority, and refused to pay the tribute which the chiefs were given no means of enforcing, or acquired lands which they held in defiance of native customary tenure.

Here, then, in my view, lies our present task in Africa. It becomes impossible to maintain the old order—the urgent need is for adaptation to the new—to build up a tribal authority with a recognized and legal standing, which may avert social chaos. It cannot be accomplished by superseding—by the direct rule of the white man— such ideas of discipline and organization as exist, nor yet by "stereotyping customs and institutions among backward races which are not consistent with progress."

Indirect Rule Sudan Style

ROBERT O. COLLINS[2]

When Great Britain found herself the ruler of a far-flung African empire from Cape Town to Cairo, she had no imperial ideology, policy, or plan as to how it should be governed. Cynical wits attributed the acquisition of Africa to an English "fit of absence of mind." The search for a coherent policy by which British administrators could govern their diverse colonies in Africa was eloquently expounded in 1922 by Lord Lugard, former Governor-General of Nigeria, in his *Dual Mandate in Tropical Africa*, in which he argued that a balance must be maintained between tradition and modernity by supporting the authority of the traditional rulers and allowing them to govern by the customary and accepted institutions of their people. The role of the local British district officers, presumably able to speak the vernacular language, would be as an adviser only, interfering as little as possible in the conduct of tribal affairs and only introducing modern ideas, customs, and technology very gradually so as not to upset the balance and to preserve law and order and, of course, British overrule. No other book of its time had such a profound influence on the formulation of British colonial policy in Africa and particularly in the Sudan, where "it passed through three stages: the first as a useful administrative device, then that of a political doctrine, and finally that of a religious dogma." The basic ideas of Indirect Rule had long been informally adopted in India, but it was Lugard who now transformed these principles into a written, practical manual for governing subject peoples in Africa. The same year that *The Dual Mandate* was published, it was applied to the rural Sudan by the promulgation of the Powers of Nomad Sheikhs Ordinance, and by 1923 the judicial powers of over 300 tribal shaykhs had been acknowledged, strengthened, and regularized.

At the time, Governor-General Sir Lee Stack recognized that Indirect Rule could be readily instituted among the tribal societies that constituted the rural

---

[2] This excerpt is taken from Robert O. Collins, *A History of the Modern Sudan* (Cambridge: Cambridge University Press, 2008). Robert O. Collins was professor of history at the University of California, Santa Barbara.

Sudan, but he was equally convinced that it was totally unsuited to the governance of the three towns at the confluence of the White and Blue Niles, inhabited by a growing number of Western-educated elite who took pride in their ethnic origins so long as they were free of what they regarded as the reactionary and unprogressive authority of their illiterate tribal elders. In order to find a place in the governance of the Sudan for this new elite, Stack promulgated the Khartoum, Khartoum North, and Omdurman Council Proclamation of 1921 which established a consultative advisory council so that this new class, what some British officials disdainfully referred to as the half-educated effendi, could now participate in the governance of urban affairs. This progressive attempt to involve the rising educated elite was eagerly abandoned, however, after the crises during the spring and summer of 1924 that swept through Khartoum and culminated in the assassination of Governor-General Sir Lee Stack in November 1924 ended his experiment with advisory councils. The tenure of his successor, Sir Geoffrey Archer, was too brief (1924-1926) for him to be concerned with the future of advisory councils, while his replacement, Sir John Maffey (1926-1933), was adamantly opposed to any advisory councils, which he regarded as containing "the seeds of grave danger and eventually present a free platform for capture by a pushful intelligentsia."

Not surprisingly, Maffey became the leading advocate for Indirect Rule, ably abetted by (Sir) Harold MacMichael who occupied the powerful position of assistant civil secretary from 1919-1925 and then civil secretary (1925-1934) throughout Maffey's years in office. They even hoped that the government's recognition and support for the local, traditional authorities would tend to neutralize the growing influence of Sayyid 'Abd al-Rahman. There were, however, numerous governors and district commissioners who were not only enthusiastic but were frequently obsessed with implementing Indirect Rule, like Reginald Davies, who served in Darfur (1920-1924) and then as Director of the Intelligence Department, which played a significant role in advising on matters concerning native policy. Together the doctrine of Indirect Rule was vigorously pursued with the promulgation of the Powers of Nomad Sheikhs Ordinance in 1927, which devolved the powers earlier bestowed on nomadic shaykhs to traditional shaykhs and chiefs of settled farming communities that suddenly transferred authority from Sudanese administering a geographically defined territory to the rulers of separate ethnic groups irrespective of administrative boundaries.

Despite the enormous appeal of Indirect Rule for British colonial officials in Africa, its implementation in the Sudan encountered severe problems. In the northern Sudan, during the Turkiya, there had been a concentrated effort to centralize government from Khartoum at the expense of tribal authorities; many were weakened, some disappeared. Similarly, in the northern Sudan, during the violent upheavals of the Mahdiya, the integrity of many tribes was shattered, including their hitherto powerful traditional rulers. The riverine Danaqla, Shaqiyya, and Ja'aliyyin, the *awlad al-bahr*, were rendered impotent in their efforts to overthrow the Khalifa, and even the Khalifa's own western kinsmen, the Baqqara of the *awlad al-ghirab*, disintegrated as a cohesive tribe when forced to immigrate to Omdurman in the early 1890s.

Moreover, in their efforts to impose security throughout the Sudan in the first decade of Anglo-Egyptian rule, the British themselves were not squeamish in deflating the authority of troublesome tribal leaders.

Unlike the northern Arab Sudan, the implementation of Indirect Rule in the African South had more far-reaching goals. The British were determined to assist the Christian missionaries, who were insufficient to turn the tide of creeping Islam into the southern Sudan. In 1922 the government promulgated the Passports and Permits Ordinance, which declared much of the South Closed Districts. This essentially excluded the most effective proselytizer of Islam, the *jallaba* merchants, while severely restricting southerners from traveling down the Nile or overland to seek work in the North. In the same year, the beginnings of Indirect Rule were found in British appeals to the southerners to reaffirm their tribal roots. In the hope of institutionalizing chiefs, the British imported chiefs' courts (*lukikos*) from Uganda and established them under the watchful eye of a British district commissioner (DC). Gradually, the combination of these ordinances and rudimentary institutions to exclude Muslims and Islam from the South, while isolating southerners in what some critics contemptuously called an anthropological zoo, became known as Southern Policy. Its British proponents vigorously pursued the extremely difficult challenge to establish the principle of Indirect Rule in the southern Sudan. Unfortunately, in many southern societies the influential tribal leaders, without whom Indirect Rule could not function, did not exist or were nonentities masquerading as chiefs. Only the Azande kingdoms along the Congo-Nile watershed had a well-defined aristocracy. The Avungura, ruled by powerful warrior kings, and the Shilluk, living by the White Nile and ruled by a divine king, the Reth, were the only southern Sudanese societies in which the imposition of Indirect Rule was not an artificial British construct.

The greatest challenge to the introduction of Indirect Rule was among the Nilotic cattle-peoples of the southern Sudan, the Dinka and the Nuer. Their numbers far exceeded the small diffuse tribes of farmers cultivating modest plots east and west of the Bahr al-Jabal and along the ironstone plateau of the Congo Nile watershed in Equatoria, where petty chieftaincies were not the ideal model for the implementation of Indirect Rule. With their vast herds of cattle, the Nilotes dominated the large savanna and swamp lands of the Bahr al-Ghazal and the Upper Nile, moving with the seasons for pasturage and water. Their inveterate raiding for cattle and distrust of strangers had earned them the reputation, in the nineteenth century, as reckless, truculent warriors.

They possessed no traditional rulers, no chiefs, only ritual specialists: the leopard-skin chiefs of the Dinka, the prophets of the Nuer. Their societies were organized by segmentary lineages, which settled disputes among themselves without the need of a chief. With no single authority through which to establish British control, let alone Indirect Rule, the Sudan government perceived no other option but force to convert the Nilotes to docile subjects. By the end of the 1920s annual punitive patrols by the Equatoria Corps had secured the subjugation of the Bahr al-Ghazal Dinka as much by waving the flag as engaging in armed combat. The Dinka, despite their large numbers, were no match for the firepower of the *Equats*. The Nuer were quite another matter.

They were more elusive, disappearing into the great swamps of the Sudd or vanishing over the Ethiopian border when threatened by government punitive patrols. Like the Dinka, they too had no chiefs, but their prophets—particularly Guek Wonding—attracted a large following by ruthlessly raiding the Dinka, now tax-paying subjects, for cattle and women and defying the authority of the Sudan government. Consequently, British officers launched the conquest of Nuerland to eliminate Guek and his following, end their Dinka raids, and enforce what came to be known as the Nuer Settlement. In the winter of 1924, heavily armed columns slogged through waterlogged plains and swamps of the Upper Nile supported by planes from the RAF. What Governor-General Sir John Maffey thought to be just another punitive patrol had become, much to his consternation, all-out war. Guek was killed in a confrontation before his sacred pyramid, and the Nuer were crushed to lay the foundations for Nuer Settlement, "which is the building up of a native administration on the foundations of tribal customs and . . . even to the point of inventing an organization . . . when they have lost their own"—Indirect Rule.

Unfortunately, the British district commissioners were ignorant of those Nuer tribal customs and organization from which they were to construct traditional tribal institutions that enabled them to rule indirectly. To sweep away the "ignorance of local beliefs and habits and insufficient understanding of savage ways of thought," Sir Harold MacMichael, acting on the recommendation of E.G. Seligman, Professor of Ethnology in the University of London, recruited Dr. E. E. Evans-Pritchard for the newly created post of Sudan government Anthropologist "to make an ethnological survey of the Nuer." The discipline of Social Anthropology was born.

In both the northern and southern Sudan, British district commissioners sought out the traditional tribal rulers. They found themselves searching for lost tribes and vanished chiefs or, as Sir James Currie, former director of education, later described the search for Indirect Rule:

"The time has long passed when it was possible to gull the Native demanding equality of economic opportunity with patter about indirect rule, or fob him off with a social scheme in which a subsidized ruler—too frequently an obsolete antiquity—dances to the pipes of young [British] gentlemen whose sole idea is that things shall 'stay put.' They cannot, by a hard fate, be squires in England, but to ape the part in Africa is fascinating."

Sir James had a particular reason to castigate the artificiality of Indirect Rule. The obsequious attempt to make Indirect Rule a reality and the Sudan safe for autocracy was inimical to modern western education whose sole intent, thought many British officials, was to create a detribalized and discontented class contaminated by progressive ideas to threaten the British status quo.

By 1935 the administration of the South had been shaped by what was unofficially known and frequently misunderstood as Southern Policy. As conceived in 1930 by civil secretary Sir Harold MacMichael, Southern Policy was to protect the backward southern Sudanese from external influences of Arabic and Islam from the northern Sudan that would undermine their traditional cultures, prevent the expansion of Islam, and undermine the prospects for the success of Indirect Rule. Very gradually, however, those northern Sudanese officials currently in the South were to be replaced by educated southerners.

Southern Policy had achieved some of its first objectives and had largely ignored the latter. Many but not all of the Arab *jallaba* had been sent packing to the North; northern government officials were rotated out of the South, but a substantial cadre remained to carry out the more mundane tasks of administration. The progressive aspect of Southern Policy, education, had failed miserably. The number of southerners enrolled in schools actually declined, for there were few prospects for graduates when reduced budgets could not provide clerks and low level officials, and even the number of southern technical staff had actually shrunk after 1932. Many members of the Political Service in the South, like their colleagues in the North, were deeply suspicious of the half-educated Sudanese, southern or northern, as potential rivals to the traditional leaders they were committed to support so that Indirect Rule could function. Progress in education was further confused by the decisions of the Rejaf Language Conference of 1928 to teach in only six vernacular languages, which severely limited instruction in some schools for those students who did not speak one of the designated six. It also introduced the sphere system, by which the government had arbitrarily separated Catholic and Protestant missions to avoid religious friction but which had transferred ancient European sectarian rivalries into southern schools, which generated unpleasant religious rivalry among the schoolboys.

In less than a year after his arrival in Khartoum, Governor-General Sir Stewart Symes sought to define his policy in the southern Sudan with particular reference to Southern Policy in a memorandum of 9 June 1935, which shortly proved to be a bundle of contradictions. Although it is quite impossible to gauge the extent by which personal bias in the Sudan government shaped policy, the profound importance of personalities in the Sudan Political Service inflated the impact of individual views upon policy decisions. Consequently, MacMichael's well-known contempt for the southern Sudanese living in what he derisively called the Serbonian Bog must have influenced his Southern Policy, just as Symes's deep dislike of the South shaped his policy of care and maintenance. As part of his progressive dismantling of Indirect Rule, he railed against the secrecy of Southern Policy, designed exclusively to isolate the South from Arab and Islamic influence by a Chinese wall that should be replaced by free access for all to the lands beyond the rivers of the southern Sudan. Opening of the South would enable tribal institutions to evolve by economic development, which, ironically, was not unlike MacMichael's vision of the progressive replacement of tribal authorities by educated southerners as the end and justification for the Southern Policy Symes was committed to destroy.

His antipathy toward the South made them impossible to achieve. He had arrived in Khartoum determined to reduce the financial burden the South imposed upon the government's budget by eliminating nonessential services. Despite his rhetoric, he was skeptical that economic development alone could overcome the endemic backwardness of the southern Sudan. Therefore, in order to reduce the perpetual annual southern deficit of some quarter million pounds, he was determined to slash administrative costs by amalgamating provinces and eliminating expensive British governors and district commissioners, a policy of care and maintenance. This made a mockery of his pious pronouncements to abandon Southern Policy, open the South to outsiders, and give them free access to trade. He believed that "the close association of individual British officers with particular tribal units . . . may be pushed too far." They should be "builders, not mere caretakers," but in fact all that Symes required of them was to be caretakers rigorously implementing his policy of just enough care and maintenance to ensure only public security and nothing more.

His obtuse failure to understand conditions in the South, its people, or his own administrators blinded him to the reality of British administration in the southern Sudan. In 1935, the South, in fact, was probably more peaceful than at any other time in this century, for which the Bog Barons were mainly responsible. The Bog Barons were former British military officers, contract men, who were recruited specifically to serve in the volatile remote regions of the southern Sudan, which British officials called the Bog, unlike members in the Political Service in the North who were regularly rotated from one post to another. Their task was to impose the authority of the Sudan government and bring an end to the endemic intertribal warfare, which they had accomplished by panache, personality, and prestige with only the assistance of a handful of local police, which had engendered mutual respect as Fathers of their People. They all were fluent in the southern vernacular languages and the customs of the people they ruled as benevolent despots. Not surprisingly, they despised Arab Muslims. Some refused to fly the Egyptian flag at their stations. Others resolutely refused to pass the test in Arabic required by all members of the Sudan Political Service. In return for being left alone in their remote satrapy, the governors and civil secretary in Khartoum ignored their insubordination and rarely ventured to tell them what to do. They were eccentric, opinionated, and paternal: Major P. M. *King* Larken and Major J. W. G. "Tiger" Wyld in Zandeland; Captain J. M. Stubbs among the northern Dinka; Captain G. R. King of the Taposa, whose word was law between Kapoeta and the Ethiopian border for forty-five years; and Lt. Col. H. A. Lilley, who ruled the Latuka during the 1930s, as did Percy Coriat among the Nuer of the Upper Nile.

In the name of economy and efficiency, Symes first began to dismantle this small but effective administration in 1936. He amalgamated, with disastrous results, the two large provinces of Equatoria and the Bahr al-Ghazal into one vast, sprawling administrative unit of 160,000 square miles inhabited by one million people dispersed into a myriad of tribes and languages. Moreover, the Sudan government had long sought to have two district commissioners in each of its large districts so that one would always be present during the annual leave, which could last as long as eight months, of the other, but in the South there was only one district commissioner for every 50,000 people. Care and maintenance was to resolve this issue by simply lumping districts together to make larger and more cumbersome administrative units with fewer officials. Moreover, this additional burden of administration had to be borne by the Bog Barons, for new recruits in the Political Service could not be assigned to administrative posts in the South where they were ignorant of the people, their customs, and their language. Even veteran district commissioners from the North were little more than a liability with no southern language: only Arabic, which was not permitted to be spoken as the language of administration. Virtually abandoned by Khartoum and isolated by geography, the Bog Barons devised ingenious and idiosyncratic innovations to meet the needs of their people with few resources that had little relevance to the doctrines of Indirect Rule. The introduction of the chiefs' courts in the South had been regarded as a major building block for Indirect Rule, but in some courts the British DC often became the chief, while in others he restrained his judicial instincts to become a bemused observer of a dysfunctional institution. Moreover, the search for the chief, particularly among the Dinka and the Nuer, often proved frustrating, for many of these societies had traditionally refused to acknowledge any single authority. When a Bog Baron arbitrarily appointed a headman paramount chief, the unfortunate fellow was often ostracized by his fellow headmen who regarded themselves as his equal. In many instances the DC found himself the tax collector, since there were few chiefs willing to take on that arduous assignment. By the end of the decade, Indirect Rule in the South had largely disappeared as an instrument of Native Administration, not by any fiat issued from Khartoum, but by the realities on the ground, which relentlessly undermined it.

Association and Indirect Rule

HUBERT JULES DESCHAMPS[3]

Ladies and Gentlemen,

When the executive council of the International African Institute conferred upon me the honor of giving the Lugard Memorial Lecture, I was so awestricken by the mere name of Lugard that the possibility of any other subject matter was immediately chased from my mind. I do not know if our President, when he gave his remarkable address to the memory of the great Lord, his predecessor, in the same city in 1952, was the victim of a similar obsession. As for me, I quickly discovered that I had something to say to Lord Lugard for a long time and that I would never have a better opportunity to do so. Please allow me then to speak to him in your presence.

Undoubtedly, being a Frenchman raised on Descartes and Voltaire, and moreover a product of this wondrous and yet abominable twentieth century, I do not especially believe in ghosts. However, my Celtic origins and my profession of historian have accustomed me to their frequentation. Therefore, in your midst and in the full light of day, and with no recourse to the subterfuges of spiritualism, I am now going to conjure up my former and highly esteemed colleague, Lord Lugard of Abinger, and address myself with respect and honesty to this venerable spirit who is so dear to us.

Lord Lugard, please be so kind to forgive me if I dare to have you come back for a moment to this abusive planet. But, knowing you quite well now, thanks to the grandiose and detailed monument of 1948 pages with which Miss Margery Perham honored you, I cannot believe that you have lost all interest in what was once the passion of your life. I rather imagine that beneath the

---

[3] This excerpt is taken from a lecture given by Hubert Jules Deschamps in Brussels on June 20, 1963, under the auspices of the Eighth Lugard Memorial Lecture. "*Et Maintenant, Lord Lugard?*" translated by Mary Paquette, was subsequently published in *Africa* 33, no. 4 (October 1963), pp. 293-305. Hubert Jules Deschamps was a governor of the French Ivory Coast.

myrtle and laurel bushes of the Elysian Fields, you are pursuing doctrinal controversies with our countless departed colleagues used to govern colonies from the time of Julius Caesar and Pontius Pilate. It is true that today the colonies themselves belong to the realm of ghosts. Therefore, I invite you to take part in a fictional dispute on an outdated topic of an eminently academic sort but serious nonetheless.

Here you are in front of me, not the Lugard of his younger days, with his unforgettable thin wolf-like face, with his nose as thin and as straight as a sword, with his awesome Turkish saber-like mustache, and with his shining dark eyes exuding a savage energy from within their deep sockets. I would no more address that Lugard than I would a black panther.

No, the Lugard who has condescended to come back among us is the founder of our Institute, its president for twenty years, a solid old gentleman—bald, calm, pale, enlightened by his lengthy experience among men. I evoke your indulgent smile for I am going to need it.

Lord Lugard, I was once your enemy. Oh, a very small enemy, so microscopic that you never chanced to see him, and one who never did you any harm. Moreover, my grudge was not against you but rather against your doctrine. You were the great victorious champion and almost the sovereign pontiff of the "indirect administration" in the 1930s when I was trying unsuccessfully to bring back assimilation.

Most of your compatriots, with a refreshing naivete, still believe that assimilation has always been the unequivocal goal of French colonization. For example, in a recent short work,—quite good, by the way—on Senegal, an English author wrote, "The French had for their goal the political and cultural integration of the colonial peoples whereas the British have always had as their final goal the preparation of their colonies for self-government and independence." Does this evident Manichaeism really take reality into account?

Has the English colonial doctrine really ever had this monolithic continuity? Our British colleagues would answer this question much better than I would. We Frenchmen who see it from the outside have a tendency to take it in as a whole and therefore to exaggerate its apparent simplicity. We find in it the spirit of Great Britain's institutions made up at the same time of respect of old institutions, of an optimistic liberalism and of a realistic empiricism. The Englishman seems to us to frown on great platonic constructions; he does not trust abstraction but, rather, puts his faith in nature. He sees the various peoples, the societies, and the institutions as living beings that he allows to grow, ready to tend to their needs, to orient them, and to use them for the best. His outlook is that of the naturalist or of the gardener. It is also the businessman's view: watch over the profits and limit the general expenses. This point of view requires that the various branches and the main office never merge. "The triumph of the British policy," writes Seeley, "consists of having separated the destiny of the colonies from that of the parent state and of having reduced to a minimum their mutual interference."

That such tendencies have had as their outcome self-government and independence is apparent to us Frenchmen, impenitent reasoners. I doubt that the good English gardener, in the golden age of colonization, concerned himself much with these outcomes. Life does not follow logic. It was enough to watch over the general development of the plants, to provide for their particular needs at the various stages of their growth, taking care to avoid any absurd and oppressive generalization. God would see to the rest for He is the only master of all ultimate ends.

I may be wrong, but that is how the promising leaf mould in which your doctrine quite naturally grew and flourished appears to me. Lord Lugard, you were acquainted with the models in India where you not only hunted the tiger with rifle but the wild boar with spear. When, after your impassioned but fruitless struggle with the slavers of Lake Nyassa, you were sent to Uganda, you displayed your skill with weapons and your persuasive authority, not to abolish the native kingdoms, but to consolidate them. You enlarged the limits of Buganda, you reconstituted the Toro and reestablished its sovereign. You refused to take the place of their rulers and you acknowledged their tribal justice. Upon your return in 1893, you formulated in *The Rise of Our East African Empire* your inflexible principle. "The object to be aimed at in the administration of this country is to rule through its own executive government."

This was the time when the French did not like you. The intervention of your Maxim machine guns in the religious wars of Uganda, then your audacious trek to Borgu, and the treaty made with the king of Nikki fifteen days before the arrival of the French officer in charge of this very same thing made you the scapegoat of our chauvinistic journalistic attacks. Thus did France have some share in your reputation, for at the same time, your compatriots discovered what you were: a hero of the empire. Chamberlain charged you with the creation of the "West Africa Frontier Force" which was to play a decisive role in the establishment of the Nigerian frontier; Bussa, where Mungo Park met his death, was to remain English. At the turn of the century, you were at the height of your glory. Kirk and Goldie were your friends; Flora Shaw sang your praise. Your eyes had lost their disquieting flame. At the age of 42, calmer but still tireless, you gained access to the government of Northern Nigeria. You had to conquer her, to organize her. Your methods were to be applied unfailingly; they were to be clarified and defined. There they were to find their perfect testing ground; a little too perfect, perhaps, because later you were to try and apply this model in different situations.

It is quite useless, except perhaps for the French public, quite ignorant about British colonization (the reverse is also true), to recall your Kano, Sokoto, and Katsina expeditions. What is important here is that you maintained the Fulani emirs in spite of how recent and questionable their power in Hausa territory might have seemed. You felt a certain repulsion for disorder, a need for efficacy, and, at the same time, a certain weakness in your means that caused you to be preoccupied primarily with "stopping disintegration." In 1906, you defined your principles in the *Political Memoranda:* recognize the native administration as an integral part of the governmental machine, while directing it in the direction of the abolition of slavery and of oppression and also towards economic development. The British governor and the district commissioner were really to be advisors and overseers. Thanks to your methods, when a revolt broke out, the emirs remained faithful. The virtue of indirect rule, at least where pacification is concerned, is thereby demonstrated. . . .

Assimilation, as I shall demonstrate later, was only rarely the official colonial doctrine of France. But it is quite true that it satisfies certain deeply rooted and constant tendencies of the French people, tendencies with origins going back thousands of years, but which the classicism of the seventeenth and eighteenth centuries expressed perfectly.

Our ancestors, the Gauls, according to all the explorers of their time, were avidly interested in novelty and were openly receptive to strangers; the Greeks referred to them as "philhellenics" or lovers of Greeks. After resisting conquest, they became subjects and then avid Roman citizens, to the point of abandoning their own language for Latin. The taste for Roman architecture and law became second nature to them. They passed this heritage on to us. We like the logical reasoning, the monuments with their sober but not cold lines, the institutions based on simple and clear principles. The Roman Empire, in uniting the various countries, left us a model and a certain regret. Moreover, all this Romanism is built on a base of Celtic anarchy with a certain flair for change and the exotic. We are quite familiar with strangers no matter to what race they belong. Add to that a dose of equalitarian and universal Christianity capping a rather pagan vivaciousness, and you will have an approximate portrait of the typical Frenchman—such, at least, as I see him in myself and in many others, either living or dead.

The first colonial efforts by France were imbued with this spirit. The expansion of the kingdom, the conversion of the savages, the absence of racism, these were the
signs. . . .

We were never to know the merits of that system because the colonies were quickly lost. This loss was to be attributed to the excesses of assimilation, and from then on, the French, for more than a century, were looking for a colonial policy. The first original effort was that of Napoleon in Egypt. An advocate of empire without ideology, and taking inspiration only from the necessity of the moment, he ordered that the Egyptian notables be kept with "the greatest possible latitude in their internal affairs"; he attended Moslem ceremonies and thanked the Prophet for his victories. But the Prophet did not protect him from Nelson.

In 1830, the French again met up with Islam in Algeria, and their first act was to ensure its protection. The local institutions were preserved on the whole. The Second Republic had only a vague recourse to assimilation. Slavery was once again and this time definitively abolished, and the colonies elected deputies to the French parliament. But no attempt was made to assimilate the Algerians. Napoleon III declared that Algeria was an Arab kingdom. The particularity of colonial legislation was recognized, and it was put into the hands of the executive and taken away from the parliament; this rule lasted a century, almost the entire duration of the colonial Empire.

A change took place at the same time in French thought. The classical and abstract concept of the "interior man" who is invariable, a product of the mathematician Descartes, started to lose ground before the discoveries of the nineteenth century. Geography, history, and sociology were on the rise. The diversity of countries, of men, and of societies was recognized. Assimilation was then as much condemned in its intellectual roots as it had already been in practice. To the universal application of principles was easily to be substituted the method based on facts. It was the colonials, the governors, the officers, and the administrators who were going to elaborate their own terms and conditions of action according to local needs.

In Senegal, Faidherbe had already based his policy on the local chieftains. He had created a "school for chieftains" to instruct the successors. Cambon, in 1881, inaugurated the policy of the protectorate in Tunisia; he maintained the Tunisian government and administration while controlling them. Lyautey, quite a bit later, used the same system in Morocco with a modernistic trend allied with an esthetic taste for the old institutions. "I am the sultan's head servant," he liked to say, and it was true. His royalist feelings, which were of no more use in France, had found their use overseas.

In Black Africa, wherever we found kings, except in the extreme cases of open struggle or a lack of traditional attachments, we maintained them, set them up on thrones and made them our chief agents, just as did the English, and for the same reasons: the facilitation of conquest and of economic administration. The only difference was that we were not tempted as you were, Lord Lugard, to modernize these antiquated states, nor to create embryos of states where none existed. We did not conscientiously seek to create the future out of the past. We preserved the latter because it was convenient, and we often let it deteriorate to the advantage of direct administration. In the same way, education, wherever it existed, was carried on in French, but that was due more to the multiplicity of languages and to the desire to form useful clerks than to a pronounced desire for assimilation.

For assimilation was then dead as far as French doctrine was concerned.

Arthur Girault, the greatest of our experts on colonial law, rather grimly established that as early as 1903. The hypocritical expression of the "policy of association" born in Indochina was substituted for it. The word "association" seemed to affirm the existence of a contract between the dominating power and the subjects, whereas it really conjured up the idea of the association that exists between a man and his horse. Your expression of the "dual mandate" was at least more honest: it indicated a mutual benefit. Your work, between the two wars, began to be recognized and praised in France. A man as authoritative as Maurice Delafosse taught us at the Colonial School as late as 1926, the year of his death, a doctrine similar to yours: to protect the native institutions and to have them evolve slowly within their natural limits, and not to create mere caricatures of Europe.

There, once more I apologize because I must enter onto the scene, and that might seem especially presumptuous since I was at that time in 1930 a young assistant administrator, lost in the Malagasy underbrush—a not too-typical figure, rather insignificant and ineffective. But among the concert of praises for your doctrine, mine was the only dissenting voice. I led a solitary attack, quite unnoticed, but firmly convinced that I incarnated the future. . . .

I maintained that the native society differed from ours not by their nature but rather by their degree of evolution. Now, because of contact with us, they are in the process of evolving at an accelerated rate. Trade, the monetary economy, the plantations, mines, and the migration of workers, the creation of cities—all these have upset the traditional societies more than did the teachers and the missionaries. The breakdown of political structures is flagrant, and it is a good thing, because they were not adapted to the new age. Education must create new social classes, already apparent and which will serve as the instruments of the future. "Colonization equals education," I wrote; even etymologically speaking, since culture naturally follows colonization . . . We still seem to control the new native societies according to principles created for primitive societies that have disappeared today. (I want to make it clear that I was not yet an ethnologist!) The idea of making them evolve "in their own milieu," without any exterior influence, is false, reactionary, and racist. "Any archaeological shoring up of tottering ruins cannot be a living and lasting work." The "imported" dogma of "indirect rule" is ill-fated. Let us turn away from the English example to meditate on that of the Roman Empire which caused us to rise from barbarism. Let us welcome the natives to us, since they are coming towards us anyway, and let us build the French nation extending to Africa. In my thesis, which I was beginning to write, I enlarged my universalism to a degree most acceptable today by concluding, "Let us be good educators and prepare good Europeans."

I did not quote you, Lord Lugard, but I attacked you in each sentence. Actually, I did not hurt you very much. As far as I know, my article was read by only one person, my colleague Geismar, who was an avid fan of yours. Between Senegal and Madagascar, we exchanged a few long impassioned letters. Indirect rule was none the worse for it. I was beaten by silence, and assimilation remained buried. It arose again much later in 1945, but really, I had nothing to do with it. My glory was purely personal, that of an unknown predecessor. And at the same time, I had a vague feeling that it was too late, and that on a planet in the process of rapid change, our great doctrinal battles over colonization would soon be relegated to ancient history with not much diffusion. You never knew this stage. In the same year, 1945, which marked the end of your era, you set out for another world, leaving behind in this one an unforgettable memory.

And now, Lord Lugard? Let us try and find the moral of this story. Time has judged the merits of our opposite views. We have to confront these views with the events that followed. Who was wrong? What remains of these monuments today? And what is their share in present-day Africa?

Here we are then in the court of History. The two parties appear: on one side, standing proudly, is indirect rule of long and glorious memory, accompanied by his two daughters, the conservation of African institutions and the controlled evolution of the role of chieftains who owe so much to you. On the opposing side, the group is less distinct: one can scarcely detect the French administrative policy previous to 1945; it differed from yours (at least in Black Africa) only in its more familiar style and less clearly defined goals. Your opposition is, rather, the assimilative tendency of the French people, however vague and intermittent its application to the colonies may have been, its juridical structure, its leaning towards vast rational constructs which led to the French Union and then to the Community of French Nations; add to it education in French, the steadfast belief in humanity, the distrust of the feudal, the nostalgia for the Roman Empire, the romantic vision of France the Liberator, all in all, a simplistic temperament plus naive convictions, all of this combination of obscure virtualities that I had tried to express with rigorous energy. To sum them up in a symbolic figure, I would say that it is assimilation—that is, the Revolution of 1789—sneaking into Africa rather late on tiptoe.

To judge fairly, we must examine not only the intrinsic virtues of both systems, but also their contact with the facts—that is, the evolution of Africa since 1945 and the present outcome.

Indirect rule was a convenient formula for submission. It caused the least possible disturbance. It tried to keep Africa on the African ancestral path. Therefore, there existed a need to know the country, to take inventory of its peoples, its political resources, its legal customs. It was the golden age of ethnologists and administrators quite taken with the exotic and the picturesque. These traditional societies, perfectly preserved, with their ancient structures, their colorful ceremonies, their noble demeanor, their palanquins, their crowns, their sacred thrones, their perfect adaptation to nature, their order, their serenity, presented to romantic minds an idealized image of long ago, the African version of Walter Scott. The lure of the past, the charm of an escape from a Europe invaded by industrial slavery and demographic inflation, was irresistible to the intellectuals captivated by esthetics. Even I, as revolutionary as I was in thought, was sentimentally seduced by this perfume of mankind of the early ages to the point, on my return to France, of giving a scandalous lecture whose theme was, "To save humanity, let us return to the neolithic age!" I suppose that my British colleagues, faithful to the crown and the venerable institutions surrounding it, must have succumbed even more so in this anachronistic universe miraculously preserved, and over which they watched with as much love as over the natural reserves. Thus they preserved the chieftains and increased the number of rhinoceri.

Unfortunately, the chieftains, as opposed to the rhinoceri, were not merely colorful. They were scarcely inclined to modify a state of affairs that was favorable to them. The careful control, where you had seen the panacea of progress, undoubtedly suppressed the most blatant abuses, the horror of the sultans' prisons, the razzias, the slave trade; it had regularized administration and justice; it had allowed material changes while maintaining social conservatism. The native societies, too well protected, continued to live apart, without any active participation in the modern world.

Evolution came from elsewhere, as I had predicted it would, and contrary to your system. The "gentlemen of the bush" that you respected as squires and the House of Lords were outdated, outclassed, and finally looked down upon as completely antiquated by the rising new class of people who were not at all titled and hereditary gentlemen: the businessmen, the store clerks, the civil servants, the wealthy planters, the influential church members, the trade unionists, the townspeople, and I should not hesitate to include in this enumeration those at the head: the intellectuals, the reasoners who will not content themselves with passive obedience. I must say that it was the honor of England to have facilitated in its universities, and sooner than us, the formation of this unruly intelligentsia. For happily, your country also had sincere liberalism in its traditions. . . .

Indeed, the conflicts were lively but rarely bloody. The state triumphed over the tribes and the chieftains, sometimes by force, sometimes by settlement, often with the aid of an English diplomatic intermediary. Some great aggregates, of artificial origin, are maintained, such as Nigeria, whose unity you cemented and where the northern chieftains exist alongside of the more equalitarian systems of the South. In spite of the differences in the political regimes and the cultural evolution that indirect rule had consolidated, the nations were born, and they have taken their first steps forward. British liberalism and a typically British insular attitude helped them: a certain detachment, a certain modest reserve with regard to other peoples; an attitude where some suffered from an adolescent timidity and others from an invincible pride; and all were undoubtedly right. It does not matter, really. The result of this reserve, of this insularity, of this reluctance to be on the lookout, was that autonomy and secession were relatively easy for you. Thus the centrifugal forces were quicker to start up in your territories than in ours, at least in West Africa. The emancipation of Ghana caused a furor, and from then on, all the neighboring countries, whether they were under the British or the French, sought to line themselves up behind independence.

On the other hand, the French system, before it died, made a last attempt at assimilation. In 1945, the French Constituent Assembly—platonic, legalistic, and steeped in geometry—tried to raise a noble architectural structure built to last for centuries, where both blacks and whites could find shelter. One dreamed rather vaguely of a new Roman Empire after Caracalla, of a French world transcending continents and races. This noble illusion, made up of a mixture of traditional French chauvinism and of a very sincere anti-racist ecumenism, had been born at the Liberation....

[O]ur nonchalant French practice with regard to the chiefdoms had, in the long run, a more positive effect on the construction of new nations than did your ingenious doctrine of the evolution of the old structures and your maternal solicitude over a good education. In our territories, the kingdoms and the chiefdoms, abandoned to their old age by our indifference, fell apart painlessly or were easily neutralized; sometimes the old institutions were suppressed, only to be retrieved by the administrations of the most modernistic chieftains; often they were simply neutralized and left to die their own death. The religious attachment to the chieftains did not evoke the favor that certain ethnological studies might have led one to believe; it even happened that in order to hasten an evolution judged to be progressing too slowly, the subjects themselves, as in the Bamileke country, had the chieftains' headquarters burned after having massacred the chieftains. Except for this and other rare examples, the 1789 of French-speaking Africa took place quite painlessly, a sign that your colorful Middle Ages had their day.

To your account must be tallied, on the contrary, the desire to create local basic constitutions, the "native authorities" and "native councils" that you often had so much difficulty in establishing in countries where anarchies abounded. The French system facilitated change but did not promote initiative. The administration, our country, was a paternal king (in the best and most common cases) but almost an absolute one; he was the last of the absolute kings and one who gave no thought to abdicating. One became concerned—and much too late—after 1945, and in too few territories, with creating rural communes to give to the people of Malagasy and to the Africans the basic sense of responsibilities; the new nations in our sector inherited rudimentary or worthless substructures. It is still the administrative system inherited from us and made African which governs the whole, often with the help of sections of the governmental party. There is a serious deficiency there: the habit of responsibility is not taken on in a day; its absence allows tyranny, or at least, it causes the leaders to increase their power since they have to face everything.

Finally, since we are counting the points, here is another in favor of assimilation: it is the diffusion of the French language and culture. I do not mean to make an allusion here to the great intellectuals. Without a doubt, men like Senghor or Alioune Diop, to mention only two, do great honor at the same time to the French University and to Africa. But the English-speaking universities also knew how to form men of the best caliber. The originality of our system is probably the diffusion of teaching in French to the primary level. "The knowledge of French," states my friend Charton, "becomes common and popular among the youngest and most active elements. It is upon a popular base of French cultural implantation that the formation of the classes and the ascension of the elite has been able to develop." Thus, we have often avoided the divorce between the masses that remain traditional and the elite that have received a foreign education. The French language has become the means of intellectual emancipation and the path that leads to unity. During a recent stay in Gabon, I found, in the smallest villages in the virgin forest, people both young and old who would speak with me in French; a Gabonese minister declared, "The United States chose English, we have chosen French." This prevented French-speaking Africa from having the feeling of giving up something of themselves. It goes without saying that the English-speaking peoples could say the same thing. A comparative study would be interesting, but difficult. In any case, the diffusion of our languages causes the linguists, after the ethnologists, to pass from applied science to pure science and history. The latter has absorbed your world and ours with all our methods and colonial doctrines. It is history who will now act as judge and decide the points.

Let us sum up the results of the match between indirect rule and assimilation; to simplify things, let us say between you and me, which magnifies my importance greatly.

Your system rested on the conviction of the differences between peoples and a respect for their ways. You believed in the possibility of making Africa evolve within the forms of the past and with the men of the past. This life apart would only lead to separation in the future. Even if you were not consciously aware of it, this centrifugal movement was the normal outcome of your premises.

The belief of the eighteenth century and of the French Revolution that I took up in my article and that the French Union tried later on to realize postulated, on the contrary, the basic similarity of the human species and its possibility of evolving on a single plane. Africa could only find its place in the modern world by an accelerated revolution replacing the old structures with modern forms. From then on, there could be no obstacle to assimilation in a same political entity.

And now, let us count up the points:

You lost on the evolution in the traditional forms, but you won on African autonomy.

I won for the victory of men and of modern institutions; I lost on political assimilation.

One to one, Lord Lugard. Match void.

Actually, we were both deceived by having too absolute of viewpoints. Men are at the same time different and similar. The Africans reacted in a normal way; they sought the same political forms as the Europeans while defending the originality of their cultures. According to Senghor, they wanted to "assimilate, not to be assimilated." The advantage that Africa had in this double point of view was that the European domination was at the same time long enough to cause a shock and an awakening and short enough for Africa not to have enough time to be abolished and yet to assimilate the new points brought in from the exterior without succumbing.

Hegemony on a Shoestring

SARA BERRY[4]

In this chapter, I will look at the early decades of British colonial rule in Africa, when administrators struggled to establish effective control with extremely limited resources. Scarcity of money and manpower not only obliged administrators to practice "indirect rule," but also limited their ability to direct the course of political and social change. In effect, I will argue colonial regimes were unable to impose either English laws and institutions or their own version of "traditional" African ones onto indigenous societies. Colonial "inventions" of African tradition served, not so much to define the shape of the colonial social order, as to provoke a series of debates over the meaning and application of tradition, which in turn shaped struggles over authority and access to resources.

The chapter is organized into four sections. The first presents my general argument about the impact of colonial rule on conditions of access to agricultural resources. The second describes the kinds of debate which arose under indirect rule over the meaning and uses of "custom," while the third and fourth illustrate their implications for the organization of native administration, and the limits of colonial authorities' control over rural economic and social life. Because of the time period covered, African countries are referred to by their colonial names.

As they moved to assert military and political control over most of sub-Saharan Africa, colonial administrators faced, from the outset, a continual struggle to make ends meet. As self-declared rulers of the African continent, Europeans assumed responsibility for governing extensive territories inhabited by scattered and diverse peoples—a vast and potentially expensive project. The British Exchequer was, however, reluctant to subsidize either the recurrent

---

[4] This selection is taken from Sara Berry, *No Condition Is Permanent: The Social Dynamics of Agrarian Change in Sub-Saharan Africa* (Madison: University of Wisconsin Press, 1993), pp. 24-35. Sara Berry is emeritus professor of African history at Johns Hopkins University.

or the capital costs of colonial administration. Partly because of financial stringency, the number of European personnel posted to colonial administrations was limited and officials were expected to raise enough revenue from their colonies to cover the costs of administering them. However confidently administrators might share Earl Grey's conviction that "the surest test for the soundness of measures for the improvement of an uncivilised people is that they should be self-sufficient," the daily struggle to wrest revenue labor and provisions from reluctant, hostile, or scattered subjects was not an easy one.

To live within their means, officials worked both to raise revenue and to keep down the costs of maintaining order and running the day-to-day business of administration. One obvious way to cut costs was to use Africans, both as employees and as local agents of colonial rule. African clerks and chiefs were cheaper than European personnel; also, by integrating existing local authorities and social systems into the structure of colonial government, officials hoped to minimize the disruptive effects of colonial rule. In other words, for reasons of financial and administrative expediency, most colonial regimes in Africa practiced indirect rule, whether or not they had articulated it as their philosophy of imperial governance.

Although colonial administrators did evolve an elaborate set of principles and institutions for formalizing the conception and practice of indirect rule, in fact they not only failed to preserve (or restore) stable systems of traditional/social order, but actually promoted instability in local structures of authority and in conditions of access to productive resources. My argument differs from those of authors who have suggested that European "inventions" of African tradition served to rigidify jural norms and practices, and hence social structures, in Africa. Colonial officials certainly tried to govern according to fixed rules and procedures which were based on what they imagined to be the stable political and jural systems of the African past, but they rarely exercised enough effective control to accomplish exactly what they set out to do.

This was so for several reasons. First, colonial administrators' own economic and political interests often had contradictory implications for their strategies of exploitation and control. Second, contrary to British expectations, African societies were not divided into neatly bounded, mutually exclusive, stable cultural and political systems; they were dynamic, changing communities, whose boundaries were fluid and ambiguous and whose members were often engaged in multiple contests for power and resources. Finally, officials' efforts to learn about indigenous societies in order to build on them frequently elicited conflicting testimony about the nature of "native law and custom." I shall elaborate each of these points in turn.

The Contradictions of Colonial Interest in African Agriculture

The financial viability of a colonial regime was likely to be both threatened and enhanced by successful African participation in cash cropping and wage employment. Whether or not a particular episode of conquest was motivated by the desire to promote European capitalist interests in Africa, once colonial rule was established, officials counted on European enterprise to generate taxable income and wealth. Trading firms, concessionaires, mining companies, and European settlers were all expected to increase the volume of commercial activity and hence the flow of taxable income generated by the colonial economy. European profits depended, in turn, on ready access to cheap African labor-farm workers and mineworkers, porters and dockhands, and producers of commodities for export or for the direct provisioning of Europe and in Africa. Africans were, in turn, more likely to offer their labor cheaply if they were hard-pressed to meet their own needs independently of trade with or employment by Europeans. In short, African prosperity threatened the profits of European enterprise on African soil.

However, Africans also paid taxes and bought European goods, and their ability to do so increased with their incomes. Thus, colonial regimes walked a tightrope between encouraging Africans to become involved in labor and commodity markets, and attempting to prevent them from becoming economically independent enough to ignore the opportunities afforded by European-controlled markets and jobs. Officials did not want to stifle the flow of African labor, produce, and tax revenue on which the fiscal and economic health of the colony depended, but they were equally anxious to minimize the cost of African labor and produce, and to limit Africans' ability to influence the terms of exchange.

Colonial administrators' ambivalence towards African agricultural growth and commercialization was expressed differently in different colonies, depending on the particular local configuration of economic activities and interests. In settler economies, such as Kenya, officials faced conflicting pressures to encourage increased African production for sale in order to generate taxable income, supply the home market, and keep down wage costs, and to suppress it in order to free up labor and protect European farmers from African competition. Officials advocated the creation of African reserves to both limit Africans' access to land and augment the flow of labor to European farms, and to "protect" Africans from dispossession or excessive exploitation. On the issue of labor recruitment, they shifted their strategies, first using African headmen as recruiters in order to forestall the abuses of commercial recruiters and then using professional recruiters or even acting as recruiters themselves when popular discontent threatened to undermine the authority of headmen and hence their effectiveness as agents of indirect rule.

In Northern Rhodesia, large tracts of land were cleared for settlers, but so few ever arrived that their labor needs were insignificant, and colonial authorities never faced the issue of restricting African cultivation in order to generate labor supplies. Instead, they wrestled with the issue of settlement patterns. For administrative purposes, it was convenient to have people concentrated in large settlements under the effective control of powerful chiefs and officials of the British South Africa Company and, later, the colonial administration waged a series of unsuccessful campaigns to prevent the dispersal of Bemba settlements. However, concentrated settlements soon led to deforestation and soil erosion. No sooner had the colonial administration moved people into newly demarcated Native Reserves in the 1930s than the resulting overcrowding led to visible signs of environmental degradation, and villagers had to be resettled within a few years.

In West Africa, there were no settlers to speak of and colonies prospered from the rapid expansion of tree crops and other forms of agricultural production for export. However, officials worried that in their rush to produce for export, farmers would neglect food crops; that African methods of production resulted in poor-quality produce which brought low prices in Europe; and that European traders' efforts to protect themselves against African competition would provoke disturbances that might threaten the smooth flow of trade. Here, too, official policy towards agriculture and commerce wavered between encouraging export crop production and African commerce and limiting it, as administrators struggled to balance competing interests and manage the contradictions of agricultural development.

The Dynamics of African Political Economies

For much of the colonial era, many Europeans assumed that African communities consisted of mutually exclusive sociocultural units—tribes, villages, kin groups—whose customs and structures had not changed very much over time. Officials could see, of course, that there was conflict among Africans at the time of colonial conquest, but they assumed they could restore order by reconstituting what they believed to have been the "closed, corporate, consensual systems" of the past. Accordingly, colonial administrators set out to discover the boundaries and customs of "traditional" communities and the "original" relations between them, in order to use tradition as the basis for their own administrative structures and practices. In attempting to construct stable, workable administrative systems in Africa, officials sometimes sought to preserve traditional structures of authority, sometimes to reorganize or completely recreate them. In Northern Nigeria, colonial officials found a system of Muslim emirates, complete with written legal codes, courts, and administrative structures, which were almost ideally suited to their purposes. Also, since a majority of the Fulani aristocracy agreed to accept British overrule in exchange for confirmation of their own authority, the process of conquest was brief and relatively smooth. However, few other systems of local government proved as comprehensive or congenial to British notions of administrative efficiency. Most African chiefs kept no tax rolls or law books; few made any attempt to separate either the principles or the practices of adjudication from those of politics or diplomacy; and many were vague about the exact boundaries of their domains. In decentralized societies, such as those of central Kenya or southeastern Nigeria, where colonial administrators were unable to find strong chiefs or hierarchical systems of authority, they created them.

In more centralized polities, chiefs who resisted or challenged colonial domination were deposed, and their governments sometimes reorganized as well, to prevent renewed dissent. For example, the British deliberately weakened Asante hegemony after 1896 by signing separate treaties with chiefs and communities formerly subordinate to Kumase and disregarding Kumase's claims to "customary" overlordship. In western Nigeria, where Yoruba states had been engaged in a series of battles and shifting alliances for most of the nineteenth century, British officials insisted on assigning them to positions in a fixed hierarchy under the supreme authority of the Alatin of Oyo, despite the fact that since the 1850s, Ibadan had been stronger than Oyo, and Ibadan's principal opponent (the Ekitiparapo, or Ekiti-ijesha alliance) was quite independent of Oyo.

In the early years of colonial conquest and "pacification," officials dealt with each area ad hoc, responding pragmatically, sometimes ruthlessly, to local conditions in their efforts to establish control and mobilize resources. By the end of the First World War, however, official thinking was converging towards a standard "mental map of an Africa comprised of neatly bounded, homogeneous tribes" and an increasingly uniform conception of their own imperial mission and how best to realize it. Lugard's *The Dual Mandate in Tropical Africa* (1923) laid out the philosophy of indirect rule, and during the next twenty years, officials labored to replicate a common system of native administration across the map of colonial Africa. In 1929, the Secretary for Native Affairs in Northern Rhodesia noted with satisfaction that, when the Colonial Office took over administration of the colony in 1924, "the tribes were in a very disorganised state," but since then a tribal organization had been "created" (quoted in Chanock 1985: 112).

In fact, precolonial communities were neither static nor internally cohesive. In central Kenya during the nineteenth century, "men and women throughout the region moved in a complex world of overlapping, layered and shifting associations," formed through migration, marriage, trade, and blood brotherhood (Ambler, 1897: 32). "As agricultural settlement steadily expanded, the patterns of [social] identity were continually recast by the evolving relations among communities" (Ambler 35). Nor were fluid, overlapping, or contested social boundaries and lines of authority peculiar to acephalous polities such as those of the Kikuyu, Igbo, or Tiv. Even as British missionaries moved into Northern Rhodesia, followed in 1895 by agents of the British South Africa Company, a major realignment was taking place among Bemba chieftaincies. As Roberts (1973) has shown in detail, the "strength" of Bemba chiefs and the cohesiveness of the tribe under the central authority of the Chitimukulu, which so impressed early British observers, rested not on any institutionalized system of central authority, but rather on a particular conjuncture of historical circumstances. In the 1860s and 1870s, shifting alliances and conflicts among neighboring peoples combined with a realignment of long-distance trade patterns to reward Bemba skills at ivory hunting and slave raiding without bringing dissident groups into their territory. This led to a temporary consolidation of Bemba power within the region, but also promoted competition among Bemba chiefs. By the 1880s, the power of the Chitimukulu was declining, and several smaller chieftaincies switched their allegiance to the increasingly powerful Mwamba. With the establishment of company control in 1895, large fortified Bemba settlements dispersed, leaving much room for the subsequent debate over which chiefs had traditional claims to authority over whom.

In Asante, since the eighteenth century, successive Asantehenes had manipulated the allocation of rights over land and people in order to consolidate and extend the power of Kumase. In 1889, Yaa Kyaa secured the throne of Kumase for her son, Agyeman Prempe I, by promising his supporters to restore to them all the land and subjects "who had been sold, pawned, confiscated or otherwise alienated from their ancestors by previous Asantehenes." After more than a century of confiscation and redistribution by several Asantehenes, Yaa Kyaa's promises left much room for debate over who was entitled to what. Similarly, in western Nigeria, much of the nineteenth century was taken up by warfare, migration, and shifting alliances among Yoruba states, which generated multiple, conflicting precedents for demarcating "traditional" social boundaries and chiefly jurisdictions.

In general, colonial regimes imposed themselves on societies already engaged in struggles over power and the terms on which it was exercised. By announcing their intention to uphold "traditional" norms and structures of authority, colonial officials were, in effect, declaring their intention to build colonial rule on a foundation of conflict and change. The result was "a blizzard of claims and counterclaims" to right over land and people, which served as "a mechanism for generating factional struggle," rather than eliminating it.

The Search for Tradition

The debates and tensions provoked by European efforts to construct stable governing structures on top of volatile African social realities were exacerbated by colonial administrators' methods of implementing indirect rule. To build colonial administration on a foundation of "native law and custom," officials needed information about traditional systems of law and authority. But few African societies, apart from those with established traditions of Islamic scholarship, possessed written bodies of legal and historical knowledge from which such information might be drawn. Officials had therefore to rely on travelers' accounts (sketchy and dated, at best) and oral testimony.

Oral evidence was gathered informally at first; later, it was gathered more systematically by official commissions of inquiry and by professional anthropologists hired by colonial regimes for the purpose. But the search for oral tradition was fraught with difficulties. Like scholars who collect oral history, colonial administrators who set out to gather information on local laws and customs were told multiple, often conflicting stories. Whichever version of customary rights and practices an official chose to believe, people were sure to challenge it—both because the past was, in fact, complex and changing, and because Africans took advantage of officials' interest in tradition to offer evidence favorable to their own interests.

When tensions rose over a particular aspect of colonial policy, the Colonial Office convened commissions of inquiry, both to investigate immediate grievances and to amass information about local customs. Though the work of these commissions contributed to the emergence of an official orthodoxy concerning "native law and custom," the evidence they collected was often full of varied and conflicting testimony. For example, in Southern Nigeria and the Gold Coast, after recurring protests both from influential Britons opposed to commercial concessionaires and from Africans who objected to the proposed enactment of a Crown Lands Ordinance for these territories, the Colonial Office convened the West African Lands Committee in 1912, to consider the "laws in force" concerning "the conditions under which rights over land or the produce thereof many be transferred," and whether those laws needed amending. Perhaps unintentionally, the committee's draft report (which was never published) summed up the colonial administrator's dilemma. In principle, "natives have rights under their own laws and customs," and, for the courts to protect them, "the appropriate custom or law must be brought to the knowledge of the court." In practice, however, the testimony offered to the courts "is often very unsatisfactory and untrustworthy."

Partly because they often received confusing or contradictory evidence on traditional norms and practices, administrators searched for common rules by which to interpret customary practices and apply them to the business of governance. In the 1920s, colonial regimes began to employ professional anthropologists to help them discover the rules and practices of traditional African cultures. Anthropologists such as Rattray, Meek, and Gluckman assumed that traditional African societies were well-ordered, self-reproducing systems whose natural evolution had been disrupted by the trauma of colonial conquest. Their self-assigned mission was to discover or reconstruct these "original" systems through fieldwork and then persuade colonial authorities to restore them, in order to put African societies back on a normal, evolutionary path towards civilization. Rattray, for example, declared that the "true Ashanti" was to be found among elderly people in remote forest settlements, isolated from the corrupting influences of commerce and colonial politics, where social interaction was still ordered according to traditional religious precepts. From his investigation of the Aba women's war in Nigeria in 1929, Meek concluded that colonial rule had weakened the religious basis of traditional law and order, undermining "what was before a well-ordered community," and threatening to replace it with "a disorganized rabble of self seeking individuals." Gluckman portrayed the Lozi kingdom as a coherent, self-contained system, in which economic, political, social, and religious practices complemented and reinforced one another in harmonious and well-ordered fashion.

By the 1920s, the study and interpretation of African custom was becoming institutionalized as part of the routine activity of colonial administration. In the Gold Coast, district officers were "obliged to take examinations in native custom, although apparently they were not required to pass them." In general, anthropological research served to reinforce the official view of African societies as clearly bounded and coherently organized. To be sure, some administrators were well aware that tradition could be invented as well as recalled. "After a review of fifty years' disputes" in the coastal Ghanaian stool of Ada, one official commented sarcastically that the Adas' "knowledge of ancient traditions is, in fact, small, but the manufacture of new ones has been raised by them to the status of a rural industry." Indeed, some saw distinct advantages in the confusion: in Ahafo, one official pointed out in 1930 that "as a result of the system of indirect rule in vogue it is extremely unlikely that any riot or disturbance should be directed against Government authorities. What disturbances occur are invariably in the nature of 'faction fights.'"

Multiple and conflicting testimonies were more likely to be dismissed as evidence of Africans' venality or obtuseness, however, than examined for the possibility that the homogeneous systems of primordial law and culture which officials had painstakingly pieced together to serve as the basis of the colonial order may never have existed in the first place. In Brong-Ahafo, "it was the conventional wisdom of the administration, apt to be produced without noticeable irony after the recital of the most baroque confusions, that in unravelling disputes about traditional issues, one must 'always be governed by well established Akan custom.'"

In short, colonial rule affected conditions of access to land and labor through the interplay of administrators' ambivalence towards African farmers' prosperity, their efforts to govern through indigenous rules and authorities, and ongoing debates over the meaning of "native law and custom." As agricultural commercialization and labor migration gave rise to disputes over the means of production, officials insisted on resolving them in terms of "native law and custom." Their insistence served, in turn, to reinforce existing linkages between farmers' access to resources, their positions in local structures of power, and their ability to win arguments over customary rules and practices. Ongoing struggles over power and the interpretation of tradition were incorporated into the rules and procedures through which officials sought to "cope with the contradictions" and "crises of accumulation" which accompanied colonial rule. Struggles over the meaning of traditional rules and structures of authority shaped struggles over resources, and vice versa.

In general, the effect of indirect rule was neither to freeze African societies into precolonial molds, nor to restructure them in accordance with British inventions of African tradition, but to generate unresolvable debates over the interpretation of tradition and its meaning for colonial governance and economic activity. As Watson remarked of the Lungu in northeastern Zambia, "in a sense, the British policy of indirect rule preserved the Lungu political system, complete with all its conflicts." In seeking to maintain social and administrative stability by building on tradition, officials wove instability—in the form of changing relations of authority and conflicting interpretations of rules—into the fabric of colonial administrations.

Indirect Rule

MAHMOOD MAMDANI[5]

How is one to understand the significance of indirect rule? As an inevitable response to prevailing circumstances, no more than a practical necessity that Lugard turned into a theoretical virtue? Or as a creative colonial response to the riddle that simply would not go away: the native question?

Those who have argued that indirect rule was no more than bare necessity have stressed two aspects of the colonial situation in the early part of this century: the lack of personnel that every colonial power faced and the extreme difficulty in communicating over long distances. Both problems were real. In 1903, when Kana and Sokoto came under the control of the British, the population of northern Nigeria was estimated at a little more than seven million. To govern this population, Lugard had at his command 231 civil European officers in 1903-1904. For the next two years, the corresponding numbers were 241 and 266 respectively. In 1906, the ratio of European civil officers was something like 1 to 2,900 square miles and 1 to 45,000 Africans.

Subordinate clerical and technical staff from Europe were hard to come by and were often absent. The death rate was high. In the four years from 1903 to 1907, 65 Europeans died and 264 returned home as invalids, victims of black water fever, dysentery, malaria, anemia, sunstroke, and bronchitis. "In 1900," claims the Nigerian scholar I.M. Okonjo, "the hopelessness of the communications system made the adoption of 'indirect' rule all but inevitable." Given the tortuously slow and difficult pace at which available transport functioned, "it was practically impossible for the high commissioner or the various heads of department to visit more than a third of provincial headquarters" in a tour of twelve months; even then, "nine-tenths of the time of a journey was occupied in actual traveling." The result was "a heavy delegation to residents and a large volume of correspondence."

---

[5] This excerpt is taken from Mahmood Mamdani, *Citizen and Subject: Contemporary Africa and the Legacy of Late Colonialism* (Princeton, NJ: Princeton University Press, 1996), pp. 72-90. Mahmood Mandani is the Herbert Lehman Professor of Government at Columbia University.

The situation in other colonies and in other periods was not that different.
...

A form of decentralized administration came to be characteristic of every colony. The unit of that administration was the district in British colonies and the cercle in French-controlled territories. The real "man on the spot," the white officer who personified colonial authority, was the British district commissioner, and the French cercle commander. The former was the legendary colonial "King in the castle"; the latter an equally famed "*Le roi de la brousse.*" Both enjoyed an enormous latitude in the interpretation of policy. The administration of every district or cercle was stamped with the personality, the style, and the point of view of its commissioner or commander. Anyone who has perused archival correspondence between the secretary in London and the governor in the colonial capital, and in turn the governor and the district commissioner in the field, cannot fail to be impressed by the division of labor in the chain of command over native policy: the colonial secretary usually confined himself to outlining the basic thrust of policy in the form of guidelines, the governor and his council established the main lines of policy, and the district commissioner was in charge of interpreting, modifying, and implementing policy in light of local conditions. Van Vollenhoven, the celebrated governor-general of Afrique Occidentale Francaise (AOF), solemnly declared that "only one's presence, personal contact counts. The circular is zero." "Few general practitioners in human history," concluded Robert Huessler in his study of northern Nigeria, "were as powerful and active in the whole sweep of community life." ...

Faced with the imperative of the native question and the cultural resistance of the African population to the policy of assimilation, the British understood better than any other colonial power the need for a policy that would harness culturally legitimate political allies—and not literate Africans ambivalent or even hostile to tradition. By 1898, Sir George Goldie, the president of the Royal Niger Company, had formulated a dictum that all company officials were required to follow: "The general policy of ruling on African principles through native rulers must be followed for the present. " Indirect rule came to be predicated on a form of decentralization that was more cultural than territorial.

More than just a search for personnel to augment the few European officials available on the ground, it was a search for institutional forms of control anchored in a historical and cultural legitimacy; summed up in the words of General Jan Smuts, "it was a shift from territorial to institutional segregation."

Institutional segregation referred to a policy of native control that would be mediated through native chiefs working through native institutions. But neither the personnel nor the institutions they worked were simply available for the picking. Even where chiefs already existed, they had to be tamed. As usual,

Lugard advised on the best practical solution: to thrash them first, conciliate them afterwards; and by this method our prestige with the native tribes would be certainly greatly increased, and subsequent troubles with them would be less likely. In reality, native institutions were given life and substance through a policy that combined a recognition of existing facts with creative modification and even outright fabrication. Whatever the mix, in every instance institutional segregation involved a shift in native policy from a civilized to a tribal orientation and a corresponding change in its social base from the educated strata to traditional chiefs. Simply put, as the link with traditional authorities was forged, so the alliance with the educated strata was severed.

By 1920, indirect rule could be said to express the general thrust of British colonial policy on the native question. Because indirect rule meant that the real locus of colonial administration was the local state, the district run by the district commissioner, it was imperative that this man on the spot be carefully identified, groomed, and placed. Both Britain and France ended the local recruitment of colonial administrators between 1890 and 1914 and reorganized the colonial administration into a formal service along lines of the upper echelon of the metropolitan bureaucracy. The corollary of district-level decentralization was that the agents of district administration were recruited, trained, and placed from the center. This was not simply a terminal shift, from local to metropolitan recruitment, but also a change in social emphasis. During the 1920s, the Colonial Office began to recruit administrators chiefly from Oxbridge. Applicants were screened through interviews and references designed to identify "those qualities of character and personality so essential in dealing with native peoples." The rationale for recruiting the new class of colonial officials from the upper classes at home was that they could be "chiefs in their own country"—men who considered it their birth right to rule, and who did so by habit. . . .

Although this system was to be applied "in its fullest" only "to communities under the centralized rule of a paramount chief, with some administrative machinery at his disposal," Lugard had no doubt that "its underlying principles" needed to be applied "to the varying extent to which it is possible to apply them, even to the most primitive communities." Lugard's point was that the implementation of indirect rule would be greatly facilitated by the prior existence of a native state apparatus, but indirect rule did not have to be restricted to these areas. For it was possible to build a native state apparatus where none had existed before. The important point was to ensure that the parameters of this state authority corresponded with that of the native community, the tribe, and then to rule through it. Between culture and territory, the former must define the parameters of decentralized rule: the boundaries of culture would mark the parameters of territorial administration. This is why to install a state apparatus among communities whose lives had never before been shaped by one was literally to invent tribes!

Not surprisingly, the tendency was for the tribe to be defined as the unit of indirect rule administration. As George Padmore noted in Nigeria, the Mecca of indirect rule, administrative units corresponded "roughly to ethnic or tribal groupings." "The notion of tribe," argues the historian John Iliffe, "lay at the heart of 'indirect' rule in Tanganyika." A 1930 *Native Administration Memorandum on Native Court,* issued in Tanganyika, explained that tribes were cultural units "possessing a common language, a single social system, and an established customary law." Based on the belief that "every African belonged to a tribe, just as every European belonged to a nation," a provincial commissioner summarized official policy: "Each tribe must be considered a distinct unit.... Each tribe must be under a chief." Yet "most administrators knew that many peoples had no chiefs." The solution of this riddle was Governor Cameron's major contribution to indirect rule administration in Tanganyika. He gave chiefs to the chiefless peoples. Admonishing an official who could not see the trees for the wood, Cameron summed up the policy in a nutshell: "Mr. Thompson must take the tribal unit." In other words, if there did not exist a clearly demarcated tribe with a distinct central authority, then one had to be created in the interest of order....

The difference between early British and French colonial experience is summed up by the following: unlike the British, who in Nigeria and Uganda worked out alliances and "treaties" with rulers of precolonial kingdoms, the French were more often than not in direct conflict with these great aristocracies. When the majority of the great African states, like the kingdoms of Segou and Sikasso and the state of Sammy, refused to submit to French claims, they were suppressed. In the words of Governor-General W. Panty in 1910, the point of direct administration was to "suppress the great native polities which are nearly always a barrier between us and our subject." To flatten all mediation between the village and themselves to one, the village chief, came to be the key object of French policy. But in reality, this objective remained elusive. Caught between an acute shortage of European administrators who were concentrated in the main towns and a turn of policy away from the previous assimilationist bent, a *de facto* recognition of chieftainship beyond the village level became inevitable. By the early 1920s, this shift had gained a theoretical recognition. The older ideal of assimilation was shed as quickly as the newer notion of association was embraced. In his influential work *Domination et Colonisation,* the conservative colonial theorist Jules Harmand distinguished "colonies of settlement from those of *domination* in which European rule was exercised over a large indigenous population." In the latter, he argued, "the social standards of the Native inhabitants were too remote from those of France for assimilation to be practicable." As an alternative, he proposed a "policy of association," which he defined as "indirect administration, with the preservation but improved governance of the institutions of the conquered peoples, and with respect for their past." The publication in 1923 of Sarraut's *La Mise en Valeur des Colonies Françaises* signaled that the policy had indeed received official sanction.

Association, as opposed to assimilation, had originally been suggested for Indochina. Only later was the policy extended to Africa, where the test case was the North African colony of Morocco. The forms of the Sherifian state were preserved throughout Morocco, as indeed they were by the Spanish colonists in the portion of Morocco they came to control. The practice in France's Sub-Saharan colonies fell short of the Lugardian stress on creating an autonomous Native Administration. The degree of autonomy varied from one situation to another, as did the level of mediation through native institutions and personnel. But the general situation was that chiefship could not be confined to the village level; a second tier of canton chiefs was also created, at first in French-controlled West Africa, later extended to French-controlled Equatorial Africa, where the *chef de terre* came to be in charge of "a group of several villages." At the same time, relations among natives came to be regulated under customary law, dispensed by various levels of chiefs under the direct supervision of the French cercle commander, as indeed it was under the supervision of white commissioners in southern Nigeria or the Cape. All in all, indirect administration in France's sub-Saharan African colonies was more a Cape-like affair than a Natal-type administration, closer to British rule in southern Nigeria than in northern Nigeria.

The British example inspired many lesser colonial powers: from the Belgians in the Congo to the Portuguese in the colonies of Mozambique, Angola, and Guinea to the Italians in Libya and even to the Americo-Liberians. The Belgians introduced indirect rule institutions in the Congo in the 1920s. The reorganization of the administration in 1918 was followed by the creation of a special legal category called native, subject to customary law and to whom the Code Napoleon did not apply. From 1921 on, all Africans were eventually required to return to the rural areas from which they were deemed to have come in the first place. The native must belong to his tribe: the notion of the native as permanently a peasant and only temporarily a worker was given legal reality through a series of decrees between 1931 and 1933. . . .

Where there was a significant settler presence, the transition from direct to indirect rule was usually an informal and protracted affair, with legal recognition following rather than clearing the ground for it. In such instances, the point of legal reform was to prune the worst excesses of indirect rule authority brought to light by popular protest. . . .

A complete reform of indirect rule leading to its full autonomy was possible only where the weight of settler interests was weak. That was, as one would expect, in the non-settler colonies. But it was also effected in those settler colonies where the relative strength of settler influence was weakened by other fractions of capital or a powerful peasant movement or some combination of the two. One example of where such a reform was effected in spite of a substantial settler presence was the British colony of Swaziland. Settlers had long opposed autonomous powers for Swazi chiefs, and the British-controlled central state had obliged in a context where Swaziland was assumed to be on a political course that would lead to its eventual absorption into the Republic of South Africa. But the unexpected victory of the National Party in the 1948 elections put into question this assumed trajectory. As the National Party consolidated its hold over the South African state, the Swazi colonial state effected a successful transition, in the form of indirect rule, from semi-autonomy to autonomy and then to independence. The shift is clear if we compare two key legislations from 1944 and 1950. The sharply limited autonomy of native rulers was reflected in the Native Administration Proclamation of 1944 in Swaziland: it gave the British high commissioner the power to appoint and depose all chiefs, including the paramount chief. The tide turned with Proclamation 79 of 1950. It recognized the Swazi king as the sole authority for issuing any of a wide variety of twenty-nine orders enforceable in the customary courts. The king and chiefs were empowered to make rules providing these did not conflict with existing laws in the country. These rules could be enforced in native courts. Another proclamation (the 1950 Native Courts Proclamation) gave the king the right to establish Swazi courts, to prescribe their rules of procedure, and to establish courts of appeal—all subject to ratification by the British resident commissioner.

A similar transition to autonomy—full-fledged indirect rule—and then to independence was attempted in South Africa when the National Party came to power in May 1948. The Bantu Authorities Act (68 of 1951) claimed to restore "the natural native democracy" to the reserves by creating a system of councils controlled by chiefs and headmen. For the first time, an autonomous Native Treasury and a Native Administration paid from it with powers to make rules in a native legislature were added to the administration of customary law, in Zululand (Natal) and in other homelands. The pace was set in the Transkei in 1956, when the Transkeian Territorial Authority was created, growing over the next twenty years from "self-government" (1963) to "independence" (1976). The Transkeian example was emulated in three other in stances—Ciskei, Venda, and Bophuthatswana—whereas developments in Zululand stopped at the establishment of an autonomous indirect rule regime.

Ironically, it is apartheid that brought to South African natives full-blown indirect rule, that system of control upheld in equatorial Africa as testimony to the true colonial genius of British imperialism; and it was apartheid that tried to keep pace with imperial-style decolonization, particularly in migrant reserve territories like Swaziland, as the "wind of change" blew across the continent. But that is where the parallel ends, for although indirect rule was successfully reformed in colonies to the north of the Limpopo through a deracialization of the state apparatus, such a reform was not within easy grasp of South Africa. Precisely that special feature in the colonial experience of South African natives, that it had come to be a colony of white settlement—a fact most often summed up in the phrase "settler colonialism" or "internal colonialism"—made such a reform difficult. For the deracialization of the system of indirect rule would require a reform of both native communities and hitherto white civil society. Entrenched in civil society and state institutions, white privilege set apart South Africa—and, to a lesser extent, Algeria and Rhodesia—from the rest of Africa.

Colonial Chiefs in the Borderlands of Northern Rhodesia and the Belgian Congo

DAVID GORDON[6]

In his study of the Luapula peoples conducted in the late 1940s, anthropologist Ian Cunnison noticed that chiefship varied on either side of the Luapula River. In Northern Rhodesia, the Eastern Lunda King Mwata Kazembe and his aristocrats were the core group of colonial chiefs. On the west bank, in the Belgian Congo, precolonial and pre-Lunda rulers called "owners of the land" had become colonial chiefs. Given what we know about the relative styles of the colonial administrations, this is not a surprising observation. The Belgian administration was known for its harsh paternalism, while the British doctrine of indirect rule encouraged rule by precolonial elites and strong men like the Lunda paramount. Yet this article argues that to understand the making of colonial chiefship we need to look beyond formal policy. Instead, the character of chiefship depended on precolonial polities at the time of conquest, the process of conquest itself, and the relative autonomy of the colonial state from expatriate commercial interests. On the Northern Rhodesian side of the Luapula River, successive Eastern Lunda rulers were able to refashion and recentralize their government during colonialism at the expense of the owners of the land: on the Congolese side of the river, by contrast, decentralized clan elders and owners of the land had opportunity to escape the rule of the Eastern Lunda, collaborate with the colonial authorities, and become independent chiefs. There was a significant divergence between colonial intentions regarding the spread of state power through chiefs and actual outcomes.

The simplest explanation for the difference in colonial chiefship was that, at the time of colonial conquest, Lunda authority was not thoroughly established on the west bank of the Luapula. To be sure, at the height of the Eastern

---

[6] This excerpt is taken from David Gordon, "Owners of the Land and Lunda Lords: Colonial Chiefs in the Borderlands of Northern Rhodesia and the Belgian Congo," published in *The International Journal of African Historical Studies* 34, no. 2 (2001), pp. 315-38. David Gordon is associate professor of history at Bowdoin College.

Lunda empire in the early nineteenth century, the Luapula River was not a significant border for Mwata Kazembe's empire. The river, lagoons, and lake acted more like an interconnecting infrastructure than a physical boundary and many chiefs west of the Luapula recognized Lunda suzerainty. However, Lunda authority was challenged during the nineteenth century. Swahili slave and ivory traders began to monopolize many of the Eastern Lunda's former trade routes. A Nyamwezi trader, Msiri, set up his capital in Bunkeya, beyond the Kundelungu Mountains that formed the western rim of the Luapula Valley, and from there asserted authority over much of the western valley. When Belgian and British forces conquered Mweru-Luapula, Lunda authority on the west bank of the river was already tenuous. It would become even more difficult to maintain with a colonial border dividing the Lunda heartland.

However, the different character of colonial chiefship on either side of the Luapula was not only a result of continuity with preconquest patterns of political organization. There were a number of leaders who could have consolidated power on the Belgian side of the Luapula. The BaYeke, for example, still had client rulers along the Luapula. The other powerful Luapula leader, the Shila ruler Nkuba, established himself in the Belgian Congo but did not secure a network of subordinate chiefs. No powerful indigenous leader similar to Mwata Kazembe emerged because little common ground or spirit of accommodation was reached between colonized and colonial elites. This was not a result of colonial policy but a legacy of conquest, or colonial "pacification," and the resultant distrust chiefs and villagers had of colonial officials. Further compromising the establishment of an arena of post-conquest accommodation was the centrality of Mweru-Luapula to the Belgian Congo's mining economy during the early colonial period: where chiefs and the resources they controlled were an essential part of the colonial political economy, colonial administrators supervised them closely, often allowing less opportunity for the consolidation of power by a single chief. By contrast, on the Northern Rhodesian side of the border where the mining economy developed in later years, Mwata Kazembe and his client chiefs managed to secure authority over owners of the land and clan elders in the early colonial period. On the west bank of the Luapula in the Belgian Congo, independent but politically weak decentralized rulers became the dominant type of colonial chief. They were drawn from a number of owners of the land and did not enjoy a significant degree of formal political power in the colonial era.

Interest in the transformation of African political leadership from precolonial rulers to colonial chiefs was first generated by proponents of indirect rule who hoped to identify an African political elite that could best be incorporated into the colonial government. With the rise of independent Africa, colonial chiefs, who had been encouraged by the colonial state to confront nationalist movements, became political anachronisms detested by the postcolonial leadership and blamed for problems ranging from "tribalism" to economic underdevelopment. A tradition of scholars inspired by the spirit of African nationalism condemned colonial chiefs as "collaborators," "colonial puppets," or "compradors." Mahmood Mamdani refers to a system of "decentralized despotism" that emerged out of the policies of late colonialism. According to such views, colonialism eroded and destroyed more balanced forms of African government and replaced them with despotic rulers. In at least one sense, these scholars are correct. Chiefship and village politics did indeed change during colonialism; the institution of colonial chiefship differed greatly from precolonial forms of governance. Most important, a colonial chief defined his sphere of rule by control over a bounded territory and not a kin group, which was the most prevalent—but not exclusive—form of precolonial governance.

Yet colonial chiefs were also more than simply part of the apparatus of the territorial colonial state and were never straightforward incarnations of colonial policy. In fact, colonial policy emerged *from* conquest and colonization; it was a theory of the dominant, but not exclusive, experience of rule in any particular colonial territory. Where conquest was incomplete and colonial administrators were dispersed, "customary" associations that surrounded colonial chiefs could create rural associational spheres that interacted with the embryonic bureaucratic state. Many chiefs maintained or reconstituted followings that extended beyond tightly bounded territories. . . .

In Mweru-Luapula, the nature of conquest and the drawing of geographic borders left certain areas with more powerful precolonial structures that could give shape to local colonial institutions. Msiri, the most powerful Katangan leader in the late nineteenth century, was the first to fall to Belgian mercenary forces. By late nineteenth century, Msiri was involved in several conflicts and had to quell frequent revolts by clients. His army was drained by an ongoing war with the Swahili trader, Simba, on Kilwa Island. In 1891, Msiri negotiated different treaties with the Congo Free State and Alfred Sharpe of the British South African Company. On the 15th of December, Captain Stairs, an English mercenary in charge of an armed Belgian force, arrived at Msiri's capital to raise the Congo Free State's flag. Desperate for war materials, Msiri conceded on the condition that he be given a supply of gunpowder. Five days later, during the to and fro of negotiations, one of Stairs' officers, Captain Bodson, shot and killed him. Although Bodson was in turn shot by the Msiri's soldiers, he allegedly managed to decapitate Msiri, take his head back to Stairs and declare, "I have killed a tiger! *Vive le roi!*" The missionary Dan Crawford, who had spent more than a year at Msiri's court, described the aftereffects of Msiri's assassination: "The population completely dispersed. No one dared walk openly abroad. The paths became lined with corpses, some of whom had died of starvation and some of the universal mistrust which keeps spears on the quiver." When Msiri died, his tribute and trade empire with its shallow historical roots disintegrated. There was no local leader left powerful enough to take advantage of colonial conquest and reconstitute a following. Instead, Dan Crawford created a community of converts out of Msiri's former subjects.

On the other side of Luapula, the conquest and incorporation of Mwata Kazembe's Eastern Lunda Empire into the colonial state was more successful. Mwata Kazembe X held back the agents of the British South African Company (BSAC) for a number of years. In 1892, Kazembe paid tribute to the BSAC representative, Alfred Sharpe. Over the next few years, he had contacts with Europeans, including Dan Crawford who visited Kazembe's capital and a rubber trader who had gained Kazembe's permission to build a house nearby. However, after the BSAC administrator Dr. Blair Watson established a post on the Kalungwishi River, near Lake Mweru, Kazembe became more antagonistic. In 1897 he refused to accept European rule and did not allow a British flag to be raised in his kingdom. He successfully repulsed an army of local and Swahili soldiers led by Watson. Two years later, in 1899, Alfred Sharpe, then the governor of Nyasaland, returned with a company of Sikhs and Nyasaland armed forces. The colonial forces killed many and burned the Lunda capital to the
ground. . . .

Unlike Msiri, Mwata Kazembe X was not killed by colonial armed forces. Yet even if he had been, the Eastern Lunda empire had far deeper historical roots in Luapula than Msiri's BaYeke empire. Lunda paramounts had suffered assassinations and coups on several previous occasions. They had been attacked by Msiri, by the Luba, and by Swahili traders, all of whom capitalized on internal divisions. Yet Lunda government was based on a resilient form of perpetual kinship and positional succession that allowed individuals to adopt positions of political office within a fictive family. Upon the death of, say, Kashiba, Kazembe's "mother," a political office was vacated and a new Kashiba could be found. Although real lineage was important in appointments to political office, fictive kinship was crucial. Lunda institutions were thereby able to withstand conquest; the Lunda elite could remake their ruling class according to a fixed constitution. Colonial conquest proved no different. Mwata Kazembe X succeeded in negotiating surrender to British colonial agents. In later years, his successor would be able to reconstitute a network of subordinate chiefs and accord them offices within the Lunda "family." On the Congolese side of the river, by contrast, the assassination of Msiri, the Nyamwezi leader of the BaYeke state, and the rupture of any ties with his clients next to the Luapula left little opportunity for a strong leader to consolidate different clan elders and owners of the land within the colonial state's apparatus.

The BaYeke, Luba, and Swahili wars just prior to colonial conquest had disrupted older patterns of allegiance and resulted in a complex and unstable political landscape when colonial officials arrived. For example, during the

Lunda-Yeke wars, local owners of the land who paid tribute to the Lunda either switched allegiance to Msiri or fled to the east bank of the Luapula beyond the reach of Msiri's army. In the early nineteenth century Kikungu, Kibale, and Kampombwe—the "Kisamamba" owners of the land, remembered by Lunda oral traditions for their treachery and mendaciousness—accepted Lunda authority and paid tribute to Mwata Kazembe. When Msiri conquered portions of the western Luapula in the latter half of nineteenth century, they left their ancestral land on the western bank of the Luapula and took refuge closer to Kazembe's capital. Thus, when the first Belgian colonial officials arrived, they found the land sparsely populated by recent war refugees and were unsure who should be appointed as colonial chiefs.

Finally, the wars of colonial conquest also disrupted older ties to the land and in a few cases allowed villagers opportunities to escape from demanding precolonial rulers. When in 1902 the British switched from collecting tax in rubber to shillings, many villagers fled to the Belgian Congo since they did not have access to shillings and their villages were burned down if tax was not paid. Rulers who had been subordinate to Mwata Kazembe took advantage of the situation by crossing into the Belgian Congo with their followers. Chief Nkuba Kawama, one of the original Shila rulers conquered by Mwata Kazembe III, fled to the Congo with his people after British colonial officials destroyed canoes for infractions against anti-sleeping sickness measures. He was joined by the Kisamamba chiefs who returned to their ancestral lands on the western banks of the Luapula River. In the newly proclaimed Congo Free State, Nkuba and the Kisamambas escaped Lunda overlordship and succeeded in being appointed as independent colonial chiefs.

The Katangan Concessionaire Regime

After conquest, the relationship of the colonial state to mining interests was a significant force in the making of colonial chieftaincies. In the Katangan province of the Belgian Congo, the administration invited expatriate capital to take responsibility for the *mise en valeur* of the colony. Large-scale expatriate capitalists played an important role in all sectors of the economy and the colonial state viewed its primary responsibility as the mediation between private, largely expatriate business interests and African society. The "marriage of iron and rye" in Prussia and the "uneasy union of maize and gold" in South Africa seem to find their counterpart in the early colonial world of Katanga with the growth of the copper industry and its insatiable appetite for cheap labor and rural produce. Demand for labor in the Katangan copper mines and fish to feed the workers were the economic forces that brought colonial capitalism to the Luapula Valley.

Rural administrative policy conformed to these needs and officials attempted to oversee all economic and political activity in the villages. An oft-cited summation of Belgian colonial policy refers to it as *"dominer pour servir,"* according to the phrase coined by the Belgian proconsul Pierre Ryckmans in 1948: authoritarian colonial rule was justified by the rapid social and economic development of the colony. Yet Belgian colonial policy, especially prior to World War II, was a melange of ideas that differed from one official to the next. . . .

Chiefs in a Northern Rhodesian Hinterland

Different patterns of conquest held diverging legacies for colonial chiefs. In the Congo, King Leopold's mercenaries had killed the most powerful ruler, Msiri, and destroyed his influence in Luapula. Village clan leaders who had previously paid tribute to Msiri now vied for influence with their new conquerors. In Northern Rhodesia, Mwata Kazembe X escaped with his life, although his capital was burned to the ground and his empire extinguished. Nevertheless, his successors were able to exploit the structures and policies of the British colonial state and recreate a local network of client colonial chiefs.

Lunda aristocrats called *abakalulwa* (or *abakalunda*) selected Mwata Kazembe from a royal patrilineage that traced descent back to "Chinyanta," whom oral traditions record as a client of the central Lunda paramount Mwaant Yaav. By the nineteenth century, three different patrilines competed for the accession to the royal office of Mwata Kazembe, with the Lunda aristocrats supposedly responsible for making the final decision. The arrangement became especially precarious in the second half of the century when Swahili and BaYeke traders backed competing candidates. However, in the colonial period, a degree of stability returned to succession when the Lunda aristocrats agreed to rotate the office between the three dominant lineages.

The success of Lunda aristocrats and Mwata Kazembe in reconsolidating power and patronage networks in the early colonial period was due to a combination of the Eastern Lunda's historical roots in Luapula and the dispersed British administrative presence. In Northern Rhodesia the colonial state was more independent of concessionaire interests and, in any event, Mweru-Luapula was more marginal to these interests. . . . Even when the copper industry in Northern Rhodesia expanded in the late 1920s, the fish of Mweru-Luapula were not considered an essential item in workers' rations, since beef was more readily available. The area was officially declared "tribal trust" to be reserved for African economic exploitation. . . . In the 1940s, as part of this modernization drive, new reforms aimed at consolidating smaller sub-chieftaincies into Native Authorities and subordinating them to Superior Native Authorities. Expert councilors were to guide these Native Authorities in what the administration considered to be a progressive and modern direction. However, the reforms of the 1940s did not involve the introduction of more democratic or representative political structures. Instead, they "modernized" the administration by introducing "progressive" elements without undermining chiefs. The changes were still built on the colonial chieftaincies created before indirect rule legislation had even been passed.

The most important Superior Native Authority in the valley was to be the Lunda Native Authority, presided over by Mwata Kazembe. The reforms coincided with the coming to the throne of a new Mwata Kazembe who had arguably more influence over the character of his chieftaincy than the colonial reforms. In 1941, Mwata Kazembe XIII, "Chinkonkole," died and Shadreck Chinyanta became Mwata Kazembe XIV, a selection applauded by the colonial administration. Previously educated and employed in Elisabethville, Mwata Kazembe "Chinyanta" could write and speak both English and French fluently. Upon coming to the throne, he appointed young men drawn from the educated elite to act as his advisors. Luminaries like the nationalist leader Dauti L. Yamba and the businessman Benjamin Kapapula were "ministers" in his Native Authority "cabinet." He wrote the first history of the Luapula Lunda in Bemba entitled *Ifikolwe Fyandi na Bantu Bandi* (*My Ancestors and My People*). He changed the name of the Lunda Native Authority to the less insulting Lunda National Association. In the Lunda National Association, chosen representatives from the region discussed policy and counseled the chief. Under his chairmanship, the association debated issues pertaining to the fishery and to village life in general. A secretary kept minutes of the meetings and sent them to the local district official. The association constructed schools, offices, a clinic, and roads in the Lunda capital, Mwansabombwe. Kazembe encouraged parents to send their children to school and visited many of the schools himself. Indeed, the leadership of Mwata Kazembe Shadreck Chinyanta set an important precedent for future inheritors of the throne. . . .

Chiefs like Mwata Kazembe collaborated on their own terms, gaining what benefits they could from the colonial administration while following a different agenda within their communities. Successive Mwata Kazembes managed to reconstitute a network of Lunda chiefs related to them through ties of perpetual kinship—the Lunda "family" did not perish with colonialism. Moreover, within the colonial state structure, Mwata Kazembe managed to subordinate independent owners of the land and elders like Mulundu, Lubunda, and Katuta Kampemba to his Lunda Native Authority. Yet in the eyes of the villagers, his authority over these elders was tenuous. These were the significant colonial transformations in the eastern Luapula Valley. Chiefs and chieftaincy changed during the colonial period, but these changes did not march to the beat of colonial policy.

Historical contingencies from below, rather than doctrines from above, were instrumental in the making of colonial chiefs. In some cases, as Mahmood Mamdani argues, colonialism "crystallized . . . and built on the range of unfreedoms unleashed in nineteenth-century conquest states. . . ." Mwata Kazembe X managed to negotiate a settlement with the colonial rulers after his defeat in 1899, and thereby provided opportunity for his successors to ensure a degree of continuity with the precolonial Eastern Lunda polity. However, such continuity was absent in the case of Msiri, executed by Leopold's mercenaries in 1895 and remembered only for his brutality. After the crushing effect of the early colonial period, the Belgian administration could not develop an indirect rule based on powerful rulers like Mwata Kazembe. Instead, in Mweru-Luapula, they based their point of contact with village society at the level of the pre-Lunda owner of the land who enjoyed little political authority and could not consolidate power on his own initiative.

British and Belgian officials envisaged their colonies in different ways and developed different administrative policies and styles. In the case of chiefship, it is unclear whether these diverse policies led to distinct outcomes. In Mweru-Luapula, chiefs who consolidated power and came to play important roles did so through opportunities during and soon after colonial conquest. The character of colonial chiefship cannot be attributed to "late colonialism" *à la* Mamdani.

Colonial chiefship was contingent on circumstance rather than structured by doctrine. The implication is that even within a single colonial territory there were chiefs with different degrees of legitimacy, a range of local followings, and a mixture of bureaucratic and supernatural powers. Mamdani has identified several important general features of colonial rule. However, in rural hinterlands where chiefs mattered, there was no generic colonialism that relied on a standard form of "decentralized despotism." The character of colonial chiefship was unpredictable; for this reason, chiefs were at best fickle allies in the attempted spread of state authority.

Suggested Readings

Daly, Martin, *Empire on the Nile: The Anglo-Egyptian Sudan, 1898-1934* (Cambridge: Cambridge University Press, 1986).

Gifford, Prosser, "Indirect Rule: Touchstone or Tombstone for Colonial Policy." In *Britain and Germany in Africa*, by Prosser Gifford and William Roger Louis (New Haven, CT: Yale University Press, 1969).

Green, Erik, "Indirect Rule and Colonial Intervention: Chiefs and Agrarian Change in Nyasaland, ca. 1933 to the Early 1950s." *International Journal of African Historical Studies* 44, no. 2 (2011), p. 249.

Low, D. A., *Fabrication of Empire: The British and the Uganda Kingdoms, 1890-1902* (Cambridge: Cambridge University Press, 2009).

Manning, Patrick, *Francophone Sub-Saharan Africa, 1880-1995* (Cambridge: Cambridge University Press, 1999).

Richens, Peter, "The Economic Legacies of the 'Thin White Line': Indirect Rule and the Comparative Development of Sub-Saharan Africa." *African Economic History* 37, no. 1 (2009), pp. 32-102.

Taiwo, Olufemi, *How Colonialism Preempted Modernity in Africa* (Bloomington: Indiana University Press, 2010).

PROBLEM III

COLONIAL RULE AND ETHNIC IDENTITY

European imperialists held firmly fixed assumptions about African institutions and identities. In their eyes, African political systems were monarchical and autocratic, while their identities were primitive and immutable. These initial convictions became reinforced by the first generation of Western anthropologists and colonial administrators who studied the newly conquered peoples of the continent. Their investigations were informed by the Enlightenment's fascination with the accumulation and categorization of knowledge, and by the nineteenth century's conflation of biology and nationalism. They compiled tribal ethnographies in an effort to both understand and govern African communities. Though their analyses could be quite sympathetic, they invariably rested on the premise that the tribe was the basic, traditional form of identity in African communities. Tribes were a primitive kind of social organization that was appropriate to technologically and politically simple communities who existed at an early stage of human development. Such views of the tribe have found support among Africans themselves, particularly those who have profited from the simplified forms of identity ascribed to them. These views continue to inform Western perceptions of African identity.

Since the end of the colonial era, however, scholars have reconsidered this static picture of African societies by probing its historical roots, seeking to understand how tribes were "made," "invented," or "imagined." This body of literature overlaps with the re-examination of "customary" and "traditional" authorities that accompanied the establishment of indirect rule throughout much of colonial Africa. One of the earliest works to question the utility of the term "tribe" was written by anthropologist Aidan Southall. He begins his essay by demonstrating the imprecision and confusion that have haunted efforts to divide African peoples neatly into separate and discrete communities. He then recounts many examples where diverse ethnic groups found themselves lumped together—for reasons of expedience or administrative ignorance—into newly identified tribes, which carried with them corporate rights and responsibilities. To Southall, the term *tribe* is inappropriate because of its imprecision and association with primitivism. While not willing to dispose of the term entirely, he warns his fellow anthropologists that it should "be applied only to the small scale societies of the past."

One of the leading critics of the use of the term *tribe* in African history was Leroy Vail. In 1989 he edited an influential collection of essays entitled *The Creation of Tribalism in Southern Africa*. In an essay originally published in that collection, Vail asserts that the tribal identities of the region emerged in the modern era: "Ethnic consciousness is very much a new phenomenon, an ideological construct, usually of the twentieth century, and not an anachronistic cultural artifact from the past." In Vail's view, tribal identities were made in the context of the nineteenth-century mining boom in Southern Africa. The intense pressure placed on men to become migrant laborers in mines created an "age of anxiety" among rural Africans. According to Vail, "rapid social and economic change eroded earlier political relationships based on clientage both within and outside of lineages, social patterns, and religious beliefs." New forms of identity emerged to replace these, the most powerful of which was tribalism: "One of the most far-reaching and important of these new forms of consciousness was a new ethnic—or tribal—consciousness." This new tribal identity was given historical legitimacy by Western missionaries and African intellectuals. But they were equally embraced by migrant laborers, whose tribal identities helped them protect their interests in their rural homelands and gain status in the multi-ethnic mining compounds in the region.

In 1984, historian Terence Ranger published a ground-breaking essay that suggested that tribal identities were one of many aspects of African culture that were "invented" under colonial rule. "The Invention of Tradition in Colonial Africa," excerpted here, explores the ways in which colonial states manipulated historic symbols and institutions to accommodate the requirements of colonial administrations. Ranger recognizes that such manipulations assumed that there was some historic precedent for the colonial efforts: "The most far-reaching inventions of tradition in colonial Africa took place when the Europeans believed themselves to be respecting age-old African customs." However, whether wittingly or not, in the process of making African culture and institutions explicable and manageable, colonial bureaucrats invariably distorted them to suit administrative needs. "What were called customary law, customary land-rights, customary political structure, and so on, were in fact *all* invented by colonial codification." Among the most influential inventions of tradition identified by Ranger in the piece is that of tribalism, which he sees as a fundamental component of the invention of customary law.

An important theme in the invention of tribalism literature is the role of middle-class Africans and European missionaries in compiling the tribal histories that came to be accepted as historical fact. Writing about the Yoruba of southern Nigeria, historian J.D.Y. Peel argues that it was Christian intellectuals who fostered ideas about Yoruba identity. Anxious to refute European notions of African primitivism, these intellectuals collected oral traditions and composed histories that treated the Yoruba as a nation in the Western sense. It was through this process that the "tribal" contours of Yoruba identity became established. As Peel puts it, "The very ethnic category 'Yoruba,' in its modern connotation, was the product of missionary 'invention.'"

The powerful influence of these critics encouraged scholars across the continent to re-examine the origins of tribal identities. But some scholars believed that this school of thought gave too much influence to colonial actors and oversimplified the complicated process of conflict and negotiation that underpinned the process. The title of Carolyn Hamilton's book *Terrific Majesty: Shaka Zulu and the Limits of Historical Invention* reflects her dissatisfaction with this approach to understanding tribal histories as colonial constructs. Her book explores the construction of Zulu identity as it has developed over the past two centuries. Hamilton shows how the Zulu became Africa's most famous tribe, and how their ruler Shaka became a notoriously brutal and tyrannical symbol of African despotism. Many writers—Western and Zulu alike—carefully crafted an image of a ferocious, Napoleonic character who forged through sheer force of will a nation out of diverse Nguni communities. But in the 1970s and 1980s, a new wave of Southern African scholarship began to deconstruct the Shaka myth, emphasizing the lack of verifiable evidence about the man, his origins, and his community. Thus, the carefully cultivated Shaka myth, and the vibrant form of identity it supported, appeared to be the quintessential example of the creation of a tribe.

But Hamilton's work questions the limits to which such inventions are possible. She believes that the powerful and enduring identity of the Zulu was not manufactured cynically by Europeans or Africans, but rather built on widely accepted events and traditions to construct a usable form of political identity. In doing so, she explicitly addresses the assertions of Ranger and others of the invention of tradition school. Such an approach, she argues, "places full control over content and form in the hands of the inventors"—usually political elites—"and ignores the ways that their versions of history are shaped by contesting and conflicting versions of the past."

The Illusion of Tribe

AIDAN W. SOUTHALL[1]

Controversial though the matter is, the most generally acceptable characteristics of a tribal society are perhaps that it is a whole society, with a high degree of self-sufficiency at a near subsistence level, based on a relatively simple technology without writing or literature, politically autonomous and with its own distinctive language, culture and sense of identity, tribal religion being also coterminous with tribal society. Some would insist on further differentiation of the tribal level of social and cultural organization, on the one hand, from the very small-scale band level characteristic of hunting and gathering peoples without agriculture, and on the other, from state or state-like organizations found at the upper limit of scale and complexity within the range of non-literate societies. Thus, Sahlins speaks of the "tribal level, as distinguished from less-developed *bands* and more advanced *chiefdoms*." This point of view has not found much favour and can be criticised on a number of counts. At the empirical level, tribes and bands do not appear as distinct as is implied, and the concept of "chief" and "chiefdom," while clear to some writers, is highly variable and inconsistent in the ethnographic literature as a whole. The empirical difficulties of distinguishing the tribal level in the broad sense have been considerable, and the addition of two further levels seems to make them insurmountable. It is not by multiplying global distinctions of this sort that we shall progress, but by dealing with more specialized categories of phenomena while retaining the general concept of tribe as a convenient initial descriptive label. Dozens of definitions could, of course, be quoted from authoritative anthropological writings, but for the most part, they add nothing to understanding and vary only in emphasis, one stressing language, another politics, another self identity, and so forth.

For present purposes, to simplify the argument, we shall use tribal society in the more inclusive sense of all those societies that exhibit the first mentioned

---

[1] This excerpt is taken from Aidan Southall, "The Illusion of Tribe," published in *The Journal of Asian and African Studies* 5, no. 1-2 (January 1970), pp. 28-50. Aidan Southall was professor of anthropology at the University of Wisconsin.

set of characteristics. On this basis, to what extent do such societies still exist? In the strict sense they cannot exist, since there are no areas of the inhabited earth unclaimed by one sovereign state or another. They can only exist in dwindling pockets so remote that such sovereign claims have not yet been made effective and can be ignored. No tribal society which has lost its political autonomy can continue to be a tribal society in the full sense of this meaning, although many of its members may retain vivid and even nostalgic memories of its former full existence and may continue to be strongly influenced by the values belonging to this former state and still endeavour to act according to them in those fields where new controls and changed needs allow them to do so. It is the melancholy paradox of anthropology that effective study of such social systems dates only from a period so late that they had already ceased to exist in this full sense, so that an element of reconstruction has always entered into the study of them in these terms. But it would be foolish to deny that the end of their existence in the full sense was the beginning of a long transitional period in which their members were in varying degrees becoming incorporated into wider systems, yet continued to retain strong elements of their former state. Neglect of this has vitiated much of the work carried out supposedly in their interests by the development disciplines. It is not only political autonomy which has been lost, though that was fundamental, and it is well to specify the changes which have generally occurred in respect of the other stated characteristics. They are no longer self-sufficient, because various pressures from without and then from within have brought them to depend extensively on goods and services that they cannot produce for themselves. Even where their material well-being is still little better than their former subsistence, they have nonetheless become involved with the wider market economy in countless seemingly irrevocable ways. By the same token, their technology is no longer simple. Even where it is little improved in efficiency, it has come to reflect in its array of tools and weapons, clothes and even foodstuffs, the vast, unseen and distant complex of the industrial world. Almost invariably some of its members have become literate, and even if they have often at the same time tended to become absentees, they nonetheless remain vital members of it and the very symbols of its passing. Furthermore, they have often, and necessarily, become literate in a foreign language. They have also adopted, of course under strong external persuasion if not pressure, new religious belief, practices, and memberships, or at least new sets of ideas, which are incompatible with tribal society. In all these ways, the close identity of language, culture, and society (if it ever existed) is now blurred and has become a series of alternatives. To say "I am a Kikuyu, a Kenyan, an African," means three very different things. The latter two identities did not exist three quarters of a century ago. What has been said here is obviously only a minimal statement of the changes that have occurred. It goes without saying that in many cases the transformation is much greater.

So far we have given a definition of what a tribal society is, conceptually, and presumably was, empirically, but have argued that it can no longer exist in this full sense, however potent many of its features may remain. The carrying over of such features into a different system is tribalism. Tribalism is usually regarded in a pejorative light and the rational basis for this is that to carry over elements specific to one system into another is inappropriate. It is in the political context that tribalism is regarded with particular disfavor, and in a number of social and economic contexts also. But those who rightly stigmatise the carryover which is tribalism in these contexts would in others often favor it, especially with respect to certain family values and to aesthetic modes of expression, as for example in music, dancing, and plastic arts. Thus President Julius Nyerere of Tanzania: "It has been said— and this is quite right—that Tanganyika is tribal, and we realise that we need to break up this tribal consciousness among the people and to build up a national consciousness." Yet on the other hand, "I have set up this new Ministry to help us regain our pride in our own culture. I want it to seek out the best of the traditions and customs of all our tribes and make them a part of our national culture." "The traditional order is dying; the question which has yet to be answered is what will be built on our past, and, in consequence, what kind of society will eventually replace the traditional one."

This is the oft-discussed problem of trying to retain the good that was in the old and grafting it on to the new. But the characteristics of tribal society, which we gave, constitute a set of highly dependent variables. Dependent variables, whether we like it or not, constitute a functional system.

We say "highly dependent" because we reject the extreme claims of total functional integration that are widely recognised as false. Tribal societies were not totally integrated. There were areas of partial integration and partial dependence in the system, allowing for the possibility of moderate change from within or without. But they were certainly quite highly integrated systems and to pick and choose among supposedly—desirable and undesirable elements in them is a fatal misunderstanding of their intrinsic nature. Of course there is continuity as well as change. There are harder and softer elements in the system. But the interdependence, although partial and not total, is nonetheless real. There is therefore some possibility of preserving some desirable elements, but it can only be done in submission to the limitations imposed by the degree of interdependence of variables. Unfortunately, this requirement is far from being taken seriously into account by the policy-makers concerned.

This is particularly relevant to those formerly tribal populations which have not lost their demographic vitality, or will to live, but rather are in many cases on the brink of, or already involved in, a dangerous population explosion, rapidly entering the modern world and usually forming the major population component of new nations, or of colonial territories in their last stages, as in most of Africa and New Guinea. The other side of the coin is the more tragic situation reported by Levi-Strauss in "A World on the Wane" of those pathetic remnants which "had learnt from the ferocious persecutions of the previous hundred years to keep themselves entirely hidden from the outer world"—people who "were neither 'true Indians,' nor, for that matter, 'true savages,' but former 'savages' on whom civilization had been abruptly forced; and, as soon as they were no longer 'a danger to Society,' civilization took no further interest in them." This is the characteristic situation of aboriginal peoples throughout the Americas, except for those who have successfully made the transition into peasantries, or, as individuals, become lost in industrial society. Such tragic situations are also reported sporadically from Africa where, according to Diamond, the Anaguta of the Nigerian Plateau *decided* not to join the modern world" but "move like ghosts on the outskirts of civilization. . . . Their culture crumbles, their population declines, their lands shrink and as an ethnic entity they change only disintegratively. They accept, they pursue their decline; for them the world ends." Or, again, the fragmentary Ik of northeastern Uganda, where, according to Turnbull, "social disintegration has gone to the limit" and "at the present rate the Ik are not likely to survive much longer." . . .

According to Steward, "the concept of primitive or 'tribal' is based on three fundamental aspects of the behavior of members of tribal societies." These are, in brief, that it is a construct representing the ideal, normative aspect of the behaviour of "all members of a fairly small, simple, independent, self-contained and homogeneous society." . . . "Tribal society is not divisible into genuine subcultural groups." Secondly, tribal culture has pattern, or configuration, some underlying unity and overall integration, and thirdly, that it is "essentially relativistic" and unique in relation to other cultures with which it contrasted. While it has been "a useful tool for analysis and comparison, especially when contrasts are sought, . . . as a tool for dealing with culture change it has found little utility." To the present writer its deficiencies are more fundamental than this, for as we shall see, the cultures which lie at the lower end of the range in terms of social scale are not, in fact, unique and independent entities which can properly be seen as unequivocally distinct from one another. Indeed, to do so is frequently to misunderstand their essential nature. On the other hand, cultures that lie at the higher end of the scale are not as homogeneous and lacking in subcultural divisions as is implied. These divergences are much too general and glaring to be regarded as permissible deviations from a consistent core.

The ideal type or analytical model of the tribe varies a good deal in the versions of different writers, as we have seen, but it is fair to say that these variations do play round recurring common themes. However, we shall give examples to document the fact that, whichever particular choice of definition is made, empirical divergences are so gross, widespread, and frequent as to render the concept of tribe as it exists in the general literature untenable. In many cases, the definitions generally current actually hinder understanding of the entities to which they are supposed to refer. The named tribes which appear in the literature frequently represent crystallizations at the wrong level, usually a level which is too large in scale because foreign observers did not initially understand the lower levels of structure or failed to correct the misrepresentations of their predecessors, or because some arbitrary and even artificial entity was chosen for the sake of easy reference, despite a realisation that it was fallacious and misleading. Furthermore, such fabrications of the foreign observer have often themselves acquired validity in the course of externally induced change and amalgamation, while the indigenous peoples concerned have also become aware of the need for larger scale as the modern world closed in upon them.

The Concept of Tribe in Africa

Since the birth of African nationalism, tribalism has always been a sore subject and for very good reasons. Some nationalists have even gone so far as to claim that tribal divisions were the deliberate creation of a Machiavellian colonial policy of divide and rule. While it is doubtful whether most colonial administrators most of the time had sufficient knowledge of the internal structure of the traditional societies they ruled and sufficient expertise in social engineering to achieve what is credited to them by this view, there is a certain element of truth in it to the extent that many of the named entities which appear as tribes in the literature appeared for the first time during the colonial period and must in this sense necessarily be considered a product of it. One of the most striking and well-documented cases is that of the Luhia in Kenya. When the German anthropologist Günter Wagner went to Kenya in 1934, Kavirondo was simply a geographical area, so named from the time of the earliest Arab, Swahili, and European traders and explorers, but not so known by any of its indigenous inhabitants. Wagner notes:

> Owing to its constant use by Europeans, the term "Kavirondo" has nowadays been to some extent adopted by the natives, but they use it with reference to the district rather than to themselves. When talking to other natives—even outside the district—they always style themselves by the name of their respective sub-tribe, such as Wanga, Vugusu, Logoli, Nyole, etc. Among politically minded natives who, for a number of years, have been pleading for a political unification of all Bantu Kavirondo tribes under a paramount chief according to the Buganda pattern, the word *avaluhia,* meaning "those of the same tribe," is propagated as a common designation

for all Bantu Kavirondo. The term "Kavirondo," on the other hand, is generally rejected in these quarters as being of European origin. (Wagner, 1949: 20)

Many other writers have pointed out that the term Kavirondo was regarded as opprobrious for various reasons, though agreement has never been reached as to its meaning or derivation.

Wagner himself, like many another ethnographer, vacillates over his use of the term tribe, applying it sometimes to one level, sometimes to another. "In pre-European days, the various sub-tribes of Bantu Kavirondo were, for their greater part, very loosely organized politically, each sub-tribe consisting of a number of more or less sovereign clans. Since British rule was established in the middle of the nineties, they have been organized into chieftaincies." However, since traditional groupings varied in size and the colonial administration aimed at uniformity and convenience in the size of administrative units, there was the usual discrepancy between the definition of groupings on the one hand and administrative chieftaincies on the other. Next Wagner distinguishes the following tribes, corresponding to what he referred to as sub-tribes in the previous passage: Vagusu, Tadjoni, Wanga, Marama, Tsotso, Tiriki, Nyala, Kabras, Hayo, Marach, Bolo and Logoli, to which must also be added the Idaxo, Isuxa, Kisa, Nyole and Samia. Among such acephalous peoples, the exact number of groups properly to be distinguished may be genuinely ambiguous and debatable in some instances, but the above list would generally be accepted. Bethwell Ogot speaks of "the seven teen Luyia tribes." Ogot further states "the name 'Baluyia' was first adopted by the North Kavirondo Central Association in June 1935. The elders rejected the name, and it was only after the Second World War that it gained general currency." This entirely accords with the experience of the present writer, who, arriving to teach at Makerere College in 1945, found that the whole group of Bantu speaking students from North Kavirondo called themselves Abaluyia and were never known as anything else.

It may be said that the Luyia people came into existence between approximately 1935 and 1945. Before that time no such group existed either in its own or anyone else's estimation. It was clearly due to the reaction of younger and more educated men to the exigencies of the colonial situation. It arose out of previous attempts at intertribal or supratribal organization and unity such as the North Kavirondo Central Association and Bantu Kavirondo Tax-payers' Association and led to further important organizations such as the Abaluyia Union, which came to represent the Luyia away from home, especially in the big towns such as Nairobi in Kenya and Kampala in Uganda. This new super-tribe was closely linked to the colonial administrative framework, being in effect based upon and in part suggested by the administrative and territorial framework of the North Kavirondo District (subsequently renamed North

Nyanza District because of the already noted pejorative aura of the word Kavirondo). In language and culture the Samia were just as much Luyia as the Hayo or Marach, but the unfortunate Samia were not only cut in two by the frontier between Kenya and Uganda, but even their Kenya half was situated administratively in Central and not North Nyanza District. Consequently Samia were never considered Luyia, and Samia away from home their own separate ethnic association.

In the original conglomeration of the Luyia in the 1930s and 40s, the Vugusu were the largest numerical component. This in itself favored secessionist tendencies on their part, since they occupied a compact territory on the north side of the Luyia area. During the 1950s, they began to agitate for, and eventually succeeded in winning, their own administrative district, which became known as Elgon Nyanza. With this the integrity of the Luyia supertribe began to crumble and it is now arguable whether the Vugusu are Luyia or not.... The fact is that many tribes have come into existence in a similar way to the Luyia, through a combination of reasonable cultural similarity with colonial administrative convenience, which in more recent times has often coincided with peoples' own sense of need for wider levels of organization to enable them to exert more effective pressure on events. The Luyia never did conform to the criteria of a tribe with which we started. Indeed, by the time they first came into existence they already diverged somewhat from every criterion mentioned.

The meaning of the name Luyia is instructive. Wagner explains (1949: 55) that "the stem -*hia* means 'to be hot,' 'to burn' and in a concrete sense the word *olu-hia* means 'fire place on a meadow,' hence 'the fire-place as the centre of public life of the clan.'" "It is at this *oluhia* that the old men of the clan community meet every morning to warm themselves and to discuss the events and news of the day as well as to settle all important matters of the clan." Despite linguistic variation between the different Luyia groups, they nearly all have this term and concept. The case of the Luyia is instructive because it is comparatively rare that an adequate documentation is available to demonstrate the process of appearance of new "tribes" with reasonable completeness. But the Luyia are far from being an isolated case and the process has close counterparts in many regions of the world.

To take an example from the other side of the continent of Africa, Labouret Fortes (1945), Goody (1957) and Tait (1961) have all extensively documented the fact that in a large and populous region, including adjacent parts of Ghana, Ivory Coast and Upper Volta, any single definitive boundary drawn between one "tribe" and another was bound to be relative, arbitrary and a misrepresentation of the facts. Colson (1951: 95) has demonstrated the same point for the Plateau Tonga of Central Africa (Zambia). It was not that these peoples were an undifferentiated mass, but that they were differentiated in many subtle and complex ways for different purposes. Any idea of the Lobi, Tallensi, LoDagaba or Konkomba as clear-cut, isolated, enclosed tribes is a complete travesty of the facts. Legitimate authority did not inhere to or flow from any one unequivocal level of organization, but was contingent upon the situation.... Much the same process of the picking up, fixing and generalizing by colonial authorities of names applied to vaguely defined peoples by their neighbors or other foreigners, seems to have occurred in the case of the Yoruba.

> The term Yoruba is sometimes said to have been derived from a foreign nickname, meaning cunning, given to the subjects of the Alafin of Oyo by the Fulani and Hausa. The Hausa word for the Yoruba language is *Yarbanci*. Yoruba has been commonly applied to a large group, united more by language than by culture, whose members speak of themselves as Oyo, Egba, Ijebu, Ife, Ilesha and the other names of the various tribes. (Forde, 1951: 1)

However, it is debatable whether the latter named entities are any more justly designated as tribes than the Yoruba as a whole. They might just as well be called city-states.

Johnson seems to agree with the Hausa or Fulani derivation of the name Yoruba, suggesting that the country was first known to Europeans from the north "for in old records the Hausa and Fulani names are used for the country and its capital; thus we see in Webster's Gazetteer 'Yarriba'" (1921: xix). This he equates with Yoruba but attempts no other derivation. But he continues, "This country comprises many tribes governed by their own chiefs and having their own laws. At one time they were all tributaries to one sovereign, the King of Yoruba, including Benin on the East, and Dahomey on the West, but are now independent." There appears to be no historical foundation for this title of "the King of Yoruba," except for the supposedly wider influence of the kingdom of Old Oyo before the eighteenth century, and the ritual focus of all Yoruba upon Ife. It is like the legendary crediting of former suzerainty over Buganda, Ankole and other Inter-lacustrine states to a supposed Bunyoro-Kitara "Empire." Here too there has been a persistent confusion between political and ritual relations.

Group names with an ecological referent are common all over the world and often show a very poor correlation with valid divisions between one tribe and another on the basis of political, social, cultural and linguistic facts. Madagascar is a striking case. There we have the following generally accepted names and meanings, which may none the less be apocryphal in some cases: *Antanala* (the forest people), *Antantlroy* (the people of the thorny cactus forest), *Antankarana* (the people of the rocks and caves), *Antanmy* (the people of the islands), *Antefasy* (the people of the sands), *Antemoro* (the people of the *coast), Antesaktt* (the people who catch small fish with the hands) *Antsihanakrt* (the people of the lake), *Betanimena* (the people of the red land), *Bezanozmw* (the bush people), and *Sttkalava* (the people of the long valleys, or of the broad and long plain). A few other Malagasy peoples have acquired non-ecological designations: *Betsileo* (the many who are not conquered), *Betsimisaraka* (the many who do not separate), *Mahafaly* (those who cause joy) and *Tsimihety* (those who do not cut their hair). It is said that growing their hair long made Tsimihety men look like women and facilitated their escape from slave raiders.

Even where these ecological terms are accurate, as in the case of Antanala, they refer to people in a particular habitat rather than to people with distinct socio-cultural characteristics. Ecology can be very important, but no one now would hold it responsible for all social and cultural differences. Other terms are vague and overlapping. Many Malagasy live on the sand besides the Antefasy, very many on the coast besides the Antemoro, and very many on red earth besides the Betanimena. The Antanosy do not, in fact, live on islands. *Antandmy* is a fair description, but these people were neither a cultural, historical nor political unity. . . . Another common basis of tribal naming which is in a sense more structurally genuine than many of those so far discussed is derived from the names of primal ancestors which appear in genealogies, myths and legends as founders of the people. It is obvious that this kind of eponymy is particularly to be expected in the case of segmentary lineage systems with their strong emphasis on genealogical reckoning. In such society's conception of itself and its past, there is usually a series of levels which phase into one another as they proceed further back in time. The nearest level largely consists of the ancestors of specific contemporary groups, whose genealogical relationships tend to express the contemporary relations of such groups and from one or other of whom every full member of the society can trace himself directly. Beyond this there is a vaguer level of tribal heroes about whose exploits, genealogical connections and even names there are differences of opinion between different members and sections of the modern community, though these are usually recognisably common variations upon central themes. Beyond this is the yet more shadowy realm of figures who represent the origins of man and society, the differentiation of human and divine, the expression of ultimate cultural meanings in symbolic form.

In these reaches all is relative, that which is "first" is so only in relation to that which followed.

> For the deeper we sound, the further down into the lower world of the past we probe and press, the more do we find that the earliest foundations of humanity, its history and culture, reveal themselves unfathomable. . . . Thus there may exist provisional origins, which practically and in fact form the first beginnings of the particular tradition held by a given community, folk or communion of faith;

and memory, though sufficiently instructed that the depths have not actually been plumbed, yet nationally may find reassurance in some primitive point of time and, personally and historically speaking, come to rest there. (Mann, 1963: 3)

Not only is the beginning thus always relative, but almost invariably there is asymmetry and contradiction associated with it.

In the case of the great Somali people, who may justifiably be called a nation as forming the basis of a new nation state, among the usual rival derivations one of the most plausible is that which traces Somali to the eponymous ancestor of most of the northern pastoral Somali. The asymmetry and contradiction lies in the fact that "the Somali nation is composed of two parts, the Somali and the Sab. Strictly, the word 'Somali' does not apply to the Sab, who say themselves that they are 'Sab' and are so described and distinguished by the 'Somali'; nor is the Sab group subsumed under the name 'Somali' in the total genealogy of the Somali nation." (Somali and Sab appear in the genealogy in the structural position of brothers, both of common descent from the Qurayshitic lineage of the Prophet Mohammed.) "The Sab stand opposed to the Somali, and are grouped with them only at a higher genealogical level, when the two ancestors Sab and Somali, are traced back to Arabian origins, in the total genealogy of the inhabitants of Somaliland" (Lewis, 1955: 15 and 1961: 12). Instances of eponymous tribal naming are very numerous among peoples with segmentary lineage organization, such as the Tiv, Gusii and others already mentioned earlier.

The difficulty of identifying one "tribe" clearly and distinctly from another is often represented as a troublesome test that the anthropologist must pass. Thus, of the Australian Tiwi, because they lived on two islands, "fuzziness on the edges of tribal territory—a chronic headache to anthropologists working with mainland tribes—did not exist" (Hart and Pilling, 1964: 11). Or again of the Tiv, "the Tiv do not present that difficulty so common in Africa: identifying the tribe" (Bohannan, 1958: 35). The difficulty is undeniable, particularly in the case of stateless societies, and meticulous exploration of the distribution, interconnections and meaning of the various elements in culture and social structure is of vital importance in such situations, but insistence on defining some global discrete entity as a tribe may simply be a refusal to recognise the fundamental characteristics of this kind of society. I have argued elsewhere (Southall, 1968) that stateless societies have the combined characteristics of: multi-polities, ritual super-integration, complementary opposition, intersecting kinship, and distributive legitimacy. The contingent nature of their structure, subdivisions and boundaries is of their essence, not something to be swept away by penetrating analysis. The representation of adjacent stateless societies as a neatly discrete series of named units is to misunderstand and misrepresent them.

Despite Bohannan's categorical statement on Tiv identity, Tiv is, in fact, a set of contradictions, as any stateless society must be when mistakenly regarded as a discrete tribe. "A Tiv is a Tiv and can prove it" because "every Tiv can trace his descent from Tiv himself." Yet this genealogy is "not in itself a record of ancestry," nor "a portrait of political structure, for its field of relevance is greater than that of the political while, on the other hand, not all political relationships are capable of expression in its idiom." For Tiv is actually the ancestor of non-Tiv peoples also, such as the Uge and Utange, and "the name of a linguistic and cultural entity which never (prior to British Administration) acted as a political unit." As with the Nguru Luguru-Kaguru cluster of Tanzania, the named entity is, quite characteristically, at once too large and too small.

The Tiwi also, despite the apparent clarity with which they are defined by the accident of island isolation, turn out on closer inspection to have just that fuzziness which Hart and Pilling deny. For the Tiwi "did little as a member of a tribe. Only when an outsider turned up did he need to think of himself as a Tiwi, and outsiders were very rare. For the rest of the time he thought of himself as a member of his band, thought of his band as his people, and of his band territory as his country.... The nine bands thus acted, psychologically, as small tribelets or semi-sovereign groups" (op. cit. 12-13). Thus Tiwi too turns out to be something of an illusion. Even the band was "a flexible and constantly shifting collection of individuals" (op. cit. 1, 12). "The casual way in which people left one band and joined another shows that the band was in no sense a tight political or legal group."

The further illusion seems to be cherished that at least with language we are on safer ground with an unequivocal factor defining clear-cut groups. "All Tiwi, of course, spoke the same language" (op. cit. 11). Yet among the Murngin, who are not so distant from the Tiwi, either culturally or geographically, "the members of each moiety are supposed to speak different languages.... Even each clan is said to have a 'language'; and some have a different dialect, but most within a given area speak the same one. The clans claim 'languages' of their own by giving themselves linguistic names in addition to group names" (Warner, 1937: 30). Rather than assume that language always defines a cultural entity, even when most other factors fail, we should assume that language is also one of the elements which groups in an acephalous, stateless society may purposefully and almost "artificially" use as a basis of distinction and identification, even when observed empirical differences are slight. "Of course," we may add, "the tribe is almost a non-existent unit among the Murngin" (Warner, 1937: 9).

> The tribes of northeastern Arnhem Land, of which Murngin is one, are very weak social units, and when measured by the ordinary def-

initions of what constitutes a tribe fail almost completely. The tribe is not the war-making group. On the contrary, it is usually within it that the most intensive feuds are found. Tribal membership of the clans on the borders of two tribes is uncertain and changing, or the people may sometimes insist that they belong to both tribes. Even clans well toward the center of a tribe's territory will, under certain circumstances, range themselves with another group. (Warner, 1937: 35)

The name Murngin is little used and the moiety names are used much more commonly.

Warner's account makes it very clear that the conventional concept of tribe was quite inappropriate to what he nonetheless called his "social Study of an Australian Tribe." He uses the name Murngin purely for convenience. "The word Murngin (fire sparks) was found as a designation only after much effort. The people do not think of themselves under this name or classification. The word has been used by me as a general term for all of the eight tribes in the area and for the groups of people located in the central part of the territory of the eight tribes. I have seized upon this name as a convenient and concise way of talking about this whole group of people; had any of the other tribes who possess the particular type of social organization found in this area been located in the center of the group, I should have used the name of that tribe rather than Murngin" (Warner, 1937: 15). Thus, Warner constantly uses the term tribe having said that "the tribe can hardly be said to exist in this area" (ibid.). Nor, of course, was the area of Warner's eight "tribes" clearly distinguished from neighbouring areas. It was simply the area within which he was able to accomplish fieldwork. The relativities of the Murngin and Tiwi situations are duplicated in other instances too numerous to mention, such as the Yir Yoront (Sharp, 1958), which chiefly show that the situation long ago revealed by Radcliffe-Brown and others is no peculiar anomaly, but far more prevalent than they can have realized.

It is not so unlike the case of the Amba in Western Uganda, who include two main groups, the Bulibuli and the Bwezi, who speak two entirely different languages. By an asymmetry that is also a further characteristic of stateless societies, while both Bulibuli and Bwezi are Amba, the Bulibuli are also known as the Amba proper. Each village is either Bulibuli or Bwezi, but Bulibuli and Bwezi villages are interspersed. Each village was an independent political unit and "warfare between various villages was a constant feature" (Winter, 1958: 138). But the village was not a "self-sufficient system of action" chiefly because "the men of the village must obtain wives from the outside"; therefore, "even the internal organization of the village can only be
understood . . . in terms of its interrelationship with the larger structure of

which it is a part" (Winter, 1958: 139). Each village had a maximal lineage as its core and villages based on maximal lineages belonging to the same named clan and exogamous group were linked together in important ways. Thus, we have again no one categorical level of organization which can properly be picked out from the rest, but rather a number of levels, all equally important for different purposes, a number of criteria defining essentially overlapping groups and categories, so that "friends on one basis are enemies on another" and conflicts become cohesion (Gluckman, 1955: 4, 19).

Needless to say, language is even less necessarily or obviously a criterion of tribe where higher levels of political specialization have been reached and diverse groups incorporated by conquest or assimilation. Thus, Alur society contained Nilotic, Sudanic and Bantu speakers, of half a dozen different languages (Southall, 1956, passim), and such situations were common in more elaborate state systems. The Azande, Lozi and many other conquering groups incorporated numerous diverse elements, which retained considerable cultural diversity. . . .

An attractively precise definition of tribe was developed by Evans-Pritchard (1940: 122). Although he defines Nuer tribes by nine very concrete and culture bound criteria (loc. cit.), the essence of the definition, which was adopted and long retained by many British social anthropologists, is contained in the simple sentence: "local communities have been classed as tribes or tribal segments by whether they acknowledge the obligation to pay blood-wealth or not" (ibid.). Evans-Pritchard applied the same criterion to the Kenya Luo and other Nilotic peoples, Lienhardt applied it to the Dinka, Middleton to the Lugbara, Tait to the Konkomba, and so on. For a while it became an article of faith in the context of a particular approach. It was most effective in relation to the immediate matter at hand—the exposition and clarification of segmentary lineage systems. Its chief disadvantages were that there were many other varieties of socio-political structure which it did not fit and that it further confused and outraged the common sense of the general reader by suddenly transforming what had always been known as single "tribes," "peoples," "societies," or "cultures," into tens, dozens and even hundreds of different distinct "tribes." For example, the Dinka were divided by Lienhardt (1958: 102) into some twenty-five "tribal groups," and the three of these which he happened to know well contained 27, 10 and 6 "tribes" respectively, suggesting that the total number of Dinka "tribes" would amount to many hundreds.

As the enthusiasm for segmentary lineage systems passed its peak, this precise but severely limited usage of the term tribe lost ground and eventually fell into disuse. In practice, the term sub-tribe is now substituted for it in the same context. Thus, Middleton (1960: 7) refers to the Lugbara as consisting of about sixty tribes, but subsequently (1963: 82) changed this to sixty sub-tribes.

The problem of ethnic classification as such is a special problem that we do not attempt to cover. We can only reiterate that no unidimensional classification of socio-cultural groups can provide an adequate basis for the comparative study of specific problems, let alone for frequency distributions, because the proper units of classification and analysis will vary according to the phenomenon and the problem studied. We must expect that comparative and generalizing studies of kinship systems or specific components of them, religious, symbolic or identity systems or specific components of them, political and economic systems or their components, and so forth, will always involve a plurality of units of analysis and fields of distribution. All attempts at establishing unequivocal, all-purpose, unidimensional classifications of socio-cultural groups involve grave danger of misrepresenting the nature of societies as anthropology knows them. To hammer home the importance of interlocking, overlapping, multiple and alternative collective identities is one of the most important messages of social and cultural anthropology. . . .

There are three sets of problems associated with the tribal concept as we have examined it: problems of definition (ambiguous, imprecise or conflicting definitions and also the failure to stick to them consistently); problems of illusion (false application of the concept to artificial or misconceived entities) and problems of transition and transformation (use of the concept of tribe unjustifiably with reference to phenomena which are a direct product of modern influences). There is a considerable overlap between the last two sets of problems. As we have seen, there are many stateless societies where inaccurate definition has simply been the product of ignorance, illusion, or inattention; but very often, the "definition by illusion" has been a definition of larger scale that became permanently adopted for administrative convenience and ultimately accepted by the people themselves. We may thus say that the problems of illusion have frequently been perpetuated by those of transition and transformation. Problems of nomenclature may seem trivial, except insofar as they breed confusion and misunderstanding among anthropologists themselves, while at the same time rendering nugatory any influence which anthropology might have upon the world of scholarship as a whole. Where unresolved problems remain, agreement upon nomenclature is unlikely. What may legitimately be demanded is that nomenclature should be clear and consistent in each discourse, so that the problems of greater moment that lie behind it can be tackled. It is simply with this in mind that we would suggest calling "tribal" that traditional form of society, which we described at the beginning. Once the empirical facts are recognized, there should be enough consensus for adequate communication despite many minor differences of opinion. Tribal society may be largely a phenomenon of the past, but it is still of enormous intellectual and human importance.

The distinguishing of individual tribal units is a different and perhaps misconceived problem as we have seen. The solution should be very simple.

Where discrete tribal units can be empirically demonstrated—well and good, where not, the temptation to speak or write as though some unique and all embracing discrete level of organization exists when the facts belie it should be resisted. The analysis and comparative study of tribal society should proceed on the basis of more specialized categories in the fields of kinship, ritual, politics, economics, language and so forth. Stateless societies cannot be expected to present discrete boundaries, except where special geographical or historical circumstances favour it. But chiefdoms and tribal states are more likely to do so the greater the degree of their political specialization. Yet by the same token they are less homogeneous and undifferentiated than has commonly been supposed. All our social and cultural constructs are bound to encounter intermediate cases when applied to empirical data, but it must be remembered that the intermediacy is as likely as not a product of the constructs rather than of the data. Nonetheless, the distinction of tribal societies in their lack of writing and records, their simple technology and direct subsistence economy, the absence of highly differentiated consumption patterns, the importance of the domain of kinship and multiplex relationships with all the institutional implications of these characteristics holds fairly well empirically.

When we move on from tribal societies in the full sense, which must increasingly be regarded as phenomena of the past, to the transitional situations that are prevalent today, there are again two main empirical types to be distinguished. There are the tribal societies that have been transitional, sometimes for long periods, in relation to the dominant influence of ancient pre-industrial states, and there are those which are transitional in relation to the post-industrial states which are almost exclusively those of the western world. This distinction has been important but is now itself becoming transitory. On another dimension there is the distinction between the transitional situation of communities, necessarily usually rural, and the transitional situation of individuals derived from such communities, which may also be urban, and indeed industrial. For the reasons already stated, it seems required by consistency and also by the human situation itself that the condition of individuals and groups in all the transitional situations of the contemporary world should now be described in ethnic and not in tribal terms. While all formerly tribal peoples are becoming increasingly subject to the ubiquitous pressures of the modern industrial world, there is the paradox that the former tribal peoples are mainly to be found within the confines of the less-developed nations, whose economic condition, radically transformed though it is, is being left relatively further and further behind by the developed nations, so that in this sense one dichotomy is being substituted for another at a higher level.

For anthropologists this involves a poignant dilemma. Their whole discipline has been reared upon the discovery and study of forms of culture and society that held up a contrasting mirror to their own. More recently they have been adjusting, albeit slowly, to the prospective resolution of this contrast and to joining in the further exploration of man and society with colleagues who have actually emerged from the other side of it. But although these colleagues from the other world, the *tiers monde,* can truly enter an international world of anthropological scholarship, their hands are still tied by the fact that their new world has a meaning for them and us which is in unexpected ways as contrasted to ours as was the old tribal world which has passed away. This imposes a heavy strain and responsibility of understanding and sympathy.

Anthropology claims to be a universal discipline. Committed above all things to cross-cultural perspectives and to the transcendence of the ethnocentric myopia, it is naturally embarrassed by the colonialist taint which besmirches it in so much of the *tiers monde.* If western, and especially American, anthropologists are to avoid the charge that they are prostituting the discipline to assuage their personality problems, they will have to take much more seriously the complementarity of the contribution required from the new breed of anthropologists whose fathers or grandfathers were members of non-literate societies. If this contribution is to be made, and anthropology to avoid drifting into a blind alley as a bourgeois, essentially Western culture bound pastime, western anthropologists will have to stop calling primitive and tribal the contemporary communities from which their colleagues of the new breed come. This may be a case in which human feelings have to prevail over strict logic. It is also essential if anthropologists, preeminently equipped and destined for the task as they should be, are to contribute to bridging and healing the widening economic and credibility gap between the *tiers monde* and the West.

If asked what terms then can we use, since even the most neutral and logical can so easily become contaminated (as the disheartening sequence of: undeveloped, underdeveloped, less developed, developing, has shown), I should have to answer simply for the strategic moment, for the present critical and vital generation, that for the present the word primitive should be dropped from the vocabulary of social anthropology, however much it wounds our romantic souls, that the term "tribe" should usually be applied only to the small scale societies of the past which retained their political autonomy, and that the new associations derived from them in the contemporary context should be referred to as ethnic groups as other members of the category are.

Ethnicity in Southern African History

LEROY VAIL[2]

Out of the crooked timber of humanity no straight thing can ever be made.
—*Immanuel Kant*

African political leaders, experiencing it as destructive to their ideals of national unity, denounce it passionately. Commentators on the Left, recognizing it as a block to the growth of appropriate class awareness, inveigh against it as a case of "false consciousness." Apologists for South African apartheid, welcoming it as an ally of continued white dominance, encourage it. Development theorists, perceiving it as a check to economic growth, deplore it. Journalists, judging it an adequate explanation for a myriad of otherwise puzzling events, deploy it mercilessly. Political scientists, intrigued by its continuing power, probe at it endlessly. If one disapproves of the phenomenon, "it" is "tribalism"; if one is less judgmental, "it" is "ethnicity." Ethnicity's emergence as a central concern for a wide range of students of African affairs is relatively recent, and its forceful intrusion upon the dominant nationalist paradigm of the 1950s and early 1960s was both unexpected and unwelcome. At that time, it was accepted that Africans were organized naturally into "tribes," but, as nationalist movements in Africa were then apparently enjoying great success, most observers believed that parochial ethnic loyalties were merely cultural ghosts lingering on into the present, weakened anomalies from a fast receding past. As such, they were destined to disappear in the face of the social, economic and political changes that were everywhere at work. People from all sectors of the political spectrum believed in this vision.

For those on the Right and in the Centre, "modernization" would do the job. Greater access to education, improved communications, and the shifting of

---

[2] This excerpt is taken from pages 1-7 and 16-18 of Leroy Vail, "Ethnicity in Southern African History," published in *The Creation of Tribalism in Southern Africa* (Berkeley: University of California Press, 1991), pp. 1-20. Leroy Vail was professor of history at Harvard University.

people from the slumbering "traditional" rural sector of the economy to the vibrant "modern" industrial sector by the beneficent forces of economic growth guaranteed that ethnic loyalties would fade away. In their place would grow a new, nation-oriented consciousness which would underpin progressive "nation-building," especially if the new nation states could make good their promises of a better life for all their citizens. Africa would be a continent of new Switzerlands in which cultural divisions would be of little political importance. For those on the Left, too, "modernization" was the key, although it was viewed from a somewhat different perspective. The break-down of "traditional" societies by the forces of new, state-sponsored welfare socialism, with its expanded facilities in public education, medicine, and agricultural programmes, would allow newly independent African states to "skip a stage" in the evolution of their societies towards socialism and to enter directly into that blessed condition. In effect, socialism would then provide the material base for a pan-ethnic class consciousness that would transcend, if not negate, cultural differences. Africa would be a continent of new Yugoslavias.

The general paradigm of "modernization," then, appealed to almost every political viewpoint. For almost every observer nationalism seemed progressive and laudable, while ethnicity—or, as it was usually termed, "tribalism"—was retrogressive and divisive. Ethnicity, however, failed to cooperate with its many would-be pall-bearers. It soon became clear that African nationalist movements, ideologically shaped by the basically negative sentiments of anti-colonialism and with little substantive philosophical content relevant to the day-to-day life of ordinary Africans living in post-colonial states, were simply unable to provide them with compelling intellectual, social, and political visions. Once the attainment of independence had made most of its anti-colonial message irrelevant, nationalist "thought" was transformed into a gloss for the manipulation of the institutions of the new nation-states on behalf of the interests of the ruling political parties in a succession of one-party states. Much state activity was devoted to the pursuit of variously defined forms of "economic development," but such development proved elusive and the much-desired economic Fruits of Independence generally failed to ripen. That growth which did occur, moreover, was usually to the benefit of the dominant political classes and possessed little popular appeal.

As a result of this quick reining in of nationalism's popular thrust within the bureaucratic structures of essentially artificial post-colonial states, ethnic or regional movements rooted in the colonial era had fresh life breathed into them and came to be seen as attractive alternatives to the dominant political parties with their demands for uncomplaining obedience from the governed. In effect, the revitalization of "tribalism" was structured into the one-party system by the very fact of that system's existence. Ethnicity became the home of the opposition in states where class consciousness was largely undeveloped.

Ethnic particularism has consequently continued to bedevil efforts to "build nations" to the specifications of the ruling party for the past two decades or more. This hard political fact has called forth ever more systematic repression of dissent by those in control of the state, thus, in effect, strengthening the appeal of the ethnic alternative. Ethnicity's future, even in countries such as South Africa, where industrialization has proceeded further than anywhere else on the continent, seems secure because it is likely to provide an important focal point for whatever opposition to the dominant political classes that might exist.

With its power to divide people politically, then, and with its sturdy resistance to erosion by the ideological forces of national or class consciousness, ethnicity came to demand close—albeit it often very grudging—attention after decades of neglect. Its source and appeal needed reasonable explanations, and interpretations of it have ranged widely, reflecting its multidimensional nature. The most prominent explanation—if only because of its widespread use—is the one that, despite the great frequency with which one encounters it in media coverage of Africa, is plainly the least satisfactory. In effect, this interpretation is a restatement of the old assumption that Africans are by nature "tribal" people and that "tribalism" is little more than an irrelevant anachronism, an atavistic residue deriving from the distant past of rural Africa. It should have evaporated with the passage of time, but, inexplicably, something went wrong, and it continues to refuse to obey the laws of social and political change. It thus remains able to motivate Africans to frequent actions of conflict and violence. Ethnic consciousness is, in this view, a form of collective irrationality. The problems with this interpretation are clear. First, it is always dangerous to assume that people consistently act out of mass irrationality. People tend to act rationally, and there is no reason on the face of it to accept that Africans are exceptions. Second, this argument is, in effect, also a tautology with no analytical power, arguing as it does that Africans act "tribalistically" because they are naturally "tribal." Third, and most tellingly, empirical evidence shows clearly that ethnic consciousness is very much a new phenomenon, an ideological construct, usually of the twentieth century, and not an anachronistic cultural artifact from the past. As an offspring of the changes associated with so-called "modernization," therefore, it is unlikely to be destroyed by the continuation of these same processes. For all these reasons, then, this interpretation must be discarded.

Other, more scholarly interpretations have been suggested to explain the origin and persistence of ethnicity in Africa. All these interpretations have two things in common. First, they derive mainly from the work of anthropologists, sociologists, and, especially, political scientists, observers who have been primarily concerned with the situation in Africa at the time they actually studied it. This has meant that their interpretations have usually been concerned with ethnicity's role at the moment of observation and its potential for the future.

As such, they usually give only brief attention to its history, presenting whatever history that might be uncovered as mere "background" to ethnicity's contemporary role. Second, all these interpretations are also marked by the fact that they have evolved out of the nationalist paradigm dominant from the 1950s into the 1970s. They implicitly accept a basically evolutionary view of human history. In this view, the future ought to be better than the past, and "better" has been identified with improvements assumed to flow from an increase in political scale and the growth of national unity—in short, from "nation-building." As a consequence, most such analyses of ethnicity are concerned with the way it has traduced the promise of modernizing nationalism and are thus predisposed to negative judgments. Their emphasis, therefore, has been on ethnicity's role as a disrupter of the promising trends of secular nationalism that seemed to characterize African politics in the late 1950s and early 1960s and to promise a rosy future.

The intellectual range of these interpretations of ethnicity has been wide. One viewpoint encountered frequently—especially within Africa itself—is that ethnicity is primarily the result of a history of "divide-and-rule" tactics which colonial governments cannily employed. European anthropologists connived at such policies by specifying "tribes" culturally within the context of a uniquely colonial sociology, thereby giving the "tribe" a real, but specious, identity. The element of truth in this explanation has made it superficially attractive, especially as the South African government today actively uses both approaches in its Bantustan policies and in its stress on the uniqueness of "tribal" culture, patent efforts to promote political divisions among the country's African population.

Yet whatever its merits, it is an explanation clearly insufficient to explain the persistence of ethnic consciousness. This is so for several reasons. First, it fails to explain why, in a particular territory throughout which the colonial state employed roughly the same divide-and-rule policies, ethnic consciousness developed unevenly, strong among certain peoples but not among others, a situation common throughout Africa. Second, it tends to depict Africans as little more than either collaborating dupes or naive and gullible people, beguiled by clever colonial administrators and untrustworthy anthropologists, a situation which empirical evidence fails to corroborate. Finally, it does not explain how, three decades after the departure of the colonialists, "tribalism," or its close kin, "regionalism," lives on as strongly as ever in independent African states, the governments of which have been actively trying to suppress it, and why in some places it is growing up for the first time. The clever blandishments of subtle European administrators are clearly insufficient to explain either the origins of ethnic consciousness or its continuing appeal today.

A second interpretation, especially prominent in the 1950s and early 1960s, arose from the study of urban sociology, especially in the mining areas of Central Africa. Intellectually, it was linked to the Dual Economy model of "modernization" theory, and it located its interpretation of the development of new ethnic consciousness in the experiences of rural people in industrial workplaces. As members of various cultural groups left their isolated rural areas and interacted with each other in industrial or urban locales, they formed stereotypes of themselves and others, and these stereotypes effectively highlighted and strengthened culturally defined distinctions amongst peoples. The tendency of employers to prefer certain ethnic groups for certain types of work and their conscious manipulation of ethnic differences to keep the workforce disunited resulted in competition between ethnic groups being built into the hierarchically structured workforce. In this view, ethnicity was a recent phenomenon of the modern urban workplace in which boundaries and distinctions between people had been built up. It was not a phenomenon of the rural areas, where people were assumed to live in accordance with prescriptive patterns derived from a "traditional" past and where they were largely isolated from peoples of differing cultures. As such, some scholars, as well as most African politicians of the time, assumed that the but recently formed ethnic identities were still malleable and that they would prove susceptible to an easy transformation into a national identity through processes of political mobilization associated with "nation-building," especially if the labour unions representing such workers could be co-opted into the national political establishment.

This interpretation is certainly valuable for its underscoring of the important point that ethnic stereotypes were indeed largely produced in work situations and in urban settings. Yet it too is unable to serve as a general explanation of ethnicity's origin or, especially, its persistence. First, by emphasizing the boundaries that the creation of ethnic stereotypes among urban Africans produced, which, in turn, created opposing notions of "them" and "us," it overlooks the more substantive intellectual content contributed by African intellectuals to the specification of concepts of ethnic self-identity within those boundaries. Positive views about one's history, the heroes of one's ethnic past, and the manifestations of one's culture, especially language, quite simply did not spring automatically from the work situation or the urban centre, yet they have all been central in defining ethnic identities and ethnic ideologies.

Second, by stressing the essentially non-rural nature of the growth of ethnic stereotypes, this interpretation implicitly accepts the notion that rural Africa was preserved in some sort of "traditional" pickle, antithetically opposed to "modern" industrial Africa and largely untouched by the forces of change associated with capitalist expansion and urbanization. Such a view of the existence of "two Africas" with but insubstantial linkages between them has by now been convincingly discredited. Quite simply, the rural areas of southern and central Africa did not remain unchanged in a brine of "tradition," with meaningful change restricted to areas of obvious economic growth. Historical change affected the rural areas as much as it did the industrial and urban areas. More to the point, empirical evidence abundantly demonstrates that it is to the rural areas that one must look for most of the intellectual content of ethnic ideologies as they developed during the twentieth century in response to such change.

A third interpretation of the growth of ethnicity is that it resulted from uneven development within African colonial territories. Certain peoples were able to do comparatively well from the educational and employment opportunities that colonial capitalism presented unevenly, with aspirant petty bourgeois groups able to establish themselves in some areas but not in others. When it became clear that the colonial era was nearing its end, these petty bourgeois groups mobilized support along ethnic lines so that they would be in a position to maximize their opportunities for access to resources and power after independence. This situation led in turn to the continuation of specifically ethnic politics in many countries of Africa, resulting in a rash of *coups d'état* and civil wars as ethnic fragments of the national petty bourgeoisie competed for their own advantage. From this perspective, ethnicity tends to be seen instrumentally, as little more than an ideological mask employed by ambitious members of upwardly-aspiring groups as a way of papering over growing class divisions within their ethnic group so as to secure their own narrow interests through demagoguery and mystification. Ethnicity, then, when ordinary people embrace it, is the very epitome of "false consciousness."

Again, this interpretation, with its emphasis on the pivotal roles of influential petty bourgeois intellectuals functioning as culture brokers and on smart politicians craftily manipulating popular opinion, especially in the post-colonial period, has obvious elements of truth in it. It also goes far towards explaining why some cultural groups who have had such a "modernizing" petty bourgeoisie within them are more "tribal" than other groups within the same country who lack such a class. Yet, on its own, it too ultimately fails to explain ethnicity's appeal. This is so because it goes too far in depicting ordinary people as being credulous, blindly accepting the ethnic party line from their devious betters. It fails to explain why, today as in the colonial period, the ethnic message should find such resonance with ordinary people. Why, in short, have ordinary people chosen so often to support ethnic politicians rather than national politicians? What is in the ethnic message that is not in the nationalist message? One must once again guard against the assumption, necessary to this interpretation, that ordinary Africans act either irrationally or sentimentally.

Finally, deriving from a Durkheimian notion of the importance of the role of the "community," or Gemeinschaft, there is the "primordialist" interpretation of ethnicity, an interpretation which now appears to be in the ascendancy amongst many scholars. Its attraction lies in its serious attempt to answer the crucial question as to why the ethnic message possesses such strong appeal.

This interpretation seeks the explanation in the realm of psychology. Africans, it is argued, were badly affected by the disruptive socio-economic and political changes of the late nineteenth and twentieth centuries. Pre-capitalist and pre-colonial hierarchies and elements of order in social life were undermined by the growth of capitalist relations and the impact of colonialism, thereby depriving people of social and psychological security. As a result, in a hostile world they have instead sought security through the invocation of a lost past of firm values as a way of recreating a life in which they can achieve emotional and, even, perhaps, physical safety. Ethnic identity provides a comforting sense of brotherhood in a world tending towards social atomization and rootlessness. Ethnic leaders represent and embody the unity of the cultural group. In this view, ethnicity is a kind of romantic rejection of the present. Enduring rather as religious fundamentalism or faith healing do in Western societies, it is a reaction to the sterility of modern positivism and has become something akin to a civil religion with great emotional appeal.

Once again, this argument is attractive, particularly as the ethnic message, once established amongst people, does appear to be a part of the natural order of the universe. It categorizes people in accordance with inevitable, largely unselfconscious ascription: people belong to tribe X because they are born in tribe X and are, regardless of personal choice, characterized by the cultural traits of tribe X. Thus one is a member of a "tribe" not by choice, but by destiny, and one thus partakes of a set of "proper" customs.

Yet there are three serious problems with this interpretation. First, the mere appeal of, or belief in, a generalized idyllic past and the presumed unity of the ethnic group seem insufficiently definite to explain the relevance to people in specific historical situations of the statements that comprise constructed ethnic ideologies. Why have vague cultural statements about language or a common history or a hero from the past succeeded in "comforting" people or mobilizing them? Does ethnicity appeal because it is intrinsically "primordial," or is it constructed as "primordial" in its discourse to render it more generally appealing? What specific messages within the ethnic ideology actually appeal the most and to whom? And why? In short, the stress upon the "primordial" aspect of ethnicity tends to overlook both the actual intellectual content of the message, which can vary from group to group, and its varying appeal among different members of the same ethnic group.

Second, by stressing the backward-looking, "primordial" aspect of ethnicity, this interpretation fails to answer the central empirical question of how the most backward-looking ethnic ideologies, with their glorification of long-dead heroes and their delight in "traditional values," have been able at the same time to contain within them a powerful acceptance of western education and skills and a willingness to "change with the times." The emphasis on the primordial past does not take into account ethnicity's forward-looking aspect which, as commentators have frequently observed, gives it a Janus-like appearance. This is so, I suggest, largely because the role of class actors in creating and shaping ethnic ideologies has been largely overlooked. It is the direct appeal of fresh ideas and institutions to certain new classes that appeared in twentieth-century Africa that has been translated into the progressive face of ethnic identity. The psychological appeal of primordialism and the concern for specific present-day interests of specific classes perhaps seem unlikely bed-fellows, but they are real ones nonetheless and must be explained.

Third, and directly related to the first two problems, the emphasis upon a comforting past projects upon African people's ideas an unconvincing stasis. It is simply impossible to accept that Africans, living through some of the most rapid changes that any people have lived through in all human history, have attached themselves blindly, like so many limpets, to a vision of the past that has little relevance to the present and the future just because it is "comfortable." As an interpretation, the "primordialist" explanation of ethnicity, on its own, is simply too ahistorical and non-specific to convince. In analyzing ethnicity's real appeal one must instead try to relate its actual assumptions about the past to the current historical reality of those accepting them. One may easily conclude then that ethnicity, or "tribalism," when analyzed abstractly, is Protean, with different appeals on different levels and in different situations. In this respect, it is quintessentially situational and multi-dimensional.

It is thus only common sense to accept that no one explanation suffices to "explain" it wholly and in every instance. But it is plainly inadequate merely to accept that all interpretations have some elements of truth within them and then try to cobble them together into an intellectual construct comprising elements of each. I would suggest, rather, that moving the analysis of ethnicity beyond the more or less ahistorical stance of the currently dominant interpretations towards a more specifically historical interpretation will shed additional light on both its origin and its continuing appeal for the peoples of southern Africa.

A History

Thus far historians have not devoted much attention to the history of ethnicity and ethnic ideologies in southern Africa. This is somewhat puzzling, especially as many have been aware for some time that ethnicity is not a natural cultural residue but a consciously crafted ideological creation. It is likely that the explanation for this relative neglect lies in the fact that historians were, like other scholars, caught up in the nationalist paradigm that dominated the entire range of African studies in the 1950s and 1960s. They thus saw studies of the growth of ethnic consciousness as parochial, misconceived, and largely irrelevant to their main concerns at that time: the recovery of Africa's pre-colonial past and the exploration of the growth of anti-colonial resistance and its flowering into progressive nationalism. In the optimistic nation-building mood of the time, studies of ethnicity were also extremely unpopular with African opinion-makers, embarrassing even to mention, and they exerted pressure against studies that might further divisiveness in the new nation states they thought they were "building." Thus, the history of ethnic identities largely remained to be written. . . .

The Situation Today

For large areas of southern Africa, independence came in the 1960s and 1970s. But the condition which stretches basic economic, familial, and welfare concerns between rural residence and work site endures down to the present. Migrant labour is still a dominant form of labour mobilization throughout the region, and the mental attitudes intrinsic to it continue. Even in situations where men have been permanently resident in the urban areas with their families for decades, these attitudes are widely found. This is so not because Africans are inherently rural people or are in close harmony with Nature, but because housing and living expenses are far lower in the rural areas than they are in urban areas. This lower cost of living serves as a constant reason for those dwelling in urban locales to keep the rural areas always in mind and to view their urban sojourn as only temporary. Thus, because at the end of one's period of employment retirement benefits are usually given in the form of a single lump sum of money rather than in monthly payments, if they are given at all, a person—whether unskilled migrant or educated white collar worker—has little choice but to return "home" to live out the rest of his days, spending as little money as possible.

The preoccupation with one's connection to the land has been overwhelming, with virtually everyone either possessing a piece of land in actuality or desiring it in his or her fantasies. This continuing fixation on land, I suggest, has resulted from decades of the existence of an oscillating workforce that has only partially proletarianized workers and from the failure to establish the sort of welfare measures that would support a fully urbanized population after retirement. The concern for land as an ultimate fall-back means of survival is clearly an economic concern, then, and, in the circumstances, it is quite understandable. Even in South Africa, the most industrialized of all the countries of the region and one in which complete proletarianization on a substantial scale in secondary and tertiary industry has existed at least since the 1940s, lack of adequate welfare and retirement measures keeps alive deep concern about access to land.

Thus the African National Congress still finds that to contend publicly that one of the fundamental roots of the political conflict between black and white in South Africa is the Native Land Act of 1913, and to talk about a land reform that would give dispossessed blacks renewed access to land, have great appeal to their constituency. Added to this economic concern is the fact that the nation states that have appeared since the 1960s have suffered profoundly from economic weakness, a weakness which has grown more serious with each passing year. Quite naturally, this has had a negative effect on the possibility of the creation of broad loyalty to the nation state itself. The nationalist message before and immediately after the end of colonialism was that the new dispensation would result in economic improvements and much increased welfare benefits. Unfortunately, this progress has not occurred, and instead the nation state's administrative structures have faltered and shrivelled.

There are thus further economic reasons why sentiments which would be described as "nationalist" do not converge with citizenship in a new nation state, as it has come to be identified as at least the occasion, and sometimes as the cause, of a declining standard of living for the majority of people. People perhaps accept that they are citizens of the country in which they live, but this acceptance of civil status does not produce the same loyalty as does their ethnic identity. There has therefore been an increased concern with ethnic identities over the past two decades, and with it has come a great acceleration in the "rediscovery" of culture for more and more ethnic groups, as the essay by Papstein explores in detail.

For economic reasons, therefore, as well as for reasons of psychological satisfaction, it seems clear that ethnic loyalties will continue in southern Africa for the foreseeable future. The exact forms of future ethnic identities are still cloudy, largely because conditions related to certain variables have changed since the development of ethnic consciousness in the colonial period, a process which has for the most part provided the model used in this volume. Education, for example, is now almost wholly under the control of the nation state, and, hence, will not be as easily employed to bring about acceptance of specific ethnic identities among children. In some countries—such as Malawi and Swaziland—the chiefs remain as influential figures in the rural areas. In others, such as Zambia, the chiefs remain, but most of their power has been taken from them. In yet others, such as Mozambique, chiefs have been abolished totally. Therefore it is likely that the symbols of ethnicity will vary from place to place and from country to country depending on the nature of local government and the way the state communicates with ordinary people.

Furthermore, the potential culture brokers are far more numerous now than sixty years ago, and they have been exposed to a far wider variety of thought, usually not associated with missions. This means that while the backward-looking aspects of future ethnic phenomena—concern for the glories of past history, culture heroes, the central importance of language, and the like—will remain pretty much the same as for examples in the past, the forward-looking aspect of the Janus of ethnicity has the potential of wide variation across the political spectrum. In contemporary Zambia, for example, a main focus of ethnic identity for the Bemba-speaking people who see themselves cut off from state power is the predominantly Bemba miners' union.

The unevenness of development that has marked southern Africa since 1886 shows no sign of ceasing now. Therefore it is likely that the content of the ethnic message itself will continue to vary from people to people, as the culture brokers craft messages that will resonate with their own clienteles. For the serious student of political history in the region, then, it will not be adequate to approach ethnicity, or "tribalism," as if all examples were essentially the same. Concern with the content of the message will be of ever greater importance if we are to understand it.

Finally, as ethnicity and parochial loyalties within the borders of nation states are likely to continue, it is important to cease approaching them from the perspective of the nation state itself. Ignoring them as embarrassing epiphenomena that should have long ago disappeared will do no good.

Condemning them as "reactionary" or "divisive" will accomplish very little. Instead, granted that it is virtually certain that the nation states of southern Africa are going to continue as institutionalized governing states in tension with those whom they govern, it will be necessary for the region's politicians and scholars alike to work towards accommodating ethnicity within these nation states. States like Lesotho and Botswana, where the nation state and ethnicity are largely coterminous, are exceptional. Multi-ethnic states like Mozambique and Zaire, Zambia and, most crucial of all, South Africa are typical. The western model of the nation state which sees it as identical with the cultural nation itself simply does not obtain in such situations and to insist upon its superior claims to legitimacy and loyalty is simply myopic. Instead, accepting that ethnicity does exist as a potent force, Africans will have to produce political solutions derived from African experience to solve African problems, and this is clearly of great importance in the evolving situation in South Africa, the political and economic centre of the region.

The Invention of Tradition

TERENCE RANGER[3]

The 1870s, 1880s, and 1890s were the time of a great flowering of European invented tradition—ecclesiastical, educational, military, republican, monarchical. They were also the time of the European rush into Africa. There were many and complex connections between the two processes. The concept of *empire* was central to the process of inventing tradition within Europe itself, but the African empires came so late in the day that they demonstrate the effects rather than the causes of European-invented tradition. Deployed in Africa, however, the new traditions took on a peculiar character, distinguishing them from both their European and Asian imperial forms.

By contrast to India many parts of Africa became colonies of white settlement. This meant that the settlers had to define themselves as natural and undisputed masters of vast numbers of Africans. They drew upon European invented traditions both to define and to justify their roles, and also to provide models of subservience into which it was sometimes possible to draw Africans. In Africa, therefore, the whole apparatus of invented school and professional and regimental traditions became much more starkly a matter of command and control than it was within Europe itself. Moreover, in Europe these invented traditions of the new ruling classes were to some extent balanced by the invented traditions of industrial workers or by the invented "folk" cultures of peasants. In Africa, no white agriculturalist saw himself as a peasant. White workers in the mines of southern Africa certainly drew upon the invented rituals of European craft unionism but they did so partly because they were rituals of exclusiveness and could be used to prevent Africans being defined as workers.

By contrast to India, once again, Africa did not offer to its conquerors the framework of an indigenous imperial state or existing centralized rituals of honour and degree. Ready connections between African and European systems

---

[3] This excerpt is taken from "The Invention of Tradition in Colonial Africa," published in Eric Hobsbawm and Terence Ranger, eds., *The Invention of Tradition* (2nd edition, 2012), pp. 211-63. Terence Ranger is emeritus professor of History at St. Anthony's College, Oxford.

of governance could only be made at the level of the monarchy; Africa possessed, so the colonisers thought, dozens of rudimentary kings. Hence in Africa the British made an even greater use of the idea of "Imperial Monarchy" than they did within Britain or India. The "theology" of an omniscient, omnipotent and omnipresent monarchy became almost the sole ingredient of imperial ideology as it was presented to Africans. For the Germans, too, the Kaiser stood as the dominant symbol of German rule. The French had the more difficult task of incorporating Africans into a republican tradition.

But serviceable as the monarchical ideology was to the British, it was not enough in itself to provide the theory or justify the structures of colonial governance on the spot. Since so few connections could be made between British and African political, social and legal systems, British administrators set about inventing African traditions for Africans. Their own respect for "tradition" disposed them to look with favour upon what they took to be traditional in Africa. They set about to codify and promulgate these traditions, thereby transforming flexible custom into hard prescription.

All this is part of the history of European ideas, but it is also very much part of the history of modern Africa. These complex processes have to be understood before a historian can arrive at any under standing of the particularity of Africa before colonialism; many African scholars as well as many European Africanists have found it difficult to free themselves from the false models of colonial codified African "tradition." However, the study of these processes is not only a part of historiography but of history. The invented traditions imported from Europe not only provided whites with models of command but also offered many Africans models of "modern" behaviour. The invented traditions of African societies—whether invented by the Europeans or by Africans themselves in response—distorted the past but became in themselves realities through which a good deal of colonial encounter was expressed.

European Invented Tradition and the African Empire

The traditions which were invented in Europe in the nineteenth century were very unevenly carried into Africa. In the 1880s and 1890s many whites were arriving in southern Africa from Europe, Canada and Australia to work in the mines; very many Africans were being drawn into the labour migrant network. But European proletarian or artisanal invented traditions were not available to fit African workers into their place in the labour hierarchy, still less to help them define themselves as artisans or workers. Instead, the revived and invented rituals of craft unionism were used by white workers to *exclude* Africans from participation. Elaine Katz in her study of white trade unionism in South Africa shows how the white miners claimed craft status. Dominated by British and Australian miners, their union was "organized on the basis of an exclusive membership restricted to white underground miners in possession of a blasting certificate." Union leaders urged an often lethargic membership to follow the Craft Banner and the brass band in Labour Day processions—rituals of worker solidarity which in that context proclaimed elite status. As John X. Merriman, prime minister of Cape Colony, remarked in 1908, white workmen who had been regarded in Europe as the "lower classes" were "delighted on arrival here to find themselves in a position of an aristocracy of colour." An extensive recent literature has shown that in the 1880s and 1890s Africans throughout East, Central, and Southern Africa were becoming peasants, their agricultural surplus expropriated through unequal terms of trade, tax, or rent and their subordinate role in a shared cultural system defined by mission Christianity. But there was little opportunity for African peasants to borrow from the invented traditions by which European peasantries had sought to defend themselves against the intrusions of capitalism. Almost everywhere in Africa white agriculturalists saw themselves not as peasants but as gentlemen farmers. Only through some of the mission churches did European peasant formulations reach Africans, and only then in transformed shape.

The closest thing to a peasant missionary church was the Basel Mission. The product of Württemberg pietism, the Basel missionaries carried with them to Africa a model of rural society derived from their defence of pre-industrial German peasant life. They proclaimed, against the threat of the industrial town, an ideal "Christian model village," a reconstituted rural "tradition" based on "the pre-industrial combination of crafts making use of natural products, [and] the extended family." They stood for "a social and economic setting "traditional" in the sense that there was direct relationship between local food production and local food supplies." The original impulse of their entry into Africa was the desire to find free land to which German peasant communities could escape. In their approach to Africans they were "a mission *from* the village *to* the village." In Germany itself the pietist model only imperfectly reflected a past that had been much less organic and coherent. In Africa there had not existed "villages" of this size or stability. The Basel Mission villages, so far from offering African cultivators a means of protecting their values, operated rather as mechanisms of authoritarian European control and of economic innovation.

Few other mission churches expressed so clearly European peasant aspirations. But many carried with them features that had been produced through European ecclesiastical responses to peasant aspiration. Thus the Church of England had responded to the tensions of an increasingly class-based rural society by developing rituals of "traditional" community, and now it introduced these harvest festivals and rogation-tide processions through the fields into Africa. The Roman Catholic Church had responded to the anarchic proliferation of local peasant shrines, cults, and pilgrimages by authorizing a popular

Marian veneration, and centralizing it at a few shrines to which the flow of pilgrims was directed. Now into Africa were introduced replicas of Fatima and Lourdes. Such centralization of ritual and cult, introduced before there was any African popular Christianity for them to respond to, acted rather to circumscribe than to stimulate African peasant imagination.

It was not the invented traditions of European workers and peasants, but those of gentlemen and professional men which were most important to whites in Africa, and which had the greatest impact upon blacks. There were two main reasons for the importance of these neo-traditions. By the 1880s and 1890s there was a surplus of neo-traditional capital in Europe waiting to be invested overseas. Production of men for service in the extended governing class of industrial democracy had been almost too successful. Younger sons, well-born orphans, the sons of the clergy had experienced the "traditions" of the public school, the regiment, the university, but were not guaranteed secure advancement in British administrative hierarchies. Such men were deployed in Africa as soldiers, hunters, traders, storekeepers, concession-seekers, policemen, missionaries. Very often they found themselves engaged in tasks which by definition would have been menial in Britain and which only the glamour of empire-building made acceptable; the emphasis which they placed on their neo-traditional title to gentility became more intense.

The second reason was that there was a desperate need in the last decades of the nineteenth century to make European activity in Africa more respectable and ordered. While life was being restructured in Britain itself, with the rise of the bureaucracy and of the service traditions in school, army, church and even commerce, most European activity in tropical Africa, whether official or unofficial, had remained tatty, squalid, rough and inefficient. With the coming of formal colonial rule it was urgently necessary to turn the whites into a convincing ruling class, entitled to hold sway over their subjects not only through force of arms or finance but also through the prescriptive status bestowed by neo-tradition.

Steps were therefore taken to ensure that the military and administrative services in Arica were related to the dominant traditions. Much use was made in the early period of colonial administration of officers of the newly efficient and honourable British army. Lugard relied upon them for "gentlemanly" administrators in Nigeria. In 1902 Lady Lugard, writing from Lokoja on the Niger, was able to describe a veritable festival of neo-tradition. To celebrate Coronation Day—the day of the first elaborate "traditional" coronation:

> We had the table patriotically decorated with roses . . . and we drank the King's health, with the band playing "God Save the King," and a black crowd of servants and others clustering round the open windows ejaculating, "Good King! Good King!" I was

myself struck with the thought as I looked down the table and noted the fine type of English gentleman's face which presented itself in rows on either side, that it really is a phenomenon of our Empire that we should be able in the heart of Africa to bring together for dinner twenty well-bred English officers of as fine a type as you would hope to meet in the most civilised centres of London.

Meanwhile, the educational system of England began to turn out civilian colonial administrators. The headmaster of Harrow declared that an English headmaster, as he looks to the future of his pupils, will not forget that they are destined to be the citizens of the greatest empire under heaven; he will teach them patriotism. . . . He will inspire them with faith in the divinely ordained mission of their country and their race.

The recruiters for the colonial service testified to the success of these endeavours. "As to the Public Schools," wrote Sir Ralph Furse, one of the chief architects of the colonial service, "they are vital. We could not have run the show without them. In England universities train the mind; the Public Schools train character and teach leadership."

But the universities too came to play their part, and soon the District Commissioner had to be a man of many parts. To qualify for appointment to the administrative branch of the Colonial Service he had to hold an honours degree in Arts from a recognised university. . . . It helped the applicant's cause if, in addition to a good degree, he had some kind of athletic record. All this produced administrators who ran their districts like lordly prefects, inventing their own little traditions to keep the fags on their toes. "D was in the habit," we are told of the district commissioner of Tunduru in southern Tanganyika, "of going for a long walk every evening, wearing a hat. When, towards sunset, he came to the point of turning for home he would hang his hat on a convenient tree and proceed on his way hatless. The first African who passed that way after him and saw the hat was expected to bring it to D's house and hand it over to his servants, even if he was going in the opposite direction with a long journey ahead of him. If he ignored the hat he would be haunted by the fear that D's intelligence system would catch up with him." But it was not enough in itself to ensure the gentility of soldiers and administrators in Africa. There was also a need to believe that many of the white settlers were also actually or potentially inheritors of the neo-traditions of governance. In the end some settler communities were successful enough to set up in Africa itself replicas of the schools whose traditions validated the British governing class.

Thus, in 1927 a plan was discussed with Eton College to found the "Kenya Public School," under the joint auspices of Winchester and Eton, with reciprocal staffing arrangements and scholarships for the children of poorer white parents. After a trip to Britain to test support for the project, the Director of

Education decided to ask "all the leading public schools to present us with pictures of their school buildings so that the boys may be constantly reminded of the great schools at home and old boys visiting the school may likewise remember their Alma Mater."

As a finishing touch the school was to be named after King George V, "as a reminder to the backward races of their participation in the Empire." But to begin with the transformation was brought about mainly by a complex system of reformulations which affected the way in which white men in Africa were regarded and the way in which they regarded themselves.

This process operated in two ways. The fact that the surplus of neo-traditional capital *was* being invested in Africa, combined with the fortune-hunting involvement of members of high society, made it possible for commentators to stress the gentlemanly element among white settlers, and to suggest that the colonial experience in itself fitted the rest to acquire gentility. Lord Bryce was struck "by the large proportion of well-mannered and well-educated men whom one came across" in the "tropical wilderness" of Rhodesia in the mid-1890s, and added that the colonial experience fostered "personality developing itself under simple yet severe conditions, fitted to bring out the real force of a man." In such circumstance Bryce was prepared to condone the rather vulgar neo-traditional enthusiasms which he himself deplored in England. He was much struck by white southern African enthusiasm for cricket, "the national game."

Even one who thinks that in England the passion for athletic sports has gone beyond all reasonable limits, and has become a serious injury to education and to the taste for intellectual pleasures, may find in the character of the climate a justification for devotion to cricket. . . . Our countrymen are not to be scared by the sun from the pursuit of the national game. They are as much Englishmen in Africa as in England.

Alongside this process of affirming and making gentility there ran another—a redefinition of occupations, so that it became gentlemanly to be a storekeeper or a prospector. Young gentlemen who migrated to Rhodesia or to Kenya may have dreamt of one day establishing a landed estate, but in the early days running a farm store and buying African agricultural produce was far more profitable than trying to grow crops oneself. It was in any case assumed that English-speaking "farmers" would be gentleman farmers, not working the land themselves, but drawing on their neo-traditional powers of command in order to manage labour. So to begin with they relied on African—or Afrikaner—knowledge of the land and creamed off the surplus of African peasant producers through trade. By so doing they performed a vital function since the labour forces of the early colonial economies depended entirely on African produced food. Hence, for a time, it was gentlemanly to run a store or to buy grain and cattle from Africans. Lord Bryce found "cultivated and thoughtful minds" in young white storekeepers in Rhodesia in 1896, or in prospectors searching for gold. The atmosphere of these early days—and the buoyancy of the neo-traditions of gentility—emerges strikingly from Colin Harding's autobiography. Harding grew up as the son of the lord of Montacute House, a young man whose main concern was with the heroics of the hunting field. "But the death of my father revealed the unwelcome fact that neither myself nor other members of my family was as opulent as expected.... Neither I nor my brothers had any profession, nor yet the means to qualify for one."

Still, "hunting teaches a man a lot." Harding arrived in Bulawayo in 1894 to find that "farming was a washout" and "men like myself were a drug on the market." "Experienced and reliable storekeepers," however, "could command almost any wage they desired." But the young gentleman did not go under. Harding set out with an old friend from the hunting field to prospect for gold. Soon he found himself set to dig a mine shaft. "It was useless for me to remind my friend that I knew little or nothing about sinking a shaft, for he shut me up with the observation that digging out gold was much the same as digging out a fox." Soon Harding was in the British South Africa Police and on his way to a properly gentlemanly administrative career.

Fairly soon conditions in Rhodesia and Kenya developed towards a more securely gentlemanly society. Asians and Greeks and Jews took over the task of storekeepers and "kaffir-traders"; political action deliberately undercut African peasant production and put labour at the disposal of the gentleman farmer. M. G. Redley thus describes the nature of Kenyan white society just after the first world war.

The main source of British immigrants with capital after the war was what has been called the "new upper middle class." Family wealth derived from enterprise in manufacturing, commerce and the professions had blurred the class distinctions of Victorian society. Public school education had provided the basis of a background for those who could lay no direct claim to gentility common with those who could. The background to post-war settlers owed much more to the mill and the factory owner's mansion, the rural rectory and the Indian Army officers' mess than to aristocratic lineage. However, gentility was a way of life with which they felt a close identity and in which they took an obsessive interest.... The upper middle class complexion of European settlement was its greatest recommendation for those who felt their status and individuality threatened in British society.

Redley describes how neo-traditions functioned to hold together the small and dispersed white rural society. Team games brought neighbours together regularly in an approved and structured way. They also allowed for symbolic expressions of protest in an idiom familiar to both settlers and administrators. Redley describes a "fancy-dress charity football match" in Nairobi in 1907 patronized by the governor, which was disrupted by leading settlers dressed as colonial officials with rows of medals made of tin lids and red tape who pegged out quarantine, forest, native and game reserves until the entire pitch was "out of bounds."

On the other hand, every project to increase the numbers of the white settler population by bringing in thousands of small yeomen or artisans foundered on the determination of those who controlled Kenyan society to keep it in the hands of "the public school educated with a patrimony, a military pension, investment income or an assurance of family support."

Europeans and "Tradition" in Africa

The invented traditions of nineteenth-century Europe had been introduced into Africa to allow Europeans and certain Africans to combine for "modernizing" ends. But there was an inherent ambiguity in neo-traditional thought. Europeans belonging to one or other of the neo-traditions believed themselves to have a respect for the customary. They liked the idea of age-old prescriptive rights and they liked to compare the sort of title which an African chief possessed with the title to gentlemanliness which they laid claim to themselves. A profound misunderstanding was at work here. In comparing European neo-traditions with the customary in Africa the whites were certainly comparing unlike with unlike. European invented traditions were marked by their inflexibility. They involved sets of recorded rules and procedures—like the modern coronation rites. They gave reassurance because they represented what was unchanging in a period of flux. Now, when Europeans thought of the customary in Africa, they naturally ascribed to it these same characteristics. The assertion by whites that African society was profoundly conservative—living within age-old rules which did not change; living within an ideology based on the absence of change; living within a framework of clearly defined hierarchical status—was by no means always intended as an indictment of African backwardness or reluctance to modernize. Often it was intended as a compliment to the admirable qualities of tradition, even though it was a quite misconceived compliment. This attitude towards "traditional" Africa became more marked as whites came to realize in the 1920s and 1930s that rapid economic transformation was just not going to take place in Africa and that most Africans had to remain members of rural communities, or as some whites came to dislike the consequences of the changes which *had* taken place. The African collaborators, playing their role within one or other of the introduced European traditions, then came to seem less admirable than "real" Africans, still presumed to be inhabiting their own, appropriate universe of tradition.

The trouble with this approach was that it totally misunderstood the realities of pre-colonial Africa. These societies had certainly valued custom and continuity but custom was loosely defined and infinitely flexible. Custom helped to maintain a sense of identity but it also allowed for an adaptation so spontaneous and natural that it was often unperceived. Moreover, there rarely existed in fact the closed corporate consensual system which came to be accepted as characteristic of "traditional" Africa. Almost all recent studies of nineteenth-century pre-colonial Africa have emphasized that far from there being a single "tribal" identity, most Africans moved in and out of multiple identities, defining themselves at one moment as subject to this chief, at another moment as a member of that cult, at another moment as part of this clan, and at yet another moment as an initiate in that professional guild. These overlapping networks of association and exchange extended over wide areas. Thus the boundaries of the "tribal" polity and the hierarchies of authority within them did *not* define conceptual horizons of Africans. As Wim van Binsbergen remarks, in criticizing Africanist historians for their acceptance of something called "Chewa identity" as a useful organizing concept for the past:

> Modern Central Africa tribes are not so much survivals from a pre-colonial past but rather largely colonial creations by colonial officers and African intellectuals. . . . Historians fail to qualify the alleged Chewa homogeneity against the historical evidence of incessant assimilation and dissociation of peripheral groups. . . . They do not differentiate between a seniority system of rulers imposed by the colonial freezing of political dynamics and the pre-colonial competitive, shifting, fluid imbalance of power and influence.

Similarly, nineteenth-century Africa was *not* characterized by lack of internal social and economic competition, by the unchallenged authority of the elders, by an acceptance of custom which gave every person—young and old, male and female—a place in society which was defined and protected. Competition, movement, fluidity were as much features of small-scale communities as they were of larger groupings. Thus Marcia Wright has shown, in a stimulating account of the realities of late nineteenth-century society in the Lake Tanganyika corridor, that economic and political competition overrode the "customary securities" offered to women by marriage or extended kinship relations. Women constantly found themselves being shaken out of the niches in which they had sought security, and constantly tried to find new niches for themselves. Later on, of course, and in the twentieth century, the dogmas of customary security and immutably fixed relationships grew up in these same societies, which came to have an appearance of *ujamaa* style solidarity; the nineteenth-century time of "rapid change," in which "formal structural factors" became relatively less important than "personal resilience and powers of decision," gave way to stabilization. As Marcia Wright remarks:

The terms of the reconstruction were dictated by the colonial authorities in the years after 1895, when pacification came to mean immobilization of populations, reinforcement of ethnicity and greater rigidity of social definition.

Hence "custom" in the Tanganyika corridor was much more of an invention than it was a restoration. In other places, where the competitive dynamic of the nineteenth century had given many opportunities for young men to establish independent bases of economic, social and political influence, colonialism saw an establishment of control by elders of land allocation, marriage transactions and political office. Small-scale gerontocracies were a defining feature of the twentieth rather than of the nineteenth century.

Some part of these twentieth-century processes of "immobilization of populations, reinforcement of ethnicity and greater rigidity of social definition" were the necessary and unplanned consequences of colonial economic and political change—of the break up of internal patterns of trade and communication, the defining of territorial boundaries, the alienation of land, the establishment of Reserves. But some part of them were the result of a conscious determination on the part of the colonial authorities to "re-establish" order and security and a sense of community by means of defining and enforcing "tradition." Administrators who had begun by proclaiming their support for exploited commoners against rapacious chiefs ended by backing "traditional" chiefly authority in the interests of social control. Missionaries who had begun by taking converts right out of their societies so as to transform their consciousness in "Christian villages" ended by proclaiming the virtues of "traditional" small-scale community. Everyone sought to tidy up and make more comprehensible the infinitely complex situation which they held to be a result of the "untraditional" chaos of the nineteenth century. People were to be "returned" to their tribal identities; ethnicity was to be "restored" as the basis of association and organization. The new rigidities, mobilizations and ethnic identifications, while serving very immediate European interests, could nevertheless be seen by the whites as fully "traditional" and hence as legitimated. The most far-reaching inventions of tradition in colonial Africa took place when the Europeans believed themselves to be respecting age-old African custom. What were called customary law, customary land rights, customary political structure and so on were in fact *all* invented by colonial codification.

There is a growing anthropological and historical literature on these processes which it is not possible to summarize here. But a few striking statements will give an indication of the argument. Thus John Iliffe describes the "creation of tribes" in colonial Tanganyika:

The notion of the tribe lay at the heart of indirect rule in Tanganyika. Refining the racial thinking common in German times, administrators believed that every African belonged to a tribe, just as every European belonged to a nation. The idea doubtless owed much to the Old Testament, to Tacitus and Caesar, to academic distinctions between tribal societies based on status and modern societies based on contract, and to the post-war anthropologists who preferred "tribal" to the more pejorative word "savage." Tribes were seen as cultural units "possessing a common language, a single social system, and an established common law." Their political and social systems rested on kinship. Tribal membership was hereditary. Different tribes were related genealogically.... As unusually well-informed officials knew, this stereotype bore little relation to Tanganyika's kaleidoscopic history, but it was the shifting sand on which Cameron and his disciples erected indirect rule by "taking the *tribal* unit." They had the power and they created the political geography.

Elizabeth Colson describes the evolution of "customary land law" in much the same way:

The newly created system was described as resting on tradition and presumably derived its legitimacy from immemorial custom. The degree to which it was a reflection of the contemporary situation and the joint creation of colonial officials and African leaders . . . was unlikely to be recognized.

The point is not merely that so-called custom in fact concealed new balances of power and wealth, since this was precisely what custom in the past had always been able to do, but that these particular constructs of customary law became codified and rigid and unable so readily to reflect change in the future. Colson remarks that colonial officers expected the courts to enforce long-established custom rather than current opinion. Common stereotypes about African customary law thus came to be used by colonial officials in assessing the legality of current decisions, and so came to be incorporated in "customary" systems of tenure.

Similarly, Wyatt MacGaffey has shown how the Bakongo peoples moved from a pre-colonial situation of "processes of dispersal and assimilation"; of "the shunting of subordinate populations of slaves and pawns"; of "a confusion of debts, assets, scandals and grievances," into a colonial situation of much more precise and static definition of community and of land rights.

In the evolution of tradition, the touchstone of merit was very often the presiding judge's concept of customary society, derived ultimately from . . . a lingering European image of the African kingdom of Prester John. . . . Court records contain evidence of the evolution for forensic purposes away from the magical in the direction of the evidential and refutable. . . . Those whose traditions lost a case came back a year or two later with better traditions.

Once again, my point is not so much that "traditions" changed to accommodate new circumstances but that at a certain point they had to stop changing; once the "traditions" relating to community identity and land right were written down in court records and exposed to the criteria of the invented customary model, a new and unchanging body of tradition had been created.

Eventually there resulted a synthesis of the new and the old, which is now called "custom." The main features of customary society, responding to the conditions that developed between 1908 and 1921, assumed their present form in the 1920s.

Around the same time Europeans began to be more interested in and sympathetic towards the "irrational" and ritualistic aspects of "tradition." In 1917 an Anglican mission theologian suggested that for the first time missionaries in the field should "collect information with regard to the religious ideas of the black man," so that their relationship to traditional society could be understood. "In the twentieth century we are no longer contented to cut the knot, as the nineteenth century did, and say: Science has put an end to these superstitions." After the first world war, Anglicans in East Africa, faced with the need to reconstruct rural society after the ravages of the fighting and the subsequent impact of the depression, began to make anthropological analyses of those aspects of "traditional" ritual which had contributed towards social stability. Out of such inquiry came the well-known policy of missionary "adaptation," which produced its most developed example in the Christianized initiation ceremonies of the Masasi diocese in south-eastern Tanganyika. More generally, there emerged from this kind of thought and practice—with its emphasis upon rituals of continuity and stability—a concept of immemorial "African Traditional Religion" which did less than justice to the variety and vitality of pre-colonial African religious forms.

African Manipulation of Invented Custom

All this could not have been achieved, of course, without a good deal of African participation. As John Iliffe writes:

> The British wrongly believed that Tanganyikans belonged to tribes; Tanganyikans created tribes to function within the colonial framework. . . . [The] new political geography . . . would have been tran-

sient had it not coincided with similar trends among Africans. They too had to live amidst bewildering social complexity, which they ordered in kinship terms and buttressed with invented history. Moreover, Africans wanted effective units of action just as officials wanted effective units of government. . . . Europeans believed Africans belonged to tribes; Africans built tribes to belong to.

We have already seen in the case of the Tumbuka paramountcy how African rulers and mission-educated "modernizers" could combine in an attempt to manipulate the symbols of monarchy. Iliffe shows how similar alliances helped to build up the ideas and structures of "tribal" tradition.

"During the twenty years after 1925 Tanganyika experienced a vast social reorganization in which Europeans and Africans combined to create a new political order based on mythical history. . . . Analysing the system [of indirect rule] one officer concluded that its main supporters were the progressive chiefs. . . . It is clear that they were the key figures in indirect rule. Its chief virtue was indeed to release their energies. . . . The native administrations employed many members of the local elite. . . . Even educated men without native administration posts generally acknowledged hereditary authority. . . . In return many chiefs welcomed educated guidance." Iliffe describes progressive chiefs and mission-educated Africans combining in a programme of "progressive traditionalism."

Just as later nationalists sought to create a national culture, so those who built modern tribes emphasized tribal culture. In each case educated men took the lead. . . . The problem was to synthesize, to "pick out what is best from (European culture) and dilute it with what we hold." In doing so, educated men naturally reformulated the past, so that their syntheses were actually new creations. One area in which African intellectuals interacted with "adaptation" missionary theory was in the invention of "Traditional Religion."

It was not until missionaries studied African religions carefully during the 1920s that most Africans dared to consider their attitudes publicly. Michel Kikurwe, a Zigua teacher and cultural tribalist, envisaged a golden age of traditional African society. . . . Samuel Sehoza pioneered the idea that indigenous religious beliefs had prefigured Christianity.

Like the missionaries, these men emphasized the function of religion in stabilizing society:

> In each district [wrote Kikurwe] men and women were busy to help one another, they taught their children the same laws and traditions. Every Chief tried as much as he could to help and please his people, and likewise his people did the same in turn, they all knew what was lawful and unlawful, and they knew that there was a powerful God in heaven.

It is easy enough to see the personal advantages which these inventors of tradition stood to gain. The successful teacher or minister who stood at the right hand of a paramount was a man of very real power. The African clergy who constructed the model of "Traditional Religion" as the inspiring ideology of stable pre-colonial communities were making a claim to do the same for modern African societies by means of "adapted" Christianity. Yet Iliffe concludes that it would be wrong to be cynical. The effort to create a Nyakyusa tribe was as honest and constructive as the essentially similar effort forty years later to create a Tanganyikan nation. Both were attempts to build societies in which men could live well in the modern world. But there was still an ambiguity in invented African tradition. However much it may have been used by the "progressive traditionalists" to inaugurate new ideas and institutions—like compulsory education under the Tumbuka paramountcy—codified tradition inevitably hardened in a way that advantaged the vested interests in possession at the time of its codification. Codified and reified custom was manipulated by such vested interests as a means of asserting or increasing control. This happened in four particular situations; though it was not restricted to them.

The Making of the Yoruba

J.D.Y. PEEL[4]

[T]he very ethnic category "Yoruba," in its modern connotation, was the product of missionary "invention." If many Yoruba have found this an unpalatable idea, the deep reason seems to be because, as commonly represented, the ethnic designation "Yoruba" belongs to a pre-colonial, traditional, or even primordial order, while Christianity belongs to an opposed global or modern order. So how could the latter engender the former? But the plain fact is that the person who has the best claim to be considered the proto-Yoruba—in the sense of being the first Yoruba effectively to so ascribe himself—namely Samuel Ajayi Crowther, was also the first Yoruba Christian of any significance. Over the subsequent century and a half, what it has meant to be Yoruba and what it has meant to be Christian have evolved in continuous interaction with one another, and neither can be regarded as having reached a definitive resting point. But a study of the first half-century of the encounter of Christianity and the Yoruba ought to conclude by showing how this course was decisively set.

The political effects of the creation of a Yoruba identity worked themselves out during the colonial period and afterward, and are not our concern here, except insofar as they have influenced later perceptions of how the process began. Here, much of the material to be considered has most often been treated as belonging to a movement of "cultural nationalism," between the late 1880s and the First World War. This has never been sharply defined, but the received account goes roughly as follows. In response to new levels of racial discrimination and social exclusion, as well as to the disparagement of their culture and collective achievements, educated or "bourgeois" Africans reasserted their dignity as a race/nation by a new insistence on the worth of what was distinctive of them. So they cultivated the Yoruba language; adopted African dress; in many cases changed their European names to Yoruba ones; collected the an-

---

[4] This excerpt is taken from by J.D.Y Peel, *Religious Encounter and the Making of the Yoruba* (Bloomington: Indiana University Press, 2003), pp. 278-309. J.D.Y Peel is professor of anthropology and sociology at the School of Oriental and African Studies in London.

cestral wisdom of their communities in the form of proverbs, stories, and poetry; compiled historical narratives from oral traditions; and even started to find merit in some aspects of traditional religion. The key question to be addressed here concerns the place of Christianity in this movement, which opens out into the broader issue of the relationship between Christianity and nationalism, whether Yoruba or any other.

The place to start is J. E Ade Ajayi's seminal article of 1961, "Nineteenth Century Origins of Nigerian Nationalism," where the term "cultural nationalism" seems to occur for the first time. Ajayi argues that nationalism had its roots in the missionary movement, which he explicitly contrasts in this respect with the movement of Islamic reform that led to the foundation of the Sokoto Caliphate. But whereas the Sokoto jihadists drew their inspiration from the transnational religious ideals of classical Islam, the missionaries were the bearers of the European idea of nation-states. As Ajayi noted, "They could not conceive of Christianity flourishing in a social or economic or even political environment that differed in essentials from the European environment." Though they themselves did not take up the task of nation-building, they sought to do so through the educated Christian class which they created.

The viewpoint from which Ajayi wrote was that of a nationalist intellectual in a newly independent Nigeria who was concerned to trace the antecedents of his country's situation as well as of his own intellectual forbears. Ajayi avoided the danger of teleology here by pointing out that this was really a "nationalism" before the nation, certainly before the Nigerian nation. Not only was the term "Nigeria" still to be invented, but the Yoruba educated class, whose project this was, had at this stage little or no sense of identification with the non-Yoruba peoples of what would become the hinterland of colonial Nigeria.

Externally, the educated circles in Lagos and Abeokuta that created "cultural nationalism" had closer links with similar groups among the Christian bourgeoisie along the coast from Freetown to Calabar, with the Creole diaspora, and even with Blacks across the Atlantic than with the non-Yoruba interior. What all these people had in common, apart from a varying mix of African and Euro-Christian cultural traditions, was a consciousness shaped by their dealings with Europeans in social settings increasingly structured by racial criteria which excluded and disparaged them. So their "nationalism" was not focused on a given political or cultural entity, but on "the African nation" ("the Negro race") in general. It was because they saw the British Empire as a valuable instrument by which Africa could be elevated to take its place among the respected nations of the earth that so many of them—Edward Blyden most conspicuously—strongly supported it. An unusual nationalism, which had so much of a disappointed imperialism about it! But any nationalism has to have some distinctive cultural content. Ajayi's essay, dealing with the whole trajectory from the mid-nineteenth to the mid-twentieth centuries, gives relatively small weight to the twenty years when "cultural nationalism" per se —"a minor cultural renaissance," he calls it—was at its height. The cultural ferment of these years received much more extended treatment from E. A. Ayandele and it is from him that most later discussion has taken its rise. While Ayandele is sometimes inclined to read too much of the later Nigerian nationalism into the movement of the 1890s, he does vividly bring out the contradictory impulses which cultural nationalism displayed—to validate African tradition and to promote the assimilation of European modernity—perhaps because the issues are often so alive and unresolved in his own texts. Yet at the same time Ayandele rarely loses sight of the Christian agenda that underlay so much of the project of the cultural nationalists. Their criticism of European missionaries, for example, did not make them less enthusiastic for mission as such, since they saw the more effective evangelization of their non-Christian compatriots as the essential foundation of cultural advance. Few figures of the movement were as assertive of the claims of the African nation as was Mojola Agbebi, but he wanted studies of traditional religion to be undertaken not as an antidote to missionary Christianity, but as "useful instruments in the hands of the aggressive missionary."

In recent years there has seemed to be some danger that the importance of the specifically Christian filiation of cultural nationalism might slip from sight. Farias and Barber, for example, describe the cultural nationalists as having to "deal . . . culturally, politically and intellectually with the incursions of European powers"—which elides the central religious terrain of argument, and rather implies that they were not themselves in many ways part of the "incursions." They acknowledge that "most of [the participants] were Christians," which makes it sound as if some were not, or as if this was an incidental aspect of the movement. But at its height, 1890-1914, virtually all the key figures of cultural nationalism were clergymen or active Christian laymen. Ironically, the best witness for the Christian inspiration of cultural nationalism is the one Muslim whose ideas are discussed in their book, the Yoruba Arabist, Shaikh Adam al-Iluri, who criticized it for making compromises with idolatry.

Christianity was integral to cultural nationalism in two main ways. First, as Ajayi argued, there was its strong link with the idea of "nation" as such.

But this has much deeper roots than the somewhat contingent one that he emphasized: the missionaries' adoption of the nation-state, as it had come to exist in early modern Western Europe, as the political norm, the "natural" environment for their kind of Christianity. After all, Christianity had existed for centuries in many other political settings. But still underlying Christianity's endorsement of the nation-state was its readiness from its earliest years to valorize the idea of the ethnos, which is the pre-political foundation of the nation state. The impulse of Christianity to translate its Gospel implies its acceptance of peoples or "nations" as naturally given units to which the Church must speak: in the New Testament the Church's mission "to the Gentiles" was literally "to the nations/peoples" (pros ta ethne). A work such as Bede's Ecclesiastical History of the English People (completed in A.D. 731, well before England had become a single political entity) is an authentic outcome of this deep disposition of the Christian religion. Islam's ideal situation stands in sharp contrast: the confessional group, or umma, was to displace the nation, and the Arabic language of its revelation was to transcend its ethnic origins and have a supra-national status.

Relationships that grow up between particular religions and peoples cannot but be reciprocal. And as peoples become nations, they tend to look toward religions in very specific ways. Since nations virtually always see themselves as standing in comparison (if not overt rivalry) with other nations, they need not only those features such as language and culture which define their uniqueness, but also some qualities that distinguish them from the others in terms of more widely shared values. Variants of the world religions are ideal for this purpose, since they offer higher, transcendent values, which can give an external, moral drive to nationhood that it is much harder to derive from mere cultural distinctiveness. From the sixteenth to the nineteenth centuries, the Protestant identity of the British nation (Scots and Welsh as well as English) did much to solidify loyalties, uniting the political class and the people, justifying action against the Catholic enemy both within (the rebellious Irish) and without (their French rivals). Modern nations are essentially in a condition of becoming, rather than of being. And the more they depend on religion for the definition of their project, the more it is that what presents itself for analysis is an articulation of two projects: the national one and the dynamic of the religion itself.

This brings us to the second way in which Christianity was integral to cultural nationalism, and also back again to the basic question of just which nation was at issue. The nation envisaged in the missionary project was an ethno-linguistic one: the Yoruba. The nation which arose from the social predicament of the Christian bourgeoisie in the towns of coastal West Africa—the "African nation"—was another name for a racial category. James Johnson gave plaintive expression to the fact that this "nation" had so little positive substance to it:

> Our life in British settlements has not been a national one, we are not a nation but a collection of individuals of different tribes, though of the same race, under a foreign government with divergent feelings and aspirations, and whom it has been difficult to fuse into one and make one great nation of. We have no national sentiment, ambition or aspiration, and no national pride and thankfulness for our great men.

Since this category had no intrinsic cultural content, the nationalists of Lagos naturally turned to the rich culture and historical experience that could give it substance, their own as Yoruba. So cultural nationalism was in effect largely concerned with consolidating Yoruba identity. Much of its historical writing, even on particular groups (and *a fortiori* in the pan-Yoruba studies such as those of J. O. George and Samuel Johnson), had as a motive to "foster unity, instead of tribal feelings, and as such gelled with the active CMS involvement in negotiations to bring the 'intertribal' wars to an end." At the same time, many of its typical manifestations had their roots in the long-term process of Christian mission rather than in the specific roots of the racial nationalism that began to show itself in the 1880s. It is thus not at all surprising that two of the early venues of "cultural nationalist" discussion were the Young Men's Christian Association of Breadfruit Church, whose pastor was then James Johnson, and the Abeokuta Patriotic Association, based at Ake Church and under the patronage of the English missionary J. B. Wood. If Robin Law is right in suggesting that it was the enactment of the Lagos Education Ordinance of 1882 which more than anything else triggered cultural nationalism, then the cause of Yoruba-language instruction was a missionary cause long before it was a "nationalist" one. Its aim was simply to enable Yoruba Christians to read the Bible in their mother tongue. . . .

Yet there was no prior Aku/Yoruba nation until it began to emerge in exile and was later re-imported to its homeland by the mission. What seems to have been decisive for the final adoption of "Yoruba" was Crowther's use of it in the title of his Vocabulary of the Yoruba Language (1843). In 1836, Crowther was still describing his hometown near Iseyin as being "in the Eyo Country." If we ask why he finally opted for the Hausa term used by travelers to the interior, rather than the one in use by his colleagues in the Sierra Leone Mission, the answer may perhaps be found in his participation in the 1841 Niger expedition. Here he and his colleague Schön spoke of the "Yaruba" when they encountered them along the Niger upstream from the confluence—both for non-Oyo groups such as "the Yagba . . . a dialect of Yaruba," and for the Oyo of the old "Yaruba kingdom." The term Aku hardly made it back to Yorubaland. So the Yoruba Mission it became, the Bible was translated into Yoruba, and Yoruba was what the converts came to understand themselves to be. They did not abandon their previous self-ascriptions as Egba, Lagosian (ọmọ Eko), Ijesha, and so forth-what missionaries (and soon literate Yoruba) often called "tribes," in the sense of sub-divisions of the nation, like the tribes of Israel. These remained the focus of people's primary loyalties, as Gollmer observed while planning, from Abeokuta, a mission station at Ijaye:

> The "feeling" which exists between the different tribes of the Yoruba nation is a drawback to the extension of mission work.

Friends at home may say, if there are so many openings in the Yoruba country, why not send some of the Abbeokuta converts to these places? This can be done and is being done. But if the Chief of Ijaye [Kurunmi] tells us, "These Egba boys [Phillips the catechist and Wilhelm the visitor] I know not," but "Thompson [the interpreter] that Yoruba man, I know he is my family," we understand what a feeling exists . . . more or less among all the tribes. . . . However[,] we trust ere long the Gospel will heal this wound and reciprocity of affection [will be] cherished among all, cementing the many Yoruba tribes into one great Christian nation.

Shaka Zulu and the Limits of Historical Invention

CAROLYN HAMILTON[5]

Making history strange poses anew the question why it is that the past is important, why history is produced both professionally—either orally or in the universities—and in non-professional contexts. There are two stock answers to this question. The first is that knowledge of the past helps society to understand the present, and thus, by implication, assists in planning for the future. The second concerns the importance of memory and the role of history in the constitution of identity. Both answers are connected to the often-asserted claim that the past provides "justification" for the present status quo. The acts of manipulating and imagining that these answers imply are now generally accepted. The central thrust of this study is to identify the constraints on these acts. The concern with limits on the manipulation of Shaka in politics and the imagining of Shaka in literature flows out of two reservations about the current theoretical literature on the making of the image of Africa. The first reservation concerns the ease with which students of ethnicity and nationalism have recourse to the notion of "the invention of tradition." As originally formulated by the essays in Eric Hobsbawm and Terence Ranger's influential edited collection, *The Invention of Tradition*, the concept derived from examinations of the way in which new traditions were created in diverse political settings: by movements of cultural nationalism, imperialist states, and radicals seeking to challenge powerful conservative rituals with counter-traditions of their own. The book showed how these traditions play an important role in the construction of ideologies of nationalism, imperialism, and radicalism, and marked an important watershed in the development of our understanding of the complex relationship between history and ideology. This work in turn stimulated a host of other studies along similar lines.

The Invention of Tradition, while oblivious neither of the processes that give

---

[5] This excerpt is taken from Carolyn Hamilton, *Terrific Majesty: Shaka Zulu and the Limits of Historical Invention* (Cambridge, MA: Harvard University Press, 1998), pp. 25-35. Carolyn Hamilton holds an NRF Research Chair in Archive and Public Culture based in the Social Anthropology Department at the University of Cape Town.

rise to such traditions nor of the preexistence of some of the materials from which they are constructed, was concerned primarily with the artificial aspects of the traditions invoked in nationalist and other struggles. While Hobsbawm and Ranger admitted that "the actual process of creating such ritual and symbolic complexes has not been adequately studied by historians," they viewed that process as determined by what is politically expedient and as constrained by prevailing political necessities. Few historians have taken up the challenge to look more closely at such processes, and to go beyond explanations grounded in current political needs. Similarly, while acknowledging that invented traditions are often "adaptations" of old ones, the contributors to the volume tended to focus on the novel aspects of the new forms rather than concerning themselves with investigation of their residual continuities with the ancient materials. They, and a good number of the studies inspired by *The Invention of Tradition*, did not examine closely what it is that determines the material selected for adaptation, and how the process of adaptation actually takes place. They did not ask what materials are available, why they are available for adaptation, and what the limitations are on their use. Finally, they did not explain why it is that traditions that are obviously mythical are believed to be true. In other words, is it possible simply to "choose your Shaka," to paraphrase Sevry, or are there constraints on these processes of invention?

The notion of "invention" can all too easily lose sight of the history of the tradition, of the way in which the tradition's (or elements of the tradition's) own past shapes its present. It further places full control over content and form in the hands of the "inventors"—usually political elites—and ignores the way that their versions of history are shaped by contesting and conflicting versions of the past. It loses sight of the struggles between existing, often opposed, bodies of knowledge, and the ways in which such contests are related to the social conditions that prevail in the worlds inhabited by their promoters. It denies the possibilities of "subjugated knowledges," and the effects these subversive texts have on the versions of the past promoted by those with political power. It sets up a crude opposition between "myth" and "reality." The argument of this study, by way of contrast, is that the image of Shaka is not an invention, either from scratch or from preexisting materials. Rather, it is an image established over time, through processes which can be charted historically and which set limits on the extent and form of its manipulation in the service of politics.

A second reservation concerns the idea of the West's' creation of the Other. Following Edward Said, it is now widely argued that "the West" invented a "primitive Other" in opposition to its "civilised self." This perspective has been extremely useful in stimulating a critique of colonial modes of representation, in drawing attention to the way in which enduring power inequalities affect knowledge of dominated societies, and in highlighting the persistent tropes used to visualize the colonized.

The great virtue of Said's study—his powerful demonstration of "the sheer knitted-together strength" of western discourse on the exotic—is also his argument's weakest point. His thesis, and the many studies that flow from it which focus on the process of "othering," can be criticized for presenting western discourse as fully systematic and invariant. As others have noted, Said's approach fails to make qualitative distinctions between a variety of texts produced under a range of circumstances for different audiences. One of the tasks of this study is to distinguish between texts produced under different circumstances, to query the very notion of a "western" discourse on the Zulu, and, more specifically, the idea of a consistent representation of the Zulu king. The coming chapters demonstrate how "western" discourses changed over time, and show how their representations were shaped by preexisting indigenous discourses, themselves far from homogeneous. The notion of the West's construction of the Other loses sight of the historiographies of the people labeled "Other," and the ways in which they have shaped the "West's" knowledge of those communities.

The argument presented here is that historically indigenous communities had a lot to say and spoke with many voices, and, more importantly, were heard. Their words were not reflected in pristine form in colonial discourse, and it may not now be possible to recover their voices, but the sediments and influences of their speech can be discerned. In some cases, this study shows, colonial researchers succeeded in recording "hidden transcripts," having access to views opposed to those of the Zulu rulers. In other cases, it reveals traces in "public transcripts" of divergent views which have been absorbed and neutralized by elites. These traces are present, I shall suggest, because the colonial worldview was not simply imported from the metropole and imposed on the colonized, nor was a new worldview suddenly "invented." Rather, it emerged out of the colonial experience, through a process of transformation and rearrangement. It was the hegemonic view because it articulated different versions of the world—including those of the colonized—in such a way that their potential antagonisms were neutralized. In some instances, of course, those traces can be detected because opposition in the past was successful or because it was dramatic and noisy. In other instances, they remained hidden while contexts of unfavorable power relations prevailed, and later, in changed circumstances, became visible. In still other cases, the colonizers actively selected elements of the new worldview which they promoted from contemporary African ideas, not as a consequence of struggles from below, but because of the power and attractiveness of indigenous concepts.

This study is critical of the crude we-they dichotomy that lies at the heart of many current discussions of colonial discourse. It does this (directly) through exploration of the complex moment when the colonial administrator Theophilus Shepstone "becomes Shaka" in order to oversee the installation of the independent Zulu king Cetshwayo, and (indirectly) through analyses of Rider Haggard's romantic African heroes and heroines. It qualifies Said's perception of an ontological and an epistemological distinction between the Orient and the Occident in "western discourse," or in this case, Africa and "the West," and acknowledges that historians' subjects' own representations have epistemological equality with those of the historians. It follows Gyan Prakash's injunction to "revisit the historical record, to push at the edges, to unsettle the calmness with which colonial categories and knowledges were instituted as the facts of history." Finally, by highlighting colonial concerns with Shaka, and demonstrating their roots in indigenous discourses, this study charts the connection between questions of rule and the first Zulu king in a manner that begins to provide a perspective on the attachment of power to the image of Shaka.

While Valentin Mudimbe is correct to argue that the foundations of discourse about Africa lie in the colonial encounter, this book stresses that we have to recognize that the origins of many of its components lie in indigenous African discourses. In making this argument, I do not claim that it is possible for us today to recover intact those indigenous discourses. I suggest that we can identify their traces in colonial and Africanist discourses, and can reconstruct more of the process of their incorporation into their present situations.

This book takes up Christopher Miller's challenge to begin breaking down the barriers between the domains of "western theory" and "African sources." Whereas Miller limits himself to an examination of the ways in which the cultural codes of "Africa" and the "West" began to play off one another in late and postcolonial times, however, this study asserts that indigenous intellectual endeavors were just as present in precolonial and first-contact times, and influenced the earliest colonial readings of Africa. The identity and desires of the colonizers were not simply projected or inscribed on Africa, nor was Africa drawn from the imagination. My study shows there was a dialogic process in the making of the image of Shaka. While Miller claims this complex intermix of conflicting codes happened only when "Senghor and Cesaire took pieces of their new Africa from Frobenius," a focus on the image of Shaka pushes back its origins to the moment of first contact. Rather than tracing small shifts in the representation of Shaka from one text to the next, and linking changes to changing politics and context—as do scholars such as Malaba, Golan, and Sevry—I seek to identify the events and historical developments that allow us to answer the question "Why Shaka?" and that set the limits on "which Shakas?"

The view of colonial discourse as systematic and universal leads commentators such as Golan and Cobbing to decry white writings about Zulu history as distortions of the Zulu past, and to depreciate the historical value of the collections of materials made by colonial officials and missionaries. Such judgments inhibit these scholars from coming to grips with the full complexity of the research efforts of a late nineteenth-century administrator such as James Stuart. As much as one ought to look at how Stuart's notion of civilization was imposed on the traditions he recorded, so too is it important to consider the way in which his ideas of "uncivilized" were shaped by the indigenous idea of buzimuzimu, translated by Stuart as "cannibalism," but glossed in other contexts by African writers as the opposite of civilized.

In advocating a reevaluation of the historical endeavors of a colonial official such as James Stuart, I am not reverting to the position of accepting Father Placide Tempels on his own terms. Nor do I accept uncritically the idea of Tempels or Stuart, rejecting the role of bringers of light in favour of becoming receivers of native wisdoms. Yet, just as Andrew Apter feels that Tempels cannot be as easily dismissed as Mudimbe would like, so, too, do I argue that Stuart should continue to command our attention, and that he offers a viable source of historical data, which, sensitively read, have a great deal to offer historians of Shakan times. To dismiss the writings of Stuart and Tempels as examples of "colonial discourse" is to close off the possibilities of recovering material about Africa's precolonial past, and ultimately to revert to a denial of that history. In cases where early African oral traditions only exist in forms recorded by white writers, then, as Greg Dening put it, "One can see beyond the frontier only through the eyes of those who stood on the frontier and looked out. To know the native one must know the intruder." Prompted by new methodological concerns about the nature of evidence, and by the crisis over the nature of "white" sources caused by the eruption of the mfecane debate, one of the main themes of this book is consideration of the many representations of Shaka in order to develop a view of how these texts might be read by historians and how they can be used as evidence about the past. In other words, it asks critical questions about the sources historians use in the reconstruction of Shakan times. It suggests that there is a far more complex relationship between indigenous narratives and colonial ones, and the processes of representation in which they engage, than Said, Martin, Malaba, Golan, and Sevry allow. It suggests that there is a historically conditioned dialectic of intertextuality between "western" models of historical discourse and indigenous traditions of narrative, and it seeks to identify some of the places where the indigenous narrative interpenetrates "modern" historical practice. This asserts the importance of history and of historicizing Shaka rather than Golan's relatively simplistic notion of the invention or reinvention of Shaka, and Sevry's idea that one can simply choose one's Shaka's or Wylie's idea that a single line of descent can be traced from Isaacs' 1836 text—the first full-length account of the early traders' contacts with Shaka—into the present.

This approach positions us to question not only the maintenance of distinctions between the fields of politics, history, and literature, but also challenge divisions implicit within each area. Chief among these is the distinction within political discourse between ideology—as in Buthelezi's Shaka Day speeches and popular culture, as expressed, for example, in the Shaka chest. Another such distinction exists within academic historical writings between historical texts and the production of the guild-trained historians—and "sources"—notably oral traditions, but also the accounts of early travelers, missionaries, and colonial officials. Within the field of literature distinctions exist between the poetry, drama, and novels produced by scholars—*La Mort de Chaka* or *Emperor Shaka the Great*—and the nineteenth-century praise poems of Shaka or even the popular 1980s television series Shaka Zulu. Each of these distinctions demands critical reassessment.

Writings on Zulu nationalism emphasize the way in which the image of Shaka is manipulated to suit current political ends. Such manipulations clearly resonate with popularly held views of Shaka, as expressed in the Shaka chest and other forms. Many commentators explain contemporary Zulu militarism associated with the image of Shaka as the result of ideological manipulations by Zulu nationalists and their supporters. This perspective, while extremely useful in drawing attention to the constructed nature of identity, fails to explain why the ideas concerned are readily accepted by ordinary people, including some Zulu speakers who are opposed to Zulu nationalism. Many Zulu speakers today claim an awareness of themselves as existing and acting in a continuous context of social relationships that began with Shaka. One of the questions that concern this study is the history of that historical awareness. It seeks to make a contribution to the understanding of ethnic politics in arguing that historicization of the image of Shaka allows us to begin to understand something of the making of popular apprehensions of Shaka. It looks at the way in which, over time, meaning has accrued to the image of Shaka.

Suggested Readings

Chimhundu, Herbert, "Early Missionaries and the Ethnolinguistic Factor during the 'Invention of Tribalism' in Zimbabwe." *The Journal of African History* 33, no. 1 (1992), pp. 87-109.

Cooper, Frederick, *Africa since 1940: The Past in the Present* (Cambridge: Cambridge University Press, 2002).

Glassman, Jonathan, *Feasts and Riot: Revelry, Rebellion and Popular Consciousness on the Swahili Coast, 1856–1888* (London: James Currey, 1995).

Mamdani, Mahmood, *Citizen and Subject: Contemporary Africa and the Legacy of Late Colonialism* (Princeton: Princeton University Press, 2001).

Spear, Thomas, "Neo-Traditionalism and the Limits of Invention in British Colonial Africa," originally published in *The Journal of African History* vol. 44, no. 1 (2003), pp. 3-27.

Vail, Leroy, ed., *The Creation of Tribalism in Southern Africa* (Ithaca, NY: Cornell University Press, 1989).

PROBLEM IV

COLONIALISM AND THE AFRICAN ENVIRONMENT

In the past thirty years, scholars have become increasingly aware of the importance of the environment as a subject of historical analysis. The field of environmental history has explored the ways in which human history has been influenced by environmental change, and the ways in which people have reshaped their environment. Interest in environmental history has been inspired in part by trends in other disciplines, such as geography and anthropology, as well as by growing public concern about contemporary environmental dangers, such as global climate change.

But much of the attention of environmental historians in Africa has focused on the colonial period. This is in part a result of availability of evidence—colonial authorities kept copious records of environmental phenomenon—but also because of the broader ideological interest scholars have expressed in evaluating all aspects of the colonial experience. Much of this scholarship has focused on the discourse of colonial environmental policy, which used the language of science, objectivity, and progress, to contrast Western environmental policies with the irrational, wasteful, and degraded land use strategies of Africans. This discourse underpinned colonial environmental policies that frequently had destructive effects on African ecology. A good deal of work has been done on colonial agricultural policies, which often had profound influences on the environment. Colonial interests in conservation of natural resources and animal species, particularly savanna mammals, also played a role in reshaping African environments. This chapter provides an overview of some of the main approaches to environmental history in Africa as they have emerged over the past generation.

William Beinart, a pioneering figure in African environmental history, begins the chapter with a historiographical introduction to the field. His piece demonstrates the historical context within which Africanists became interested in studying environmental history. He notes that in general, historians of the African environment during the colonial era share a common goal of subverting the claims to objectivity that underpinned colonial environmental policies. "Such approaches are beginning to assume the status of a new paradigm and have successfully inverted colonial stereotypes which celebrated Western knowledge and bemoaned Africans as environmentally profligate."

Leroy Vail describes how colonial policies precipitated an environmental catastrophe in eastern Zambia. In what was northern Rhodesia, British administrators attempted to secure African labor for European plantations, reserve fertile land for white settlers, and discourage Africans from hunting wildlife. They passed laws which required Africans to live in compact, easily policed settlements, and cut off their access to firearms, which were crucial to the hunting and trading economy. These policies had disastrous effects on the local environment. "The refusal to allow Africans to hunt and the insistence upon closely settled communities led to the development of large areas of bush in which an ever-growing animal population dwelled and set the stage for one of the major ecological reverses in eastern Zambia's history, the spread of tsetse fly and, with it, human and animal sleeping sickness." According to Vail, the effects of these ecological traumas continued to inform the region's poverty long after independence. Through the misguided, selfish policies of colonial agents, "The land had been rendered barren and desolate, and the finely balanced relationship between man and his environment that had existed in the area prior to the mid-nineteenth century was undermined, involving it in a process of underdevelopment still unreversed today."

Vail's scathing critique of colonial policies was part of a new wave of historiography that placed the blame for modern ecological problems squarely at the foot of the European rulers. One common element of this body of scholarship was the emphasis on misguided colonial understandings of African ecologies. In their groundbreaking environmental history of the French territory of Guinea, *Misreading the African Landscape: Society and Ecology in a Forest-Savanna Mosaic,* anthropologists James Fairhead and Melissa Leach demonstrate the fundamental misconceptions that guided conservation efforts in the West African region of Kissidougou. There, early French officials encountered an environment in which a patchwork of small forest groves stood among a savanna that they assumed had once been filled with trees. They understood the forest mosaic to be a degraded forest, which had resulted from ecologically destructive agricultural policies of local farmers. But Fairhead and Leach found that what colonial authorities viewed as "degraded" areas was, in the eyes of local farmers, "half-filled and filling with forest, not half-emptied and emptying of it." French interpretations of local ecology were informed by their desire to maximize forestry and cash crop cultivation by African farmers. But "by treating forest islands as relics, and savannas as derived, policy-makers may have been misreading Kissidougou's landscape, by reading forest history backwards."

Such scholarship emphasizes the unwillingness of colonial observers to integrate indigenous understandings of the environment into policy-making. However, JoAnn McGregor's study of conservation efforts in colonial Zimbabwe demonstrates that African ideas about land use and resource allocation were far from monolithic. Responses to colonial "common sense" land use initiatives were informed by political and social concerns. In the Shurugwi region of Zimbabwe, discourses of land use and management—like the supposedly scientific discourses that guided colonial policies—were embedded with conflicting subjective interests which militated against a single form of "indigenous knowledge." As she puts it, "Local narratives of ecological change and accounts of the success or failure of interventions there were colored by local politics and the particular configuration of alliances with the state."

In a similar vein, Helen Tilley observes that environmental studies of the colonial era too often treat the policies of colonial authorities as monolithic. Far from ignoring local knowledge, colonial officials proved willing at times to learn from African farmers. Tilley shows that colonial governments had contradictory policies and diverse interests that allowed for indigenous knowledge to inform decision making at times. According to Tilley, "it was research officers associated with agricultural departments who first began to undermine widespread assumptions of tropical Africa's natural fertility and drew attention to the relative inferiority of the soils. . . . They also began to speak in positive rather than pejorative terms about the techniques associated with African agricultural practices." Thus the "misreading the landscape" model overstates the inflexibility of colonial authorities and their monolithic approach to policy-making.

African History and Environmental History

WILLIAM BEINART[1]

Human beings are, before anything else, biological entities as Crosby reminds us. Their interaction with other species and with the natural environment, and their appropriation of the natural resources without which life is impossible, must be a central element in history. Significant sorties have been made over this terrain in a variety of historical writing, and more so in other disciplines. With respect to Africa, environmental issues have been a perennial concern for historical and physical geographers, anthropologists, archaeologists, and medical scientists. Historians and social scientists, however, have often been uneasy about incorporating environmental questions into their work, and not only because of disciplinary divisions and their lack of familiarity with the subject matter. Some earlier Western intellectual traditions evinced a strong environmental determinism to explain different forms of society, racial characteristics and social division. . . .

The new environmental history has in certain respects run in parallel with trends in African history because it shared many well-established Africanist moral concerns and perspectives: an essentially corrective and anti-colonial approach which emphasized African initiative in the face of European conquest and capitalist exploitation. It has been intellectually more congenial for Africanists to reintroduce environmental issues within this framework. At the same time, focus on environmental questions has extended the range of African studies, providing further scope for interdisciplinary interaction with geographers as well as natural and medical scientists. There are deep wells of accumulated research in such fields.

Environmental concerns have necessitated moving from well-thumbed administrative files to explore new archival sources. They have opened the way

---

[1] This excerpt is taken from a public address that was originally published as "African History and Environmental History," in *African Affairs* 99 (2000): 269-302, and subsequently web-published on the H-Environment web site. William Beinart is the Rhodes Professor of Race Relations at Oxford University.

to consideration of fascinating non-human agents in history such as fire and water, animals, insects, and plant invaders. They have raised further questions for oral fieldwork which are strongly familiar to the great majority of Africans who, until recently, lived in rural settings. Both African people, and the settlers and colonists who came to the continent, debated environmental issues intensely; nature and landscape have also been evoked in many different modes of cultural expression. An environmental approach facilitates the mining of rich but still neglected seams of intellectual and cultural history—from African fables and eco-religions to colonial fascination with botany and wildlife.

Colonialism and the Causes of Environmental Degradation

A number of interlinked lines of analysis in recent African environmental history bear considerable import for understanding the relationship between coloniser and colonized, white and black. Such approaches are beginning to assume the status of a new paradigm and have successfully inverted colonial stereotypes which celebrated Western knowledge and bemoaned Africans as environmentally profligate.

First, historians have explored the environmental consequences of colonial incursions including appropriation of natural resources such as wildlife, forests, minerals, and land by companies and settlers. This process was at the heart of European expansion from its very inception: a core myth of the foundation of Madeira, one of the first extra-European islands colonized, was a seven year fire by which this densely wooded landscape was cleared for settlement. Spanish *conquistadores* claimed tracts of the Americas, not only by reading proclamations and warfare, but by symbolically striking trees, or lopping branches with their swords.

Some Africanist writing shared what John MacKenzie calls the apocalyptic vision of global environmental history based on the profoundly disruptive colonial encounters in the Americas and Australia. Kjekshus' *Ecology Control and Economic Development in East Africa* (1977) is a sombre account of early colonial rule in Tanzania, sketching the impact of war and diseases such as smallpox and jiggers. Critically, he argued that colonialism spread the endemic tsetse fly and trypanosomiasis, causing sleeping sickness among people and effectively excluding cattle from large areas. Ecological catastrophe was reflected in a period of demographic halt or decline, perhaps comparable to the period of the slave trade in parts of West Africa. Leroy Vail painted a similar picture of the colonial intrusion into eastern Zambia. Colonial policies which curtailed hunting, encouraged concentrated village settlement, and stimulated labour migration exacerbated the effects of the nineteenth century Ngoni invasion by expanding the area dominated by bush, wildlife, and tsetse.

In the *Empire of Nature,* MacKenzie himself vividly illustrates the predatory character of settler and imperial hunting in southern Africa, which catastrophically reduced wildlife and was responsible for final extermination of a couple of mammal species, the quagga and blue antelope. Had other key species such as the elephant and lion been limited to the present day boundaries of South Africa, they may have been lost. Even where African chiefs such as Khama in Botswana and Lobengula in Zimbabwe, who retained independence till the late nineteenth century, tried to limit and control the process, they had little success. Environmental decay is discussed in many studies of partial displacement, or compression, of African societies into smaller areas of land as a result of settler colonialism from the Cape to Kenya. Water, the staff of life in more arid zones, was also directly appropriated. In South Africa, settler farms were often named after the captured fountains—Grootfontein, Brakfontein, Modderfontein—which initially sustained them. By the mid-eighteenth century, as the trekboers moved into the dry interior of South Africa, nearly 50 percent of new farm names were water-related.

Second, while colonial states in Africa facilitated appropriation of natural resources, some also became concerned about environmental regulation, including forest protection, game preservation, and soil and water conservation. They also attempted to eradicate, through environmental management, human and animal diseases, such as malaria, trypanosomiasis, and tick-borne maladies, whose complex ecological etiology was becoming apparent. . . .

Conservationist interventions, linked with other priorities of agricultural development, social control and segregation, also fed into wholesale attempts to change African patterns of land use. Such prescriptions, whether attempts to corral transhumant pastoralists into sedentary modes of life, or villagize societies with scattered settlement, have been seen in themselves as a major cause of rural degradation, both social and environmental. Officials and scientists often misconstrued local systems of resource use in attempts to protect nature from people, and assumed that labour for major physical interventions such as ridging and terracing was freely available.

Such resettlement and engineering projects, rooted in a scientific and modernizing logic, have been subjected to particularly critical scrutiny because they outlived the colonial era and remained central in the development strategies of independent African states and international agencies. Scholars have pointed to continuities in justificatory discourse, and in the patterns of "purposive rationality" espoused by bureaucrats in the post-colonial era. While they may have proposed very different property regimes, socialist experiments such as *Ujamaa* villages in Tanzania could share a similar approach to physical planning. In drawing together such critiques of "authoritarian high-modernism" on a global level, James Scott uses *Ujamaa,* alongside Soviet collectivization, colonial agricultural schemes, and the city of Brasilia, as key examples. Displacement necessitated by major engineering projects such as big dams seemed to advertise the arrogant aspects of modernity.

Third, the inadequacy of colonial and Western science has frequently been stressed, an argument strengthened by the failure of major schemes even after independence. While political resistance and bureaucratic incapacity played a part in the mishaps of planning, nevertheless lack of research, misunderstanding, scientific hubris, and technical weakness have all been demonstrated by researchers. Interventions designed to control trypanosomiasis by the slaughter of game or removal of people in the early decades of this century may have facilitated its spread. Kate Showers argues that faulty contour banks in lowland Lesotho, one of most eroded landscapes on the continent, caused more problems than they solved; storm water welled up behind them, broke through and caused new gullies. Ridges, encouraged and enforced in fields in many parts of British central Africa, could collapse in sandy soil, or, as in the lower Tchiri valley of Malawi, provide a nesting ground for white ants. The Nile perch, introduced into Lake Victoria in the 1950s to provide the basis for expanded commercial fisheries, ate indigenous cichlid fish which were not only at the heart of local supplies for consumption but ecologically unique on account of their diversity.

The devastating Sahel famines of the 1970s triggered renewed debates about the spreading Sahara in West Africa. French colonial scientists and their successors had linked deforestation caused by African agrarian and pastoral systems with desertification, drought, and famine. In *Adapting to Drought* (1989), a micro study of the Manga Grasslands in northern Nigeria, Mortimore, raised questions about the concept of desertification. He suggested that ecological change at a local level was still ill understood, that African people were undeservedly characterized as misusing natural resources and were highly adaptive in their approach. The boundaries of the grasslands he examined were much the same as reported by the Anglo-French Forestry Commission of 1937; drought could be associated only in a limited sense with anthropogenic factors. Much of the emergency, he argued, was caused by changes in rainfall patterns: "any farmer or stockowner in the Grasslands would call the problem underprecipitation, not overexploitation."

A further striking example, which has rapidly achieved paradigmatic status in the literature, is Leach and Fairhead's West African research on *Misreading the African Landscape*. They illustrate how, over many years in Guinea, French colonial officials and subsequent experts interpreted the patches of forest to be found in the savannah zone as evidence of deforestation and framed their interventions with this in mind. By contrast, Leach and Fairhead found that "elders and others living behind the forest walls provide quite different readings of their landscape and its making. At their most contrasting, they bluntly reverse policy orthodoxy, representing their landscape as half-filled and filling with forest, not half-emptied and emptying of it. Forest islands, some villagers suggested, are not relics of destruction, but were formed by themselves or their ancestors in the savanna. And rather than disappearing under human pressure, forests, we were shown, are associated with settlement." Scientists, they argue, could not easily divest themselves of colonial assumptions about the destructiveness of African agricultural methods especially where land was perceived to be short. Outside experts drew on a long line of orthodoxies in which Africans were depicted as botanical "levelers." Such analyses have emphasized that scientific understanding has been embedded in broader political and cultural agendas and that interventions have seldom been socially neutral.

Fourth, as a corollary, the validity and salience of local knowledge about the environment, and means of living in it, have become an increasingly rich area of research as well as a powerful ideological statement about the right to manage resources. It is a point made with equal force in respect of Australian aboriginal people or Native Americans, although, because so many of them were comprehensively dispossessed, the argument has potentially different and greater policy import in Africa and Asia.

Perhaps it is not coincidental that some of the most trenchant statements have come from West African contexts, in that this region was least affected by settler colonialism and maintained particularly innovative forms of African agricultural production. In his influential book *Indigenous Agricultural Revolution* (1985), Paul Richards explored the capacity of West African smallholders to make "the best of natural conditions," "capitalizing on local diversity." "This ecological knowledge" he argued, was "one of the most significant of rural Africa's resources" and was by no means simply a "hangover from the past." He focused on food crop strategies, especially low-technology wetland rice cultivation in Sierra Leone, where "people's science" was at work in the deployment of locally evolved seed varieties to cater for small shadings in natural conditions. Any outside aid, he argued, should work flexibly with local knowledge and techniques; oral and practical skills should not be shouldered aside simply because their practitioners were unqualified in science or had limited literacy. His research fed into concerns articulated by Calestous Juma in *The Gene Hunters* about the intellectual property rights of local people everywhere both over wild and cultivated species in the face of a new international "scramble for seeds."

Local knowledge has also been addressed in debates about the thorny question of the environmental vulnerability of common property regimes. These remain of central importance not only because so much of Africa, especially its pastureland, remains to some degree common, but also because a number of African governments are moving towards systematic policies of privatization; decisions in this sphere may have an impact on millions of people. In its older forms, the argument against commons was often a commentary on the "backwardness" of Africans, their cattle complex, and the apparently irrational imperatives of pastoral activity in which accumulation was measured in animal numbers at the cost both of their quality and that of the pasture. In its modern form, captured in Hardin's "Tragedy of the Commons," actors are seen as rational individuals who maximize exploitation of a free common resource at the cost of the resource itself. This analysis implied that African people overstocked not simply because of traditional attitudes but because individuals could accumulate without bearing the costs of maintaining the common pastures.

Africanists have tended to reject such simple renditions of the problems of common management. Counter-arguments have noted that private landholding has clearly been no guarantee against environmental degradation: there are many examples where freeholders or capitalists have mined the land and moved on. White farmers in South Africa on privately owned land have certainly been subject of a powerful environmental critique for overstocking their pastures since the late nineteenth-century. Borehole development and the government's Tribal Grazing Land Policy implemented in Botswana from the 1970s resulted in partial privatization of grazing land, at the cost, Pauline Peters shows, of intensifying both inequality and degradation. Moreover, people have gained access to commons as members of communities, with traditions of socially circumscribed usage; traditional authorities, customs, and religious ideas often reinforced constraints on exploitation. Systems of dispersing herds over wide areas, or moving animals seasonally between pastures, were commonplace in Africa.

Nor was it clear that African pastures were, in general, degraded. In a key article on overgrazing controversies, Homewood and Rodgers argued that there was limited evidence of serious degradation in common management systems. They questioned calculations of fixed carrying capacities for East African pastures and suggested that overgrazing was frequently invoked but not botanically demonstrated. Referring to Baringo district in Kenya, they maintained that "the history of the area is more suggestive of a series of oscillations in stock numbers and vegetation conditions precipitated by . . . climatic fluctuations governing this semi-arid area, rather than a long-term trend of anthropogenic environmental destruction."

An avalanche of studies in range ecology has developed such findings. At the heart of these new approaches is the idea of disequilibrium. Ecologists will search in vain, it is suggested, for a stable ecosystem with a predictable and optimum balance of "climax" vegetation. Range management practised by African pastoralists allowed for high-risk accumulation and heavy stocking at favourable moments, and also rapid loss in times of drought. Attempts at controlled management or stock limitation were not only likely to be resisted or to backfire, but were ecologically unnecessary. Evidence suggested that pastures could recover during periods of lighter stocking. These were powerful arguments against interventionist strategies and in favour of close attention to local techniques of management.

With respect to communal areas of Kwazulu, South Africa, which had long been seen as highly degraded, Shackleton suggested that the particular type of grass cover established through long and heavy common usage, though different, was not less productive. It apparently sustained consistently high stocking levels over a long period and local people had, by implication, found a way of maximizing pasture use with relative environmental safety. In Nigeria, Bourn and Wint found that much of the recent increase in livestock numbers was taking place not in semi-arid pastoral zones but in areas of population increase and agricultural intensification, as part of mixed farming regimes, and as a response to local tsetse clearance. Livestock, Mearns noted, were often good for the environment. Not only could common grazing lands be more productive than private ranches, but domestic animals could enhance soil fertility through spreading dung, and control bush encroachment. In sum: the economic and social benefits, especially for poor people, of access to commonage for their animals, vital for multiple uses such as draught, milk, meat as well as exchange, were not necessarily measured in environmental costs.

South Asian and Latin American literature about the "environmentalism of the poor," which adds a directly economic interpretation to the celebration of local knowledge, provides a parallel. In this argument, poor people, especially in rural areas, who are more immediately dependent on natural resources such as water, trees, or soil for sustenance have an overwhelming interest in retaining them in usable form as well as maintaining equitable access. In Africa also, many examples could be found of "indigenous" soil and water conservation.

Ecofeminist perspectives have informed an increasing appreciation of women's local knowledge about nature. Vandana Shiva elaborated gendered analyses of science as a patriarchal practice which facilitated projects of "domination and destruction, of violence and subjugation, of dispossession and the dispensability of both women and nature." Women, by contrast, have been presented as more benign in working with nature, and their local knowledge more replete with organic metaphors. Anthropologists have long recognized African women's role in the front line of managing nature, as the continent's main cultivators, and the specific content of their ideas and practices is increasingly being explored. Simultaneously, however, scholars are emphasizing that, in particular regions and societies, women's ideas varied considerably. While ecofeminism might provide some framework for examining these, it has served as a rhetorical and mobilizing set of ideas, rather than a sharp analytical tool: "by essentializing the relationship between women and nature, [ecofeminism] has represented history in generalized ways which entrap women in static roles."

Fifth, interpretations of the impact of demographic growth in Africa have changed significantly within this new environmental literature. Colonial ideas about population, especially up to the 1930s, were not uniform. While specific degraded reserve areas were judged overpopulated, Africa as a whole was sometimes conceived of as underpopulated. However, after the Second World War, colonial officials, and American foundations dispensing aid, increasing viewed population growth as a problem both for social and environmental reasons, because it would undermine development expenditure and exhaust natural resources. William Allan, a Zambian official with a deep understanding of African agricultural systems, nevertheless thought that the system of *citemene*, in which trees were lopped and burnt to form a rich ash bed for millet production, had become unsustainable because of population increase. Overpopulation ran in tandem with overstocking as an explanation of degradation.

These neo-Malthusian ideas have been challenged at many different levels: rich Western countries, it was argued, consumed more than even the most rapidly expanding populations of the South; a more equitable distribution of global wealth would in itself defuse the population explosion. Boserup made a positive correlation between population growth, agricultural intensification, and innovation. This has been extended and developed with respect to environmental impacts. Tiffen, Mortimore, and Gichuki demonstrate in their book *More People, Less Erosion* that peasants greened their land in Machakos district, Kenya, over a period of fifty years from an environmental low-point in the 1930s, despite increases in population. A key factor in their analysis is not only the significance of local knowledge in managing environments, and relatively cautious state policies, but the scale of investment and innovation in both intensified agriculture and conservation that accompanied denser settlement.

Sixth, scholars have systematically illustrated the centrality of conflicts over environmental issues in rural anti-colonial movements and rebellions. These were often of great moment precisely because natural resources were so central to the lives of rural African people. In late nineteenth-century West Africa, chiefs resisted attempts by the colonial state to assert control over forests. Disputes over management prompted them to make common cause with coastal lawyers and proto-nationalists such as Casely-Heyford. More robust colonial development and conservationist strategies, in both British colonial and settler territories following the Second World War, triggered widespread protests and helped to drive peasants into the arms of nationalists.

In Zimbabwe, conflicts over the threatened clearing of the Matopos National Park, near Bulawayo, and related interventions fed into the remarkable *Sofasonke* resistance movement in late 1940s. The National Democratic Party later found the neighbouring area a fertile ground for recruiting; tax collections were boycotted, dipping tanks destroyed and conservation regulations ignored. Joshua Nkomo addressed meetings in the park and Rhodes's grave was attacked. In the lower Tchiri district of Malawi, agricultural and conservationist planning was supported by the modernist chief Tengani, formerly an employee of the South African Railways, who tried to impose his own draconian discipline, time-keeping and agricultural rules on his people. This combination of colonial and local chiefly state, Elias Mandala demonstrates, fueled widespread dissidence. Nor have conservationist interventions been absent from analyses of the origins of Mau Mau in Kenya. Chieftaincy was often a lightning rod for such conflicts both because of the intercalary role of traditional authorities and their responsibility for many aspects of environmental management.

And last, the fortunes of African societies have long been enmeshed in wider economic and social forces; environmental degradation has been strongly linked with these processes which are also sometimes seen as intensifying African susceptibility to environmental calamity. Mandala's investigations of rural economy and ecological management in the Lower Tchiri valley in Malawi demonstrates how international and regional processes shaped its people's options in responding to floods in the 1930s; many men were pushed into the sub-continental labour market. Watts argues that the transformations wrought by colonialism and cash cropping hamstrung established strategies to cope with famine in northern Nigeria. Drawing on Amartya Sen's idea of entitlements to food, rather than drought, as the major cause of famine, Megan Vaughan and others have explained the centrality of markets, and economic and gender differentiation, in mapping susceptibility to hunger. Civil conflicts bred in the Cold War had far-reaching environmental repercussions: warring parties, linked to global markets, shot out elephants for their ivory in Angola and Mozambique. Millions of refugees placed intense pressure on resources in receiving areas. Debt, structural adjustment, the collapse of civil authority, and warlordism have prompted the stripping of natural resources for export and compounded environmental losses.

Ecology and History: The Example of Eastern Zambia

LEROY VAIL[2]

The focus of this study is the area between the Luangwa River and the Zambia-Malawi border. Prior to the arrival of the Ngoni in the area around 1855, it was inhabited by the Chewa and Nsenga peoples, who lived in the southern part of the plateau between the Luangwa escarpment and the border, by the scattered Tumbuka, who lived to the north of the Chewa on the plateau, and by the small Ambo, Kunda and Senga groups, who dwelt in the Luangwa Valley itself. The plateau enjoys a moderate climate, ample rainfall and a soil more fertile than that of most of Central Africa. It was thus able to support a relatively large population. In the early nineteenth century the Portuguese explorer Gamitto visited the area and was impressed by the density of the population and the area's natural wealth. As he wrote in 1832: "The country which the Cheva occupy, although much smaller than that of the Marave, is without doubt much more extensively peopled and cultivated. . . . The Chewa . . . have great wealth which they use in the satisfaction of their primary needs." The area at that time was peaceful and the land productive, enabling the Chewa to trade with neighbouring peoples for goods locally unobtainable. Ivory and slaves, for example, were traded eastwards to the chieftainship of Mwase Kasungu in exchange for salt. Tobacco and dried fish from the Luangwa Valley were traded for iron implements that were made in great numbers on the plateau. The area was so well regulated, according to Gamitto, that the people left "their harvest, still in the ear, in heaps on the village roads; they take from them what they require and are not afraid of theft." Further, there were no creatures "that destroy their gardens, and so they sow and reap without any damage except that caused by weather." The people's wealth lay not only in their fertile land, but also in their numerous herds of cattle. Once off the plateau, however, Gamitto

---

[2]This excerpt is taken from Leroy Vail "Ecology and History: The Example of Eastern Zambia," published in the *Journal of Southern African Studies* 3, no. 2 (April 1977), pp. 129-155. Leroy Vail was a professor of history at Harvard University.

descended into the Luangwa Valley, with its far sparser human population and a wealth of game that he thought unparalleled in any other area he had seen.

Into this country the Ngoni of Mpezeni penetrated in the mid-nineteenth century, bringing disruption in their wake. The Ngoni at that time were a warrior people who measured their wealth in cattle. The cultivation of crops was left largely to those people assimilated into the Ngoni system by capture, conquest, or clientage. Their arrival in eastern Zambia caused much disorganization in this area and the adjacent parts of Mozambique and Malawi. Livingstone, travelling through the country some thirty years after Gamitto, noted the changes that had occurred. The Ngoni were pillaging the Chewa, and the abundance of food reported by Gamitto was a thing of the past. To defend themselves, the Chewa had crowded into stockaded villages, and they enjoyed little freedom of movement.

In subsequent years, as the Ngoni of Mpezeni settled permanently in eastern Zambia, a distinctive settlement pattern emerged. For reasons of political cohesion and safety the Ngoni and their assimilated people lived in a thickly-settled area surrounded by broad, empty zones, once inhabited but no longer so. The new settlement pattern upset the old balance and, as it turned out, set the stage for severe ecological reverses in the colonial period. In the areas surrounding the Ngoni heartland, the bush regenerated. Animals soon moved in, creating hunting areas for the Ngoni. In the settled areas, the density of people and cattle reached unnaturally high levels. This was partly because the Ngoni preferred to live in a relatively compact area, but it was also because many people living to the west, near the Luangwa Valley, had fled to Mpezeni's country to escape the slave-hunting ravages of the part-Portuguese *prazo-holder,* Jose de Araujo Lobo, popularly known as Matekenya, who lived near Zumboy. In the mid-1890s a prospector visiting Mpezeni's country described the impact that the high density of people and cattle had had upon the land:

> Before us lay an undulating valley some miles in breadth, which, as the heavily timbered hills on either side proclaimed, had once been covered with forest, but was denuded of every vestige of a tree. Village after village surrounded by waving cornfields and green plains dotted with herds of cattle stretched away into the distance.

While the Ngoni enjoyed security in their area, the remainder of eastern Zambia suffered from the attacks of the Bemba, of Matekenya's forces, and of both the Mbelwa and Mpezeni Ngoni. The pattern of closely settled stockaded villages with large tracts of empty land between them became general. Into this situation the British penetrated in the mid-1890s, harbingers of capitalism and colonial administration and their attendant consequences. By this time

Mpezeni's people needed release into the surrounding areas, uninhabited now for some decades, as the soil of the heartland was becoming exhausted. A similar situation existed to the northeast, in the area of Mbelwa's Ngoni, and the necessary population release had been achieved successfully in the years after 1896. In eastern Zambia, however, governmental policy frustrated a similar easing of the pressure, thereby causing considerable stresses in the area. Additionally, the establishment of the colonial administration coincided with other events destined to accelerate the impoverishment of the people.

The 1890s were a disastrous decade for Mpezeni's people. Around 1893 a scourge in the form of jiggers attacked them. This was the South American sand jigger *(Pulex penetrans)*, which had spread throughout Africa from a beachhead on the Angola coast made in 1872. This vicious insect reached the Tanganyika-Nyasa Corridor area in 1892 and Mpezeni's country in the following year, bringing much debilitation in its wake. At about the same time, the great rinderpest epizootic swept through the area, decimating the wild game, which had provided an important source of protein to the local people, and killing large numbers of the Ngoni's cattle, their main form of wealth. Following hard upon these natural disasters came the military defeat of the Ngoni by forces of the British Central Africa Protectorate, fighting on behalf of the British South Africa Company, which had been granted administrative authority over the area by the British Government. The defeat of the Ngoni leadership in 1898 was accompanied by a further pillaging of the already depleted cattle herds. In 1906, eight years after the debacle, the African population of the area possessed only about 2,000 head of cattle, but a tenth of what they had held before their defeat by the Europeans. Thus rinderpest and Europeans had, together, destroyed the economic base of Ngoni society and rendered it peculiarly vulnerable to what the twentieth century was to bring.

The dramatic impoverishment of eastern Zambia's people was underscored by certain administrative decisions affecting not only the people themselves, but also the environment in which they lived. The Europeans who came to Central Africa in the 1880s and 1890s were eager to suppress the slave trade to release labour for wage employment. Further, as they were generally few in number, they desired usually to avoid trouble with the local population. They were also intent on gaining full control over the lucrative ivory trade. It was natural, then, that one of the key policies of British officials in Central Africa was to deny guns and powder to the local people. In accordance with Article 10 of the Brussels Act of 1890, Harry Johnston, the Commissioner of British Central Africa, in 1891 promulgated extensive gun laws curtailing the sale of firearms and powder to Africans and placing heavy restrictions upon the use of those already in African possession. At about the same time Europeans came to fear that excessive hunting was dispossessing Africa of her wild game, and in 1896 Lord Salisbury suggested that the issuance of licenses would control overshooting. The rinderpest epizootic, which killed many hundreds of thousands of animals in Central Africa, gave impetus to Salisbury's idea, and in 1897 the British Central Africa administration set up its first game reserve and promulgated restrictive Game Laws. Soon afterwards, Major Hermann von Wissmann, explorer, hunter, and Governor of German East Africa, urged international co-operation to save Africa's game. The British South Africa Company's response was to establish the Mweru Marsh Game Reserve in 1899 and to issue a set of Game Laws. In 1900 a conference on the protection of African wildlife was held in London, and this gave international sanction to the idea of conservation of animals in Africa. By 1902 a game reserve was established in the Luangwa Valley to preserve a rare type of giraffe.

For the people of North Eastern Rhodesia these decisions meant several things. First, the laws prohibiting the hunting and trapping of animals and forbidding the sale of gunpowder to Africans, promulgated at the very time that their cattle had either been seized or killed by disease, cut off a traditional source of protein. Nutritionally the people were worse off in 1900 than they had been in 1890. Secondly, during the dry season the people had traditionally hunted game, particularly the elephant. In this way, in addition to obtaining meat for food and ivory for trade, they kept in check the animal population. With the establishment of game and gun laws to protect wildlife and gain control over the ivory supply, the animals began to multiply rapidly. Whereas the plateau area had been reported by Gamitto as free from "creatures that destroy ... gardens," by 1909 the rapidly growing animal population was a major nuisance to the people and a threat to their sustenance. The most frequent complaint made to touring government officers was about damage done to gardens by wild animals, notably elephants and bushpig.

While government ordinances interfered with the food supply of the people and caused it to be threatened by wild beasts, the colonial administration also made other decisions respecting land alienation and village settlement, and these too had deleterious effects upon local standards of living. The Ngoni had concentrated people into large villages and had located these villages in a sharply restricted area. Surrounding areas were allowed to revert to bush. With the destruction of Ngoni power in 1898, though, there was no longer a compelling reason for the people to remain clustered together. Nor was there a need for non-Ngoni peoples to remain in their stockaded villages. With the increase in security, those who had hitherto lived in compact settlements began to spread out. Such a dispersal was not welcomed by authority, however. The collection of tax, one of the administration's main preoccupations, was far easier if all the people of an area dwelled in a single, large village. Also, as the administration was short-staffed, it wanted to employ traditional authorities as agents in its rule. It was noted as early as 1899 that "the natives, no longer fearing their chiefs, refuse to obey them, and consequently it is difficult for the Chartered Company's officials to obtain a hold over them." For greater influence and effectiveness the traditional authorities would have to rule over compact villages rather than scattered settlements. Amalgamation of the scattered people into larger villages thus became one of the administration's basic policies. Laurence Wallace, the Administrator of North Eastern Rhodesia, summed up this policy in 1908:

> The chiefs and headmen cannot control their people when scattered in small villages and single huts.... If the people collect into larger villages, the chiefs and headmen look after their villages, hear the small milandus (cases), and help the Boma by reporting crimes and in the collection of Hut Tax.

Thus, for administrative convenience the Administrator imposed and maintained a fundamentally abnormal settlement pattern upon the people, who were obliged to dwell in villages in numbers excessive for harmonious social life and efficient production.

In addition, especially around Fort Jameson, land alienation affected the lives of the people. In 1895 the British South African Company created the North Charterland Exploration Company by granting a concession of 10,000 square miles to the north of the Mozambique border, between the Luangwa River and the border with British Central Africa. This company sought to attract European settlers to raise cattle. Because cattle raising required extensive ranches, and because the most fertile areas of the concession were densely populated by Africans already, it was natural that a conflict between the company and the people over land tenure should have developed. From an early day the company pursued a policy of land alienation and establishing Native Reserves on the Southern Rhodesian model, with certain land seen as "European" and other land seen as "African." The policy's full impact was not felt until the inter-water years, but as early as 1903 the company established a reserve to free certain land for cattle raising. In fact, however, the large numbers of European settlers for which the company hoped did not arrive, and the land that was set aside for them tended to revert to bush, natural havens for the wild animals then increasing in the area.

The conflict over land was complicated by the British South Africa Company's tax and labour policies, policies dictated largely by the needs of growing capitalism in the South. Partly to raise money for the costs of administration and partly to stimulate the flow of labour to a Southern Rhodesia that was labour-poor because the Shona people there preferred a flourishing peasant economy to wage employment, the North Eastern Rhodesian administration decided as early as 1898 to institute a five-shilling hut tax. As employment opportunities were almost non-existent locally, and as markets for peasant production were exceedingly limited, the men of the area had little choice but to leave their families behind and journey to Southern Rhodesia to work, usually for periods of two years, but frequently for longer. The removal of the labour power of the healthy young men of the area had grave results for the local economy. In the first place, the prevailing method of agriculture involved a system of rotating cultivation, necessitating the clearing of fresh land each year to maintain the overall fertility of the soil. With the young men, to whom fell traditionally the task of clearing new land, absent, the people's ability to open fresh land lessened and productivity diminished. Cultivated areas became smaller and, as the lands became exhausted, crops poorer. In areas that in earlier times produced food surpluses there developed a situation of precariously balanced food supplies. This was especially noticeable in the Luangwa Valley, but it also occurred on the more fertile uplands. Secondly, the men's labour was also removed from the villages. There, the men had had the task of periodically rebuilding the houses. With the majority of men absent, and with deforestation a great problem in the African reserves. houses were used for too long and became dilapidated. This resulted in the proliferation of the *nkhufu* tick *(Ornithodoros moubata),* which inhabited dirty houses and caused the dreaded relapsing fever. Lastly, the removal of the men deprived rural society of its most vital element. Women and children and the aged, who comprised the majority of those left behind in the villages, were unable to organize and make function village life and so ensure adequate agricultural production. Instead, women contracted illicit unions in the absence of enough men, and these resulted in litigation and recriminations which strained village life. The constant absence of between 50 and 70 percent of the adult male population over a period of over fifty years could not but spell disaster for the fabric of rural life.

In almost every sphere, the rhythm of life was adversely affected, and the people left in the villages suffered increasingly both from the lack of food and the lack of energetic male labour. Nutrition became a problem as food supplies shrank and as animals which had earlier provided protein were under the protection of the law. The women and the children who remained in the villages eked out their existence by growing what they could and by supplying cheap labour to the local settlers. Early in this century, then, the essential characteristics of the colonial era had been impressed upon eastern Zambia. But the double impact of colonialism and capitalism was still new. As time passed, the pattern was etched deeper and deeper into the land and its people as the policies already accepted had their full impact and as new policies were implemented.

The refusal to allow Africans to hunt and the insistence upon closely settled communities led to the development of large areas of bush in which an ever-growing animal population dwelled and set the stage for one of the major ecological reverses in eastern Zambia's history, the spread of tsetse fly and, with it, human and animal sleeping sickness. Tsetse flies and trypanosomiasis both have a long history in Africa. In the nineteenth century European explorers found tsetse flies in Central Africa, particularly in the hot river valleys. There the flies lived on the blood of wild animals, especially buffalo, kudu, eland, warthog and bushpig. Without these game species, together with a suitable habitat, the tsetse disappears. The type of tsetse found in eastern Zambia, *Glossina morsitans*, was restricted in its habitat to areas where bush provided the light shade that it needs to survive. The great rinderpest epizootic had killed off most of the tsetse's natural hosts, and by 1896 eastern Zambia was largely free from the creatures. Thus, even in the Luangwa Valley, where game habitually abounded, cattle were raised by the local people successfully.

Protection of game and amalgamation of villages, coupled with the large-scale emigration of men from their villages, gave the opportunity for a remarkably quick regeneration of both bush and wild game following 1896. Harry Johnston, the first Commissioner of British Central Africa, had understood that the great enemy of tsetse was man and had advocated the destruction of Africa's wild animals to rid it of its tsetse problem. As he wrote:

> We must encourage the unchecked increase of the negro population in British Central Africa, for the presence of millions of men with strong arms . . . will soon dispel malaria, the Tsetse fly and other drawbacks to the utility of British Central Africa. . . . The Tsetse fly loathes the presence of man . . . and we have only to get those great riverain plains and lakeshores densely peopled to be able to chronicle its complete extinction.

His successors ignored his insight, however, and soon after the establishment of a game reserve in the Luangwa Valley an official reported that game was everywhere increasing in numbers. This is attributed to the . . . strict application of the Game Laws, to the general disarmament of the natives and the fact that there has been no disease amongst the game for many years. . . . The increasing numbers of natives killed by lions and the spreading of tsetse fly areas are undoubtedly connected with an increase of game throughout the country, and I am of opinion that the general protection of game is complete.

At the same time, game and tsetse were both reported to be spreading out of the Luangwa Valley focal areas onto the plateau to the east. And with the spread of the tsetse came the death of African-owned cattle that were infected with cattle trypanosomiasis, the parasite for which tsetse is the vector. From about 1905 onwards, official reports speak of the spread of tsetse and the dying out of African stock. The recrudescence of tsetse and the spread of cattle trypanosomiasis did not greatly concern the British South Africa Company's administration initially, as the fly was still far from European herds. Soon, however, the approach towards North Eastern Rhodesia of human trypanosomiasis, the dreaded sleeping sickness, shattered the administration's calm. Around the turn of the century the West African form of the disease, caused by the parasite *Trypanosomiasis gambiense,* suddenly appeared in the Uganda area, carried by the vector *Glossina palpalis.* Hitherto an endemic disease of low incidence, in its new environment it became a vicious epidemic affliction, and by 1909 an estimated 200,000 people had succumbed. This horrible epidemic greatly frightened the Colonial Office, and it sought to prevent the spread of the disease to other parts of the African empires. The threat to North Eastern Rhodesia appeared to come most directly from the Congo Free State. Here the disease arrived in its epidemic form from the Atlantic coast in the 1890s, reaching the areas near Lakes Tanganyika and Mweru by 1901. As most of the labour recruited for the Katanga mines then came from North Eastern Rhodesia, the fear grew that men returning home from the mines might carry the disease with them. The fear was substantiated in 1906, when the disease was reported at Lake Mweru itself. In 1907 an expedition under Dr Allan Kinghorn, of the University of Liverpool, arrived in North Eastern Rhodesia to try to stop the disease's advance at the Luapula Rivers.

At that time research into the cause of sleeping sickness was yet in its infancy. The cause of the disease, the parasite *Trypanosomiasis gambiense,* had been identified in 1901 by Everett Dutton, and in 1903 the Nabarro-Castellani-Bruce mission to Uganda had detected *Glossina palpalis* as its vector. The conclusions had been generally accepted, and an assumption grew that the causes of the disease had been wholly identified. Unfortunately, this was a false assumption. There was another parasite, *rhodesiense,* as yet unidentified. Its vector was *G. morsitans,* not *G. palpalis.*

G. morsitans was the very type of tsetse then rapidly spreading throughout North Eastern Rhodesia from its river valley focal areas. While Kinghorn and his colleagues were working against *T. gambiense* and *G. palpalis* along the Luapula, *T. rhodesiense* suddenly appeared well to their east, in Nyasaland, causing great concern to North Eastern Rhodesia's administration and ultimately bringing about the demise of one of the territory's infant industries.

In 1908 human sleeping sickness appeared at Dowa, in Nyasaland, hundreds of miles behind Kinghorn's battle-line. In 1909 an African youth, Chimpeni, died of the disease after reportedly being bitten by a *G. morsitans* in North Eastern Rhodesia's Petauke District. Soon afterwards a European, O. Phillips, died of the disease after a journey through the Luangwa Valley, where, in Petauke District, a *G. morsitans* bit him. As *G. morsitans* was not yet recognized as a vector for human trypanosomiasis, the local administration's first reaction was to place the responsibility for these two cases upon Nyasaland, suggesting that both people had travelled through Dowa. Under Southern Rhodesia pressure, however, it finally agreed to send an expedition into the Luangwa Valley in search of sleeping sickness and *G. palpalis.* This expedition was not encouraging in its results. Although no *G.palpalis* could be found—for none existed there—three indigenous cases of sleeping sickness were discovered at Nawalia, in Serenje District, in the middle of the Luangwa Valley. Two of the afflicted persons had never ventured further than ten miles from home. Further investigations uncovered another eleven cases, but still no *G. palpalis* came to light, much to the investigators' bafflement. Dr. Bagshawe, the Director of the Sleeping Sickness Bureau in London, supported by the Colonial Office, criticized the administration's doctors' astonishing lack of imagination and suggested that *G. morsitans* might be the vector in the Luangwa Valley. In response to this pressure, the administration closed the Luangwa area to the public, established a "Sleeping Sickness Zone," and accepted an expedition under Dr. Kinghorn to investigate.

This expedition proved of great importance to medical history, for in August 1911 Kinghorn identified the trypanosome carried by *G. morsitans* as the cause of the local type of sleeping sickness. Kinghorn also reported that about 50 percent of the animals in the Luangwa Valley harboured trypanosomes and suggested that the local people be permitted to shoot the game from the area and burn the bush to destroy the fly's habitat, both suggestions that were rejected by the local administration. In subsequent years both cattle and human trypanosomiasis became entrenched in eastern Zambia. The factors that encouraged its spread: protection of game, emigration of men, and the amalgamation of villages, all remained government policy. Thus, governmental decisions had given trypanosomiasis a head start by perpetuating and deepening the imbalance between man and the wild animals and bush that had begun in Ngoni days, and the disease made rapid headway under this protection.

This scare about the spread of sleeping sickness and the uncertainty about its vector brought an end to the European cattle industry in North Eastern Rhodesia, contributing directly to developments that were to worsen further the way of life of the people in the North Charterland Concession. With the end of the cattle industry, the settlers of North Eastern Rhodesia turned first to cotton and then to tobacco as a new source of income. Wanting the best possible land for these crops, the settlers and the North Charterland Company together pressed for the removal of Africans from good land into reserves. In 1910 the British South Africa Company, which held a third of the company's shares, agreed. In June 1913 a proposal to establish a complete system of reserves was presented to the area's chiefs, but the outbreak of World War I and the need for war carriers prevented the implementation of the plan until after the war's end.... World War I witnessed a rapid acceleration of the decline in the living standards of the people of North Eastern Rhodesia. Throughout the war, years' reports constantly tell of increasing tsetse infection and the death of cattle. Wild animals continued to multiply, bringing more and more destruction to African gardens and grain storage bins. The war's demands for carriers resulted in most of the men of eastern Zambia's being called from the villages to move supplies to the East African front. Thus, the labour available to cut new gardens and repair houses was further severely curtailed. After the war, inflation sent the cost of goods up over pre-war levels by as much as 250 percent, an increase in the hut tax from 5 shillings to 10 shillings was implemented, and the great Spanish influenza pandemic made its devastating appearance. In the Luangwa Valley the general misery was compounded by an outbreak of bubonic plague and a fresh epidemic of sleeping sickness. The war, then, marked a deepening of the patterns of deprivation that had been sketched out in the years before 1914. More than this, it marked the start of a twenty-five year period of accelerated ecological dislocation when, after the war, the colonial administration implemented its policies with a new vigour to the detriment of the physical and social health of the people .

This article has argued that certain policies of the colonial administration of eastern Zambia, based on convenience or fear, greed or ignorance, when combined with the impact of a growing South African capitalism, contributed to the fundamental deterioration of eastern Zambia, a deterioration which, in the form of erosion, tsetse fly, human sleeping sickness, and depopulation, is still in evidence today, particularly in the Luangwa Valley. Gun control laws stemming from the Brussels Act of 1890; game control policies arising from the London Convention of 1900; village amalgamation policies formulated to bolster waning chiefly authority and facilitate the collection of taxes: all of these placed the villagers out of harmony with the countryside. The imposition of a hut tax to stimulate labour migration, coupled with systematic labour recruitment drives which lasted well into the 1950s, deprived the land of its most productive labour power as the young men journeyed to Southern Rhodesia, leaving their families behind. The villages sank into decline as the women and children were unable to maintain them. Houses were used for too long, and *nkhufu* ticks, with their relapsing fever, gained a foothold. Sanitation pits were not properly maintained, and as the population grew, so did malnutrition and disease. The policies Government espoused at the behest of the North Charterland Company divided the land in an unjust manner, with the Africans granted as little as possible in order to generate labour for the Europeans. Africans were not permitted to grow cash crops so they would have to work on the European plantations. Land reserved for Europeans reverted to bush and provided havens for game, tsetse and trypanosomiasis. The land allocated to Africans, pathetically overcrowded and overworked, yielded to the seasons' rains and winds. Deforestation and erosion resulted in the desolate conditions of the late 1930s.

The period from 1898 to 1939 was a time when mistake followed upon mistake. Only after forty years of error did the colonial administration attempt to turn the processes it had been instrumental in accelerating. But the programme of rebuilding, impeded by a lack of money and the demands of World War II, was slow and uncertain. Too late were markets for African-grown crops provided; too late were "European" lands returned to the Africans; too late was it accepted that large, compact villages were unsuitable for the local environment; too late did the colonial regime put men before animals. As a result of the colonial experience, eastern Zambia was an area which provided much support for the nationalist movement when Federation was broached, with the movement's promises to rid the land of its colonial legacy.

Misreading the African Landscape

JAMES FAIRHEAD AND MELISSA LEACH[3]

Kissidougou's landscape is striking. Over open expanses of grassy savannah tower patches of dense, verdant, semi-deciduous rainforest. These forest islands, scattered over the gently rolling hills, are generally circular, perhaps a kilometre or two in diameter, and most conceal at their centre one of the prefecture's 800 or so villages. Apart from these islands, dense forest vegetation is found only in narrow strips along streamsides or swampy valley bottoms. This landscape resembles that in many parts of the West African forest-savanna mosaic or "transition" zone, which stretches along the northern fringe of the forest zone from Sierra Leone eastwards to Nigeria and beyond.

Since the first French occupation in 1893, Guinee's administrators have been convinced that these forest patches are the last relics of an original dense humid forest which once fully covered the landscape. They suppose that inhabitants have progressively converted this forest into "derived" savanna through their shifting cultivation and fire-setting practices, preserving only the narrow belts of forest around their villages. From the outset, this "savannisation" has been a major policy concern because of the threat it posed to the local agricultural and tree crop economy and to regional climate and hydrology. Today, and with the addition of global environmental concerns, the degraded and degrading landscape of Kissidougou attracts major international funding for environmental rehabilitation. These concerns are not unique to Kissidougou: they have been expressed throughout much of the transition zone, and elaborated during a century of scientific investigation.

Our research was originally conceived to engage with natural science and policy debates concerning savannisation, in a landscape the broad vegetation history of which seemed well known. We were broadly interested in the social dynamics of deforestation: in how different inhabitants understood this process

---

[3]This excerpt is taken from Fairhead and Leach, *Misreading the African Landscape Society and Ecology in a Forest-Savanna Mosaic* (Cambridge University Press, 1996), pp. 1-21. Melissa Leach and James Fairhead are professors of anthropology at Sussex University.

and responded to it technically and socially. Put crudely, we sought to elucidate its social causes, consequences and ramifications, and especially to identify how wider issues in the region's political economy articulated with these.

Early in the research, however, it became clear that the very pattern and direction of vegetation change in Kissidougou's forest-savanna mosaic was open to dramatic reappraisal. As this book explores, elders and others living behind the forest walls provide quite different readings of their landscape and its making. At their most contrasting, they bluntly reverse policy orthodoxy, representing their landscape as half-filled and filling with forest, not half emptied and emptying of it. Forest islands, some villagers suggested, are not relics of destruction, but were formed by themselves or their ancestors in savanna. And rather than disappearing under human pressure, forests, we were shown, are associated with settlement, and come and go with it. In short, it became clear that by treating forest islands as relics and savannas as derived, policy-makers may have been misreading Kissidougou's landscape, by reading forest history backwards.

That a landscape could become subject to such conflicting readings invites—even demands—consideration of the worlds which have generated them. In Kissidougou, our research agenda thus broadened not only to address what could be said about the making of this landscape and what its inhabitants made of it, but also to consider critically what scientists and policy-makers had made of it too, and the social contexts which had generated these different views.

Considering all landscape interpretations as in part socially constructed does not, however, negate the fact that certain readings can be demonstrated as false, and that historical evidence might support some more than others. Indeed if, as we shall argue, the views driving policy are demonstrably false but have brutal instrumental effects, it is the clarification of "real" history which renders apparent the power relations of which these views are part. This issue is more than academic. The view of Kissidougou's landscape as degraded and degrading has justified state action to take resource control from local inhabitants, and repressive policies to reorientate what has been seen as destructive land management. Many aspects of local land use have been criminalised. Setting bush fires—whose timely application has been a central feature of villagers" land management—carried the death penalty in the 1970s.

Formal fines and informal extortion by environmental services further tax an already cash-poor population. A landscape filling, not emptying, of forests under local land management would have very different implications.

The Making of a Landscape

A fundamental element of this study has therefore been to establish with as much precision as possible the course, pattern, and causes of vegetation change in Kissidougou's forest-savanna mosaic. Clearly, this first involves attention to evidence of vegetation change, which we have compiled from documentary, photographic, and oral accounts during the last century and before. It also involves attention to specific land management techniques, grounded in farmers' ecological knowledge, and to the social and economic relations which have conditioned land use. It is important at the outset to clarify the particular perspectives which we have taken in analysing these issues.

Land Management and Socialised Ecology

This study adds to a now large literature which attempts to document the agro-ecological knowledge of African farmers. In general, this literature demonstrates the sophistication of local land, soil, and vegetation management techniques, and the wisdom and creativity of farmers; in effect, the operation of a dynamic indigenous science.... When considering the ecological concepts and explanations employed by Kissidougou's farmers, however, it has not always been straightforward to understand these in terms familiar to the Western scientific literature on forest-savanna ecology.

This problem stems, at a fundamental level, from the framing of scientists' and inhabitants' explanations within very different root assumptions concerning the relationship between social and ecological processes. In short, since the Enlightenment, Western science has conceptualized natural and social phenomena as being of a different order—as a priori separate. It is assumed that "natural" phenomena can be investigated as separate from human society, except in as much as people and their social world are subject to "nature" and act on "it." Boundary problems are interesting, but do not undermine the conceptual scheme. It is partly this perspective which circumscribes the concerns of ecological science in the forest-savanna transition zone, encouraging ecologists to break down their consideration of vegetation into "natural" forms and processes involving plants, animals, soils, water and so on as if uninfluenced by people and society—so-called anthropic factors.

Ecologists who seek out untouched nature—pristine forest—against which to assess human impact are drawing on and reaffirming this divide; they may be disappointed, but not conceptually challenged, when they find pottery sherds in their soil pits beneath "natural" vegetation. Nature is an essential reference point against which to discuss human impact. Kissidougou's forest islands have proved a prime subject for this view, considered by ecologists as islands of more original, albeit threatened nature: the legacy of a natural "climax" vegetation remaining within an otherwise abused landscape. This ideal of nature has, of course, been central to conservation policies which have commonly deemed the exclusion of people as necessary for the preservation, or reestablishment, of nature.

Treating nature and people as opposed, and people's society as phenomenologically different, does not of course foreclose on analysis which theorises the relationship between "nature" and "society," culture and environment, or people and habitat (human ecology and cultural ecology). It does, however, structure the ways that such relationships are theorised.

Whatever the merits or otherwise of this perspective, one must recognise, first, that not all people conceive of social and ecological relations in this way: of nature and society/culture as separate objects of analysis which can be examined on their own, and in interrelationship. In many African societies, such a distinction is alien; categories of thought are structured in very different ways which crosscut a nature-culture divide.

Indeed unversed in western views about the nature of nature, Kissidougou's rural inhabitants, we shall suggest, broadly associate the presence of forest not with a near "natural" state, but with a "settled" state. And rather than seeing savanna as a cultural artifact (derived savanna, abused nature), savanna is associated more with vagrant, mobile, and impermanent lifestyles; with the human world perhaps of hunters, the mad, pastoralists, and refugees. One might be tempted to equate settlement with "social," and vagrant with natural, but when one sees that it is not just human life which has a settled existence and forest association, but also many land spirits and termites, which also live in "villages" associated with denser vegetation, such an equation becomes more problematic.

Furthermore, even if these conceptual categories were treated as analogous, one would find a second order of difference. While in western thought nature and society are, in their ideal form, inherently distinct, albeit acting on each other, for Kissia and Kuranko these potentially analogous concepts are inherently indistinct, moral, and fallible. Cycles of birth, growth, maturity and death common to people, land spirits and termites, and to animals, crops, and plants, can directly interfere with each other and must be scrupulously and actively maintained as separate. Space for human settlements and reproduction must be established as very separate both from the settled life of spirits and termites, and from the vagrancy of animals and crops. The problem is not how to theorise the interaction of these (the subject of western human ecology) but how to prevent it.

That inhabitants' categories cannot be fully understood in terms of western ones is noted in works throughout the West African region, and elucidating such differences has been the stuff of much social anthropological inquiry.

Such studies underscore how attempts to consider local representation in terms of these modern western categories obscure inhabitants' own perspectives on social and ecological relations. The relevance of this critique has, however, often been overlooked in the study of farmers' agro-ecological knowledge. Indeed, the extent of attempts to overcome western scientific categories can be used to distinguish two broad genres in the analysis of what has come to be termed "indigenous technical knowledge" or ethnoscience, at least when focusing on soil and vegetation phenomena. In such studies, the first and predominant analytical strategy has been to consider the wisdom of "folk" representations in terms of the conceptual apparatus of western natural sciences. This has evaluative aims, seeking to assess the validity of indigenous knowledge, and how it can be brought into a productive partnership with western science in environmental management and development processes.

A second genre, more firmly rooted in social anthropology, takes the more comparative perspective, asking how agro-ecological concepts (in natural science as much as ethnoscience) develop and make sense within their particular socio-cultural and economic, as well as ecological, milieu. From this perspective, for example, instead of searching for, and failing to find, the local equivalent of a western concept of plant "disease" to explain poor yields, it would be appropriate to investigate the broad ways in which farmers consider plant health. If farmers do not recognise disease, analysts would not deduce ignorance and hence the need to teach about it, but instead seek out other explanatory frameworks in which farmers consider ill health, with which scientists might be able to establish dialogue. To take a second example, instead of seeking out local knowledge of soil nutrient cycling, texture, and morphogenesis in exploring "indigenous knowledge" of soil quality, this perspective would hope to comprehend the operation of the field of local concepts pertaining to site productivity; concepts which may have no equivalents in western agricultural science. In Kuranko-speaking areas, as we will suggest, ideas of past habitation and of soil "maturity" and "oiliness" which have little obvious relevance to agronomic science are fundamental for comprehending farmers" rationales.

In attempting to evade the centrisms of the evaluative perspective, this genre explores the references or allusions which local ecological explanations make to other phenomena and everyday experiences, including those perhaps concerning human health, wellbeing and social life. Identifying these metaphors may be essential to comprehending what is being said. Attention to such "metaphors," moreover, can show up relationships which are considered to be stronger than mere likeness; where social and ecological processes are linked together intercausally. Thus when fishing fails, Kuranko might say that the water is "tied," when hunting fails that the bush is "tied," and when a woman "fails" to become pregnant, that she is "tied." Certain activities can provoke a state of tying across all of these domains; if, for example, a menstruating woman enters a fishing pool, both she and the water may simultaneously become tied. Treating tying merely as metaphor would obscure this, as well as hiding common aspects of fishing and hunting ecology in local representation: for example, when a senior hunter dies, both fishing and hunting immediately become tied. Importantly, attention to such links throws into relief particular ways that representations of ecology might be socialised. In contrast, the first, evaluative genre obscures how agroecological reasoning helps to constitute and reproduce the socio-political conditions within which it gains its sense, as well as the social implications of differing "ecological" opinions and assertions.

While much of western science examines natural and social phenomena separately, it is conventionally the disciplines of human and cultural ecology which have examined their interaction. Often locked into the nature-culture impasse, works in this genre have rarely sought to reflect on alternative ways in which "ecological phenomena" are "socialised," and social phenomena ecologised. The dominant perspective in these sciences, which became popular from the late 1950s, "suffered from a naive organismic view of society and a functionalism that saw culture as having adaptive value with respect to the general goals of living systems." Myth, ritual, and symbolic systems were thus examined for the regulatory role they played in shaping land use and understanding, such that ecological and social systems remained in equilibrium; equilibrium which was, in the most extreme versions, seen to operate through cyclical and homeostatic mechanisms. In Kissidougou, it is this kind of theoretical position which has enabled some studies to postulate the past existence of an equilibrium between a functional social order and "nature"—in its iconic form of a full forest cover.

Supposed forest degradation is thus explained in terms of emerging social dysfunction, and a breakdown of the culture-nature equilibrium. Such views of change in terms of "disruption" or "breakdown" of the systemic order, and a subsequent dialectic in which "culture" and "environment" are out of synchrony, are inherent to this approach. As Amanor argues, however, this perspective on ecology in effect "robs society of its history" replacing it with another "history" which obscures the parameters of local struggles. Furthermore in that the functional equilibrium of society and environment seen as worked out in unconscious ways, lying above human cognition, these cultural ecology perspectives tend either to silence local people's own analyses, or to co-opt them by reinterpreting them. In reducing "human organisation and consciousness to a regulative mechanism for preserving an equilibrium," functional equilibrium models rob people of their action and consciousness. As will become terribly apparent in the Kissidougou case, this is not merely academic debate. Social science analyses which draw on such functionalist models have become the complement to natural science in sustaining policy views of degradation. In contrast, local peoples" own theories concerning social and ecological issues carry very different implications for issues of agency, cause and responsibility in explaining vegetation change.

At the same time as theories of equilibrium have made a major impact on cultural ecology, ecologists themselves have been questioning their applicability to the natural world, refashioning their view of nature in the process, albeit within the society-nature distinction. This rethinking has involved a shift in fundamental assumptions about the orderly functioning of biophysical systems, which had been enshrined in the dominant perspectives of systems ecology. New attention has been given to issues of inherent instability, non- and disequilibria, chaotic fluctuations and the role of specific contingent events in ecosystems. This undermines classical representations of ecosystems in terms of tendency to equilibria, and of universal laws—such as of plant succession to climax vegetation—conditioning their structure and function. Sometimes heralded as a "new ecology," giving the semblance of providing a coherent alternative, this rethinking arguably amounts less to the provision of a single alternative than to freeing ecological reasoning from the strictures of unified theory, enabling theoretical pluralism. While they still examine the world within the conceptual nature-culture dichotomy, these views of nature nevertheless deny visions of society and ecology as in functional equilibrium. Correspondingly, they compromise managerial perspectives, whether in cultural ecology or policy, which assume that society can necessarily predict and manage ecological relations for stability.

We will argue that a more pluralistic ecology and appreciation of non-equilibrium issues provide conceptual space for reevaluating vegetation dynamics in the forest-savanna transition zone. When freed from its nature/culture straitjacket, this perspective enables better comprehension of local ecological reasoning, and reappraisal of people's roles in achieving environmental stability or directing change. This book therefore moves with others in this trend towards pluralism within ecological science, but simultaneously makes the case for an incorporation of land users' own perspectives and conceptual frameworks.

A pluralistic ecology also allows appreciation of actual environmental histories, rather than marginalising these to a narrow interest in intra-system oscillations as equilibrium perspectives do. As Worster points out, "Abstracted from time . . . ecosystems may have a reassuring look of permanence; but out there in the real, the historical, world, they are more perturbed than imperturbable, more changing than not." . . . In the case of Kissidougou, the past century has seen some major changes in the wider political economy. These include the effects of three severe political regimes: the rise and decline of Samori Toure's Dioula state (1860s-1893 in Kissidougou), the French colonial administration (1893-1958), and the state socialist "revolutionary" First Republic under Sekou Toure (1958-84). They include some major economic changes: for instance the early use of Kissidougou as a labour reserve during nineteenth-century slavery and early colonial rule, and the rise and fall of rubber, oil palm product and coffee export economies. In some periods populations have increased, but in others they have declined due to war and economic or political outmigration, and seasonal migration patterns have altered. Our historical analysis will trace how these changes have articulated with local social relations in influencing land use, an in the making of the forest-savanna landscape. The effects of environmental policy are themselves an important influence, since the environmental service has been one of the more penetrative arms of state intervention in Guinee's rural areas during the past century. Studies in environmental history have examined the history of colonial and post-colonial environmental controls and regulations and some have examined these in interaction with local land-use practices. But in following this analytical tradition, caution is needed in ascribing too great or direct a role to policy in the making of the African landscape. The effects of environmental policies must be contextualised in relation not only to the many other processes involved in shaping the environment, but also to the ways that villagers have dealt with, resisted, subverted or lived with them. . . . A central aim of this book is to recover the landscape readings of Kissidougou's inhabitants, and to put them into wider circulation. In establishing competing claims to truth about forest-savanna dynamics and landscape history, and in carrying very different implications for the control of rural resources in their links to particular institutions, inhabitants' landscape readings might also be considered as part of (a very different) discourse. Yet during investigation we heard less a single truth than contested opinion. Among the prefecture's Kissi- and Kuranko-speaking farmers, there is a plethora of ways of representing landscape history and dynamics which can vary in their implications for different people: for example for the resource control and claims of different women and men, and of longstanding citizens or recently arrived strangers. It would thus be wrong for us to portray a homogeneous "local" perspective on landscape and its making. Rather, we attempt to give a sense of the terms, operation and discursive structuring of local debate.

Conservation, Control, and Ecological Change

JOANN MCGREGOR[4]

Settlers' rapacious and destructive use of resources was the main environmental issue for Southern Rhodesian officials in the first decades of the twentieth century. Deforestation on a previously unknown scale had accompanied the expansion of mining, because the mines depended on abundant timber for construction and fuel. Miners' legal rights ensured them access to wood and other resources free of charge on gold belt title land, and elsewhere they paid only minimal fees. Mine timber contractors commonly chose to cut in African areas, where they could easily avoid tariffs, and by the 1920s, Native Commissioners in mining districts were complaining of "utter denudation of timber," though they were powerless to control it. Timber on European farms, in contrast, had a degree of protection through private title outside the gold belt and, later, by virtue of farmers' increasing political influence.

Officials also criticised crude settler agriculture which was eroding and depleting the soil, destroying wetlands and river banks, and silting up streams. Though for many settlers, farming "meant only cutting down trees and selling wood, or cultivating a small patch of mealies," others were cultivating to "get rich quick"—at the cost of "mining" the soil of its value.

Agricultural, irrigation, and forestry officials argued that this environmental destruction threatened future production and the future of the colonial project itself. Severe regional droughts in the 1920s and the dramatic loss of top soil on white farms in the rains of 1928 served to reinforce these views." Officials' anxieties, however, did not simply reflect the misuse of Southern Rhodesian resources, but were shaped by and themselves reinforced regional and Empire-

---

[4]This excerpt is taken from JoAnn McGregor, "Conservation, Control and Ecological Change: The Politics and Ecology of Colonial Conservation in Shurugwi, Zimbabwe," published in *Environment and History* 1, no. 3, Zimbabwe (October 1995), pp. 257-279. JoAnn McGregor is Reader in Human Geography at the University College London and Deputy Chair of the Board of the *Journal of Southern African Studies*.

wide alarm. Epitomising this attitude, the editor of the *Rhodesian Agricultural Journal* in 1928 raised the prospect not of national, but global deforestation within 37 years. The body of technical officers in Southern Rhodesia were part of an expanding scientific community who debated and published on the relationships between vegetation cover, soil erosion, rainfall, and climate. Deforestation and soil erosion were blamed for declining rainfall, drought, and desert encroachment. The ideas of the time were misleading in their understanding of the relations between forests, hydrology, and climate and exaggerated in their conclusions, for example about the physical effects of deforestation per se. However, their alarm provided a basis for intervention.

From the late 1920s, a barrage of conservation legislation was put on the statute book: the Water Act of 1928 was followed in 1929 by the Native Reserves Forest Produce Act and the Game and Fish Preservation Act. If the timing and context of much of the legislation reflected the ideas of a regional scientific culture, Southern Rhodesian segregationist politics and the interests of different segments of Rhodesian settler society can explain its implementation. The conservationist goals of the various Acts implied a common interest in the preservation of the colony's resources for future generations, yet the discourse surrounding enactment and implementation increasingly placed blame on African misuse of the environment and justified unequal restrictions.

The Native Reserves Forest Produce Act (NRFPA) was the first piece of conservation legislation which provided for state regulation of resource use specifically within the native reserves. It banned tree cutting for any purpose other than the "direct fulfillment of subsistence needs," protected selected valuable species against felling for any purpose at all, and regulated timber concessions by means of an application procedure operating through Native Commissioners.

There was no doubt that the legislation threatened miners' access to timber in the native reserves. To secure its passage, the Act's supporters from the Departments of Agriculture and Native Affairs cast the regulations as intended to preserve trees for future mining use, attributing the blame for deforestation to Africans, particularly their use of fire and shifting cultivation. The Chief Native Commissioner Sir H. J. Taylor explained to Parliament:

> The Native Reserves Forest Produce Act aims at conserving and developing the woodlands of native reserves, a chief asset of the natives which needs protection from the natives themselves as much, perhaps, as from other exploitation.

The Water Act restricted cultivation within 30m of a water course on the grounds of erosion control. It was enforced in the native reserves in association with land use planning after 1929, when the designation of arable blocks on the dry watersheds restricted cultivation of wetlands except in the form of small dry season vegetable gardens (the effects of which are described below). This legislation was not enforced against settler agriculture.

Conservation legislation was enacted as the depression was deepening, as the commitment to racial segregation was renewed and state "development" of the increasingly crowded African reserves was bringing technical officials into contact with African producers in a new way. White farmers fiercely opposed further land allocation to Africans and, fearing competition, fought against these "native development" programmes. In the face of opposition from settlers, officials in the Native Affairs Department emphasised how conservation interventions would obviate the need to allocate further land to Africans and justified their "development" policies by emphasising their conservationist value. New discriminatory maize and cattle marketing legislation in the 1930s secured markets and elevated prices for white farmers whilst it simultaneously undercut African production. The unequal application of conservation legislation also helped shore up European agricultural and mineral production.

Some headway was made with voluntary conservation schemes for the white agricultural sector. The country's first Irrigation Officer, responsible for soil erosion, was appointed in 1921 and, as the result of his efforts, one tenth of settler agricultural land was contoured by 1936. After financial incentives for conservation were introduced in the same year, this figure rose more quickly to a quarter of all land by 1938. In the native reserves, contouring programmes began only in 1936 and the alliances and coercion used in implementation are described below.

The success of incentive schemes for settlers, however, was not matched by the enforcement of restrictions on settlers' resource use. The new legislative controls on cutting by miners and timber contractors were a case in point. Native Commissioners argued that there was a trade-off between conservation and development, and most prioritised the latter. Some were loathe to forego the sizeable revenue from timber tariffs which funded "development" in the reserves. Others waived tariffs on the grounds that free timber reciprocated the "development" miners brought to the country by providing jobs or by "opening up" formerly remote areas; deforestation in these instances was portrayed as the cost, even the necessary cost of improvement. At other times, tariffs were waived as it was feared they would "bear harshly" on the mine in question. "Conservation" in these instances took second place to miners' economic interests and the developmental project of colonialism, yet the existence of environmental regulations (even if unenforced) could be upheld as a step in the right direction.

In contrast to this leniency towards settlers, the Act was used to levy tariffs on Africans selling firewood, because their "flagrant profiteering" constituted "unfair competition" for European vendors. Blanket restrictions on peasant farmers cutting live trees were also included under the Act, but these controls remained hortative as they criminalised every African household and the Native Department had neither capacity nor strong inclination for such a project.

After the mid 1920s, officials increasingly argued that Africans caused more severe damage to natural resources than settlers. For example, in a review of forestry in the country, the Chief Forest Officer explained:

> It is common knowledge that the native method of cultivation, i.e. clearing and burning together with uncontrolled grazing for pasture causes more damage to forest growth than can ever occur through mere extraction by felling.

This shift in the representation of the causes of environmental problems in official discourse can be interpreted as expedient in segregationist Rhodesian politics: it allowed the passage of legislation threatening to miners' interests and justified inequitable enforcement of controls. But the increasing emphasis on African misuse of the environment also reflected regional trends and was part of a wider colonial scientific culture. Backward native populations' wasteful destruction of natural resources was a dominant theme of Empire-wide discourse in the 1930s: it became part of officials" training, was repeated in conference presentations, technical reports, and scientific journals. The fact that these views were "scientific" and were propounded by scientists gave them weight and an appearance of objectivity.

Hegemonic colonial views on African misuse of the environment were not, however, uncontested: technical officers disagreed over which aspects of resource misuse were the most important and even over whether African agriculture was a conservation issue at all. Although agriculturalists had called for controls on forest use, in general they were less concerned about deforestation than forestry officials. Emery Alvord, American missionary and later Agriculturalist for the Instruction of Natives, was principally interested in agricultural improvement rather than conservation *per se*. He found Rhodesian technical officers' conservationism exasperating and complained retrospectively of their "tree conservation complex," elaborating that, "It was the fixed obsession of official opinion that all trees must be preserved. No thought or consideration was given to proper land utilisation. . . . Significantly, Alvord's influence dominated policies of rural improvement in the reserves from 1920 to 1938.

The effect of conservation policy in this period was a failure to redress the major environmental problems, particularly those caused by miners, though changes to settler agriculture were significant after financial incentives were provided. Legislation was enacted, then enforced, in support of various settler interests. The prioritisation of "development" over conservation when they were perceived to conflict further ensured that conservationist restrictions on settlers were ineffective. The "vexed question" of mine timber was only resolved with comprehensive legislative controls enacted under the Forest Act of 1948, by which time the controls were partially redundant because miners' need for timber had in any case been drastically reduced by the National Electricity Grid." The next section turns to a case study of the District where conservation initiatives for the native reserves were piloted, to consider their impact and local interpretations.

State Intervention and Ecological Change in Shurugwi

In the reserves, officials feared environmental problems per se, and their consequences for productivity. Shurugwi was considered to be one of the worst cases, portrayed in the 1920s as teetering on the brink of ecological and economic disaster. Alvord, for example, held that "destructive tillage," "misguided" agricultural practices, and a "traditional" way of life had ruined the land. Ironically, Chief Native Commissioner Taylor made Alvord's appointment to the post of Chief Agriculturalist for the Instruction of Natives in 1926 partly in response to an article published in the Phelps-Stokes Education Report, which asserted that African methods of cultivation had been condemned too hastily in the past.

Although officials portrayed African agriculture as unchanging, the first three decades of the century had seen far-reaching transformations to agricultural practices which preceded state agricultural intervention. On the sandy soils of the midlevel of central and southern Zimbabwe, extensive, shifting dry land cultivation had become increasingly important where previously intensive wetland ridging had dominated, and metal ploughs caught on quickly after 1910. Far from being timeless customary practices, the growing emphasis on shifting and dry lands were new developments, made possible when people could move out of their defensive hilltop settlements. The changes were attractive as they improved returns for labour and gave younger men an unprecedented autonomy from their elders. In Shurugwi's characteristically fissive and decentralised Karanga chiefdoms, these changes undermined the control of chiefs, headmen, and household heads over both people and land use. Although the new dry fields were more drought-vulnerable, freshly cleared fields were relatively fertile, shifting reduced the impact of weeds, and the millets and sorghums grown in a good year could be stored for several seasons. Maize could be sold on a large scale to the new markets of the settler economy in the "decade of peasant prosperity" from 1915-1925 which preceded the Maize Control Acts of the 1930s.

Officials" descriptions of African agriculture and of environmental change can be misleading because they portray shifting cultivation as universal and "traditional"; because they fail to consider practices in relation to the economic constraints of land, labour, capital, and markets or to the ecological constraints of infertile soil, abundant weeds, and patchy and variable rain; and because they present all cutting and burning of trees as a bad thing. Later documents ignore, downplay, or misrepresent the effects of land alienation and land use policy.

Colonial land policy had a dramatic effect on the patterns of agricultural change underway in the native reserves. The implementation of segregationist land policies speeded up after the Native Reserves Commission of 1914-1915 and involved "squeezing" people into reserves, causing land scarcity and much hardship as Shurugwi's inherently infertile soils were quickly exhausted. The population of Shurugwi reserve more than doubled over the five years from 1923-1928 and was to receive further evictees in subsequent decades.

However, environmental degradation was more than just a process of spatial marginalisation, whereby the poor were forced by land appropriation into small areas of poor quality land and were then compelled to extract their surplus by degrading their environment. Though ecological changes did stem from congestion and segregation, their particular form was shaped by state interventions in the reserves and the way these were manipulated at local level. The policy of centralisation implemented from 1929 onwards was particularly important in this respect.

Centralisation involved reorganising land use, separating blocks of arable and grazing land on either side of a central linear village located on the watershed. The project was justified in different ways to different audiences and changed over time. Similar policies were already underway in the Southern Africa region for diverse reasons. One tradition of settlement planning was that of strategic village consolidation for subjugation and administrative control. Another tradition was the planning and layout of "model villages" by missionaries as part of their endeavour to civilise. Centralisation was also to become a standard part of agricultural improvement packages in the region.
. . .

Big men with sizeable cattle herds and the ability to command labour had been able to benefit from this programme to introduce improved seed and manure-fertilisation, which was particularly suited to relatively well-watered environments such as Shurugwi where yields were constrained by poor, sandy soils. They welcomed the demonstrator "because he had knowledge" and were attracted to the idea of consolidating grazing land which Muhloro and Alvord discussed at length together, because it "stopped you getting into trouble for herding your cattle in someone else's land."

Headmen were used by the state to collect taxes after 1914 and had gained the title "owner of the book" *(sabhuku),* so had an administrative interest in the new layout centralisation introduced. One kraalhead emphasised this point:

At first we refused to go into lines. . . . But then some headmen [*sablmku*] joined the demonstrators. The chiefs were adamantly against the idea. It was the *sablmku* who was responsible for collecting taxes. It was going to make their job easier if we were in a line and orderly.

But headmen could also benefit in other ways. They were able to use centralisation to gain control over evictees and other immigrants who flooded into the reserve. They could also use it to try to reassert their authority over juniors and former dependants who had taken advantage of the new opportunities and independence provided by the settler economy. Moreover, headmen could secure privileged land rights for themselves in the face of increasing scarcity. Unlike later centralisations, state agents did not allocate individual holdings within the arable block and some headmen themselves secured sizeable land holdings—several times larger than the supposedly reduced, egalitarian and intensively used plots. As headmen often owned sizeable cattle herds, they and other big men also stood to gain disproportionately from any improvement to pasture, controls on residence, or cultivation in grazing land. . . .

This alliance between some state-salaried headmen *(sabhuku)*, a handful of wealthy Christian progressives, and the Native Department undermined the authority of the local chief Nhema, who tried to obstruct the scheme. Nhema's inflated status as "paramount" over other chiefs had been brought about by the colonial state, but the authority his title conferred was contested by other chiefs in the district, and was nominal in many ways; headmen and other chiefs had a marked degree of autonomy. The influential headman Muhloro was head of one of the many houses of the Nhemachiefly lineage, and acted explicitly against the incumbent chiefs' wishes in adopting land use planning. Nhema's adamant resistance to centralisation was short-lived and the following year he gave enthusiastic support, bringing about an alliance with Muhloro and the state which gave him economic and status benefits. Alvord did not initially interpret the chief's interest as derived from enhanced authority and control over people, but attributed it to seeing the tangible benefits of fatter cattle. However, in 1931, he noted that centralisation was considered:

> most beneficial . . . much satisfaction was expressed in the fact that headmen now know where each man on his book is living and where he has his lands and cattle with the result that all headmen and chief Nhema have better control over their subjects than before.

In official eyes, Nhema ceased to be the "conservative reprobate steeped in superstition, witchcraft and taboos," and was thereafter "intelligent" and "ambitious for his people."

Whole communities were centralised after a headman's or chiefs' decision. Many said they heard of the scheme only as an order from the demonstrator, headman, or chief: "It was not a question of what we did or did not want, it was an order!" Coming as it did in the wake of the first phase of forced labour recruitment following land alienation, evictions, and taxation, many felt their best tactic was to comply with the demonstrators' "new laws." "As it was the headman who was told how many men were needed for forced labour *[chibaro]*, and as he selected them, so you had to keep friendly with the headman," one old man explained. The experience of prior state compulsion was emphasised in many of the oral accounts of this early phase of state intervention, although historical studies tend to downplay the use of force in the "protective" phase of official development ideology in the 1920s and 1930s and stress its use only when compulsion became explicit policy in the 1940s.

This enthusiastic adoption of centralisation by some headmen in northern Shurugwi is not typical of other parts of Shurugwi, or of other parts of the country. Some chiefs and headmen in the district opted for a populist strategy of resistance. One chief resisted for six years and centralisation was only brought about in 1935 following his arrest and the appointment of a new chief. From this part of the District, some saw chief Nhema as a "yes man" and sellout: one old man joked that Nhema only wanted the village lines so that he could move up and down them drinking beer. Another leader evicted into the area accepted centralisation as a necessary cost of obtaining land, whilst headmen remaining on land alienated to Europeans similarly accepted it as a potential means of avoiding eviction or because they thought they had no choice.

The policy was not perceived as environmentalist in intent, and its adoption was not based on a consideration of its conservation value. Moreover, its impact was rarely perceived as conservationist—even by the scheme's supporters. Mr. Mulausi, the first agricultural demonstrator in Shurugwi, was responsible for implementing centralisation and was an ardent advocate of its value from a "development" point of view, because it marked the acquisition of new knowledge and orderly villages, but nonetheless recounted how the "conservation phase" came after the new village lines had been created. As an administrative measure, centralisation could facilitate the introduction of other policies by the state, including conservation policies, but, in itself, had no direct conservation value. As centralisation was implemented around the country, the state increasingly used conservation arguments in its justification: these suited the segregationist land policy, had administrative appeal, created a sense of urgency and later added weight to justifications for the use of force. . . .

Though centralisation brought about many negative environmental changes, it did not herald environmental collapse. Land became scarce and was increasingly unproductive if used permanently without labour intensive fertility inputs; however, the other resource scarcities perceived by officials were not experienced by many living in the reserve at this time. The clearance of trees had religious and ecological implications, but did not create economic scarcities: wood was still available from rocky parts of the landscape (kopjes and incised river valleys) whereas parts of the landscape which did not have a high physical stock of trees were nevertheless highly productive of woody biomass. There were even complaints about too many trees in some places.

People could generally still find the timber, fuel species, and other forest produce they wanted, as long as they had the time and labour to collect it. Grazing land supported herds of increasing size and some small game was still available in the reserve. Old people commonly recalled that they were scared of tracts of unoccupied forest, which were reputed to harbour thieves, feared spirits, and wild animals. They were not, therefore, unanimously grieved in seeing the reduction of the woodlands.

Not all deforestation was a bad thing to everyone. Interpretations of ecological change occurring in centralisation's wake often emphasised the violation of the spiritual order and physical destruction or profanation of specific sacred sites which occurred in the process of state intervention. Some described the village lines themselves as an offence to the rain god at Matopos, and to ancestral and land guardian spirits. Some described how the deforestation which accompanied state intervention caused sacred springs and forests to dry out and sacred river pools to silt up, so transforming and making "salty," dry and dirty the moist, cool habitats preferred by spirits, and leading to their departure. Some sacred woodlands were cut down as the landscape was reorganised, whilst lion spirits *[mhondoro]* in those which remained were said to have begun to depart after this period. The breach of "traditional" ecological controls was disrespectful of the ancestors and the order they upheld through elders.

These explanations were not universal. Some people used deforestation as a metaphor for development rather than profanation and portrayed life in the bush as the epitome of backwardness. The departure of the old order—symbolised by deforestation and the new watershed village lines—was neither regretted nor regarded as a problem by everyone. One master farmer recounted how "centralisation was a good thing: it was good to control grazing, farm properly and have smart villages. People objected at first because they didn't understand these things." Others spoke favourably of applying the demonstrators' knowledge, referring to past ways disparagingly or merely emphasising how times had changed. Many explained how they got used to the lines over time.

Dispute over the interpretation of environmental change was important in local politics because of the relationship between maintaining the fertility of the land and legitimate "traditional" authority. Prior to state intervention, local authority was legitimated by establishing one's ancestors as indigenous or as having been given land by the autochthonous and previously land-holding

Rozvi. Such a history gave privileged access to land spirits (ancestral spirits and/or lion spirits known as *mhondoro* which in Shurugwi were usually Rozvi spirits). Edicts from *mwari*, the rain god of the Matopos, reinforced the importance of respecting local spirits. The moral code of environmental practice and ritual, which local leaders and spirit mediums upheld, not only invoked communal environmental benefits such as rainfall and fertility but also defined a relationship of control over both territorial resources and people.

Such local authority was profoundly challenged by the opportunities which accompanied the political and economic changes of the early colonial period. Large-scale immigration of evictees with their own leaders posed further challenges to local authority, as did heightened competition over resources. In response, some local chiefs, headmen, and cult messengers began to exhort traditional ecological controls with renewed vigour, underlining their own legitimacy as autochthons, elaborating in greater detail the fate of those punished by land spirits, and beginning to threaten, introduce, or step up fines or other punishment for breach of the rules.

Existing local leaders required incoming evictees and other immigrants to recognise their authority. "Newcomers" were supposed to respect the chiefly and autochthonous land spirits, and to obey the moral code of environmental practice. However, immigrants could use the fact that they were outsiders to claim that they did not know the ecological regulations, or that the rules were not for them: they cut in sacred woodlands and used forbidden species. Those who came in sizeable groups with their own leaders sometimes set up their own rain shrines, organised their own ceremonies and made contact with the messengers of the *mwari* cult. Breakaway factions of local families could also establish themselves independently. Some Christian churches set themselves up in opposition to "traditional" religion and provided further reasons for noncompliance with the existing order. In this context, the state could provide a more effective and less easily contested authority over people and resources than "traditional" land guardianship. As described above, some headmen chose to invite and effectively manipulate centralisation in their own political and economic interests. . . .

Local narratives of ecological change and accounts of the success or failure of interventions are coloured by local politics and the particular configuration of alliances with the state. As retrospective accounts, they are also influenced by current attitudes. But evidence from official accounts also has to be handled with extreme care: just as centralisation's supporters saw the value of the lines in terms of "staying tidily *[kugara kuchena],*" officials who argued that centralisation was "successful" in Shurugwi often used aesthetic criteria as evidence, such as the orderliness of the lines of houses, and saw the new organised landscape as itself symbolising development. Others pointed to the administrative benefits rather than positive environmental change as justification. The argument that rural afforestation was a success could be based on the fact that trees were planted—even if they were not used because there was no demand for them at the time. More generally, the reports themselves are often contradictory. Technical officers had an interest in identifying problems which their professional training and state intervention would solve: reports often exaggerate problems caused by "traditional" practices to reinforce the need for a more far reaching state natural resources strategy. The visit of an investigatory Natural Resources Board team to Shurugwi in 1942 was 13 years after the first villages were centralised and 8 years after the majority had been laid out. The Shurugwi diary noted:

> This reserve was the first to be centralised and it is claimed that thereby the conditions in it have been greatly improved—indeed it has often been cited as an example of what centralisation can do. Quite apart from the merits of centralisation the fact remains that the whole area is in desert conditions. . . . To save this reserve . . . it seemed to the board that nothing short of withdrawing it from occupation for a sufficiently lengthy period to give it time to regenerate would suffice.

These accounts contradict other reports lauding the achievements of centralisation in conservationist terms. The exacerbation of some environmental problems subsequent to the implementation of "conservation" and land policies did lead to some questioning of policies and the knowledge on which they were based. However, the outcome of such questioning in this period was to heighten prejudice against African agriculture and to reinforce the need for technocratic solutions. The conservationist and increasingly technical debate allowed African demands for land to be circumvented and provided a justification forth need to educate and change practices by force. This trend culminated in the 1950swith the apogee of technocratic policies—the Native Land Husbandry Act.

Conclusions

Official readings of the landscape were made in a political context of segregation and racial dominance. They drew on scientific understandings promoted by their technical training and a hegemonic colonial ideology of disrespect for African production. Within this context, however, representations of ecological change were nonetheless much contested. "Conservation" arguments were used in a variety of ways in Southern Rhodesian politics. Officials came to use the interest of "conservation" to justify centralisation after it had already been introduced for other reasons: it added legitimacy to "development" policies at a time when they were not otherwise politically acceptable to settlers. At the same time, however, conservation policies were dropped when they were perceived to conflict with settlers' interests which were defined as "developmental"—for example, continuing to allow miners access to trees in the reserves on the grounds that they were bringing development to the colony. Conservationist arguments later provided the cutting edge to arguments for the use of force to implement state intervention, whilst a conservationist interest in transforming land use within the reserves conveniently diverted attention from African demands for more land.

Conservation interventions in the native reserves were drawn into local level struggles over political authority and themselves provoked new struggles. Local leaders' control over land, resources, and people had been derived from privileged access to land spirits. Their authority was inherently contestable, and became subject to particular challenges in the early colonial period. Early state interventions were manipulated by some local leaders to their own economic and political ends rather than for the mutual benefits of conservation. Officials' repeated assertions of an environmental crisis were partly legitimations for successive state interventions; they also described the product of state land and conservation interventions. Despite being interpreted by officials as laying the basis for conservation within the reserves, land use policy led to new ecological problems. Woodland was cleared as fields were shifted up the watershed to newly cleared dryland blocks which were later crudely contoured whilst wetland fields were abandoned. However, this did not necessarily amount to a crisis of the same type as officials portrayed. At the same time as natural resources experts wanted to evict Shurugwi's population to allow the "desert" to recover from misuse, local people tell a different story. Although land and particularly wetlands had become scarce, and land alienation and eviction had caused bitter resentment and much hardship, the reserve was not on the verge of ecological collapse and many environmental resources were not scarce in economic terms.

Local representations of environmental change are no less political and no more universal than official accounts. For old people in Shurugwi, the process of deforestation and moving into village lines epitomised the departure of the old order and the entry of the new. Whilst for some this had brought with it environmental decline and deep offence to ancestors and spirits, for others, notwithstanding the exhausted soils produced by land scarcity, it marked the acquisition of new knowledge, a modern way of life and the abandon of former backward ways.

Africa as a Living Laboratory

HELEN TILLEY[5]

Looking closely at agricultural research in tropical Africa provides a significant corrective to several recent interpretations of science in colonial contexts. Many historians and anthropologists, reacting against older, imperialist views featuring "backward" and resistant natives and "progressive," enlightened colonial officials, have emphasized colonialists' "misreadings of the African landscape." They argue that scientists helped to *construct* inaccurate "environmental orthodoxies" that became "received wisdom," and which had negative consequences for Africans that often extended into the postcolonial period. Among the earliest proponents of this view was the ecologist, John Ford, who was himself employed for over twenty-five years, between 1938 and 1965, by various colonial states and research institutes in British Africa. In 1971, with funding from the Wellcome Trust, Ford published *The Role of the Trypanosomiases in African Ecology: A Study of the Tsetse Fly Problem*, a historical account that quickly and deservedly became a classic in African studies.

Ford's book appeared just as a new wave of historical research documenting colonialism's adverse effects came to prominence. Imperial control was still being challenged actively in Zimbabwe, Namibia, and Mozambique, while apartheid in South Africa showed no signs of waning. Although he was not the first to focus on environmental or epidemiological issues, Ford certainly offered the most ambitious and far-reaching account to date. He also introduced key vocabulary and angles of analysis that were picked up and developed by scholars working in social, medical, and environmental history. Ford explained in the book's preface that he had written his study because, "Many years ago I began to have doubts about *official colonial doctrine* concerning the importance of the tsetse in tropical Africa." Given his desire to offer a critical account of colonialism, Ford pointed the finger at his own colleagues: "It is a curious

---

[5]This excerpt is taken from Helen Tilley, *Africa as a Living Laboratory: Empire, Development, and the Problem of Scientific Knowledge, 1870-1950* (Chicago, 2011), pp. 117-34. Helen Tilley is associate professor of African history at Northwestern University.

comment to make upon the efforts of *colonial scientists*," he wrote, "that because of *preconceived notions* about Africa and Africans . . . basic circumstantial epidemiology has often been wrongly described." According to Ford, these workers' principal failures were fourfold. First, "Western science continues to make a piecemeal approach to disease whenever and wherever it breaks out." Without recognizing the need for an "ecological" framework and "for joint investigation by zoologists, ecologists, and parasitologists," he argued, "the colonial governments in Africa . . . left to the new countries a legacy of ideas that had little relevance to the biological processes with which they had unwittingly interfered." Second, he believed officers had "almost entirely overlooked the very considerable achievements of the indigenous peoples in overcoming the obstacle of trypanosomiasis to tame and exploit the natural ecosystem of tropical Africa by cultural and physiological adjustment in both themselves and their domestic animals." Third, officials made "erroneous" assumptions about their own effects and, as a consequence, pursued "misdirected" efforts to control the disease. "Unfortunately, with very few exceptions, it was psychologically impossible for men and women concerned in imperial expansion in Africa to believe that their own actions were more often than not responsible for the manifold disasters in which they found themselves caught up. The scientists they called in to help them were as ignorant as they of the problems they had to tackle." And finally, he asserted that officials pursued an overconfident and misguided quest to "eradicate" tsetse flies and find a "permanent cure" for trypanosomiasis. "The real problem is not how to get rid of tsetse flies or how to cure sleeping sickness and the infections of domestic animals, but how to apply techniques of control in such a way that an expanding economy is not hampered by their mishandling."

Ford was implicitly arguing in his 1971 book that new states in tropical Africa ought to pay attention to what today might be called *subaltern* strategies of disease control. He spelled this out a few years later in a volume edited by anthropologist Paul Richards: "If there is any lesson to be learned from the results obtained by applied science in tropical Africa in the twentieth century, it is that vast projects designed to solve artificially isolated problems do not work except with the willing collaboration of the people they are intended to help." It was no accident that Ford stressed the inadequacies of the laboratory and its methods in his critique. He had been trained as a field scientist at Oxford University, circa 1929 to 1938, under the tutelage of Charles Elton, among others, and it was only by working in the field that he had an opportunity to speak to "the local people" and hear what evidence they had to offer on the history of trypanosomiasis in the areas where they lived.

What Ford left out of his narrative, however, was any discussion of the terms of his own employment. Had he explored this, he would have had to acknowledge that his book was in many respects an outgrowth of what he had been hired to do. As E. B. Worthington reported to the Colonial Office in his 1948 "progress report" on the East African "research and scientific services," one of the main studies being done in the realm of tsetse and trypanosomiasis research was an examination of the "Relationship of Tsetse to its Environment, including Man, Animals, Vegetation and Climate. This, the broad ecological approach, is the special task of Mr. Ford." Worthington also drew the office's attention to "an important paper" that Ford and two of his colleagues had recently published, as an example of cross-disciplinary research, in which they "gave a general account of some of the main problems involved [in tsetse and trypanosomiasis control], and detail[ed] the approach to these problems (a) through the trypanosomes, (b) through the tsetse flies, and (c) through broad ecological relationships." This research method seemed one of the more promising lines of work, *but*, stressed Worthington, "It is desirable to re-emphasize that, in spite of long years of hard work by many investigators, there is still a great deal of knowledge lacking on the innumerable questions of how tsetse flies and trypanosomes live in relation to their environments."

Ford's arguments have been perceived by many to be a radical departure from colonial thinking. I would suggest instead that key elements of Ford's work were less a rupture with the colonial era and more an expression of continuity. After all, he derived his evidence from his own extensive fieldwork and from a close reading of the published accounts of technical officers who had been employed in the colonial service. It was they who had also done many of the oral interviews and field studies on which Ford's analysis rested. Ford was not so much rejecting as he was embracing "official colonial doctrine" when he took up these research questions.

Ford's influence among a handful of social scientists in the 1970s—Helge Kjekshus, Paul Richards, and Leroy Vail, for instance—and a wider group of medical and environmental historians in the 1980s, including Maryinez Lyons and James Giblin, was profound and helped to establish a research agenda that re-examined colonial history along new lines. No longer was the aim of research to help colonial states or the imperial project; now scholars undertook studies that focused on Africans' agency and, often, on the negative effects colonialism had on peoples' lives. Kjekshus, for instance, was one of the first historians to examine at length the demographic effects of the rinderpest cattle epidemic that spread across eastern and southern Africa in the late nineteenth century. Using a vocabulary and periodization very similar to Ford's, he argued that colonial conquest had touched off a demographic and "ecological collapse," largely because officials had "fail[ed] to consider the African positively at the centre of administration and development." Quoting Julius Nyerere, the first president of independent Tanzania, Kjekshus concluded that "development means the development of people." Kjekshus believed that because African states were no longer under the yoke of colonialism that they could now "question older assumptions about the unadaptive nature" of "traditional" economies" and acknowledge that Africans' pre-colonial systems of environmental control had been based on "change and adaptation." Like Ford, Kjekshus held out an implicit hope that subaltern populations might become central to development strategies.

Paul Richards, in turn, took up the question of Africans' environmental knowledge, calling it "folk ecology" and "people's science," and wrote one of the first (post-independence) anthropological studies of West African "indigenous agriculture." Richards was well aware that he was following in the footsteps of certain technical officers and scientists during the colonial period; in fact he took a great deal of interest in these precedents, but his examination of the colonial past was more utilitarian than comprehensive. His central preoccupation was to explore "the relationship between science and development—more especially the relationship between environmental science and prospects for increased food production in West Africa [today]." To do this he framed his argument in terms of the differences between "scientific universals and ecological particularism." "Following John Ford, I have argued that West African farmers are especially good) at solving ecological problems of the kind that arise when human and "wilderness" ecosystems intersect, and ii) at exploiting the risk-spreading possibilities of ecological boundaries and landscape sequences." The goal, in other words, was to ensure that people who lived on the land and generated their livelihoods from it received support for the tools and ideas they had developed across the generations. This was necessary not just to redress the balance of power but also because these methods worked. Richards's historical analysis, however, led him almost incidentally to offer a very interesting insight about "scientific" studies of "local practices" during the colonial period: they sometimes resulted in the authors "discovering" the value of these practices and "reinvent[ing] traditional agriculture!"

A body of work that has built on these themes emerged in the mid-1990s and has straddled the fields of African environmental history, social anthropology, and development studies. According to Melissa Leach, James Fairhead, and Robin Mearns, among others, "the origins and persistence of received wisdom about environmental change in Africa lie in the substance of science, on the one hand, and in its social and historical context on the other, including the effects it has through development in practice." Subscribing to many of Ford's initial criticisms, they argue that "colonial scientists" "had little evidence to support their hypotheses about African environments . . . [which] [n]evertheless . . . became institutionalized in the colonial agricultural, forestry, livestock and wildlife departments, forming the rationale for intervention." Labelling this knowledge environmental "orthodoxy," they conclude that it often rested on "bad" science and on "racialist, pejorative views" of Africans and prevented more locally sensitive policies from gaining sway. When competing perspectives did exist, those who "challenge[d] the prevailing orthodoxy found their views either suppressed or unable to influence higher levels in the institutional hierarchy."

Rather than embrace these critiques wholesale, this chapter examines instead the ways that scientists working in British Africa helped to *deconstruct* late nineteenth-century ideas about the tropics and early twentieth-century assumptions about the unproductive and wasteful nature of indigenous agricultural practices. Indeed, it was research officers associated with agricultural departments who first began to undermine widespread assumptions of tropical Africa's natural fertility and drew attention to the relative infertility of the soils. Along with a handful of field ecologists, they also began to speak in positive rather than pejorative terms about the techniques associated with African agricultural practices. The fact that these ideas originated during the colonial period requires us to reinterpret the interplay between science and empire in new ways.

As British Africa was subjected to scientific scrutiny, the politics of knowledge increasingly took center stage. The agricultural research described in this chapter repeatedly pushed back against the wholesale transfer of European norms to African environments and offered a wide range of different approaches to modernization and development. As part of this process, Africans' subaltern, or orally transmitted, knowledge became an object of scientific study, a pattern I refer to as *vernacular science*. While none of the British scientists involved in these activities was moved to call for the end of empire, many were keen to criticize how it worked in practice. They also often inadvertently opened up a space to reconsider and even redefine state and imperial aims. The nature and scale of the problems research officers and anthropologists were forced to confront in the African "field" led them to adopt conceptual and methodological tools that attempted to bridge previously distinct areas of disciplinary expertise and cross the boundaries that separated one kind of problem from another. Although these perspectives did not always fundamentally reshape the views of policy makers in the metropole or redirect all the scientific and technical work within colonial states, they were enormously significant in shifting evaluations of African expertise from the negative to the positive.

The Political Economy of Bioscientific Research

Africa's environments were fundamental to the colonial project for one reason: resources could be extracted or utilized to yield revenue for the colonial state, which was essential to the maintenance of the empire. As British officials soon discovered, however, turning resources into revenue was a difficult business. Tensions between social needs and commercial uses, conservation and exploitation, and differing systems of knowledge complicated the equation. Colonial states sought to make tropical Africa's natural economy more profitable; they also aimed, in principle if not always in practice, to enhance the well-being of their inhabitants. The dual aims of wealth and welfare, along with the structural asymmetries inherent in the imperial project, forced colonial administrators to confront a series of questions that were politically charged and epistemologically fraught. What were the best uses of different kinds of land? Which productive systems would be the most lucrative, and which the most beneficial? What were the best measures of agricultural success? Implicit in these questions was a default assumption that officials would have the means to implement the findings of scientific studies and be able to control the outcome of these experiments. In much the same way that colonizers" attempts to rule indigenous peoples often backfired, leading to social resistance, wars, and weakened states, their efforts to manage the natural world sometimes exploded in their faces, turning what many thought would be a relatively easy extraction of resources and profits into an intricate courtship dance with nature itself. As Worthington observed in his memoirs, "The ecology of land use could only be learned on the spot and the environment had a way of kicking back at mistakes. From the late nineteenth century on, geographical descriptions of tropical Africa typically included inventories of potential crops, mineral deposits, and pharmaceutical specimens. Colonies were regarded as "sources of supply of foodstuffs and of raw materials for the industrial enterprises of the mother land." In Africa, the British articulated their imperialist vision in unambiguous and unapologetic terms. During a 1907 tour of East Africa, for example, Winston Churchill described tropical Africa as Europe's future breadbasket and claimed that it would soon "play a most important part in the economic development of the whole world." Nature's apparent abundance lay open to exploitation, and environmental scientists were brought in to find the best ways to make it both pliable and portable.

Agricultural Departments and the Place of the "Native"

Colonial administrators were expected to create a viable "export trade" in their territories and to extract wealth from Africans by means of economic coercion, including land appropriation, forced labor, and requirements that cultivators grow specific crops. The severity of these interventions varied from territory to territory. The atrocities of King Leopold's regime in the Congo attracted the greatest attention in Europe, but British policies and practices were socially disruptive too. By the turn of the twentieth century, Britain's tropical African colonies had begun to undergo an "export boom" in agricultural and mineral products. Many of these commodities—palm oil and kernels, rubber, cotton, groundnuts, timber, coffee, cocoa, and metals—were fed directly into industrial production in Europe and elsewhere: oils for food, soaps, and manufacturing; cocoa and coffee for the chocolate and drinks industry; cotton for clothing and fabric; and rubber for vehicle tires and for belts to transmit motive power to machinery in factories. Tropical Africa's trade statistics were still much lower than many other regions of the world, but exports from this region had already surpassed those from the British-controlled islands in the Caribbean, and this rapid growth seemed to imperialists a positive sign of things to come.

Agricultural departments were founded between 1890 and 1914, usually in tandem with forestry, meteorological, and geological research. Botanical stations were central to these efforts, and from the early 1900s the Colonial and Foreign Offices promoted "agricultural and forestry surveys." Initially, governors faced serious obstacles in finding the funds to support territory-wide research. When Harry Johnston was appointed High Commissioner of British Central Africa in 1891, he founded a "scientific department" for the study of its plant, animal, and mineral resources, a project that addressed geographical and anthropological questions as well as economic ones. The naturalist-turned-administrator was responsible for establishing East Africa's first botanical stations, in Nyasaland and Uganda, and for recruiting Alexander Whyte, a botanist with experience in Asia, to oversee their crop experiments. Funding for science was not forthcoming, so Johnston had to pay for many of the scientific instruments himself, and he secured financial support from both the Royal Geographical Society and the Royal Society. State building was an expensive business, and scientific research was not always the top priority Lack of funds also plagued Kew Gardens' studies in British Africa. The same year Johnston moved to Nyasaland, Britain's prime minister, Lord Salisbury, wrote privately to Kew's director urging him to consolidate the information its correspondents had collected over the years: "A proper knowledge of the Flora of Tropical Africa would do much to aid the development of the territories over which this country has recently acquired an influence." By 1900, however, the treasury had yet to approve any grant for this effort, and the second volume of the *Flora of Tropical Africa*, which had been completed in 1898, was "still unpublished." In the eyes of Kew's director, William Thiselton-Dyer, these delays raised serious questions about Britain's commitment to development. "It is, of course, a waste of time tendering to Her Majesty's Government such advice as is contained in [these reports], unless there is a real desire to deal with our immense responsibilities in Tropical Africa in a practical spirit." Thiselton-Dyer argued that colonial governors should be provided with funds to undertake field surveys. Metropolitan bodies like Kew, he stressed to Joseph Chamberlain in 1900, could only offer advice "of a vague and general kind. A man of trained experience brought face to face with the problem on the spot is in a very different and more effective position. . . . The appropriate methods [of agriculture and forestry] vary in different cases, and it requires a skilled expert to work them out locally."

At the same time, Harry Johnston was trying to drive home the significance of systematic scientific fieldwork to the imperial project. Soon after his appointment as Special Commissioner to Uganda in 1899, he asked his technical officers: "What resources does the country at present possess for the development of a profitable trade?" In a special dispatch to the Foreign Office in 1901, just a few months before he returned to England to attend the inaugural meeting of the African Society, he contended that research should be coordinated at the imperial level and asked the Foreign Office to discourage scientific exploration "at the hands of persons not connected to the Administration." Johnston said he would welcome and support "experts" appointed by the Foreign Office to conduct field research, but he would guard against "persons who wish to acquire knowledge for purely selfish purposes, or who wish to enrich museums outside the British Empire . . . or merely to drive a lucrative trade in specimens." In addition to worrying about their profit motive and affiliation with competing imperial powers, Johnston charged that "nearly all these individuals give untrue descriptions of the country, because their presence in it has been brief and their capacity for forming a correct opinion naturally poor." In his eyes, long experience in the field was an important prerequisite for producing accurate and true knowledge.

For all his reputation as a proponent of "constructive imperialism," Chamberlain initially seemed to undervalue the kind of scientific fieldwork Thiselton-Dyer and Johnston were advocating. For two years after his appointment as commissioner, Frederick Lugard lobbied Chamberlain to recognize "the necessity of hiring a small scientific staff" for the purpose of "development and conservation" in Northern Nigeria, but each year the funds he set aside in the budget for a "Department of Scientific Research" were "over-ruled" by the Colonial Office. Chamberlain justified this decision by remarking that "the expenditure of a small sum would probably effect little or no good." Lugard, however, finally succeeded in getting Chamberlain to approve a preliminary field survey. The natural inventory, conducted along the lines that Kew's officials had suggested, would focus not just on the size and location of forests and types of soils but also on the "crops . . . actually grown at the present time by the natives in different parts, and [their] methods of cultivation." Until the survey had been completed, Chamberlain and Lugard agreed, it was inadvisable to start new agricultural projects.

As they received field reports from the different territories, imperial officials and advisors began to articulate general principles that were supposed to guide the development of agricultural industries. Northern Nigeria played a key role in this process because its reports conveyed the unexpected news that the region's "inhabitants are as a rule good agriculturalists" who achieved "splendid" results with both local staples and newly introduced cash crops, including cocoa and coffee. The social reformer Edmund Morel made a similar observation after touring this region: "In the northern part of Zaria and Kano the science of agriculture has attained remarkable development. There is little we can teach the Kano farmer. There is much we can learn from him." Chamberlain's successor at the Colonial Office, Alfred Lyttelton, announced that "the only sound plan" of agricultural development "is to begin by carefully taking stock of *existing* industries, and to aim, in the first instance, at improving and developing these (where they are capable of development) before proceeding with attempts to introduce new products." Colonial states, he continued, should also take into account "the character of the inhabitants and their existing agricultural development." This approach was designed to enable frail colonial states to avoid provoking social unrest. Equally important, it would allow Britain to keep pace scientifically with its European competitors in the region, especially Germany.

Other European colonial powers were also moving toward the study of "native agriculture" at the turn of the twentieth century. As Christophe Bonneuil and Mina Kleiche have shown, French administrators had begun to point out the practical problems associated with ignorance of "native" practices. In 1906, Yves Henry, an agricultural director for French West Africa, criticized experiment stations in the region for failing to account for "the environment in which [Africans] live and the procedures they use in order to make the land productive (*mettre en valeur*)." "The three elements of our public riches are: the producer, or in other words, the *indigène*, the productive milieu, or rather the landscapes and climate, and finally the product, its nature and means for improvement. Through the system of experiment stations, it is possible to know only some part of the third element, while one gains very limited knowledge of the second and virtually nothing of the first." Henry and his colleagues were convinced that uninformed interventions were likely to fail. In one of the first articles to address African agriculture, the botanist Auguste Chevalier suggested that "judicious observations of the cultural procedures that [Africans] employ, the [crop] rotations they practice, the yields they obtain, and the distinctions between the varieties that they cultivate . . . will often help the colonial to avoid useless groping and will guard against applying procedures associated with European culture prematurely. Before the First World War, however, no European power incorporated this kind of research into a systematic strategy of agricultural development. In British Africa, neither the agricultural departments nor the Colonial Office adopted a consistent or coherent approach. Agricultural activities proceeded in an ad hoc fashion, and only a few scientific studies were supported through botanical stations and field surveys. As part of the state-building process, all territories tended to encourage their subjects to cultivate cash crops well before administrators had an adequate understanding of land tenure or subsistence agriculture. By default and by design, scientific concerns were subordinated to colonial states' economic priorities.

Fieldwork, Interdisciplinary Collaborations, and Emergent Critiques

Even during the interwar period, field research was not given the high priority that many scientists and some officials in Africa believed it should be accorded. The proposal to create an integrated scientific and research service within the Colonial Office was never adopted; neither were a series of recommendations, endorsed by the participants at the 1927 Imperial Agricultural Research Conference, to establish a chain of research institutes within the colonial territories. Yet the projects that were implemented often had significant effects on imperial thinking. Research completed during these decades reached beyond the boundaries of specific territories and shaped both metropolitan policies and inter-territorial practices. Importantly, scientific studies drew attention to contradictory elements and fault lines within existing programs in colonial agriculture. Most apparent in these reports was the tension between promoting commodity crops for export and supporting "native agriculture." The alternative approaches that field scientists and specialists promoted might be described as "bottom-up development schemes," although the contemporary ethos of participatory development that aims to allow producers a role in decision making was absent from their recommendations The emergence of this perspective was made possible by an interesting confluence of factors that expanded opportunities for scientific fieldwork in diverse African environments. Above all, this included the metropolitan push to augment the technical services themselves. Between 1918 and 1931, employment in the agricultural, medical, survey, forestry, and game departments more than tripled across British Africa, a growth unparalleled in any other decade during the colonial period. A growing number of officers were assigned to the production of knowledge, rather than restricted to imperial management tasks. Although their numbers remained small compared to their counterparts elsewhere in the British Empire, their work had a disproportionate impact on imperial thinking and policy making. Staff members who remained in the same area for years became intimately acquainted with the place and its indigenous inhabitants. Staff retrenchments during the 1930s made research officers" results more prominent, since their numbers remained relatively stable compared to other officials, and their studies came to be seen as benchmark examples.

Acting in concert, statesmen and scientists began to push for research institutes and scientific investigations within British Africa that could serve more than one territory. Not only were technical officers forced to agree on shared problems, a process that involved controversies over definitions, but also they became more aware of the need to account for local differences. When the directors of agriculture from Tanganyika, Kenya, Uganda, and Zanzibar met in 1921 to discuss the Amani Agricultural Station, which Britain inherited from the Germans, one of their biggest concerns was that its investigations might fail to address the "considerable variety in natural conditions" throughout "these vast, new countries." While they endorsed the idea of increasing the amount of research done in the region, they doubted that a "centralized" approach would yield the sort of knowledge they needed to do their jobs well. The drive to localize knowledge was just as strong an imperial imperative as the desire to standardize and systematize it.

At the same time, because individual territories had so little funding at their disposal, state leaders encouraged interdepartmental collaborations in research, which they referred to as scientific "teamwork." A handful of metropolitan advisors were beginning to promote field sciences, which stressed multidisciplinary investigations that made connections between natural and social phenomena. Upon his appointment as director of Amani in 1927, William Nowell spent five months touring the six East African territories and learning about the distinct research needs of their agriculture departments. Besides short-term crop studies, which were well established, he stressed the urgency of embarking on long-term investigations, especially "a description of East Africa in which the inter-relations between geological structure, soil, climate, vegetation, animals, and man and his industries would be worked out." He told a gathering of naturalists in London that "while this proceeds, valuable information may be obtained by a shorter route through ecological studies." By the late 1920s, plans were circulating in Britain and its African dependencies for three multiyear research projects featuring teamwork, ecological methods, and ethnographic sensitivities based at the Amani Agricultural Station, the Tsetse Research Department in Shinyanga, Tanganyika, and the Ecological Survey in Northern Rhodesia. The histories of these projects and the fortunes of the African Survey were closely intertwined. All three projects received grants through various metropolitan funding schemes, including the East African loan of 1926, the Empire Marketing Board, and the Colonial Development Fund. These initiatives became hallmarks of bioscientific research in colonial Africa during the interwar period.

Both the British government and the League of Nations increasingly supported scientific coordinating conferences in specific territories and metropolitan centers. At these events, technical officers were able to pool information, consider common problems, and share ideas and strategies. Inadvertently, these conferences created a forum for individuals to criticize the status quo. The most prevalent and enduring criticism was the lack of scientific knowledge required to inform policy and practice. In a memorandum on agricultural research prepared for the 1927 Colonial Office conference, William Ormsby-Gore declared: "Our ignorance about the soils of the tropical Empire is profound. The only book on the soils of Tropical Africa is the work of an American." Britain must rapidly increase the scale and pace of its "acquisition of scientific knowledge of our resources," he contended. As Ormsby-Gore and others found, the new knowledge they sought could take Agricultural departments in unexpected directions.

Those who worked in tropical Africa were occasionally nervous about the lead taken by South Africa in agricultural research, arguing that the divergent natural and social conditions facing colonial states required different research priorities and policies. In 1929, after South Africa hosted the fifth Pan-African Agricultural and Veterinary Conference, the South African government proposed to Britain's Colonial Office that it coordinate botanical and agricultural research for the entire continent. South African officials argued that this plan would take some of the financial burden off cash-strapped colonial dependencies and would put at these territories' disposal the far more numerous research workers based in South Africa. Several directors of agriculture in East and West Africa objected to this move. Tanganyika's director explained to the Colonial Secretary that "there is at present a sharp divergence of outlook between the centre and the South of Africa." The biggest problem, in his view, was South Africa's overemphasis on white settlers' efforts to the detriment of African agricultural development. "I feel our delegates would be more at home, and could better express themselves at conferences where native work and European work are given equal prominence. . . . We should preferably more strongly develop our own conference" system. No further pan-African agricultural conferences were organized in South Africa in the 1930s, while the East African coordinating conferences flourished and had significant effects on both agricultural and epidemiological research. Conflicts still arose among the East African states because of Kenya's settler politics and the overwhelming support it provided to white farmers, but these were easier to adjudicate since colonial dependencies were more on a par, economically and politically, with one another than with South Africa.

The final factor that affected both scientific research and agricultural development was the Depression. Charlotte Leubeuscher, an advisor to the African Survey, assessed the situation in 1934: "One of the paramount facts by which one is faced in Africa is the enormous development that has occurred in almost every province of economic and social life, as compared with pre-war times, a development that has been pushed forward impetuously in the years from 1920–29 and was brought to a sudden, in some cases catastrophic, stop in 1930 by the economic world crisis." The Depression had a direct and almost immediate effect on each territory's export revenue. In British West Africa, export income was cut in half between 1929 and 1931. The situation was just as dire in East Africa, which already had lower levels of revenue. Only Central Africa (limited to Northern Rhodesia and Nyasaland) experienced a slight increase in exports, mostly from Northern Rhodesia's emerging copper mining industry.

As the economic historians Michael Havinden and David Meredith have pointed out, the Depression had particularly acute consequences for government finances in British Africa. By 1936, territorial governments were spending between one-fourth and two-fifths of their budgets on serving their debts, a far higher proportion than the British territories in the Caribbean and Asia. The dramatic declines in colonial treasuries affected Africa's white settlers and indigenous inhabitants unevenly. Recent historical research disaggregating African and European producers has shown that at some times and places the economic crisis conferred greater power on African producers and rural communities within local economies. When subsistence agriculture, non-cash exchange, mixed cropping, and flexible production were all part of the equation, the economic downturn could mean opportunity rather than calamity. For the research officers and administrators who were responsible for studying and attempting to remedy the situation, dire circumstances could justify strategies that might have been dismissed in territories with more capital.

Officials at the Colonial Office and Kew Gardens were already reluctant to promote plantation-based agriculture in the West African territories, since they thought it unlikely that large numbers of white settlers would ever live there and the region lacked the transportation networks that a profitable export trade required. As early as 1888, Alfred Maloney, the governor of Lagos and an avid botanist, sought to persuade the Colonial Office that agricultural diversification was the best strategy. "Blind adherence to one industry only means commercial ruin, as was proved, to the cost of many, in some of our colonies. "Eggs-in-one-basket" policy has proved disastrous." Pursuing a policy of diversification would require information about which crops might thrive in specific regions.

Suggested Readings

Anderson, David M., "Depression, Dust Bowl, Demography and Drought: The Colonial State and Soil Conservation in East Africa during the 1930s." *African Affairs* 83, no. 332 (1984), pp. 321-43.

Beinart, William, and Peter Coates, *Environment and History: The Taming of Nature in the USA and South Africa* (Routledge: London, 1995).

Giles-Vernick, Tamara, *Cutting the Vines of the Past* (Charlottesville: University of Virginia Press, 2002).

Griffiths, Tom, and Libby Robin, eds., *Ecology and Empire: Environmental History of Settler Societies* (Edinburgh: Keele University Press, 1997), pp. 215-28.

Kjekshus, Helge, *Ecology Control and Economic Development in East African History* (Heinemann: London, 1977).

Leach, Melissa, and Robin Mearns, eds., *The Lie of the Land: Challenging Received Wisdom on the African Environment* (Oxford: James Currey, 1996), pp. 73-90.

Mackenzie, A. Fiona D., *Land, Ecology and Resistance in Kenya, 1880-1952* (Edinburgh: Edinburgh University Press, 1998).

Maddox, Gregory, James Giblin, and Isaria N. Kimambo, eds., *Custodians of the Land: Ecology and Culture in the History of Tanzania* (London: James Currey, 1996).

Tiffen, Mary, Michael Mortimore, and Francis Gichuki, *More People, Less Erosion: EnvironmentalRecovery in Kenya* (Chichester: John Wiley, 1994).

PROBLEM V
AFRICAN NATIONALISM

When the Second World War broke out in 1939, few people in Africa imagined that they would live to see the end of European empire. But within three decades the majority of Africans were living in independent nation-states, while guerrillas were challenging settler regimes in South Africa, Rhodesia, and the declining empire of Portugal. The wave of nationalism that swept the Europeans from Africa was nearly as sudden and unexpected as that which had brought them to power in the final decades of the nineteenth century. The first stirrings of nationalist consciousness emerged in the 1930s, as the great depression put enormous pressure on African workers in growing colonial cities. The Second World War mobilized African populations as labor and as soldiers, instilling in many an expectation that victory would bring a new relationship with their colonial masters. After the war, inspired by the example of British India, which won its independence in 1948, African leaders became increasingly clamorous for their freedom. When the British Gold Coast colony became Ghana in 1957, it sparked a rush to decolonize that would ultimately see all of Africa independent of foreign rule by 1975. When South Africa became a democracy in 1994, the continent's long road to national liberation was widely viewed as complete.

Scholars agree for the most part on the chain of events that led from world war to independence. The problem of nationalism is one of emphasis. Were these new states of Africa nations in the European sense? Did they consist of congeries of disparate tribes—as colonial observers asserted—or diverse peoples who still shared a historic sense of unity and desire for liberation, similar to that held by European nationalists of the nineteenth century? Was African nationalism a product of the Second World War, or did its roots lie deeper in colonial history? And which groups within African societies provided the initiative and leadership for national liberation? These are not mere academic questions, as the legitimacy of virtually all post-colonial governments rested on claims they made about their roles in the nationalist movements.

The early leaders of the new African nations were almost all middle-class politicians who were literate in Western languages. These men successfully negotiated the independence of their nations by making arguments about national self-determination and personal liberty. At independence, they ruled governments whose borders, administrative structures, and armies bore a striking resemblance to the colonial state they had opposed. The first reading in this chapter, from Frantz Fanon's *The Wretched of the Earth,* is a criticism of the "bourgeois nationalism" of the men who took power in these new states. Its author was a French-trained psychologist from the Caribbean island of Martinique. Writing in the late 1950s, he witnessed the struggle against European rule firsthand and knew some of the leading figures of the liberation movements. But Fanon worried that African nationalism—with its emphasis on glorifying the African past and its willingness to accept the existing colonial state system—was in danger of becoming the mirror image of the colonial rule it sought to abolish. He warned that nationalist movements threatened to replace the colonial elite with a virtually identical African elite. If the nationalist struggle were left in their hands, he warned, that "national consciousness, instead of being the all-embracing crystallization of the innermost hopes of the whole people, instead of being the immediate and most obvious result of the mobilization of the people, will be in any case only an empty shell, a crude and fragile travesty of what it might have been." To Fanon, legitimate national identity would emerge from the struggle against a common oppressor. He believed that the diverse ethnicities and cultures of the African colonies would not act as a barrier to forging a new national identity. "A national culture is the whole body of efforts made by a people in the sphere of thought to describe, justify, and praise the action through which that people has created itself and keeps itself in existence."

These issues became of concern to scholars before the liberation struggle had run its course. Professor Terence Ranger, writing as nationalist sentiment was gaining momentum in Rhodesia, published a study that asserted that nationalism in that colony had deeper roots than colonial critics suggested. Ranger argued that the rebellion against the rule of the British South African Company of 1886 had established an important precedent among the people of the colony, who worked across "tribal" lines against their common enemy. Memory of this cooperation would loom large in the second "Chimurenga" that would ultimately lead to majority rule in Zimbabwe. As Ranger put it, "the environment in which later African politics developed was shaped not only by European initiatives and policy or by African cooperation and passivity, but also by African resistance. In this sense at least there is certainly an important connection between resistance and later political developments."

While not directly contradicting Ranger, Martin Kilson regarded African nationalism as emerging from the international wreckage of the Second World War. He sees the movement as having brought together leadership from the urban, westernized African elite, as well as "traditional" authorities. The nationalists straddled both worlds and were able to unite opposition to colonial rule through political shrewdness that, in the end, challenged the traditional authorities and allowed them to harness the benefits of modernization for the betterment of themselves and their new African nations.

But was this anti-colonial movement "nationalist" in the European sense? Bruce Berman uses the example of the anti-colonial movement of Mau Mau in Kenya to consider the relevance of the term "nationalism" to the process of African decolonization. Berman draws on the work of the highly influential historian of nationalism, Benedict Anderson, to explore the degree to which Kikuyu nationalism—as reflected in Mau Mau—follows the pattern whereby nationalism took hold of the public imagination in Europe. For Anderson, the crucial development of national consciousness in Europe was the emergence of "print capitalism," the commodification of newspapers and books that were widely absorbed in a common language. This created a literate public which became conscious of their part in a larger "imagined community" of like-minded readers. Berman finds the Mau Mau example to be a mixed bag, with elements of Anderson's formula—including the rise of Kikuyu print capitalism and a literate political class—chafing against other aspects of colonial nationalism that are missing. "While Mau Mau was clearly not a tribal atavism seeking a return to the past, the answer to the question of 'was it nationalism?' must be yes and no." Berman found that, while Mau Mau proved incapable of crossing ethnic boundaries to make alliances with non-Kikuyu groups, Kikuyu nationalism did emerge against the backdrop of a thriving Kikuyu print culture which encouraged the emergence of a new "imagined community."

Finally, Basil Davidson observes that in the eyes of many African subjects, nationalism became conflated with anti-colonialism. In this, he disagrees with those authors who see in these movements incipient nations. "The jubilant crowds celebrating independence were not inspired by a 'national consciousness' that 'demanded the nation'; . . . they were inspired by the hope of more and better food and shelter." Davidson lays much of the blame for the problems of the post-colonial states on the lack of vision, primarily on the part of colonial authorities, who until the last minute remained blinded to the direction that the nationalist movement was taking. Thus he recognizes that the process of decolonization shaped the ways nations and national identity came to be understood in the post-colonial era.

National Consciousness

FRANTZ FANON[1]

In this chapter we shall analyze the problem, which is felt to be fundamental, of the legitimacy of the claims of a nation. It must be recognized that the political party which mobilizes the people hardly touches on this problem of legitimacy. The political parties start from living reality and it is in the name of this reality, in the name of the stark facts which weigh down the present and the future of men and women, that they fix their line of action. The political party may well speak in moving terms of the nation, but what it is concerned with is that the people who are listening understand the need to take part in the fight if, quite simply, they wish to continue to exist.

Today we know that in the first phase of the national struggle colonialism tries to disarm national demands by putting forward economic doctrines. As soon as the first demands are set out, colonialism pretends to consider them, recognizing with ostentatious humility that the territory is suffering from serious underdevelopment which necessitates a great economic and social effort. And, in fact, it so happens that certain spectacular measures (centers of work for the unemployed which are opened here and there, for example) delay the crystallization of national consciousness for a few years. But, sooner or later, colonialism sees that it is not within its powers to put into practice a project of economic and social reforms which will satisfy the aspirations of the colonized people. Even where food supplies are concerned, colonialism gives proof of its inherent incapability. The colonialist state quickly discovers that if it wishes to disarm the nationalist parties on strictly economic questions then it will have to do in the colonies exactly what it has refused to do in its own country. It is not mere chance that almost everywhere today there flourishes the doctrine of Cartierism.

The disillusioned bitterness we find in Carrier when up against the obstinate determination of France to link to herself peoples which she must feed while

---

[1] This excerpt is taken from Frantz Fanon, *The Wretched of the Earth,* copyright © 1963 by *Présence Africaine.* (Used by permission of Grove/Atlantic, Inc.) Frantz Fanon (1925-1961) was born in the French Caribbean territory of Martinique. He was a psychiatrist, diplomat, activist, and writer.

so many French people live in want shows up the impossible situation in which colonialism finds itself when the colonial system is called upon to transform itself into an unselfish program of aid and assistance. It is why, once again, there is no use in wasting time repeating that hunger with dignity is preferable to bread eaten in slavery. On the contrary, we must become convinced that colonialism is incapable of procuring for the colonized peoples the material conditions which might make them forget their concern for dignity. Once colonialism has realized where its tactics of social reform are leading, we see it falling back on its old reflexes, reinforcing police effectives, bringing up troops, and setting a reign of terror which is better adapted to its interests and its psychology.

Inside the political parties, and most often in offshoots from these parties, cultured individuals of the colonized race make their appearance. For these individuals, the demand for a national culture and the affirmation of the existence of such a culture represent a special battlefield. While the politicians situate their action in actual present-day events, men of culture take their stand in the field of history. Confronted with the native intellectual who decides to make an aggressive response to the colonialist theory of pre-colonial barbarism, colonialism will react only slightly, and still less because the ideas developed by the young colonized intelligentsia are widely professed by specialists in the mother country. It is in fact a commonplace to state that for several decades large numbers of research workers have, in the main, rehabilitated the African, Mexican, and Peruvian civilizations. The passion with which native intellectuals defend the existence of their national culture may be a source of amazement; but those who condemn this exaggerated passion are strangely apt to forget that their own psyche and their own selves are conveniently sheltered behind a French or German culture which has given full proof of its existence and which is uncontested.

I am ready to concede that on the plane of factual being the past existence of an Aztec civilization does not change anything very much in the diet of the Mexican peasant of today. I admit that all the proofs of a wonderful Songhai civilization will not change the fact that today the Songhais are underfed and illiterate, thrown between sky and water with empty heads and empty eyes. But it has been remarked several times that this passionate search for a national culture which existed before the colonial era finds its legitimate reason in the anxiety shared by native intellectuals to shrink away from that Western culture in which they all risk being swamped. Because they realize they are in danger of losing their lives and thus becoming lost to their people, these men, hotheaded and with anger in their hearts, relentlessly determine to renew contact once more with the oldest and most pre-colonial springs of life of their people.

Let us go further. Perhaps this passionate research and this anger are kept up or at least directed by the secret hope of discovering beyond the misery of today, beyond self-contempt, resignation, and abjuration, some very beautiful and splendid era whose existence rehabilitates us both in regard to ourselves and in regard to others. I have said that I have decided to go further. Perhaps unconsciously, the native intellectuals, since they could not stand wonderstruck before the history of today's barbarity, decided to back further and to delve deeper down; and, let us make no mistake, it was with the greatest delight that they discovered that there was nothing to be ashamed of in the past, but rather dignity, glory, and solemnity. The claim to a national culture in the past does not only rehabilitate that nation and serve as a justification for the hope of a future national culture. In the sphere of psycho-affective equilibrium it is responsible for an important change in the native. Perhaps we have not sufficiently demonstrated that colonialism is not simply content to impose its rule upon the present and the future of a dominated country. Colonialism is not satisfied merely with holding a people in its grip and emptying the native's brain of all form and content. By a kind of perverted logic, it turns to the past of the oppressed people, and distorts, disfigures, and destroys it. This work of devaluing pre-colonial history takes on a dialectical significance today.

When we consider the efforts made to carry out the cultural estrangement so characteristic of the colonial epoch, we realize that nothing has been left to chance and that the total result looked for by colonial domination was indeed to convince the natives that colonialism came to lighten their darkness. The effect consciously sought by colonialism was to drive into the natives' heads the idea that if the settlers were to leave, they would at once fall back into barbarism, degradation, and bestiality.

On the unconscious plane, colonialism therefore did not seek to be considered by the native as a gentle, loving mother who protects her child from a hostile environment, but rather as a mother who unceasingly restrains her fundamentally perverse offspring from managing to commit suicide and from giving free rein to its evil instincts. The colonial mother protects her child from itself, from its ego, and from its physiology, its biology, and its own unhappiness which is its very essence.

In such a situation the claims of the native intellectual are not a luxury but a necessity in any coherent program. The native intellectual who takes up arms to defend his nation's legitimacy and who wants to bring proofs to bear out that legitimacy, who is willing to strip himself naked to study the history of his body, is obliged to dissect the heart of his people.

Such an examination is not specifically national. The native intellectual who decides to give battle to colonial ties fights on the field of the whole continent. The past is given back its value. Culture, extracted from the past to be displayed in all its splendor, is not necessarily that of his own country. Colonialism, which has not bothered to put too fine a point on its efforts, has never ceased to maintain that the Negro is a savage; and for the colonist, the Negro was neither an Angolan nor a Nigerian, for he simply spoke of "the Negro." For colonialism, this vast continent was the haunt of savages, a country riddled with superstitions and fanaticism, destined for contempt, weighed down by the curse of God, a country of cannibals—in short, the Negro's country. Colonialism's condemnation is continental in its scope. The contention by colonialism that the darkest night of humanity lay over pre-colonial history concerns the whole of the African continent. The efforts of the native to rehabilitate himself and to escape from the claws of colonialism are logically inscribed from the same point of view as that of colonialism. The native intellectual who has gone far beyond the domains of Western culture and who has got it into his head to proclaim the existence of another culture never does so in the name of Angola or of Dahomey. The culture which is affirmed is African culture. The Negro, never so much a Negro as since he has been dominated by the whites, when he decides to prove that he has a culture and to behave like a cultured person, comes to realize that history points out a well-defined path to him: he must demonstrate that a Negro culture exists. And it is only too true that those who are most responsible for this racialization of thought, or at least for the first movement toward that thought, are and remain those Europeans who have never ceased to set up white culture to fill the gap left by the absence of other cultures. Colonialism did not dream of wasting its time in denying the existence of one national culture after another. Therefore, the reply of the colonized peoples will be straight away continental in its breadth. In Africa, the native literature of the last twenty years is not a national literature but a Negro literature. The concept of negritude, for example, was the emotional if not the logical antithesis of that insult which the white man flung at humanity. This rush of negritude against the white man's contempt showed itself in certain spheres to be the one idea capable of lifting interdictions and anathemas. Because the New Guinean or Kenyan intellectuals found themselves above all up against a general ostracism and delivered to the combined contempt of their overlords, their reaction was to sing praises in admiration of each other. The unconditional affirmation of African culture has succeeded the unconditional affirmation of European culture. On the whole, the poets of negritude oppose the idea of an old Europe to a young Africa, tiresome reasoning to lyricism, oppressive logic to high-stepping nature, and on one side stiffness, ceremony, etiquette, and scepticism, while on the other frankness, liveliness, liberty, and—why not?—luxuriance: but also irresponsibility.

The poets of negritude will not stop at the limits of the continent. From America, black voices will take up the hymn with fuller unison. The "black world" will see the light and Busia from Ghana, Birago Diop from Senegal, Hampate Ba from the Soudan, and Saint-Clair Drake from Chicago will not hesitate to assert the existence of common ties and a motive power that is identical. . . .

If the action of the native intellectual is limited historically, there remains nevertheless the fact that it contributes greatly to upholding and justifying the action of politicians. It is true that the attitude of the native intellectual sometimes takes on the aspect of a cult or of a religion. But if we really wish to analyze this attitude correctly, we will come to see that it is symptomatic of the intellectual's realization of the danger that he is running in cutting his last moorings and of breaking adrift from his people. This stated belief in a national culture is in fact an ardent, despairing turning toward anything that will afford him secure anchorage. In order to ensure his salvation and to escape from the supremacy of the white man's culture, the native feels the need to turn backward toward his unknown roots and to lose himself at whatever cost in his own barbarous people. Because he feels he is becoming estranged, that is to say because he feels that he is the living haunt of contradictions which run the risk of becoming insurmountable, the native tears himself away from the swamp that may suck him down and accepts everything, decides to take all for granted and confirms everything even though he may lose body and soul. The native finds that he is expected to answer for everything, and to all comers. He not only turns himself into the defender of his people's past; he is willing to be counted as one of them, and henceforward he is even capable of laughing at his past cowardice.

This tearing away, painful and difficult though it may be, is however necessary. If it is not accomplished there will be serious psycho-affective injuries and the result will be individuals without an anchor, without a horizon, colorless, stateless, rootless—a race of angels. It will be also quite normal to hear certain natives declare, "I speak as a Senegalese and as a Frenchman . . ." "I speak as an Algerian and as a Frenchman . . ." The intellectual who is Arab and French, or Nigerian and English, when he comes up against the need to take on two nationalities, chooses, if he wants to remain true to himself, the negation of one of these determinations. But most often, since they cannot or will not make a choice, such intellectuals gather together all the historical determining factors which have conditioned them and take up a fundamentally "universal standpoint."

This is because the native intellectual has thrown himself greedily upon Western culture. Like adopted children who only stop investigating the new family framework at the moment when a minimum nucleus of security crystallizes in their psyche, the native intellectual will try to make European culture his own. He will not be content to get to know Rabelais and Diderot, Shakespeare and Edgar Allen Poe; he will bind them to his intelligence as closely as possible. . . .

But at the moment when the nationalist parties are mobilizing the people in the name of national independence, the native intellectual sometimes spurns these acquisitions that he suddenly feels make him a stranger in his own land.

It is always easier to proclaim rejection than actually to reject. The intellectual who through the medium of culture has filtered into Western civilization, who has managed to become part of the body of European culture—in other words who has exchanged his own culture for another—will come to realize that the cultural matrix, which now he wishes to assume since he is anxious to appear original, can hardly supply any figureheads which will bear comparison with those, so many in number and so great in prestige, of the occupying power's civilization. History, of course, though nevertheless written by the Westerners and to serve their purposes, will be able to evaluate from time to time certain periods of the African past. But, standing face to face with his country at the present time, and observing clearly and objectively the events of today throughout the continent that he wants to make his own, the intellectual is terrified by the void, the degradation, and the savagery he sees there. Now he feels that he must get away from the white culture. He must seek his culture elsewhere, anywhere at all; and if he fails to find the substance of culture of the same grandeur and scope as displayed by the ruling power, the native intellectual will very often fall back upon emotional attitudes and will develop a psychology which is dominated by exceptional sensitivity and susceptibility. This withdrawal, which is due in the first instance to a begging of the question in his internal behavior mechanism and his own character, brings out, above all, a reflex and contradiction which is muscular.

This is sufficient explanation of the style of those native intellectuals who decide to give expression to this phase of consciousness which is in the process of being liberated. It is a harsh style, full of images, for the image is the drawbridge which allows unconscious energies to be scattered on the surrounding meadows. It is a vigorous style, alive with rhythms, struck through and through with bursting life; it is full of color, too, bronzed, sunbaked, and violent. This style, which in its time astonished the peoples of the West, has nothing racial about it, in spite of frequent statements to the contrary; it expresses above all a hand-to-hand struggle and it reveals the need that man has to liberate himself from a part of his being which already contained the seeds of decay. Whether the fight is painful, quick, or inevitable, muscular action must substitute itself for concepts.

If in the world of poetry this movement reaches unaccustomed heights, the fact remains that in the real world the intellectual often follows up a blind alley. When at the height of his intercourse with his people, whatever they were or whatever they are, the intellectual decides to come down into the common paths of real life, he only brings back from his adventuring formulas which are sterile in the extreme. He sets a high value on the customs, traditions, and the appearances of his people; but his inevitable, painful experience only seems to be a banal search for exoticism. The sari becomes sacred, and shoes that come from Paris or Italy are left off in favor of pam-pooties, while suddenly the language of the ruling power is felt to burn your lips. Finding your fellow countrymen sometimes means in this phase to will to be a nigger, not a nigger like all other niggers but a real nigger, a Negro cur, just the sort of nigger that the white man wants you to be. Going back to your own people means to become a dirty wog, to go native as much as you can, to become unrecognizable, and to cut off those wings that before you had allowed to grow.

The native intellectual decides to make an inventory of the bad habits drawn from the colonial world, and hastens to remind everyone of the good old customs of the people, that people which he has decided contains all truth and goodness. The scandalized attitude with which the settlers who live in the colonial territory greet this new departure only serves to strengthen the native's decision. When the colonialists, who had tasted the sweets of their victory over these assimilated people, realize that these men whom they considered as saved souls are beginning to fall back into the ways of niggers, the whole system totters. Every native won over, every native who had taken the pledge not only marks a failure for the colonial structure when he decides to lose himself and to go back to his own side, but also stands as a symbol for the uselessness and the shallowness of all the work that has been accomplished. Each native who goes back over the line is a radical condemnation of the methods and of the regime; and the native intellectual finds in the scandal he gives rise to a justification and an encouragement to persevere in the path he has chosen. . . .

The native intellectual nevertheless sooner or later will realize that you do not show proof of your nation from its culture but that you substantiate its existence in the fight which the people wage against the forces of occupation. No colonial system draws its justification from the fact that the territories it dominates are culturally nonexistent. You will never make colonialism blush for shame by spreading out little-known cultural treasures under its eyes. At the very moment when the native intellectual is anxiously trying to create a cultural work, he fails to realize that he is utilizing techniques and language which are borrowed from the stranger in his country. He contents himself with stamping these instruments with a hallmark which he wishes to be national, but which is strangely reminiscent of exoticism. The native intellectual who comes back to his people by way of cultural achievements behaves in fact like a foreigner. Sometimes he has no hesitation in using a dialect in order to show his will to be as near as possible to the people; but the ideas that he expresses and the preoccupations he is taken up with have no common yardstick to measure the real situation which the men and the women of his country know. The culture that the intellectual leans toward is often no more than a stock of particularisms. He wishes to attach himself to the people; but instead he only catches hold of their outer garments. And these outer garments are merely the reflection of a hidden life, teeming and perpetually in motion. That extremely obvious objectivity which seems to characterize a people is in fact only the inert, already forsaken result of frequent, and not always very coherent, adaptations of a much more fundamental substance which itself is continually being renewed. The man of culture, instead of setting out to find this substance, will let himself be hypnotized by these mummified fragments which because they are static are in fact symbols of negation and outworn contrivances. Culture has never the translucidity of custom; it abhors all simplification. In its essence it is opposed to custom, for custom is always the deterioration of culture. The desire to attach oneself to tradition or bring abandoned traditions to life again does not only mean going against the current of history but also opposing one's own people. When a people undertakes an armed struggle or even a political struggle against a relentless colonialism, the significance of tradition changes. All that has made up the technique of passive resistance in the past may, during this phase, be radically condemned. In an underdeveloped country during the period of struggle traditions are fundamentally unstable and are shot through by centrifugal tendencies. This is why the intellectual often runs the risk of being out of date. The peoples who have carried on the struggle are more and more impervious to demagogy; and those who wish to follow them reveal themselves as nothing more than common opportunists, in other words, latecomers. . . .

We must not therefore be content with delving into the past of a people in order to find coherent elements which will counteract colonialism's attempts to falsify and harm. We must work and fight with the same rhythm as the people to construct the future and to prepare the ground where vigorous shoots are already springing up. A national culture is not a folklore, nor an abstract populism that believes it can discover the people's true nature. It is not made up of the inert dregs of gratuitous actions, that is to say actions which are less and less attached to the ever-present reality of the people. A national culture is the whole body of efforts made by a people in the sphere of thought to describe, justify, and praise the action through which that people has created itself and keeps itself in existence. A national culture in underdeveloped countries should therefore take its place at the very heart of the struggle for freedom which these countries are carrying on. Men of African cultures who are still fighting in the name of African-Negro culture and who have called many congresses in the name of the unity of that culture should today realize that all their efforts amount to is to make comparisons between coins and sarcophagi.

There is no common destiny to be shared between the national cultures of Senegal and Guinea; but there is a common destiny between the Senegalese and Guinean nations which are both dominated by the same French colonialism. If it is wished that the national culture of Senegal should come to resemble the national culture of Guinea, it is not enough for the rulers of the two peoples to decide to consider their problems—whether the problem of liberation is concerned, or the trade-union question, or economic difficulties—from similar viewpoints. And even here there does not seem to be complete identity, for the rhythm of the people and that of their rulers are not the same. There can be no two cultures which are completely identical. To believe that it is possible to create black culture is to forget that niggers are disappearing, just as those people who brought them into being are seeing the breakup of their economic and cultural supremacy. There will never be such a thing as black culture because there is not a single politician who feels he has a vocation to bring black republics into being. The problem is to get to know the place that these men mean to give their people, the kind of social relations that they decide to set up, and the conception that they have of the future of humanity. It is this that counts; everything else is mystification, signifying nothing.

In 1959, the cultured Africans who met at Rome never stopped talking about unity. But one of the people who was loudest in the praise of this cultural unity, Jacques Rabemananjara, is today a minister in the Madagascan government, and as such has decided, with his government, to oppose the Algerian people in the General Assembly of the United Nations. Rabemananjara, if he had been true to himself, ought to have resigned from the government and denounced those men who claim to incarnate the will of the Madagascan people. The ninety thousand dead of Madagascar have not given Rabemananjara authority to oppose the aspirations of the Algerian people in the General Assembly of the United Nations.

It is around the peoples' struggles that African-Negro culture takes on substance, and not around songs, poems, or folklore. Senghor, who is also a member of the Society of African Culture and who has worked with us on the question of African culture, is not afraid for his part either to give the order to his delegation to support French proposals on Algeria. Adherence to African-Negro culture and to the cultural unity of Africa is arrived at in the first place by upholding unconditionally the peoples' struggle for freedom. No one can truly wish for the spread of African culture if he does not give practical support to the creation of the conditions necessary to the existence of that culture; in other words, to the liberation of the whole continent.

I say again that no speech-making and no proclamation concerning culture will turn us from our fundamental tasks: the liberation of the national territory; a continual struggle against colonialism in its new forms; and an obstinate refusal to enter the charmed circle of mutual admiration at the summit.

Early Nationalism in East and Central Africa

TERENCE RANGER[2]

On the particular [question of primary resistance and modern mass nationalism], there has been very considerable scholarly disagreement. One school of thought would emphatically differentiate the initial violent reactions from later manifestations of opposition and particularly from nationalism. Nationalist movements, they contend, are essentially modernist in outlook and are directed towards the concept of a territorial loyalty. Primary resistance movements, on the other hand, were inherently backward-looking and traditional, not only tribal but emphatic of the most "reactionary" elements in tribal life. Such movements, it is held, repudiated those within African societies who wished to come to terms with modernization and to accept education, the missionary influence, and the new commercial and technical opportunities. Resistance movements of the early colonial period were romantic, reactionary struggles against the facts, the passionate protest of societies that were shocked by a new age of change and would not be comforted.

[I disagree with this argument and] it seems worthwhile to see if it is not possible to establish some "historic connections" between primary and secondary resistance. No such argument has yet been propounded for East and Central Africa, and probably no argument in the same sort of terms can be propounded. But it seems worthwhile to see if it is not possible to challenge the assumption of hiatus in East and Central Africa also. This paper is an initial exploration of such possibilities.

The argument for East and Central Africa has to begin, I think, by establishing what is perhaps an obvious but yet insufficiently appreciated fact: namely, that the environment in which later African politics developed was

---

[2] This excerpt is taken from pages 438, 439-40, 442-51, and 631-637 of Terence Ranger, "Connections between Primary Resistance Movements and Modern Mass Nationalism in East and Central Africa: Part 1," and "Connections between Primary Resistance Movements and Modern Mass Nationalism in East and Central Africa: Part 2," by Terence Ranger, originally published in *The Journal of African History* 9, no. 3 (1968), pp. 437-53, and *The Journal of African History* 9, no. 4 (1968), pp. 631-41.

shaped not only by European initiatives and policy or by African cooperation and passivity, but also by African resistance. In this sense, at least, there is certainly an important connection between resistance and later political developments.

An example of this which I have elaborated elsewhere is that of the Ndebele of Southern Rhodesia. Their uprising in 1896 was defeated, but they came out of it with some political gains. Before 1896 the Ndebele state had been in ruins; its white rulers had broken up all its institutions, confiscated all Ndebele land and nearly all Ndebele cattle, and disregarded every Ndebele political authority. The 1896 rising at least showed the whites that this had been unwise. The Ndebele were still a formidable military foe; it took many men and much money to defeat their rising, and even then it had not been convincingly defeated by the end of the 1896 dry season. Rhodes faced a long, drawn-out war of attrition in which the authority of the British South Africa Company might well have collapsed through bankruptcy or British political intervention. So he negotiated with the Ndebele. They thus won in 1896 what they had not had in 1893—a voice in the settlement. The policy of the British South Africa Company was one defined as being to restore to the Ndebele indunas as much of the powers they had possessed under Lobengula as was possible; they received official salaries. So was struck an alliance between the Ndebele chiefs and the Rhodesian administration, which still has important political consequences today.

But it was not only the attitudes of defeated African societies and those of apprehensive white settlers that were affected by resistance and rebellion. There was a complex interplay between so-called "primary" resistance and manifestations of "secondary" opposition. We have seen above that many scholars have employed a rather rigid periodization in their approach to African nationalist historiography. The period of resistance is followed by hiatus; then arises the new leadership. But we must remember that the effective establishment of colonial rule throughout southern, central, and eastern Africa took a very long time to achieve. Primary resistance to it was still going on in some areas while "secondary" movements were developing elsewhere. Independent churches, trade unions, welfare associations, and Pan-Africanist movements all existed at the same time as expressions of tribal or pan-tribal resistance. This fact was important in forming the attitudes of the more radical "secondary" politicians.

[I refer once again] to the Rhodesian case, one which refers back to Ndebele resistance. In June 1929 the first militant African trade union was holding its meetings in Bulawayo; weekend after weekend, it hammered away on the theme of African unity, appealing not only to the pan-tribal union movements of South Africa but also to successful examples of continuing armed resistance. "If Lobengula had wanted to he could have called every nation to help him. He did not. That is why he was conquered. In Somaliland they are still fighting. That is because they are united. Let us be united."

It will be seen, therefore, that there is a long ancestry behind the attention currently paid by nationalist leaders to the heroic myths of primary resistance. When a man like Nelson Mandela seeks inspiration in tales "of the wars fought by our ancestors in defense of the fatherland" and sees them not merely as part of tribal history but "as the pride and glory of the entire African nation," he is echoing the response of many of his predecessors.

In all these ways, then, resistances formed part of the complex interaction of events which produced the environment for modern nationalist politics. I now want to turn to a more complex and interesting argument. This argument runs that during the course of the resistances, or some of them, types of political organization or inspiration emerged which looked important ways to the future, which in some cases are directly, and in others indirectly, linked with later manifestations of African opposition.

The point can be well illustrated in the cases of the two greatest rebellions in East and Central Africa, the Ndebele-Shona risings of 1896-7 and the Maji Maji rising of 1905. The main question about these risings is not so much why they happened as how they happened. How was it possible for the Ndebele and their subject peoples to rise together in 1896 when in [their previous war against the settlers in] 1893 the subject peoples had abandoned their overlords? How was it possible for the Ndebele and the western and central Shona to co-operate in the risings in view of their long history of hostility? How was it possible for the Shona groups to cooperate among themselves in view of their nineteenth-century history of disunity? How was it possible for the very diverse peoples of southern Tanzania to become involved in a single resistance to the Germans? Finally, how was it that these apparently odd and patchwork alliances offered to the whites a more formidable challenge than had the disciplined professional armies of 1893 or the Hehe wars?

In the Rhodesian case, part of the answer certainly lies in the appeal back to traditions of past political centralization. But in both Rhodesia and in Tanzania, the main answer lies in the emergence of a leadership which was charismatic and revolutionary rather than hereditary or bureaucratic.

In times of emergency, the African societies of East and Central Africa could draw upon a number of traditions of such charismatic leadership. Two emerge as particularly important in connection with the sort of large-scale resistance we are discussing. The first of these is the prophetic tradition. Many African societies of East and Central Africa had religious systems in which specialist officers played an institutionalized prophetic role, speaking with the voice of the divine either through possession or through dream or oracular interpretation. Such prophet officers have usually been regarded by scholars, in common with "traditional religion" as a whole, as conservative and normative forces. The prophet has been thought of as the ally of the established political order and as the guardian of its customary moral norms. But, as I have argued in a recent paper, the prophetic authority could not be so confined; the claim to speak with the voice of the divine was always potentially a revolutionary one, and if the prophet could invest the ordinary operations of a society with divine sanction he could also introduce new commandments. In his brilliant Malinowski Lecture of 1966, I.M. Lewis has suggested a typology and spectrum of possession and prophetic movements which throws a good deal of light on the point I am trying to make. His spectrum ranges from hysterical possession cults on the periphery of religious practice to fully institutionalized tribal religions at the center, in which the messianic revelations of moral teaching shrink into creation myths and myth charters of the establishment. Lewis goes on to discuss the complex relationship of such establishment religions, "which celebrate an accepted code of public morality," with the messianic tradition. Establishment religions, he suggests, may have sprung from or may precede a messianic movement; there are nearly always within them "undercurrents" of messianism and opportunities for the rise of "revitalizing prophets"; and often, where the establishment religion itself seems incapable of revitalization, it is surrounded by peripheral cults in which the innovatory vitality of prophetism is still present. "It seems probable," he writes, "that such displaced and peripherally relegated cults may provide the kind of institutional continuity which, in appropriate historical circumstances, enables new messianic cults to develop."

Something of the same pattern can be seen for the most striking mass primary resistances of East and Central Africa. Certainly it seems to hold for the two great risings already discussed—the Shona-Nedebele and the Maji Maji rebellions. I have argued at length elsewhere that what I described as the "traditional" religious authorities were the main coordinators, and in a real sense the leaders, of the risings in Matabeleland and Mashonalond, and that the priests of the Mwari cult in the first province, and the spirit mediums of the Chaminuka-Nehanda hierarchies in the second, were the main vehicles of cooperation between the various elements engaged. Perhaps in these articles I have emphasized the "traditional" character of this religious leadership too much. Certainly, it was important that they presented themselves as survivors from the imperial past of the Shona—the one cult so intimately identified with the old Rozwi empire and the other with the Mutapa dynasty and its outriders. But at the same time, the emergence of these religious leaders as leaders also of a widespread rebellion constituted what Gann has described as a "theological revolution." Contemporary white observers stressed that the Mwari cult had previously been concerned with matters of peace and fertility and that its militant, authoritarian character in 1896 took them by surprise; no doubt there was both ignorance and naiveté in their idea of its earlier total severance from politics, but there seems no question that the power and the nature of the authority of Mwari priesthood underwent significant development in 1896. Nor does there seem much question that this "theological revolution" took the form ascribed by Doutreloux to the prophet movements. The Mwari priests and the spirit mediums imposed new regulations and prohibitions upon their followers; to enter the rebellion was to enter a new society and to become subject to a new "law;" the rebels were brought into the fellowship of the faithful by the dispensation of "medicine" and promised immunity from bullets; they were promised success in this world and a return from death to enjoy it. (When the religious leaders were attempting in 1897 to bring into being a Rozwi "front" in all the areas of Mashonaland as a means of coordinating the secular side of the rising after the withdrawal of the Ndebele aristocracy, they promised that all Rozwi who were killed should be resurrected and participate in the coming golden age.) The religious leaders moved out of the limitations, which, as well as the advantages, were implied by their connection with specific past political systems and speak to all black men. And they are, to an extent, successful. For a time, the charismatic leadership of the prophets brings together Ndebele aristocrats, subject peoples, deposed Rozwi chiefs and Shona paramounts; as one scholar puts it, "the proud Matabele chieftains now agreed to operate under the supreme direction of an ex-serf, a remarkable man who in "normal" times would hardly have acquired much political influence." In the case of the Maji Maji rising, the evidence presented by Iliffe suggests a possible combination of both the prophetic and the witchcraft-eradication elements in the inspiration and coordination of the rising. Clearly, the Kolelo cult played an important part. It was influential over a wide area and provided centers to which large numbers of people went to receive medicine and instructions which they distributed on return. The evidence is perhaps sufficient to conclude that the Kolelo cult provided a machinery that could reach the peoples of the Rufiji complex and perhaps further afield. Like the Mwari cult, the Kolelo belief involved priest-interpreters of the oracle; like the Mwari cult also, its normal preoccupation was with fertility and the land. And, as Iliffe tells us, some "evidence suggests that in the period before the rebellion, the Kolelo cult was transformed from its normal preoccupation with the land to a more radical and prophetic belief in a reversal of the existing order by direct divine intervention." The prophets of the new development commanded revolt in the name of the new God, who would come to live in the land. "He will change this world and it will be new. His rule will be one of marvels." They provided protective medicine; they prescribed a new form of dress and imposed new prohibitions; they promised invulnerability or resurrection. The drinking of the holy water was a sign of entry into a rebel communion. The appeal was to all Africans. "Be not afraid," the message ran, "Kolelo spares his black children."

At the same time there seems to be evidence to suggest that the innovatory potentialities of witchcraft-eradication movements were also being used. The Vidunda understood the *maji* in the context of an attack on sorcery, Iliffe tells us:

In southern Ubena a series of anti-sorcery movements had entered from the east, from Ungindo and the Kilombero. Maji Maji was also brought by Ngindo, and it seems that the pattern of Bena response followed that normal with a *mwavi* medicine, the hongo administering the maji to the assembled people in the presence of the chief. It seems very probable that both the rebellion and subsequent movements were drawing on an established pattern of indigenous millenarianism. Just as the rising in the Rufiji complex became associated with the cult of Kolelo, so its expansion appears to have taken place within the context of recurrent movements to eradicate sorcery.

My own work on subsequent witchcraft-eradication cults in the Rufiji complex and in the Maji Maji area generally leads me to suppose that the ability of such movements to pass rapidly across clan and tribal boundaries, and to sweep people into a unity which overrides suspicions and allegations of sorcery, was indeed an important element in the 1905 rising.

In the first part of this article a number of possible connections between the last-ditch resisters and the earliest organizers of armed risings, and later leaders of opposition to colonial rule in East and Central Africa, were explored. It was argued that African "primary" resistance shaped the environment in which later politics developed; it was argued that resistance had profound effects upon white policies and attitudes; it was argued that here was a complicated interplay between manifestations of "primary" and "secondary" opposition, which often overlapped with and were conscious of each other. Then the argument turned to a more ambitious proposition, namely that during the course of the resistances, or some of them, types of political organization or inspiration emerged which looked in important ways to the future; which in some cases are directly and in others indirectly linked with later manifestations of African opposition.

Half of the case for this assertion was set out in the first article, and the character of the organization and aspirations of the great resistance movements was discussed. It was argued that they attempted to create a larger effective scale of action; that they endeavored to appeal to a sense of Africanness; that they displayed an ambiguous attitude to the material aspects of white colonial society, often desiring to possess them without abandoning the values of their own communities at the same time; that they attempted to assert African ability to retain control of the world by means of a millenarian message. In all these ways, it was asserted, they were *similar* to later mass movements.

There is undoubtedly a link between these resistances and later mass movements of a millenarian character. Nor is this link merely a matter of *comparing* the Shona-Ndebele or Maji Maji risings with later prophet movements or witchcraft eradication cults. There is often a quite direct connection.

The most direct connections, of course, are provided by examples like that of Nyabingi, which provided the basis both of "primary resistance" and of persistent twentieth-century millenarian manifestations. Next come movements like that of the Mumbo cult in Nyanza province, Kenya. The Mumbo cult has recently been examined in a very interesting paper by Audrey Wipper. It arose among the Gusii, apparently around 1913, after the defeat of various "primary resistances." It reached peaks of activity in 1919, in 1933, and to a lesser extent in 1938 and 1947; it was one of the movements banned in 1954. Thus in point of time it bridged the period between the suppression of the Gusii risings of 1904, 1908, and 1916 and the emergence of modern mass nationalism. In character it was strikingly similar to the sort of movement we have already discussed. Although arising among the Gusii, it was "a pan-tribal pagan sect," creating its own society of true believers, whom it bound by its own codes of conduct and to whom it promised eventual triumph and reward. The colonial period, in its mythology, was merely a testing period devised by the God of Africa to sort out the true believers from the fainthearted; before long, those who remained true would enter into the wealth and power of the whites. Mumbo had the most direct links with the period of primary resistance. The Gusii's most venerated warriors and prophets, noted for their militant anti-British stance, were claimed by the movement, Miss Wipper tells us:

> Zakawa, the great prophet, Bogonko, the mighty chief, and Maraa, the *laibon* responsible for the 1908 rebellion, became its symbols, infusing into the living the courage and strength of past heroes. Leaders bolstered up their own legitimacy by claiming to be the mouth-piece of these deceased prophets.

Indeed, if Miss Wipper is right, we are close here to the idea of an "alternative leadership," stemming from traditions of resistance and opposed to officially recognized authority. Especially successful in effecting such aims were the descendants of the prophets and chiefs concerned. Thus, with the progeny of the Gusii heroes supporting the sect, a physical as well as a symbolic link with the past was established. Here was a powerful symbolic group whose prestige and authority could well be used to arouse, strengthen, and weld the various disunited cults into a solid anti-British position. Miss Wipper makes the important point that the cult looked back only to those figures who themselves stood out from and tried to transform traditional small-scale society; "it looks to the past for inspiration and to the future for living. Its goals are Utopian and innovative rather than traditional and regressive," involving attacks upon small-scale traditional values as well as upon European values. It would seem it is justifiable to apply the word "radical" to the cult, and to claim that "the history of African nationalism in the district must be traced back to its emergence."

Similar examples of direct "physical" and indirect "symbolic" connection with primary resistances can be given for Christian independent church movements. In the first category comes, for instance, Shembe's Nazarite Church in Zululand. This impressive manifestation of Zulu, rather than South African, nationalism referred back to one of the most dramatic occasions in the history of Zulu nationalism, the Bambata rising of 1906. It was physically linked to this rising through the person of Messen Qwabe, one of its leaders. Shembe himself proclaimed, "I am going to revive the bones of Messen and of the people who were killed in Bambata's rebellion." All five sons of Messen have joined the church, which was given posthumous spiritual approval by their dead father, and it is taken for granted that all members of the Qwabe clan will be members of it. In the second category comes Matthew Zwimba's church of the White Bird, established in 1915 in the Zwimba Reserve in Mashonaland, which appealed to the memory of the 1897 rising by regarding all those who died in the fighting in the Zwimba area as the saints and martyrs of the new church. It is important to note also that Zwimba regarded himself as very much a modernizer and succeeded, at least for a time, in establishing himself as the intermediary between the chiefs and people of Zwimba and representatives of the modern world.

It can be shown, then, that some at least of the intermediary opposition movements of a millenarian character, which are usually, by common consent, given a place in the history of the emergence of nationalism, were loosely linked, as well as essentially similar, to some movements of primary resistance. Can we go further than this? It would be possible to argue, after all, that whatever may be the interest of such millenarian movements in the history of African politics, they have not in fact run into the mainstream of modern nationalism and in some instances have clashed with it. A movement like Dini Ya Msambwa might be cultivated for short-term purposes by a political party—as KANU is said to have cultivated it in order to find support in an otherwise KADU area—but it can hardly be thought to have had much future within the context of modern Kenyan nationalism.

It seems to me that there are a number of things to be said at this stage. I have argued that modern nationalism, if it is to be fully successful, has to discover how to combine mass enthusiasm with central focus and organization. This does not mean that it needs to *ally* itself with movements of the sort I have been describing that succeeded, on however limited a scale, in arousing mass enthusiasm. Indeed, it will obviously be in most ways a rival to them, seeking to arouse mass enthusiasm for its own ends and not for theirs. But it would be possible to present a triple argument at this stage. In the first place, one could argue, where nationalist movements do succeed in achieving mass emotional commitment, they will often do it partly by use of something of the same methods, and by appealing to something of the same memories as the movements we have been discussing. In the second place, where nationalist movements are faced with strong settler regimes in southern Africa, they will tend to move towards a strategy of violence, which is seen by them as springing out of the traditions of "primary resistance." And in the third place, where nationalist movements fail, either generally or in particular areas, to capture mass enthusiasm, they may find themselves opposed by movements of this old millenarian kind, some of which will still preserve symbolic connections at least with the primary resistances.

The new mass party in East and Central Africa, as it spreads to the rural districts, comes to embody much of the attitude which has hitherto been expressed in less articulate movements of rural unrest. It often appears in a charismatic, almost millenarian role—the current phrase, "a crisis of expectations," which politicians from Kenya to Zambia employ to describe their relations with their mass constituents, is not a bad description of the explosive force behind all the movements we have described. Often, the party locally—and nationally—appeals to the memories of primary resistance, and for the same reason as the millenarian cults did: because it is the one "traditional" memory that can be appealed to which transcends "tribalism" and which can quite logically be appealed to at the same time as tribal authorities are being attacked and undermined. My own experience of nationalist politics in Southern Rhodesia certainly bears out these generalizations. It was the National Democratic Party of 1961 which first really penetrated the rural areas and began to link the radical leadership of the towns with rural discontent. As it did so, the themes and memories of the rebellions flowed back into nationalism.

> In rural areas, meetings became political gatherings and more, the past heritage was revived through prayers and traditional singing, and ancestral spirits were evoked to guide and lead the new nation. Christianity and civilization took a back seat and new forms of worship and new attitudes were thrust forward dramatically. The spirit pervading the meetings was African and the desire was to put the twentieth century in an African context.

So Mr. George Nyandoro, grandson of a rebel leader killed in 1897, and nephew of a chief deposed for opposition to rural regulations in the 1930s, appealed in his speeches to the memory of the great prophet Chaminuka, round whom the Shona rallied in the nineteenth century; so Mr. Nkomo, returning home in 1962, was met at the airport by a survivor of the rebellions of 1896-7, who presented him with a spirit axe as a symbol of the apostolic succession resistance; so the militant songs copied from Ghana were replaced by the Old tunes belonging to spirit mediums and rebel leaders.

It is natural that a nationalist movement that is still engaged in an increasingly violent struggle for independence will turn even more exclusively to the tradition of resistance. This has certainly happened in Southern Rhodesia, for example. The present phase of guerrilla activity in Rhodesia is called by the nationalists "Chimurenga," the name given by the Shona to the risings:

> "What course of action will lead to the liberation of Zimbabwe?" asks a Zimbabwe African National Union writer. It is not the path of appeasement. It is not the path of reformism. It is not the path of blocking thirds. It is the path of outright fearless defiance of the settler Smith's fascist regime and fighting the current war for national liberation. It is the path of direct confrontation. It is the path of Chimurenga.

Nationalism in Sierra Leone

MARTIN KILSON[3]

A much neglected feature of the study of colonial change in Africa has been the transformation of the traditional *elite*. As a group they claimed a disproportionate share in modern social change, owing largely to their role in local colonial administration. Their position enabled them to retain traditional authority while simultaneously pursuing wealth and power in the modern sector of colonial society. Among the sources of new wealth available to chiefs were:

1. direct money payments by governments
2. tax extortion
3. salary payments by native administrations, and
4. the commercialization of chiefs' customary economic rights

The colonial transformation of traditional rulers had a considerable impact upon their relations with the peasantry. The chiefs, exposed to both colonial administration and the market economy, became a mediating agency through which much of modernity—especially its socio-political orientations—reached the masses in rural society. The particular use chiefs made of this function, especially the furtherance of their own modernization, influenced the changing political relationships between them and the peasantry.

The chiefs often abused local tax administration and perhaps the most important consequence of this was the emergence of a characteristically modern group conflict in local African society. This conflict was characterized by a form of rural "radicalism," which in some instances constituted a virtual peasant revolt against traditional rulers and authority.

In Sierra Leone this rural radicalism was evident in the 1930s, and it was

---

[3] This excerpt is taken from Martin Kilson, *Political Change in a West African State: A Study of the Modernization Process in Sierra Leone* (Cambridge, MA: Harvard University Press, 1966), pp. 53-54, 60-67, 68-72, and 89-93. Martin Kilson is professor emeritus of government at Harvard University.

particularly strong in the immediate postwar years (1946-51) and has sometimes flared up since then. On one occasion (October 1950) it took the form of a violent riot which involved some 5,000 peasants and hinterland town-dwellers in Kailahun District. Commenting on this riot in his annual report to the governor, the chief commissioner observed that "the extent and violence of the rioting, which spread from Kailahun to outlying towns and villages . . . with casualties and considerable damage to property, made it necessary to summon police help from Freetown." In late 1955 and early 1956 a recurrence of rural radicalism approximated a peasant revolt properly so-called; the commission of inquiry described it as a "mass disobedience to authority." The disturbances, known commonly as tax riots, involved "many tens of thousands" of peasants and hinterland town-dwellers and entailed widespread property destruction (especially chiefs' property—e.g., cattle, surplus crops, modern homes), with damages estimated at £750,000.

As regards the political meaning of this rural radicalism, it is perhaps best described . . . as peasant rebellion. The previously mentioned peasant riots seldom entailed demands for the destruction of the existing system of traditional authority . . . but instead were aimed at ameliorating aspects of its use. Such a distinction assists us in grasping the rather peculiar ambivalence of many Africans (literate and illiterate, rural and urban-dwelling) toward traditional rulers. In the words of Lucy Mair:

> In the eyes of the same persons, the chiefs may be symbols of reaction, symbols of group unity, and symbols of pride in national history. That is why there has been no move to eliminate them from the political system altogether.

The chiefs' involvement in cash crop production and marketing created a competitive relationship between chiefs and the peasantry that had no precedent in tradition. The relationship was essentially modern or Western in nature. It stemmed from the money economy and related institutions established by colonial rule. It depended upon colonial legal and political support. Since there was no basis in the indigenous scheme of things for legitimizing this economic role of chiefs, the peasantry could not be expected to relate to it in traditional terms.

As it happened, the peasantry viewed the chiefs' role in the cash economy in modern competitive terms. It was seen as an unfair competitive advantage. As early as 1903, a Sierra Leone government report to the Colonial Office recognized this situation: "The chiefs cannot understand . . . that their young men prefer leaving their villages for work on the railway and in Freetown; but, considering that they got a good wage for their labor, from 9d. to 1s. a day, they naturally prefer it to unpaid labor in their villages under their chiefs." Similarly, a correspondence to the *Sierra Leone Weekly News* in 1930 related the economic relationships between chiefs and peasants in the following terms:

> The protectorate youths are forced to come to the Colony proper because of the almost inhuman oppression that seems to be going on. The natives are forced to make the chiefs' farms, to do all public buildings for the chiefs, all government buildings, and the monies for all work done are paid to the chiefs; and if they refuse to turn up or are late, they are fined heavily; and they have to provide their food whilst doing these public works. Over and above that, they are fined heavily at court even beyond their means, and if they can manage a little time to make a small farm, the chiefs portion is also demanded. If you produce a good quantity of rice in your farm, the chief is sure to know it, and some charge is brought against you to take all that rice away. . . . Further, if you show any attitude of resistance or unwillingness to conform to the chiefs' dictates, you are either recommended for imprisonment or for deportation.

Although the average peasant's attitude toward the chiefs' advantage in the market economy was essentially economic in origin, it eventually became part of a wider outlook which would prove a basis for political action. A district commissioner's report for the year 1921, for instance, . . . mentioned that the "collection of tribute is the most fertile source of abuse and complaint."

The transmutation of specific economic grievances into a broader social and political consciousness, however, had to await the penetration of local African society by the middle-class nationalism of the post-World War II period.

The participation of chiefs in the colonial economic system has made it exceedingly difficult to categorize them simply as a "traditional *elite*." In reality they are both traditional and modern authorities. This situation has both weakened and strengthened their authority and power, depending upon the particular combination of modern circumstances confronted by chiefs at any given point in time.

As regards their authority, chiefs had superficially the best of both worlds: they freely invoked either traditional or modern justifications as circumstances required. In reality, however, this double standard was not easy to uphold unless the peasant masses remained unqualifiedly attached to traditional authority. The fact of the matter was that the same forces of change that made chiefs what may be called a tradition-modern *elite* equally influenced the peasantry and undercut or questioned allegiance to traditional authority. As we have shown, some peasants considered the chiefs' role in the modern economy an unfair competitive advantage and refused, often in violent ways, to accept it.

As regards their power—i.e., the physical means enabling chiefs to command or influence people—there is little doubt that traditional rulers became essentially modern. Most if not all of their traditional sources of power (e.g., slavery, war making, economic preemption) were either destroyed or regulated by the colonial state. What remained of these (e.g., customary rights of tribute, labor, land rights) was closely articulated to the colonial processes of social and economic change that they can scarcely be called "traditional."

The political implications of this situation are, I think, crucial for understanding the role of traditional rulers in African political change. The traditional rulers may be expected to support that political arrangement which will enable them (1) to maximize modern sources of their power and (2) simultaneously maintain as much as possible of traditional authority. Under colonial rule this political arrangement prevailed in its purest form: *ergo*, the accommodation by chiefs to the colonial system. Similarly, in the period of nationalist political change one can expect to find the traditional rulers shifting, especially as the central political power shifts, slowly but definitely away from accommodation to colonial rule toward a shrewd selection of political alliances among competing nationalist groups. Again, this shift will be governed by the chiefs' calculation of which nationalist group will best enable them to maximize modern sources of power and simultaneously retain much of their traditional authority.

Apart from the manner in which the chiefs' authority and power were modernized, a number of other circumstances enabled chiefs to pursue the political strategy I attribute to them. For one thing, the new *elite* nationalist leaders were frequently the direct kin of traditional rulers. They were thus disposed to assist chiefs in making the transition from traditional to modern society while at the same time upholding the traditional authority of chiefs. The fact that the kin of chiefs have become political leaders in emergent African societies is itself linked to the greater opportunities chiefs had to take advantage of social change. Their favored status under colonial administration and the wealth they derived from it enabled traditional rulers to provide their kin with the best education available. In the Sierra Leone Protectorate and elsewhere in Africa the educated kin of chiefs were among the first African professionals and the first senior African members of the colonial civil service. From these preferred positions they readily moved into nationalist political leadership.

Another factor that enabled traditional rulers to pursue the political strategy sketched here is that, though traditional values were shaken by social change, their hold on the rural masses did not dwindle completely. Despite the important occasions of peasant rebellion against certain uses of traditional authority in the context of modernization, the masses displayed the ambivalence toward chiefs and traditional authority that we have already noted. Thus there is still a real sense in which chiefs continue as the sole legitimate representatives of traditional values (especially as they relate to personal or group allegiances to authority) in the eyes of most people. In the context of modern political change this was a fact of considerable significance. The nationalistic new *elite*, in its attempt to secure mass political support beyond the urban centers of its own origin, normally accommodated its political organization, methods, and policies to the strategic position held by chiefs in local society, such was particularly the case for the Sierra Leone People's Party, the dominant party in the rise of postwar nationalism in Sierra Leone.

Usually the more advanced elements among the new African "social categories" arising under colonialism and afterward have been regarded as essentially a "new *elite*." ... The new African *elite* was distinct from the lower strata of the *elite* as well as from the bulk of the African population. By virtue of their occupation, wealth, and prestige, senior civil servants, wealthy merchants and traders, wealthy planters, bankers, contractors, some manufacturers, African managers in European firms, the political *elite*, and members of the liberal professions constituted a veritable upper class. Those engaged in such occupations were not merely functionally distinct from the lower level of the new *elite* (e.g., junior civil servants, clerks, tailors, carpenters, seamstresses, masons, medium traders); they were equally distinguished by their affluence and style of life and by their significantly higher level of education. They were also differentiated from the lower level of the new *elite* insofar as they normally dominated the development of modern nationalist politics.

The new African *elite* ... was a politically conscious group which entered politics to advance its overall position in society and ultimately to become a ruling or governing class. ... It employed politics to become a ruling class or a politically effective group within the ruling community. In the context of colonial modernization, the African middle class's attempt to become a ruling class meant that it had to (1) replace the expatriate ruling oligarchy as the "standard setting" group and (2) appropriate for itself the prestige of the traditional *elite* as the most legitimate authority in the eyes of the black masses who still resided largely in traditional society.

The first of these requirements of ruling-class status was met by the upper level of the new *elite* through the political nationalism that they created and organized. To meet the second requirement, they often returned to traditional society in order to assume the symbols, titles, and other badges of prestige and rank which still carried weight with the common man.

It is not altogether correct to say that this group's success displaced the upper strata in traditional societies. Although there has certainly been a good measure of *elite* displacement under colonialism and since, traditional forces have qualified the process of displacement at several crucial points. First, traditional rulers have been able to modernize themselves to the point of assuming many new-*elite* attributes. Second, a not inconsiderable proportion of the professional and business elements among the new *elite* are the offspring of traditional rulers. Third, the new-*elite* persons of commoner origin have sought the symbols and badges of prestige, status and rank controlled by the traditional *elite*. This process has been particularly evident in West African states and in East Africa, especially Uganda.

Accordingly, what emerged in the new African societies was a legitimate ruling class which was a peculiar African amalgam of the traditional *elite* and upper level of the new *elite*. Marriages and the school system probably brought them together. Even more important perhaps was the sharing of political power.

The main phase of the development of the new *elite* in Sierra Leone coincided with the rise of anti-colonialism. World War I marked a watershed for both of these developments. The old middle class of the late nineteenth and early twentieth century, whose style of life may be described in terms of "bourgeois, old style," emphasizing thrift and hard work as the conditions for getting ahead in modern society, gave way at this time to a different type of middle-class outlook which focused upon the resources of the colonial government as the more effective means of advancement. This change in middle-class outlook was partly related to the fact that increasing numbers of professional Africans found government service the most suitable outlet for their skills. In 1925, for instance, 57 percent of the medical doctors in Sierra Leone were so employed. This, in turn, whetted the appetite of the new *elite* for more government jobs, as well as for direct government assistance in training and preparation for government posts.

Stripped to its essentials, the anti-colonial nationalism that emerged after World War I was merely the ideological projection of middle-class Africans for new jobs and related perquisites which only the government could provide. Inevitably, this nationalism confronted the sizable expatriate personnel who claimed the most desirable posts in the colonial establishment, as the main barrier to its goal. This barrier, it was soon discovered, could be overcome only with the demise of the colonial regime itself. Hence the anti-colonial orientation of African nationalism.

The National Congress of British West Africa founded in Accra, the Gold Coast, in March 1920, with branches in Sierra Leone, the Gambia, and Nigeria, was the major organizational expression of the new middle-class nationalism after World War I. The aims of the NCBWA covered the whole gamut of essentially middle-class needs, among which were greater African representation in central colonial government, expansion of the franchise, and the establishment of a British West African University to give British Africans technical and scientific training, and especially the training necessary for the holding of positions in the Colonial Service. Only a small portion of these aims was even partly achieved during the 1920s and 1930s. At the end of World War II, however, the authorities moved toward greater African representation in central government, which widened the possibilities for greater use of government resources for the development of the African *elite*.

This development, as the *elite* saw it, was basically a matter of the replacement of expatriate personnel at all levels of the colonial establishment. In Sierra Leone this policy of "Africanization" commenced in the late 1940s and by the end of the 1950s had no small achievement to its credit. . . . Professional Africans were the main beneficiary of this increase. By 1956 some 80 percent of the medical doctors were in government service, compared to 57 percent twenty-one years earlier, and in 1960 nearly 40 percent of the lawyers were so employed. Furthermore, a majority of the doctors and lawyers pursued private practice along with government employment. Africanization also applied to the training of professionals. Whereas the colonial government in Sierra Leone had sent fewer than one hundred students overseas for education in the period 1943-49, the Sierra Leone People's Party (SLPP) government, elected to office in 1951, had sent over three hundred students for higher education overseas by 1959. The SLPP government also assumed full financial responsibility for Fourah Bay College (now the University College of Sierra Leone) during this period; today most students at the College receive government scholarships.

The SLPP government has also extended wide assistance to the business community among the African *elite*. In the mid-1950s the government announced that it was government's policy to encourage private enterprise and by the end of the 1950s a number of measures had been instituted to this end.

Manufacturing machinery was purchased and sold to African capitalists at less than original cost; African produce firms were given special consideration by the Sierra Leone Government Produce Marketing Board when purchasing cash crops for export; the Development of Industries Board was established to provide loans and easy credit to African businessmen; a variety of assistance, including credit, was extended to the large cash crop planters organized into cooperatives; and, finally, government pressure was brought to bear upon expatriate firms to expand their African managerial personnel and to upgrade it without let or hindrance.

With the establishment of the independent state of Sierra Leone in April 1961, the new *elite*, now with a governing class, obtained incomparable opportunities for further development. But it was no longer quite so easy for the new *elite* to justify claims upon government resources precisely in the same nationalistic mode that prevailed before independence. The range of self-serving policies that the new *elite* could have been accepted by the African majority in the pre-independence period as being in the public interest was much more limited in the post-independence era. Yet there will always be a lot of room for maneuver by the *elite* in this regard.

For instance, it is certainly arguable that the use of government resources to expand professional categories like that of medical doctors was as much in the public or national interest as it was in that of the new *elite*. Throughout

West African states medical doctors shun many crucial areas of medicine because, as a report of the Nigerian government has noted, they "offer very little or no scope for remunerative practice."

In 1958 such important medical fields in Nigeria as pathology, dermatology, malariology, nutrition, anaesthetics, among others, had only a few or no practitioners. This situation necessarily affected the efficiency of any developing state in tropical Africa and cannot be left wanting; and to the extent that it is attended to, the result is as much in the public as in the new *elite*'s interest.

Yet every instance of government assistance to the professional and business categories of the *elite* could hardly be rationalized invariably in this way. Much of this assistance was purely and simply self-serving, with little or no gain for the public interest. Even so, it must be recognized that what we call public interest was a meaningless notion separate from specific group or class interest; the evaluation of the claims of both upon government resources must, therefore, take into consideration the relative nature of the relationship between them. As one scholar has put it:

> Private groups have a remarkable facility in the rationalization of private gain with the public interest. The principal driving forces in politics are class interests and group interests; they make themselves felt, regardless of the kind of government or social organization that exists. Yet the promotion of the public good cannot be accomplished apart from class or special interest. The public good is, after all, a relative matter.

Nationalism and Mau Mau

BRUCE BERMAN[4]

What was Mau Mau? What was its significance in the history of Kenya or, more broadly, the history of colonial Africa? What can an understanding of Mau Mau tell us about the colonial confrontation of African "tradition" and Western "modernity"? Almost forty years after the colonial authorities in Nairobi declared a state of emergency to crush what they insisted was a savage and wholly evil secret cult, conclusive answers to these questions remain elusive. "The horror story of the Empire in the 1950s," as John Lonsdale calls it, continues to be a source of political and intellectual controversy. During the 1970s and again in the mid-1980s, Kenyan intellectuals and political figures clashed over conflicting interpretations of Mau Mau, with many aging ex-Mau Mau fighters also jumping into the fray The historical and fictional writings on Mau Mau of Kenya's leading intellectual dissidents, Ngugi wa Thiong'o and Maina wa Kinyatti, were factors in their detention and exile. Academic interest in Mau Mau has surged once more, with a whole series of monographs and papers appearing since 1986 which explore yet again its nature and place in the politics of colonial and post-colonial Kenya.

Central to the debates over Mau Mau is the nature of its relationship to nationalism in Kenya. Was it a parochial tribal uprising or the central episode of Kenya's national liberation struggle? Were the Mau Mau forest fighters tribal traditionalists or nationalist patriots? Despite its military defeat by Imperial forces, did Mau Mau force the British into social and political reforms which led to independence under an African government? If Mau Mau fought for national liberation, why was it unable to articulate a trans-ethnic national ideology? This article addresses these questions through a critical examination of the conflicting interpretations of Mau Mau's relationship with nationalism, fol-

---

[4] This excerpt is from Bruce Berman, "Nationalism, Ethnicity, and Modernity: The Paradox of Mau Mau." *Canadian Journal of African Studies/Revue Canadienne des Études Africaines* 25, no. 2 (1991), pp. 181-206. Bruce Berman is professor emeritus in the Department of Political Studies at Queens University in Ontario, Canada.

lowed by a plausible reconstruction of the relationship suggested by an understanding of the internal conflicts in Kikuyu society in the first decade after World War II.

Mau Mau: Anti-Nationalism or Militant Nationalism?

In the late 1940s colonial officials first became aware of what they believed was a secret organization among African farm labourers on the European estates of the Rift Valley which they named "Mau Mau." Through the years of the Emergency from 1952 to 1960, and into the first years of Kenya's independence after 1963, the dominant interpretation of this phenomenon focused on its essentially tribal and religious character. This view, with variations, comprised the conventional wisdom about Mau Mau shared not only by colonial officials in Nairobi and London, white settlers, and missionaries, but also by journalists and academic commentators from Britain and several other countries.

In the most coherent official version, Mau Mau was depicted as a savage, violent, and depraved tribal cult, an expression of unrestrained emotion rather than reason. It sought to turn the Kikuyu people back to "the bad old days" before enlightened British rule had brought the blessings of modern civilization and development. . . . As the British parliamentary delegation which visited Kenya in 1954 put it:

> Mau Mau intentionally and deliberately seeks to lead the Africans of Kenya back to the bush and savagery, not forward into progress.

Depraved, murderous, and wholly evil, Mau Mau had to be totally destroyed.

This characterization of Mau Mau, repeated almost daily for several years in press conferences, news briefs, and interviews from government information agencies in Nairobi and London, and widely disseminated in print and broadcasts by the press throughout the world, became and remains, especially in Englishspeaking countries, the image of the phenomenon in popular culture. . . .

Mau Mau's atavistic mind and tribal scale made it the enemy, the very antithesis, of nationalism. Mau Mau could not be an expression of nationalism because it led away from everything the latter represented as an essential part of the modernization process.

> No Western observer, not even those on the anti-colonial left, saw Mau Mau as the political expression of national integration. . . . The movements' symbols had nothing "Kenyan" about them. Mau

Mau, uniquely, seemed to be a core radicalism which rejected the nation. (Lonsdale, 1989: 7)

By the mid-1960s this interpretation began to be challenged by a revisionist version of Mau Mau which depicted it as an essential, if radical, component of African nationalism in Kenya....
The second challenge to the interpretation of Mau Mau as atavism is a thoroughly academic monograph, based on extensive documentary analysis and numerous interviews with African political figures, composed by John Nottingham, a maverick colonial administrator who had rejected the official version of Mau Mau, and Carl Rosberg, a political scientist from the University of California at Berkeley. They state their revisionist purpose right at the outset:

> "Mau Mau" is identified with the militant nationalism and the violence which characterized the politics of central Kenya before and during the early years of the Emergency.... This book presents an alternative interpretation of "Mau Mau," in which we will be concerned with the modern origins of African politics and their pattern of development, with particular emphasis on the politicization and mobilization of the Kikuyu people.... In our view, the outbreak of open violence in Kenya in 1952 occurred primarily because of a European failure rather than an African one; it was not so much a failure of the Kikuyu people to adapt to a modern institutional setting as it was a failure of the European policy-makers to recognize the need for significant social and political reform.

... How could such divergent, indeed contradictory, characterizations of Mau Mau develop as successive influential explanations of the phenomenon, with the "militant nationalism" model largely supplanting the "atavistic tribalism" model among Africanists by the end of the 60s? The matter becomes even more compelling when one examines the explanations more closely and finds that they are in fact based on essentially identical premises about modernity, development, and nationalism. This paradox reveals some of the crucial difficulties involved not only in understanding Mau Mau, but in understanding the phenomenon called African nationalism....
For most of the first decade after 1945, British political development policy had no clear role for African nationalism, but by the early 1950s nationalist organizations were disrupting British hopes for a very gradual process of national development and devolution of power in which they could hand-pick and train their successors. The problem with African nationalism was neither the legitimacy of its existence nor the acceptability of its goals, but its premature, excessive, and confrontational demands. It became clear in colony after colony,

however, and in Kenya by 1957-58, after African political activity was permitted to resume at the end of the military phase of the Emergency, that nationalist intransigence rendered official plans for political development irrelevant. Thus, by the mid-1950s British policy increasingly accepted African nationalism and moved to co-opt its leaders and organizations into collaboration in the project of national development. . . .

Collaboration with modernizing nationalist leaders and their organizations became even more important in the face of the possibilities of social decay and disorder attendant on rapid social change which uprooted Africans from the comforting communal microcosm of the tribe. Development produced a dangerous period of transformation in which men were mobilized out of the sacralized traditional world but not yet fully absorbed into the wider identities and secular orientation of modern national society. Amongst migrant labourers and cash-crop farmers, urban factory workers, government clerks, and teachers, there were thousands of transitional men, "nomads of the spirit in search of a new identity." The volatility of these rootless masses, their potential for violence and disorder, stimulated a profound ambivalence in both colonial authorities and social scientists. Mobilization was an essential part of the modernization process, but it was of critical importance that the mobilized were reattached as quickly and securely as possible to the institutions and identities of class and national citizenship. Failure to do so could mean either a turning backward towards a recharged tribalism and its fragmenting hostilities or towards a revolutionary communism aided and abetted by the Soviet Union. The watchwords of political development became order and integration, and nationalist movements and parties became critical agencies for the completion of a successful passage of transition.

Nationalist leaders also assumed a critical role in the process of attaching Africa's masses to new institutions and values. Often graduates of the metropole's finest universities, they were assumed to be thoroughly modern and secular men. Moreover, the shared model of development conceptualized their great personal authority as charismatic leadership essential for guiding Africans over the leap of allegiance, the orientational upheaval, between the opposed categories of traditional, tribal authority, and the legal-rational authority of the modern nation-state . . . [w]hile nationalist organizations and leaders could be assimilated to the rationalist social engineering of nation-building, nationalist passions could not. Colonial officials and political scientists alike shared an aversion to the fervent emotions, deep personal identification, and self-sacrificial commitment also identified with nationalism. In the aftermath of World War II, these sentiments seemed not only irrational but pernicious and destructive. . . .

The question remains as to whether there is a more effective way of understanding the passions of nationalism that will help analyze the character of

Mau Mau and its relationship with nationalism in Kenya. The necessary conceptual tools can be found, I believe, in Benedict Anderson's *Imagined Communities*, one of the most important theoretical essays on nationalism in recent years. In both those attributes which conform to and those which diverge from Anderson's construction of nationalism, one can understand the distinctive character of Mau Mau and its ambiguous relationship to the more typical forms of what he calls "anti-colonial nationalism."

Anderson stresses the importance of historical sequence and precedent for understanding the development of the successive forms of nationalism and the nation-state, which is its institutional container. Rather than originating in the primordial past, both are seen as the product of little more than two hundred years of development. He identifies the origins of nationalism and the modern state in the "creole nationalisms" of the Americas, North and South, and their movements for independence from 1775 to 1830. These revolutionary new nations provided a model that was widely discussed in Europe and available for emulation:

> Out of the American welter came these imagined realities: nation-states, republican institutions, common citizenships, popular sovereignty, national flags and anthems, etc., and the liquidation of their conceptual opposites: dynastic empires, monarchical institutions, absolutisms, subjecthoods, inherited nobilities, serfdoms, ghettos, and so forth. . . . In effect, by the second decade of the nineteenth century, if not earlier, a "model" of the independent national state was available for pirating.

. . . The most recent variant of nationalism, according to Anderson, is the anticolonial nationalisms of the twentieth century, for which all of the previous forms have provided accessible models of nationalism, nation-ness and the state in an international environment in which the sovereign nation-state is the dominant, indeed, unchallenged norm. This nationalism is grounded in the experience of literate and bilingual indigenous intelligentsias fluent in the language of the imperial power, schooled in its "national" history, and staffing the colonial administrative cadres up to but not including its highest levels. These new nations have been essentially isomorphic with previous imperial administrative units. This perspective allows us to understand how the senior imperial administrators from the metropole were able to conceive the project of modernization and nation-building to transform colonies into nation-states, even in advance of the demands of indigenous nationalist movements.

To deal with the critical problem of the passions of nationalism, Anderson stresses the importance of understanding the nation as an imagined community:

> It is imagined because the members of even the smallest nation will never know most of their fellow members, meet them, or even hear of them, yet in the minds of each lives the image of their communion. . . . It is imagined as a community, because, regardless of the actual inequality and exploitation that may prevail in each, the nation is always conceived as a deep, horizontal comradeship. Ultimately it is this fraternity that makes it possible, over the past two centuries, for so many millions of people, not so much to kill, as to willingly die for such limited imaginings.

Unlike the rationalism of liberalism and Marxism, nationalism is much concerned with ultimate meanings, death and immortality. Rather than a political ideology, it has more in common with kinship and religion. It replaces the religious vision of immortality with a secular one based on the nation:

> If nation-states are widely conceded to be "new" and "historical," the nations to which they give political expression always loom out of an immemorial past, and, still more important, glide into a limitless future. It is the magic of nationalism to turn chance into destiny.

Language plays the central role in the creation of the imagined community in so far as it is printed and related to the spread of mass literacy. "Print language is what invents nationalism, not a particular language per se." In the European experience a diversity of dialects was reduced to a much smaller number of standardized print vernaculars, while in the creole nations of the Americas and the colonial empires of the twentieth century, the print language was primarily that of the imperial metropole. In all of these instances, the growing number of readers formed the embryo of the nationally imagined community, with the production and consumption of novels and newspapers being particularly important in making possible the imagining of the nation.

The role of print language in the development of nationalism is closely linked to the development of what Anderson calls "print capitalism." Printing and book production was one of the key industries of early capitalism. The principal consumers of literature were the growing middle classes, with the bourgeoisie being the first class to achieve solidarity on a largely imagined basis rooted in universal literacy. Finally, print language is also crucially connected to the development of the modern state. The schools and universities run by the state not only spread universal literacy, but also create the studies of history, literature, and folklore through which the nation takes on concrete and permanent existence, and can systematically reproduce itself from generation to generation. The use of the language as a language of administration shapes the consciousness of the imagined national community within the state cadres. The linkage of print language and the state transforms ethnicity into nationalism and makes the possession of a sovereign state the universally demanded norm for every imagined community. . . .

Anderson stresses that in the development of colonial nationalism "to an unprecedented extent the key early spokesman . . . were lonely, bilingual intelligentsias unattached to sturdy local bourgeoisies," whose pilgrimage among administrative posts ending in the colonial capital was critical to their imagining of a nation,. This was not true, however, for the Kikuyu or for Kenya as a whole through most of the colonial period. The intelligentsia and administrative cadres among the Kikuyu were intimately connected with the development of a petty bourgeoisie. In the particular circumstances of Kenya as a colony of white settlement, the Kikuyu servants of the colonial state consisted of local chiefs and headmen, who never served outside of their original areas, and literate clerks and artisans, who encountered their counterparts from other peoples in Kenya only when they worked in the urban crucible of Nairobi and a few of the other major towns. The pilgrimage for both the Kikuyu new wealthy and new poor was a more restricted circuit between the reserves established by the colonial state, the white settler estates and towns of the Rift Valley, and the capital. From the 1920s, however, the developing elite of accumulators was internally split by a cleavage between the collaborationist chiefs and their families and supporters and a younger and more populist element organized in the Kikuyu Central Association and willing to confront colonial authority over the issue of the "stolen" lands alienated to white settlers and the missionary attack on the Kikuyu custom of female circumcision. At the other pole of the class structure, growing numbers of impoverished Kikuyu were leaving the home territories, now increasingly crowded within their fixed boundaries, to seek land and work as squatters or wage labourers on settler estates or as largely unskilled workers in the towns.

The increasing disparities of wealth and property and developing conflicts within and between the developing social classes in Kikuyu society were expressed in a vigorous internal debate, largely invisible to the British in Kenya and only now being reconstructed, over the meaning of Kikuyu-ness, the nature of the community, the value of tradition, the involvement in new forms of production and exchange, and the degree of acceptance of and assimilation to European culture. Thus, the chiefs and their supporters opposed the more militant Kikuyu Central Association through the pointedly named "Kikuyu Loyal Patriots." Meanwhile, in the aftermath of the breach with the mission societies over the custom of female circumcision, two independent school associations were formed calling themselves the Kikuyu Independent Schools Association and the Kikuyu Karing'a (pure or authentic) Schools.

From the beginning, print-language and literacy in both English and Kikuyu played a crucial role in defining the terms and content of the debate. The developing petty bourgeoisie was commonly referred to as the athomi (literally, "the readers"). In 1928 the KCA began publishing a Kikuyu-language journal called Muigwithania ("The Reconciler"), with Kenyatta as its first editor. An article in an early issue on the word "association" told the readers not to say "that you do not belong to that Association. You are members of the Association since you are all Kikuyu Karing'a (real Kikuyu)." In 1938 Kenyatta published in English his ethnography of the Kikuyu, written during his studies at the London School of Economics with Bronislaw Malinowski, which provided a vigourous defence of Kikuyu custom against European criticism and provided in permanent printed form his version of a pre-colonial pastoral. In this key text of an emerging Kikuyu imagined community, as well as in other writings of the period, there is a strong element of "redemptive criticism," a "present employment of the past in the hopes of reshaping the future."

By the late 1940s the Kikuyu were a deeply divided people, increasingly in conflict among themselves as well as with the colonial political and economic order. In three centres of growing unrest, a growing mass of the dispossessed and impoverished confronted the leadership of the chiefs and the athomi. In the Rift Valley, an increasing number of squatters were expelled from settler estates for refusing to accept ever-tighter restrictions on their herds and use of settler land. In the overcrowded reserves, small peasants desperately clung to fragmented and eroded holdings no longer capable of supporting a family, while wealthy landowners sought to expel tenants and dependents to regain land for more profitable uses. In Nairobi, a largely Kikuyu labour force struggled with growing impoverishment, inflation, and unemployment. The struggle over authentic Kikuyu-ness, over the character of the imagined community, continued unabated. At this point, however, the conceptions of propertied civic virtue . . . began to mock the majority rather than to inspire; . . . those who had the most cause to fight colonial rule had the least chance to merit responsibility. Those whose deeds might deliver power would have no chance to enjoy it. That was the Kikuyu tragedy, a struggle over the moralities of class formation, not mental derangement" (Lonsdale, 1990: 417).

The situation was complicated by the emergence of the Kenya African Union, the first attempt at a pan-ethnic "national" political organization. In this organization we do find an expression of a more typical anti-colonial nationalism. KAU had a multi-ethnic, although largely Kikuyu, leadership of bilingual literates of the type upon which Anderson focuses. It was committed to a very different vision of the imagined community, a multi-ethnic Kenya, and to moderate constitutional politics which accepted the premises of the colonial state's version of modernization and nation-building. However, the failure of the KAU to attain any significant reforms or redress of grievances from the colonial authorities discredited petty bourgeois leadership and shifted the political initiative to younger and more militant figures within the African trade union movement, among the squatters on the settler estates in the Rift Valley and in KAU branches in Nairobi and the Kikuyu districts of central province. In 1950 these leaders embarked upon the campaign of mass oathing to silence the opposition and unify the community. The development of what became known as "Mau Mau" thus threatened both the propertyholding elders and petty bourgeois athomi who claimed the authenticity of Kikuyu civic virtue and authority, and their class counterparts among other ethnic communities in Kenya, who joined together in the leadership of KAU. . . .

While Mau Mau was clearly not a tribal atavism seeking a return to the past, the answer to the question of "was it nationalism?" must be yes and no. What the British called Mau Mau, and by constant repetition imposed on the consciousness of both Kenya and the outside world, was no single thing, but rather a diverse and exceedingly fragmented collection of individuals, organizations and ideas, out of which no dominant concept of a Kikuyu imagined national community had emerged. At the same time, if Mau Mau was not a nativistic revival or atavistic revitalization movement, it did emerge out of a bitterly contested process of reinterpreting and reconstructing tradition that embraced the colonial authorities as well as Kikuyu factions, Leakey as well as Kenyatta; and in which cultural beliefs and symbols were profoundly important. Mau Mau was part of a struggle over the dimensions and meaning of Kikuyu ethnicity and its problematic relationship with both the internal cleavages of class and the wider solidarities of a Kenyan nation.

The colonial authorities' version of Mau Mau as a conspiratorial secret cult attached to it an illusory unity of organization and ideology. The official version also played loosely with the historical sequence of events, focusing on the limited degree of organization and unity achieved by the forest fighters under Dedan Kimathi and General China, adding the connections to the Nairobi "Central Committee," combining both with the "evidence" of oaths often extracted from detainees under torture, and then projecting all of this backward to characterize "Mau Mau" before the Emergency. What the accumulated evidence records, instead, are largely failed efforts to define a Kikuyu nationality linked to a militant populist politics of the poor. How this was to relate to the other imagined communities in Kenya in an independent nation state was not clearly thought through. What is interesting is that the ideological cleavages of contrasting visions of the Kikuyu and Kenyan nations were reproduced within the structure of the Land and Freedom Army itself in conflicts between the literate leaders like Kimathi and Karari Njama and many of the primarily illiterate rank and file of peasants and dispossessed squatters led by men like Stanley Mathenge. "This boiled down, in essence, to the rejection by the non-literate leaders of the state-building, parliamentarist 'Freedom' component, in favour of the peasant/land component, in the forest fighters' 'nationalism'" (Maughan-Brown, 1985: 47). The forest fighters' own name for their movement, *ithaka na wiarhi*, is perhaps better translated, according to Lonsdale, as "freedom through land" or "land and moral responsibility," which invokes the highest civic virtue of Kikuyu elderhood, rather than the more common "land and freedom" which invites the retrospective connotation of "land and national independence" (Lonsdale, 1990: 416 note 118), and thus expresses the distinctive cultural content of Kikuyu internal conflicts as much as an anti-colonial liberation struggle. . . .

Ironically, it was the Emergency which secured the victory of the very different nationalism of the multi-ethnic dominant class that came to power with independence, while Kenyatta's conviction and imprisonment for organizing Mau Mau probably saved his position as the national leader. The elite nationalism of this class was definitively formed during the Emergency itself among the Kikuyu loyalists and the educated elites from other ethnic communities, who shared literacy in English and who travelled their national pilgrimage in less than a decade through increasing access to the bureaucracy of the colonial state and to the expanding "national" political institutions at the centre, created by repeated rounds of constitutional reform. Simultaneously, with the detention or confinement in the reserves of the bulk of the Kikuyu labour force in the colony, replacements were found among other ethnic groups, while economic reforms both raised wages and increased peasant access to cash crop markets—all of which provided a substantially widened base of support for "nationalist" goals when African political organizations were again permitted after 1957. The pressure of this multi-ethnic elite forced the pace of British withdrawal, undermined the political position of white settlers and ultimately made independence under a "multi-racial" regime impossible (Berman, 1990: chapter 9). In them, the British found, rather unexpectedly, the "political class" to whom they could safely turn over power, and belatedly discovered in Kenyatta the moderate modernizing national leader.

The Black Man's Burden

BASIL DAVIDSON[5]

The activists of the 1950s plunged into their chosen road of nationalism, seeing this as the only available guarantee of a route open to progress. They accepted the aim of building nation-states on the British model (or, later, on the French) because, as it seemed to them and as they were strongly advised, there could exist no other useful objective. Nkrumah's advice that they should seek the political kingdom, and all would then be added to them, expressed a central maxim of which the truth appeared self-evident: once sovereignty was seized by Africans no matter under what conditions, the road to freedom and development would be theirs to follow.

That this acceptance of the postcolonial nation-state meant acceptance of the legacy of the colonial partition, and of the moral and political practices of colonial rule in its institutional dimensions, was a handicap which the more perceptive of the activists well perceived. They foresaw some of its possible perils, and they warned against these perils. In accepting the British government's offer of 1951 to make him leader of a Gold Coast (Ghana) government pledged to an eventual African independence—a long step forward at the time—Nkrumah told his voters that "there is a great risk in accepting office under this new constitution which still makes us half-slaves and half-free." There would be a great need for "vigilance and moral courage" to withstand the consequent temptations of "temporary personal advantage." This was because "bribery and corruption, both moral and factual, have eaten into the whole fabric of our society and these must be stamped out if we are to achieve any progress."

No doubt it was inevitable that such warnings fell on deaf ears. Along with the nation-state as necessary aim and achievement, the legacy of the partition was transferred practically intact, partly because it seemed impossible to reject

---

[5] This excerpt is taken from Basil Davidson, *The Black Man's Burden: Africa and the Curse of the Nation-State* (Random House, copyright © 1992), pp. 162-67, 173, 180, 182, and 185. Basil Davidson (1914-2010) was a journalist and scholar who published more than thirty books on African history.

any significant part of that legacy, and partly, as one is bound to think in retrospect, because there was as yet no sufficient understanding of what the legacy implied. There were political thinkers, true enough, who understood that the colonial partition had inserted the continent into a framework of purely artificial and often positively harmful frontiers. There were others who perceived that a petty-bourgeois nationalism was bound to remain a nationalism subordinate to external powers organized on a capitalowning and capital-commanding basis. But they were few, and their voices feeble in the great resounding chorus of anticolonial agitations that was now heard on every side. This chorus had little to say on the subject of nationalism. As a mobilizing and emotively compelling slogan, nationalism had small meaning in the Africa of the 1950s. Its history was as little known as its credentials. Outside the boundaries of thought in a few old nations like Asante, nobody was thinking about the implications of nationhood. The implications that counted were those that linked the slogans of nationalism to a removal of the colonial incubus, to the arrival in Africa of that dispensation of *uhuru*, of freedom, so warmly praised in the wartime propaganda of British imperial agencies. The war had become a *vita vya uhuru*, a war for freedom, and if *uhuru* meant anticolonial nationalism, then let it be so. The already veteran anticolonialist of Nigeria and later president Nnamdi Azikiwe put the matter well when speaking in Washington in 1949. Asked what forces had impelled the struggle of Africans for anticolonial independence, Azikiwe replied by quoting a comment of Eleanor Roosevelt's made during the Second World War. She had affirmed that "we are fighting a war today so that individuals all over the world may have freedom. This means an equal chance for every man to have food and shelter and a minimum of such things as spell happiness. Otherwise we fight for nothing of real value."

In its essence, this 1950s nationalism had far less to do with any national cause than with demands of a social nature and content. "One thing's certain," wrote Jacques Rabemananjara, the Malagasy nationalist, in 1958, "in today's political vocabulary the word nationalism means, generally, the unanimous movement of coloured peoples against Western domination. What does it matter if the word doesn't really describe the phenomenon to which we like to apply it?" What fired the activists, in short, was never an imagined spectacle of the beauties of the sovereign nation-state, but the promise that the coming of the nation-state would strike away the chains of foreign rule and all that these had meant in social and moral deprivation. It has been in this large sense that the language of European nationalism, as applied to Africa, had been consistently misleading. Their poverty of thought about the implications of accepting the sovereign nation-state on the European pattern may be held against the activists; but this poverty was not without its advantages.

Generally, they remained free of the kind of millenarian romanticism which so monstrously inflamed the nationalists of Europe in the nineteenth century, above all in the Germanspeaking states. The violence and death so accurately forecast in the strange but influential writings of Heinrich von Kleist (1777-1811), portending dogmas of the "national will" that were going to end in mass murder, had no echo here. There might be good reason to fear that there would be nationalists in a future Europe who "will know nothing of reverence for anything," as the poet Heine warned against Kleistian thoughts, and "who will ravage without mercy, and riot with sword and axe"; and this prophecy was to be horribly realized a century later. Nationalism in Africa, or whatever was labeled as such, has since then led to plenty of horrors and miseries. But there is nothing in the African nationalist documentation, or in one's memories of what was otherwise said or advised, to give any ground for grim disasters. African nationalism was the product not of a Kleistian chauvinism but of a mixture of antiracism, and, which amounted in practice to the same thing, of anticolonialism. "Let freedom come," and freedom would bring its own good solutions.

This pragmatism, or if one prefers it this poverty of ideological thought, was the natural and direct fruit of African nationalism's being, all through its early and introductory phases, the impulse and achievement of what can broadly be called the "social struggle." Like the European movements of the 1840s, it was always the "labouring poor" whose involvement and effort in the 1950s gave the tribunes of the "national struggle," who were the educated elite in one manifestation or another, their ground to stand on. Without the mass pressure that surged into the streets of colonial cities and made its impact felt even in remote corners of the bush, the educated elite would have remained upon the sidelines of everyday life, genially teased and tolerated by colonial officials of a liberal sort, or else jeeringly ignored and pushed aside by officials of another kind.

As it was, the activists were given power by the pressure of a social struggle, with the ambitions of nationalism very much in second place; and this simplicity of "basic idea," in the familiar terminologies of European nationalism, may be seen as a blessing. It certainly helped to obscure the implications of the nationstatist legacy, but it also meant that African nationalism stayed quite largely immune to the eruptive territorial ambitions and rivalries that have sunk European nation-statism so often into pits of internecine bloodshed. With some minor exceptions, arising largely from claims determined by the arbitrary and inappropriate nature of the imposed frontiers, the record of the modern African nation-state over its forty or so years of life has not led to interstate warfare and, for reasons inherent in its nature that will become clear, is quite unlikely to do so in the future. In all essentials of mobilizing efficacy, African nationalism for long remained close to the social struggles that had given it scope for development.

And so long as this was so, of course, the activists of those times could feel that they need not fear the constricting embrace of a purely nationalist project. They could look beyond that project to the consummation of social struggles which should be far more liberating for their peoples. "Self-government will not necessarily lead to a paradise overnight," commented a Nigerian nationalist as early as 1950, "nor will it turn African nationalist leaders into angels. But it will have ended the rule of one race over another, with all the humiliation and exploitation which that implies. It can also pave the way for the internal social revolution that is required within each country"of a decolonized Africa. The thought was not even a controversial one, as between left and right: all notable nationalists thought and said much the same thing, even if they often put it differently. The same meeting in England which heard the Nigerian I have just referred to was also warned by the staunchly conservative nationalist Dr. Kamuzu Banda of Nyasaland (later president of Malawi). He said, also in 1950, that imminent self government "in Central Africa today would mean delivering the Africans into the hands of white minorities inspired by the same Herrenvolk ideas as the South African Nationalists," by which, of course, he was referring to the Afrikaner white National Party of apartheid. The immediate need was not self government "but a quickening of educational and political development." . . .

Accepting the nation-state that was offered to them, the pioneering nationalists saw no useful alternative and asked no further questions about its credentials or potentials.

And would the great "transferring powers," Britain and then France, have had useful answers to such questions, supposing that these had been posed? It seems not. The authoritative Lord Hailey in his majestic many-volumed survey of Africa and its administrative problems, published at various times between 1938 and 1950, had almost nothing to say about the nationstate and its potentials for good or evil. Lesser authorities did no better, and even those European parties of the left sympathetic to African aspirations, notably the British Labour Party, had little to offer save bromides of goodwill. For this they can scarcely be blamed, if only because knowledge of African realities, in those late colonial times, was in practice restricted to persons able to travel to distant colonies and then able, moreover, to gain access to administrative information. As such persons were never welcome, their coming was rare and their access rarer still.

Even so, in retrospect, it is bound to seem strange that the whole project of nation-statism, of promoting nationalism as a means of promoting nation-states, was so little inspected by British authorities. The French, of course, could and did argue that they were not promoting nation-statism in "their Africa," but the elevation of their colonies to membership in La plus grande France, so that the only nationalism that could count in those colonies would have to be French nationalism. But the British in authority ardently believed in the project of African nation-statism. "The objectives of our colonial policy have been summed up in a number of different formulae," affirmed Sir Hilton Poynton, a former administrative head of the British Colonial Office, speaking in 1978 after a long and successful career, "but the shortest and simplest is 'Nation-building.'" And by this, Sir Hilton clearly meant the "building" of separate nation-states as the successors and inheritors of colonial states.

But would a multiplication of new nation-states be helpful to peace and progress? Nobody seems to have asked, much less answered. And yet the great "transferring powers" were singularly well placed to know that nationalism could "ravage without mercy and riot with sword or axe," as well as with weapons far more dreadful than any known in Heine's time. After all, Europe had just emerged from the latest horrors of nation-statist violence sung to the tunes of Hitler's favorite marching song: "Today Germany is ours, tomorrow the whole wide world." But all that seems to have been forgotten, or at any rate forgotten in African contexts; and insofar as the British took notice of nationalism in Africa, they followed their policy in India and treated it as a subversion better handled by the police until, toward the eleventh hour, they declared that promoting nationalism had been their policy all along. . . .

When it came to choosing interlocuteurs who could and did really speak for their peoples, and who were therefore likely to dominate the political scene after the "transfers of power," but for whom the primacy of external interests was not acceptable, the process went sorely astray from an imperial standpoint. This is a fact which also has its bearing on the poverty of political debate. Senior colonial officials during the 1950s were by far the best informed actors on that scene. But once it came to weighing up the credentials of anticolonial Africans, and the ideas for the future that those Africans might have and mean to promote, the narrowness of these officials' powers of judgment became painfully apparent. Plunged with the advent of anticolonial nationalism into an unfamiliar world of politics, these senior officials had entered terrain they neither understood nor were qualified to measure. . . .

It is consequently fruitless to believe that the end of political empire was a program arranged and designed to give colonized peoples "the best possible start" to their independence. Much was said and done, true enough, to present the imperial withdrawal as a process planned and prepared in advance, and any subsequent mishaps and miseries were to be explained as entirely the fault of Africans failing to carry out "the plan." But the full extent of any plan, most obviously in the French empire, was to conserve as much as possible of the colonial legacy; and even that much of a plan, when perceived, looks like mere opportunism.

In the great example of Nigeria, for instance, local historians well qualified to judge have reached the conclusion that "no conscious British initiative to liquidate the empire was apparent at the Nigerian end." Successive steps and constitutions transferring power simply went with the winds and tides of momentary pressure. The spokesmen of nation-statism were given their head, earlier in the nonsettler colonies, later in those with significantly large white settler minorities. They were then left to make the best they could of the "existing units of territory" in such ways as to ensure that these units remained separate from each other, no matter what arguments there might be, or might have been, for restructuring or federalizing them. Against the 1950s leaders of nationalism, the real count is not that they failed to foresee the traps and snares that lay ahead, but that they all too easily accepted what was offered to them. They accepted the colonial legacy-whether of frontiers or of bureau-dictatorship-on the rash assumption that they could master it. But as things turned out, it mastered them. Critics have said that the pioneering nationalists of the 1950s should have better considered where they were heading and have understood that nation-states fashioned from the structures and relationships of colonial states, and thereby produced from European and not from African history, were bound to be heading for trouble. This is asking a great deal of men and women to whom the lessons and examples of European history had been invariably presented as the sum and summit of all useful experience; moreover, as far as the crucial economic structures and relationships were concerned, these in the 1950s were little understood anywhere. . . .

Such considerations apart, it is a misreading of the history of those years to suppose that the nationalists, or at any rate the best of them, nourished any great illusions as to the obstructive nature of the colonial legacy they were going to accept. Its economic implications may have largely escaped them, just as these escaped their imperial rulers; but they thoroughly understood its political and moral implications, for it was from those implications that they, as the objects of colonial rule, had suffered. At the same time it needs to be recalled that any informed "looking ahead" was difficult or impossible if only because, to the very last, colonial governments in all the empires hugged closely to their chests whatever sound information their administrative files might contain. They camouflaged their social and economic problems with clouds of condescending propaganda. Or they simply denied that these problems existed. They preferred among the nationalists the boneheads to the brilliant, or at least the convenient to the awkwardly questioning. And they generally behaved as though every arrangement for decolonization must be expected in any case to end in tears. . . .

Down the line of agitation and organization, among the mass of rural and urban supporters of the anticolonial movements, there was small sign of any developing loyalty or attachment to this or that colony-turned-nation. What the multitudes wanted, by all the evidence, was not a flag for the people or an anthem for the people, nearly so much as they wanted bread for the people, and health and schools for the people, while caring precious little, as these same multitudes would overwhelmingly prove in the years ahead, about winning frontiers for the people. The jubilant crowds celebrating independence were not inspired by a "national consciousness" that "demanded the nation," any more than were the Romanian peasants and their coevals in the nation-states crystallized some decades earlier from Europe's old internal empires. They were inspired by hope of more and better food and shelter.

Suggested Readings

Anderson, Benedict, *Imagined Communities: Reflections on the Origins and Spread of Nationalism* (London: Verso books, 1983).
Balandier, George, "Messianism and Nationalism in Black Africa." In Van den Berghe, *Social Problems of Change and Conflict* (San Francisco: Chandler Publishing, 1965).
Coleman, James, *Nigeria: Background to Nationalism* (Berkeley: University of California Press, 1963).
Cooper, Frederick, *Africa since 1940: The Past in the Present* (Cambridge: Cambridge University Press, 2002).
Egerton, Roger, *Mau Mau: An African Crucible* (New York: Free Press, 1989).
Gifford, Prosser, and William Roger Louis, eds., *The Transfer of Power in Africa: Decolonization, 1940-1960* (New Haven, CT: Yale University Press, 1982).
Henderson, Ian, "The Origins of Nationalism in East and Central Africa: The Zambian Case." *The Journal of African History* 11, no. 4 (1970), pp. 591-603.
Mazrui, Ali, *Nationalism and New States in Africa from about 1935 to the Present* (Nairobi: Heinemann, 1984).
Ranger, T. O., *Revolt in Southern Rhodesia* (Evanston, IL: Northwestern University Press, 1967).
Shepperson, George, and Thomas Price, *Independent Africa: John Chilembwe and the Origins, Setting, and Significance of the Nyasaland Native Rising of 1915* (Edinburgh: Edinburgh University Press, 1958).
Vail, Leroy, ed., *The Creation of Tribalism in Southern Africa* (Ithaca, NY: Cornell University Press, 1989).

Africa in 1914

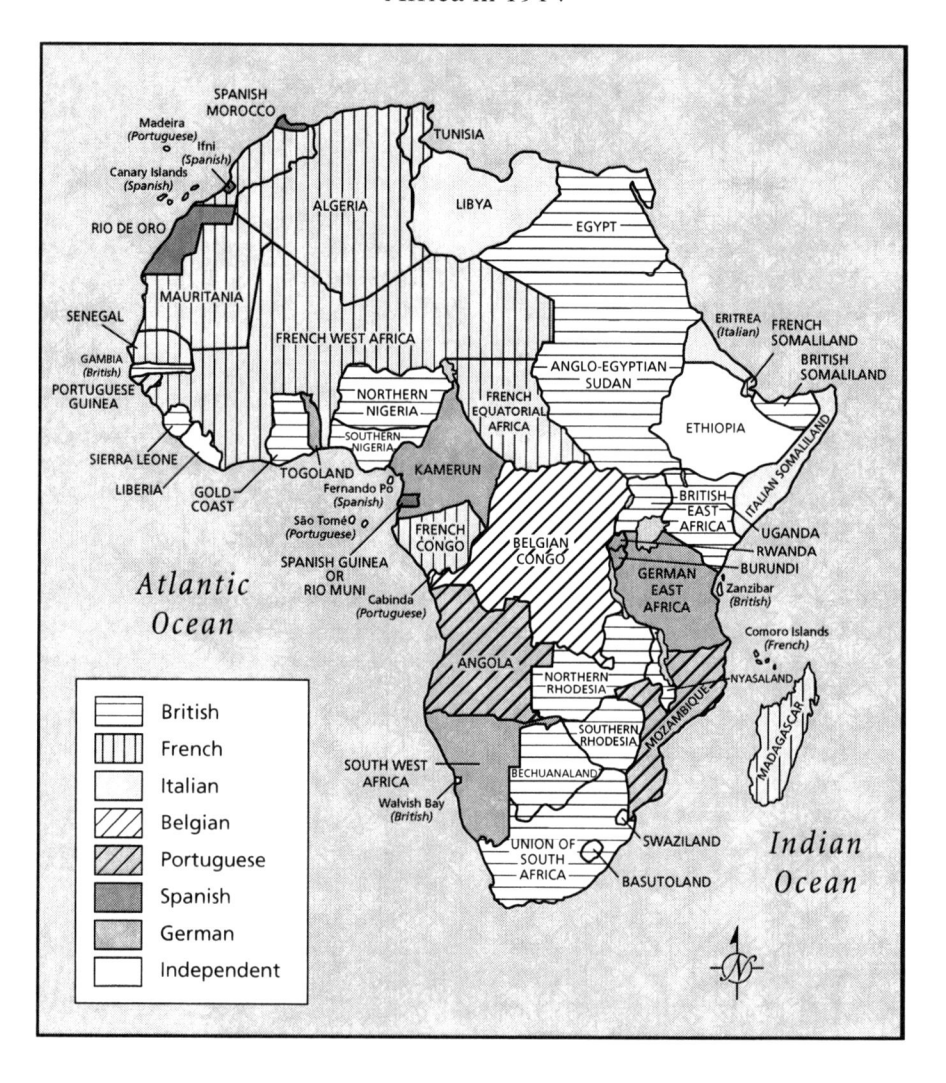

PROBLEM VI
EXPLOITATION OR DEVELOPMENT?

While there were apparent economic motives behind some imperial annexations, many territories were acquired with little or no clear idea of their economic potential. Though British and French politicians hoped to discover a "New India" in the vast interior of West Africa, or King Solomon's mines in the South, overall the colonial powers found that their new colonies offered uneven economic opportunities. With their publics at home clamoring for their new territories to pay for themselves, colonial administrators began pressuring African peoples to provide cash crops or labour to develop sources of revenue. This strengthened the growing connection between the industrial economies of the West and the predominantly agrarian, pastoral, and trading societies of Africa. Africans were forced to pay taxes in cash as a spur to get them to work on plantations or in mines. New ports emerged on the continent's coasts and main waterways to extract the growing flow of agricultural and mineral resources. Colonial governments built roads and railways—often with impressed African labour—to expedite the export of these raw materials. Upon independence, African colonies had thriving metropolises, railways, and harbors. The new nations exported minerals and cash crops, many of them introduced during the colonial era, for a global market.

This chapter presents diverse evaluations of colonialism's economic impact on Africa. To the men who built these empires, and their subsequent supporters, colonial rule modernized primitive subsistence economies. In the process, European expertise and capital bestowed upon Africa the infrastructure requisite for real economic development. Other scholars argue that the colonial relationship "underdeveloped" African economies by forcing Africans to produce primary products for an export market, thereby stunting real economic growth.

The imperialists viewed the jarring economic transformation as part and parcel of bringing Africans into the modern world. To the colonialists and the

Africans who benefited from their association with the Europeans, the century of colonial rule was one of enlightenment and development that laid the foundation for the participation of the independent African states in a wider and increasingly interdependent world. Writing during the terminal phase of African empires, L. H. Gann and Peter Duignan argued that colonialism was more constructive than destructive. Rejecting those who regarded European colonialism in Africa as exploitive, they asserted that colonial rule was actually a burden upon Europe to the advantage of Africa. In their view, European rule did not deprive Africans of any form of wealth that they had previously enjoyed. Rather, it provided the infrastructure of twentieth-century Africa—roads, ports, and hydroelectric plants—that allowed for the more efficient extraction of Africa's resources, to the benefit of European and African alike. Writing in 1967, when settler regimes still ruled in Rhodesia and South Africa, they argued that regions with large scale European migration enjoyed levels of education, medical care, and infrastructure that would have been impossible to achieve without European rule.

D. K. Fieldhouse is more cautious. On the one hand Africa has suffered from its inferior economic position relative to Europe, and the West has clearly played an exploitive role in this relationship. But he asserts that European colonialism was not responsible for this predicament. Rather the continent's problems are the result of Africa's failure to possess the tools that would allow it to compete effectively in the world market. Western capital, technology, and markets were necessary to unearth Africa's untapped resources. After Africa's occupation, Europe received only limited economic advantages from Africa that it did not already possess. Fieldhouse points to the example of the nation of Liberia to support his argument. While never formerly occupied by an imperial power, Liberia exhibits conditions of underdevelopment similar to those of its neighbors, which were all former colonies. In Liberia, as in all of Africa, "exploitation" was a consequence of the already underdeveloped economic position of Africa prior to European intervention and would have occurred whether Europe colonized Africa or not.

Michael Crowder regards the economic impact of colonial rule on African society as much less significant than either Gann and Duignan or Fieldhouse demonstrates. In his examination of West Africa under colonial rule, Crowder acknowledges that in certain areas, European incursions had dramatic consequences. But this was limited to those regions that the Europeans found specifically important economically—the cocoa of the Gold Coast and the coffee and palm regions of Nigeria. For those peasants who produced crops for the European market, the social transformations that emerged as a result of taxation and the construction of railways, ports, and roads were profound. Nevertheless, even in these areas the colonial powers did little to improve growing techniques, and the money the Africans earned from the colonial economy did little to improve their standard of living. For those Africans who lived outside the regions of European economic interest, the changes rendered by colonial rule were limited, while the greatest source of frustration came from that small group of African businessmen who were excluded from a share in the profits being made by Europeans.

Walter Rodney is one of the most famous and influential scholars to weigh in on the question of colonial economics. The title of his popular polemic, *How Europe Underdeveloped Africa*, effectively conveys his view of the question. According to Rodney, European colonialism was an advanced stage of a 400-year exploitive relationship between Africa and Europe. Beginning with the slave trade, Europe had inexorably expanded its control over African economies, stunting their natural growth to the benefit of Europe's economic miracle. Therefore, Europe must bear the moral and economic responsibility for contemporary African underdevelopment. To Rodney, "underdevelopment" was not just the creation of economic poverty under exploitive rule but the reversal of all previous social and economic development that Africa had achieved prior to the European presence. What Gann and Duignan describe as Europe's beneficial economic intervention in Africa—the cultivation of such primary products as coffee, rubber, and cocoa—Rodney regards as the pinnacle of exploitation, since such commodities were exchanged for Europe's manufactured goods, the terms of trade always being to the detriment of the Africans. Such endeavors may have speeded up economic growth, but at the cost of economic exploitation and the deterioration of the social values associated with "traditional" African life.

A. Adu Boahen takes a more balanced approach. He recognizes that colonialism was certainly a watershed in the history of the African continent, and the economic dependence of Africa on Europe will continue for the foreseeable future. But colonialism's impact on Africa has both debits and credits, for while it exploited and scarred, colonialism also created and developed. According to Boahen there is no easy answer, and one must examine both the positive and the negative aspects of colonial rule, a conclusion that may very well satisfy no one.

Finally, writing half a century after the first African colony won its independence, historian Gareth Austin evaluates from a broader perspective the influence of colonialism on African economies. In examining the subsequent development in the new African nations, Austin poses the question, "Did colonial rule put African countries on a higher or lower path of economic change?" He asserts that previous scholarship has focused too closely on the colonial period and argues that the trajectory of many African economies was already established before the colonial conquest. Thus, while colonial rule did initiate important innovations in African economies, its long-term impact must be weighed against more profound trends in the continent's economic development.

The Burden of Empire

L. H. GANN AND PETER DUIGNAN[1]

The history of Africa, the argument goes, is obviously the history of Africans, not that of its conquerors, and against the vast time span of Africa's past, the imperial period is but a brief interlude. Western conquest in Africa, starting in the 1870s and 1880s, therefore formed but an episode. The "new imperialism" arose from the inner needs of an overripe capitalist system, which called for protected markets and even more for new opportunities for Western investors" growing stock of capital. Relying on their temporary military superiority, the whites conquered Africa and introduced new techniques of government and economic exploitation. Under the imperial aegis, Africa nevertheless remained poor. Its economy, where not deliberately distorted to suit the victor's purse, was stagnant. African living standards were stationary or declined.

Western man, the argument continues, used the peoples of Africa and their natural riches for his own selfish purpose. His activities therefore help to account for Africa's present backwardness. Empires in Africa greatly contributed to the accumulation of Western capital resources and present-day Western prosperity. One continent's loss was another's gain. But Africa, at long last, revolted against the white conqueror and has achieved its political liberation, with the exception of a few remaining bastions of Western rule. This victory forms only one of the many struggles in the emancipation of underprivileged classes and races all over the world. African political independence, however, is meaningless without economic independence. Economic, or even cultural, colonialism continues to threaten emergent Africa, and the battle must continue until the levers of financial, commercial, and industrial power pass into black hands and until the last remnants of Western colonialism are liquidated.

We believe that many of these views are wrong and that others stand in need of modification. We are critical of what seems an unduly philanthropic

---

[1] This excerpt is taken from L. H. Gann and Peter Duignan, *Burden of Empire: An Appraisal of Western Colonialism in Africa South of the Sahara* (New York: Frederick A. Praeger, 1967), pp. v-vii, 229-31, 234, and 236-52. L. H. Gann and Peter Duignan were both senior fellows at the Hoover Institute.

approach to world affairs, of an outlook which springs from a justifiable attempt at cultural self-criticism—commendable within limits— but which nevertheless is as much a distortion as the old-fashioned flag-waving view of history.

We hold that cultures differ objectively in the number of choices which their members can make and in their ability to develop man's potentialities. Matabele society, for instance, possessed some admirable features. Warriors belonging to the ruling stratum were trained to display courage, fortitude, and self-respect. But the number of effective alternatives open to a Matabele fighting man . . . was very limited. He might earn renown in battle. He could accumulate wealth in the shape of horned beasts. He could marry many wives and, if successful, gather a large following of kinsmen and captives. But these achievements exhausted the limits of his choice. This is hardly surprising; the resources of Matabele society were small. Drought might destroy the crops, disease might strike down the cattle, and war and pestilence might wipe out a whole community. The margin of survival remained small even at the best of times, and there was relatively little room for innovation or experiment. It is our contention that imperial rule helped to bring about major social, economic, and ideological changes which in turn vastly extended social opportunity. The Matabele warriors' modern descendant can make a living as a teacher, a trader, a bus owner, a civil servant, a farmer, or a tailor. This advance was not only relative, but absolute. It was made possible by a great cultural transfusion in which the West took the leading part and which was not limited to technical factors alone.

In the race for development, the Union of South Africa had many advantages. The country contained more people of European ancestry than all the rest of the continent together; the young dominion therefore commanded the greatest reservoir of human skills and capital existing in Africa. South Africa had a developed transport system. There was an efficient public service and, by African standards, a fairly productive agriculture; there were some excellent ports; there was a developed system of trade and finances. South Africa, moreover, possessed great mineral riches; the country's gold resources kept their value during periods of depression, when the price of commodities such as copper, maize, or peanuts rapidly dropped. Not surprisingly, South Africa attracted more than twice as much money as all the rest of British Africa. From the mid-1920s to the mid-1930s, South Africa thus nearly doubled the value of its gold output. Mining supplied the government with an enormous amount of revenue and also provided funds for development of other industries.

Copper production in the Belgian Congo made similar progress. Development began in a small way during the first decade of the 1900s. Organized mineral production was incompatible with a "robber economy" based on the export of ivory and wild rubber. The original abuses practiced under the Congo

Free State administration disappeared, and after 1908 a more orderly Belgian colonial administration enforced a more sensible policy of economic development. In 1910, a southern railway reached Elisabethville, provided the mines with an outlet for their products to Beira in Portuguese East Africa, and enabled the Belgian mines to import coal from Southern Rhodesia as well as stores and mining equipment from South Africa. World War I stimulated activities, and in 1918 over 20,000 tons of copper were turned out. The slump occasioned a serious setback, but world capitalism surmounted the crisis. In 1936, output reached well over 100,000 tons, and by 1958 copper output amounted to 237,000 tons. The Congo also became the world's greatest producer of industrial diamonds and one of Africa's largest suppliers of hydroelectric power. Mining development went with improved social legislation; the Belgians proved intelligent employers, and after thorough investigation during the late 1920s, the Belgian administration came out with model labor laws for its territory.

South and South Central Africa thus developed into major mineral exporters. Mining dominated the local economy, and minerals from the southern portion of the continent accounted for most of sub-Saharan Africa's foreign trade. Other territories made advances as well. The proclamation of imperial rule over the Gold Coast encouraged an influx of European capital. Foreign entrepreneurs imagined that deep-level mining might also create a second Rand on the West Coast. British and South African investors, however, suffered many disappointments. The gold-bearing strata proved insufficiently rich, and the African people were too numerous and tenacious to give up long-established rights. Gold mining nevertheless made some advance; by 1935, about 41 percent of the country's exports consisted of minerals, mainly gold and diamonds. Gold mining, together with the need to secure a firm hold over the Ashanti, also caused the government to embark on railway building. The opening of the forest by railways, and later by motor roads in turn, gave great stimulus to the production of cocoa on the part of individual peasant owners.

All Marxist and many non-Marxist economists believe that a country that makes a living by selling raw materials to foreigners necessarily stays poor. Prosperity supposedly cannot be gained without factories, especially steel mills and machine-tool manufactures. There is, however, no justification for this belief. The doctrine rests in the highly ethnocentric assumption that the chronological pattern of the British industrial revolution must prevail all over the world. . . . The question of priority also needs to be considered. Modern Zambia may well make money in manufactures, but this does not mean that Northern Rhodesia would have done better in the 1920s and 1930s, at an early stage in its development, by directing funds into factories. Thirty years ago, the country lacked an economic infrastructure; manufacturing would have been expensive in social as well as economic terms and might merely have led to a dead end.

The next point concerns the general relationship between colonial capitalism and secondary industry. Marxist arguments notwithstanding, a capitalist economy does not necessarily preclude industrial development in colonial or ex-colonial territories. South Africa and Southern Rhodesia both started as mining and farming countries. In time, they built up factories and steelworks with money made in primary industries, an economic policy which they shared with countries as diverse as Australia and the United States.

Large-scale mining, moreover, was not confined to purely extractive processes, but also set off development in what might be called the "nonmetallic" sectors of the economy. Here a distinction must be made between simpler forms of enterprise, such as alluvial gold washing, and complex ventures, such as the deep-level excavation of copper, vanadium, or gold. The technology of alluvial gold production is comparatively simple and requires little capital. Many African communities in countries as widely separated as Ghana and the ancient kingdom of Zimbabwe knew the art of washing the yellow metal and worked this natural resource. That does not mean that mining of this type, needing little capital and often stopping short of processing the extracted raw material, did not contribute to economic well-being. In East and Central Africa, indigenous miners sold their gold to Arab or Portuguese traders and thereby acquired more consumer goods than they would otherwise have enjoyed. Large-scale mining, however, made for much greater changes. The mines created markets for more agricultural produce. The flow of investment was not confined just to sinking shafts and driving tunnels. Smelters and electrolytic plants went up in the bush. Mining gave rise to railway development, to road construction, and to the provision of port facilities. Money went into workshops, electric power plants, waterworks, and cement factories. The concentrations of population created a demand for permanent housing. The emergence of townships, large and small, required public utilities and public services. Development, in turn, attracted a multitude of people eager to meet the growing demand for building material, food, fuel, clothing, and all kinds of services. Banks and trading stores opened their doors. White and black farmers alike found new opportunities for selling their grain and cattle, and "the basis was thus laid for a multiplier-accelerator process of economic growth."

[Some scholars] express indignation over the figures devoted to African wages. [They] point out that only £2 million in money and rations went to Africans working on the mines, out of a gross value of output amounting to £36,742,000. The mine owners, however, also had a case. The mines . . . paid £3,600,000 into the public coffers. The government spent some of this on projects benefiting Africans on the Copper Belt, a contribution to African living standards ignored by the conventional Marxist argument. Wages for unskilled men were small because the supply of such labor was large and its competence was low. But African copper miners went to work because they wanted to; in

Northern Rhodesia there was no compulsory labor of the type practiced under the fully collectivist system that then prevailed in the Soviet Union. The Central African mines, with their high level of technology and their paternalistic outlook, also eschewed the kind of underground labor on the part of women and children that was utilized during the early industrial revolution in Great Britain. The African proletariat in some ways, therefore, paid a lower price for incipient industrialization than did the British workers in the eighteenth century. African mine workers on the Copper Belt enjoyed a higher standard of living than they did in their native villages; they received better housing and food than at home, so much so that their average physical well-being consistently improved in employment.

For many decades, mining dominated the cash economy of sub-Saharan Africa. From the first decade of the 1900s, however, agricultural exports began to rise sharply, and agriculture rapidly increased in relative importance. Much of this development centered on South Africa, by far the most advanced country and the most important pioneer on the African continent. Yet economic growth in many other parts of Africa also went forward at a rapid pace. There is, accordingly, no justification at all for the view, fashionable among critics of the colonial system in the 1920s and 1930s, that saw Africa as nothing but a stagnant pool, whose people, under the imperial aegis, either stood still or were retrogressing. Africa's agricultural progress was all the more surprising in view of the many natural obstacles faced by cultivators black and white alike. Many parts of Africa suffer from alternating cycles of drought, followed by heavy tropical downpours that leach the soils. Erosion forms an ever present threat to inexpert farmers. The peoples of Africa faced all kinds of human, plant, and animal diseases peculiar to tropical areas. Development was desperately hampered until Western research found means of coping with afflictions such as malaria, sleeping sickness, and parasites attacking cattle. The lack of transportation facilities further impeded development. Most parts of Africa lacked good riverine communications; because of the great distances, inland producers in the past could rarely market their crops. The imperial impact vastly changed this situation. The period from 1880 to 1920 was the great age of railway building in Africa. By the end of the 1930s, about 32,000 miles of railroad track were in operation, about two-thirds of which served South Africa, the Rhodesias, the Congo, and the Portuguese colonies.

The steam locomotive helped bring about a social revolution. An ordinary freight train used nowadays in Africa will do the work of 15,000 to 20,000 carriers for one-fifth to one-tenth the cost. The steam engine thus relieved the sweating African porter from his age-old labors; for the first time in the continent's history, farmers could produce economic crops away from coastal and river ports. Africa's scarce manpower could at last be used in pursuits more profitable to the economy than head porterage. In the 1920s and 1930s, motor trucks and bicycles also began to make their appearance in the bush. The new means of locomotion might in some ways be called "markets on tires," providing backward farmers with new incentives for turning out more and better crops.

Agricultural development in twentieth-century Africa stood, so to speak, on three legs. There was cultivation by African peasants; there was farming by European settlers; there were some large-scale plantations run by big concessionary companies. Of all these, African enterprise was by far the most important, but it was also the form of enterprise that varied most extensively in methods, technical skill, and output. African peasants faced many obstacles. They had to contend not only with the difficulties of nature but also with lack of physical and social capital. Throughout most of Africa their work continued to depend on hoes and axes and on the unaided power of the human muscle. In most parts of Africa, tribesmen lacked incentives for intensive cultivation. Land was plentiful; whenever cultivators had exhausted the fertility of their gardens, they moved on, allowing nature to restore the fertility of the soil. As long as the supply of land seemed unlimited and storage facilities and markets few or nonexistent, African cultivators would only have wasted time and effort by producing more specialized crops. Where conditions became favorable, however, African farmers did make use of new opportunities and in some areas made astonishing progress.

One of the best-known success stories concerns the development of cocoa in the Gold Coast (now Ghana). The Gold Coast had an ancient tradition of overseas trade. The commerce in palm oil and other commodities had created a certain amount of capital. Long-standing links with the Western world and improved railway and port facilities created under British aegis put bush farmers in touch with metropolitan customers. Contacts with other countries also introduced new cultivable plants, including the cacao tree. The colony's agricultural department provided valuable help [for cocoa production], and by 1935-1936 output amounted to 285,351 tons, that is, nearly half the world's supply. Cocoa enabled the Gold Coast to pay for substantial imports of cement, machinery, flour, and so forth, commodities unknown to the country in the 1890s. Carriers and canoes gradually gave way to steam locomotives, trucks, and bicycles, and conditions of life underwent a major transformation.

African society at the same time experienced a new kind of social differentiation. The old pattern of a small family farm, run entirely by the labor of the peasant's own kinsfolk, gradually disintegrated. The majority of growers came to rely on hired labor; some accumulated great wealth, but others fell into poverty. West Africa as a whole now had to face the problem of migrant labor, with the additional disadvantage that small proprietors could not afford welfare facilities remotely comparable to those provided by big European-owned mining companies. The growers also believed that foreign buyers combined to keep down cocoa prices. In 1937, most of the big European firms entered into an agreement to restrict competition and to prevent local prices from rising above the world market level. The African growers, to their good fortune, were not then tied down by any official distribution monopoly, and they retaliated by refusing to sell to the buyers" combine. Some European firms, moreover, remained aloof from the restriction scheme, and in the end the two parties to the dispute concluded a truce which once again allowed cocoa to be sold abroad. There were many other difficulties, but by and large African agricultural enterprise made considerable progress, especially on the West Coast; the black farmer became what he had never been before in the history of his continent—a factor of some importance in the world economy.

In relation to the enormous size of the African landmass, white agricultural enterprise remained restricted in extent, being confined to a few relatively limited areas. . . .

[In its early days] South Africa never experienced any large-scale white immigration, and economic progress remained relatively slow. Cape farmers turned out limited quantities of grain, fruit, vegetables, wine, and livestock for local consumption and for ships plying the Indian trade. But the settlers who pushed inland had to rely largely on grazing of a simple type, requiring many acres. Territorial expansion in most parts of South Africa thus owed its primary impetus to cattlemen rather than to capitalists with land as the prize of victory. Technically backward as the settlers might have been, their economic and military potential nevertheless remained far superior to that of the Bantu. The black tribesmen thus lost control over most of the available land, and South Africa became the only region on the continent where the overwhelmingly greater part of the available acreage passed into white ownership.

After about the middle of the nineteenth century, moreover, European farmers at the Cape strengthened their economic potential and found a modest kind of prosperity. Growing ports and expanding mining compounds furnished farmers with additional markets. Engineers put up roads, bridges, railways, and dockyards. The growth of shipping and banking helped to put the country in touch with new customers overseas. Some farmers began to work out more intensive methods, and various technological improvements made their appearance in the countryside. Landowners experimented with new products such as mohair and ostrich feathers, while South African Merino wool acquired a recognized place on the world markets. In the twentieth century, technological change acquired increasing momentum. Agricultural mechanization and progress in agricultural processing industries such as fruit canning, tobacco manufacture, and meat refrigeration vastly added to the country's wealth. Farmers developed better methods of plant selection, stockbreeding, and soil management. Veterinary surgeons learned how to cope with various kinds of animal diseases. Despite large remaining islands of backwardness, South

Africa developed into the most skilled and most versatile of Africa's agricultural exporters.

[Another] instrument of progress was company enterprise. Big business preferred to put its resources into mines and railways and, in South Africa, into factories. There were, however, some notable exceptions. Unilever in the Congo and the Cameroons Development Corporation in West Africa promoted extensive agricultural enterprises. Liberia also owed much of its development to similar foreign initiative. In 1926 the Finance Corporation, a Firestone subsidiary, concluded an agreement with the Liberian government and advanced money to the small, financially unstable republic. . . . The Liberians secured sufficient cash to satisfy some of their creditors and attained the unusual distinction of being one of the few nations to repay their war debts to the United States in full. Firestone received extensive land and tax concessions and in turn initiated the world's largest rubber undertaking. Furthermore, the company acquired a good reputation as an employer. It paid its workmen much more adequately than the government and other local entrepreneurs and also subsidized wages by bonuses for increased output and by selling low-priced food to its employees. Plantation labourers could work their own plots in spare-time hours; debt peonage was strictly avoided. The company put up hospitals, built roads, and established a public radio service and other undertakings. Firestone had sufficient perception to encourage independent rubber production in Liberia, proving thereby that company enterprise need not necessarily conflict with private initiative. The company provided free rubber seeds to independent growers, as well as high-yielding clones, or buds, and trained instructors to advise on methods.

In summary, the inter-war period saw tremendous economic growth in Africa. There is, accordingly, no justification for the view of this period of African history as one of imperial neglect in contrast with Communist progress. True enough, development was uneven. Large areas of Africa were little affected by change; only South Africa, the oldest white-settled area on the continent, managed to build up substantial industries, while the continent as a whole remained a primary producer that devoted its resources to the export of minerals and crops. Africa did, however, see vast additions to its real resources in the shape of railway lines, roads, mines, plantations, hydroelectric plants, and other assets. These economic changes came about without large-scale liquidations and without forced labor of the Stalinist variety. Imperial rule indeed shielded sub-Saharan Africa from other foreign pressures and prevented internecine struggles; colonial Africa bore but a minor military burden; it operated with a relatively small and inexpensive state machinery, so that comparatively few resources were diverted into civil service and defense expenditure (the Gold Coast had fewer than 150 civil servants in the 1930s).

The new enterprise, by the very speed of its impact, created a host of social tensions. The clash of black peasant agriculture, white farming, and company ventures, for instance, might engender sharp competition for labor and natural resources. Competition, on the other hand, might also imply cooperation. Firestone's activities, to a certain degree, assisted indigenous Liberian rubber producers; white Rhodesian tobacco farmers bought native-grown maize. The various new enterprises in some ways complemented one another. Critics of existing colonial practices often erred, therefore, when they advocated reforms in terms of a rigid either-or choice and contrasted black with white farming or primary with secondary industries as mutually exclusive categories.

Contact with the white man, whether as merchant, mine owner, farmer, or manufacturer, also brought about economic changes of a more intangible kind. Europeans taught African villagers the art of storing ideas. In the past, tradition had depended on memory and word of mouth; the old knew most and the young least. Now missionaries and others showed how words might be committed to paper and permanently preserved. Not only were labor migrants enabled to communicate with their fellow villagers back home by means of inky marks on paper, but they were also enabled to read books and newspapers. Of equal significance was the creation of a vernacular literature which began, as in Europe, with translations of the Scriptures and the compilation of hymnbooks in indigenous languages. Cash-books and catechisms both demand literacy of their users, and these skills in turn helped to speed up economic transformation.

In addition, economic change spread new ways of measuring time and space. The Africans, of course, could reckon time quite adequately for their purposes; they divided the year into months and seasons, or they used the growth cycle of a crop, with the day further subdivided by the sun's position or what people would normally be doing at that hour. But in villages there were neither printed calendars nor mechanical clocks. Time was an everlasting stream. The white man's beliefs, however, were very different. Time to the European was something that could be minutely subdivided, a commodity for sale. . . . The new space-time concept slowly influenced African thought in general and in turn contributed to the great economic transformation that was beginning to change the face of Africa.

The Myth of Economic Exploitation

D. K. FIELDHOUSE[2]

The most dangerous and commonly held myth connected with the modern empires is that they were great machines deliberately constructed by Europe to exploit dependent peoples by extracting economic and fiscal profit from them. Its corollary is that the new states had a moral claim to be compensated for losses suffered in the past by being helped to become advanced industrial economies. None denied that it was desirable for wealthy industrial states to help those with primitive economies, but to base their claim to assistance on the premise that they were exploited in the past was wrong. The myth of imperial profit-making is false.

To start, the modern empires were not artificially constructed economic machines. The second expansion of Europe was a complex historical process in which political, social, and emotional forces in Europe and on the periphery were more influential than calculated imperialism. Individual colonies might serve an economic purpose; collectively, no empire had any definable function, economic or otherwise. Empires represented only a particular phase in the ever-changing relationship of Europe with the rest of the world; analogies with industrial systems or investment in real estate were simply misleading.

Yet though the colonial empires were undoubtedly functionless in origin, this is not to say that they did not later provide an economic return, a "profit," to their owners. Certainly, many colonial enthusiasts in Europe alleged that they could and did. Were they right?

To answer this question requires a careful analysis of its meaning. It is, in fact, highly theoretical. An industrial company exists to produce profits; colonies were human societies belonging to a different order of things. It is really as meaningless to ask whether a colony such as Nigeria was "profitable"

---

[2] This excerpt is taken from D. K. Fieldhouse, *The Colonial Empires: A Comparative Survey from the Eighteenth Century* (New York: Delacorte Press, 1967), pages 380-87 and 389-94. D. K. Fieldhouse was the Vere Harmsworth Professor of Imperial and Naval History. He is currently professor emeritus of Jesus College, Cambridge.

to Britain as to ask whether Wales or England was. In each case some form of "advantage" was obvious. But this was not necessarily economic; and if it was, it cannot necessarily be called "profit" and need not result from "exploitation." In short, such concepts reflect a perverted form of thinking about colonies, forms derived from the "mercantile" theories of the first empires. The fact that they were commonly held does not make them true. The task of the historian is to analyze the various forms of "profit" Europe may have gained from her colonies; to compare these with countervailing disadvantages; and to decide whether, on balance, empire gave economic advantages that Europe would not otherwise have obtained.

The crux of the matter is to define what empire meant in economic terms. A colony differed from an independent state only in that it was governed by an alien power; colonial status was primarily a political phenomenon. This immediately limits the field of inquiry, for it excludes all those influences exerted by Europe which fell short of full political control: "economic imperialism" and "informal empire," for example. If an empire generated "profit," this must be directly attributable to alien rule. The question can therefore be redefined: what economic advantages did Europe extract from her colonies which she could not have gained from other countries, however similar in other ways?

There were at least six obvious ways in which this might be done. The first was simply to loot an occupied country of its treasures. This was very rare in the modern empires. Few new colonies possessed hoarded wealth on the scale of Mexico, Peru, or India in the past: there was little that could profitably be seized from African or Polynesian chiefs. Moreover, although "pacifying" armies were often barbarous in their methods, they were normally under direct metropolitan control, and conquest was quickly followed by civilized methods of government. The rape of Bengal in the 1760s was not repeated after 1815.

A more sophisticated way of extracting profit before 1815 was to transfer colonial revenues to the metropolitan treasury. This also became very rare. From 1831 to 1877, the Dutch transferred Indonesian surpluses through the "Culture System"; the British East India Company and other chartered companies sometimes paid dividends out of colonial taxation; but no normal colonial government ever did so. Some demanded contributions to defence costs; the French confused things by integrating the accounts of some colonies with their own. But most colonies were left to use their own revenues and were more likely to receive subsidies than to be robbed of surpluses.

A third possible source of imperial advantage was to transfer money or goods from colony to metropolis as interest on loans, payment for services rendered, the pensions and savings of colonial officials, and the profits made by business firms. Much has been made of this "drain," particularly by Indian historians, but the Indian case is misleading. The greater part—interest charges, profits of alien enterprises, etc.—would have been equally due from independent states that borrowed in the British capital market or in which British firms operated. The net "drain" was therefore the cost of services, such as the Indian army, which Britain controlled and which India might not otherwise have chosen to pay for, and the transferred salaries of alien officials. The damage to India was not the absolute cost but the loss of currency and international exchange by a country short of both.

A fourth possible form of exploitation was the imposition of "unfair" terms of trade on a colony. This had been the basic device of the "mercantile" empires, and, in its pre-nineteenth-century form, may well have provided artificially high profit levels for metropolitan merchants and producers. But no modern empire operated a comparable system of monopoly. By the 1860s the old controls had been dismantled. Although tariff preferences, shipping subsidies, navigation acts, and import quotas were soon disinterred, no country ever entirely closed colonial ports to foreign competition. Even the proportion of colonial trade which fell to the parent states was unimpressive. Britain's share of her empire's trade fell from an average of 49 percent in the decade after 1854 to 36 percent in 1929-33; thereafter, even revived protection only increased it slightly. France kept a larger share, always more than half, of the trade of her colonies; even so, the proportion declined with time. Most other empires had a similar experience. Only the United States and Russia, who entirely enclosed their colonies within domestic tariff systems, really had a commercial monopoly, and this probably benefited the dependencies as much as the metropolis. Although modern protectionism harmed the interests of colonial subjects as much as it did metropolitan consumers, it was at least reasonably impartial, and the losses of colonial consumers were compensated by guaranteed and preferential markets in Europe. It is therefore unlikely that "neo-mercantilism" produced substantial net "profits" for metropolitan countries.

By a curious paradox, however, it has been argued that during their era of free trade the British "exploited" colonies by making it impossible for them to protect their own industries against her exports, so holding back their industrial progress. This did not apply to the settlement colonies, which were allowed their own protectionist policies from 1859, but may have been true of others. India was again the test case, since she was the only British dependency in the nineteenth century with the evident capacity to develop large-scale mechanized industry. There is no doubt that free trade had serious consequences for her. In the early nineteenth century, free import of British cottons destroyed Indian hand-loom weaving on a commercial scale; thereafter, the British ban on protective tariffs held back mechanized cotton production and kept the market open for Lancashire. Indian cottons were not protected until about 1926, and textile imports from Britain then dropped significantly. India consumed £40,729,000 out of total British manufactured textile exports of £195,805,000 in 1913, but only £11,373,000 in 1934. To some extent, enforced free trade may have had similar effects on other nascent Indian industries and on the economic growth of other British dependencies.

Yet it is impossible to be certain that these disadvantages were specifically the result of British imperial authority, for other and totally independent states were also forced, during the nineteenth century, to reduce or abolish import duties in the interests of British exports. China, for example, was restricted by treaty after 1842 to a maximum tariff of 5 percent on all imports. An "open door" might, in fact, have been imposed on any weak state by European powers; an independent India might have been as unable as China was to protect her own industries against foreign demands for freedom of access. Thus the "open door" was a typical product of Europe's general preponderance. Formal empire was one way of imposing it, but by no means the only way, and the benefits resulting from free commercial access to non-European states cannot be regarded as an exclusively imperial "profit."

The most commonly alleged form of imperial profiteering was to "exploit" the natural endowments of dependencies—oil, minerals, natural rubber, ivory, etc. If these were extracted without giving compensating advantages, an ex-colony might hypothetically find itself robbed of assets which might otherwise have financed the creation of a modern industrial economy. . . . Examples of "exploitation" on this scale are, however, difficult to find. Extractive industries were never entirely insulated from their environment. All had to use local labor. They paid wages lower than they paid to Europeans but vastly higher than those normal in subsistence economies. All had to build modern communications and other amenities, which benefited the colony as a whole. Some part of company profits were always spent locally, lubricating the colonial economy. Most overseas companies had to pay taxes to the colonial government. Thus no extractive industry failed to provide some advantages to the dependency in which it operated. The question is whether these were enough: whether an independent state could have gained more.

The question was pragmatic rather than moral. The value of natural endowments was, for the most part, created by demand elsewhere; in most cases, only alien capital and skills could give them commercial value. What tax was due to the indigenous owners of the soil? The only useful yardstick was what happened in comparable independent countries; evidence provided by states such as Persia and the Latin American republics suggests that this would have been small simply because their bargaining power also was small. Independence enabled ex-colonies to impose stricter terms on foreign companies, but these were matched by the higher demands also made by previously independent states after 1945. If neither was able to undertake such complex economic operations on its own account, its demands were limited by the fact that Europeans might cease to operate altogether.

It is impossible, therefore, to measure the "profit" Europe gained from "exploiting" the natural resources of her dependencies because they were formal colonies. By mid-twentieth-century standards Europeans showed a cavalier disregard for the interests of other societies, taking what was profitable and putting back only what was necessary. Yet this had little to do with political empire and was not limited to it. One-sided use of natural resources reflected an imbalance of power between the west and the non-industrialized areas of the world; and while this lasted, no non-European society had sufficient bargaining power to impose fully equitable terms.

The last and most sophisticated way in which empires have been alleged to give economic profit was through the return Europeans could obtain by investing capital in colonies, higher than what they could get at home. . . . This theory was based on the Marxist principle of "surplus value" and turned on the greater profitability of using capital in tropical lands, where labor was cheaper than in industrialized Europe. Lenin, for example, argued in 1916 that the growth of industrial monopoly and "finance-capitalism" in western states created an enormous "superabundance of capital." This could not profitably be invested at home without raising wage levels, and therefore reducing profits, simply because the labor supply could not be expanded. The rest of the world lacked capital but had ample labor and raw materials. European capital could generate a higher surplus value there than at home, and this enabled metropolitan capital to go on accumulating. If it could not go abroad, capital would stagnate and capitalism would crack. Lenin predicted that in course of time the nonindustrial world would be entirely absorbed by European "imperialists" (finance-capitalists), and that this would lead to wars for imperial redivision, which would destroy capitalist society and usher in the socialist revolution.

Shorn of its ideological trimmings, Lenin's theory simply asserted that the combination of cheap labor, political power to make it work at subsistence wages, and commercial monopoly to exclude foreign rivals generated excess profits for European empires. The desire for these advantages led to tropical colonization. Was he right?

He was wrong on one point at least, for, as has already been seen, it is impossible to explain the expansion of European empires after 1815 in terms of economic need: there simply was no correlation between the time-scale of European "finance-capitalism" and imperial expansion, nor between colonies and areas of greatest investment.

The advantages which Lenin thought European capital engaged in the colonies received from imperial political power were in fact of little significance. Labor was certainly cheap by European standards: otherwise, many of these enterprises would have been unprofitable. But low wages were not created by political power: they reflected the social environment of a subsistence economy. In the period before about 1906, many colonial governments provided forced or semi-forced labor; but this was also a period of generally low company profits. Thereafter, colonial governments tended to impose restrictions on labor contracts and conditions of work, both tending to raise labor costs. Europeans could have "exploited" native labor more effectively if they had not been policed by imperial administrations sensitive to humanitarian public opinion at home, and they often did so in independent Latin America and the Middle East. Nor did empire provide a degree of commercial monopoly sufficient to enable capitalists to sell at monopolistic prices at home or in the colonies. European investors showed no marked preference for their own colonies and often got higher returns by operating in foreign empires. Conversely, the really artificial prices were those set by agreement between companies of different nationalities, especially the oil companies, which transcended imperial systems. Thus, while colonial governments often provided a convenient framework of political security within which private companies could work satisfactorily, formal empire was in no sense necessary for profitable European activity overseas.

Second, the relative profitability of investment in Europe and in tropical dependencies was determined by many complex factors and varied immensely from time to time. Changing economic and political conditions within Europe sometimes encouraged investment at home, sometimes overseas. Another important influence was the relative demand for the products of the advanced economies and those of primary-producing countries, in which a large proportion of "colonial" investment was made. When the terms of trade favored primary producers, investment in tropical colonies was obviously more profitable than when the terms favored manufacturing states. During the half century before 1914, European demand for minerals, tropical vegetable oils, and food increased considerably, and the terms of trade normally favored primary producers. This enabled the more fortunate European companies producing such goods to make spectacular profits. Between 1914 and 1939, however, the terms of trade normally favored industrial producers, with the result being that the relative advantage of investing in primary-producing countries was less. After 1939, the war and postwar demand for primary products again favored the overseas investor, though by the later 1950s his advantage was declining. Such trends cannot confidently be translated into statistics, but some indication of their importance can be gained from estimates of the relative percentage rate of profit gained from investment in industrial concerns operating in Britain and in British companies operating overseas between 1953 and 1961. In 1953, British industrialists gave an average net profit of 12.5 percent on their capital (ordinary capital plus capital and revenue reserves), compared to 21.5 percent from overseas companies. In 1961, British industrials were yielding 12.4 percent but overseas companies only 13.7 percent. In the same years, the terms of trade, taking 1937-8 as 100, had moved in Britain's favor from 119 to 103.

Such figures are far too limited to prove anything, but they do suggest, in conjunction with other evidence, that the profitability of investment in primary-producing non-European economies, many of which were colonies, depended more on international economic factors than on the special advantages which Lenin thought colonies provided for their masters. By comparison, the political status of non-industrialized countries was of little importance, and empire could not of itself generate super profit for European capital.

If Europe benefited economically from other parts of the world by "exploiting" them, it was because of her immense military and economic preponderance. Empire, in the formal sense, was merely one form in which this was expressed, and had no colonial empires been created in the nineteenth-century Europe would still have taken whatever economic assets she needed and dictated the terms on which she did so.

In fact, no meaningful balance sheet can be constructed, even in economic terms. One or two small or short-lived empires almost certainly cost their owners more than they repaid. Certainly the German and Italian empires did so, because their colonies lacked natural resources, and because they were in any case destroyed before high initial expenditure could be written off against long-term advantages. All other empires were too complex for such definite verdicts to be made. Most colonies were "unprofitable" during the period of initial conquest and while later internal rebellions lasted. But there were few such expenses between about 1920 and 1939; and apart from obvious metropolitan expenditure (grants-in-aid, payment for services in particular colonies, etc.), the cost of colonies depends on what proportion of total imperial expenditure (on defence, for example) is debited to them. Hence no one can determine whether the accounts of empire ultimately closed with a favorable cash balance.

This is unimportant, for the value of the colonial empires was not to be measured in money. Colonies were seldom deliberately acquired to produce wealth, and they were retained irrespective of their "profitability." Empire in the modern period was the product of European power: its reward was power, or the sense of power. The end of empire did not mean economic loss to the onetime imperial states; on the contrary, it meant that the economic advantage of operating in other parts of the world was no longer offset by the cost and inconvenience of political responsibilities. Only the minority of private investors and others, whose assets or business concerns were hampered, destroyed, or taken over without proper compensation by the new states, actually lost through decolonization. The West retained its economic preponderance: some even held that the margin of wealth between advanced and "developing" countries widened as empire ended. If Europe in fact derived her wealth from her colonies, their loss made remarkably little difference to her.

Yet the West undoubtedly suffered from the end of empire, for Europe and America lost some part of their political power and self-assurance. The world

no longer consisted of colonies unable to complicate international politics: the United Nations provided a forum in which the new states could challenge overwhelming power by appealing to alleged moral standards and the principle of one state, one vote. The powers were no longer free to use their military power to support their interests: the Suez crisis of 1956-7 marked the end of "informal empire" in its nineteenth-century form. The world was no longer ringed by the western bases and colonial armies which had enabled it to impose its will on all continents. Europeans had lost the freedom of movement and economic activity which empire had given them. They were now dependent on a multiplicity of small and often chauvinistic states who needed western enterprise but also resented it and complicated its operations. But above all, the end of empire deprived the West of status. The countries of Europe were no poorer than they had been before, but they were infinitely smaller. They had been the centers of vast empires, but now they were petty states preoccupied with parochial problems. Dominion had gone and with it the grandeur, which was one of its main rewards.

The Economic Impact of Colonial Rule in West Africa

MICHAEL CROWDER[3]

The economic impact of colonial rule on African society was much less profound than colonial administrators liked to think. The period 1919-39 was one of *immobilisme* in which what little change there was did not stand comparison with what was taking place in the outside world. The railway systems had for the most part been completed by 1918—only the introduction of the motor vehicle was a significant factor for change in this period. The African found himself the simple producer of raw materials for which Lebanese were the agents of sale and European companies the exporters. Conversely, these same companies imported the goods which the African bought, mainly at the shops or through the agencies of Lebanese traders, with the money he earned from the sale of his crop. Only in rare cases did the African survive as an importer, almost never as an exporter, and in neither role was he significant after 1920. Except in the cocoa-producing areas of the Gold Coast and Nigeria, the African was squeezed out of his precolonial role of middle-man between peasant producer and expatriate exporter by the Lebanese. This meant that the African's role in the colonial economy became almost exclusively that of petty trader and primary producer of cash crops on his own account or as labourer on the farms of others, African or European, in the case of the few plantations that existed in French West Africa. A small number were employed in mining industries in Ashanti, Jos, and Enugu, on the railways, and as casual labourers in the urban centers. The income they derived from the colonial economy was for the most part so low that it brought about no significant change in their standard of living. Only cocoa and coffee fetched high enough prices to affect the traditional socioeconomic structure of the peoples producing it. The other

---

[3] This excerpt is taken from Michael Crowder, *West Africa under Colonial Rule* (Evanston, IL: Northwestern University Press, 1968). Michael Crowder taught African history at several universities, including the University of Ibadan and the University of Botswana. He was a fellow at the Commonwealth Institute.

cash crops, most of which had, like palm products, groundnuts and cotton, been exported before the imposition of colonial rule, fetched such low prices that the peasant produced just enough to pay taxes and satisfy his immediate needs for imported cloths, utensils, and foodstuffs like sugar. The narrow range of goods in the Lebanese stores was not substantially **different from those which the African middleman used as the basis of barter in pre-colonial times.**

For the African peasant, the growing of cash crops during the colonial period was, except in the cocoa and coffee-producing areas, primarily geared to paying taxes and supplementing the subsistence economy with imported luxuries. If the price for cash crops was low, his marginal propensity to produce cash crops for sale over and above those necessary for the purposes of paying taxes fell also, for the peasant could provide most of his basic needs from internal sources. Even when the price for crops was high, immense effort was required, in terms of labor, to produce larger quantities. This problem was solved, partially, by the importation of labor from other areas. This migratory labor was available, as we have seen, because of taxes imposed on peoples inhabiting areas on which no cash crops would grow. In certain areas, the peasant would involve himself in commitments based on the previous year's price for a crop and be forced to produce greater quantities of his cash crop in order to meet them if it fell. Where immigrant labor was scarce, he would have to transfer labor from the subsistence crops to the cash crops. In parts of Senegambia this situation, aggravated by the long-standing dependence on imported goods, reached the point where peasants were importing rice, which they could grow themselves, and going without food for nearly two months a year because they had neglected the subsistence economy in favor of the cash crops. Counteracting the propensity of the peasant to abandon cultivation of the cash crop in favor of subsistence crops was his tendency to incur debts to the Lebanese traders, who were quite aware that indebtedness was one of the only ways over and above taxation that could force him to produce for a low price. The French, however, resorted to the introduction of compulsory production of crops in areas where the peasant would otherwise have refused to grow them because of the low price. Thus, anxious to be independent of cotton supplies from outside the French empire, the administration in French West Africa forced the peasant to produce it under threat of imprisonment if the quality was not good enough or the quantity insufficient. The ease with which people moved out of the cash economy into a purely subsistence economy also related to the dependence their society had built up on imported goods. In Senegal, where by the time of the Depression many families had been involved in the export of groundnuts to Europe for over seventy years, imported cloths, utensils, and rice had become part of their way of life. But even they, despite predictions of famine and political upheaval, were able to revert to subsistence production in 1932. Millet, manioc, and taro were substituted for imported rice. Home-grown tobacco replaced imported varieties. Honey was gathered in place of sugar, and local soap and perfumes were produced again; thus the subsistence economy was stimulated.

The extent of the involvement of the peasant in the cash crop economy was limited by the extent of the colonial transportation system. Vast areas, such as Bornu in Nigeria, remained largely untouched by it because no railway passed through them, and not until after the Second World War did long-distance road haulage of the low-priced cash crops pay. Even the term *cash* applied to these crops is inappropriate, for in many areas the exchange of "cash" crop for imported goods was largely by barter. It was the migrant labourer rather than the peasant farmer who became the pioneer of currency as a means of exchange.

Just how little the bulk of the people were affected by the European-dominated import-export economy is brought out by Governor Clifford's report to the Nigerian Council in 1923:

> The vast majority of the indigenous population are still independent of the outside world for all their essential supplies. They can and do spin their own thread, weave their own garments, provide their own foodstuffs, and even, when the necessity arises, forge their own tools, and make their own pottery. For them imports from Europe are still, in the main, luxuries with which, if needs must, they can wholly dispense; and the sole exception to this in pre-war days, was imported spirits of European manufacture.

And for these latter they had "illicit" substitutes. Twenty years later, with regard to the whole of British West Africa, the Leverhulme Trust Commission reported that "all Africans are, to a very large extent, and very many of them wholly, outside the system of money economy which dominates the economic life of Europe and the rest of the world." The African, encouraged in times of good prices to produce cash crops, and ignorant of the fluidity of prices on the world commodity markets, was easily convinced that he was being robbed and deceived by the whites if they offered him a low price, and refused to continue production unless under pressure of taxation, indebtedness, or force.

The African Peasant and New Crops

The colonial regime did little to improve the growing techniques of low-value export crops: they remained the same as in precolonial times. For most peasants, the European agricultural officers were an irrelevance. There was of course no attempt to improve the methods of production of subsistence crops, as the Germans had done in Togo. Thus the peasant, whether farming for himself or working on the farms of others, did not gain any new knowledge of agricultural techniques under colonial rule. Even the labourer on European plantations used for the most part his traditional instruments and stayed there as short a time as possible, learning nothing about improvement. Rather, the peasant was allowed to exhaust the land. In Senegal, for instance, large areas, like the Baol, have been reduced to semi-desert by the cultivation of groundnuts. As early as 1925, certain areas of Senegal like Thies and Diourbel were exhausted and the peasants had to move eastwards, following the railway to earn enough money to pay taxes and buy imported goods.

The colonial administration did nothing to prevent situations such as that in Gambia, where rice that could have been grown by the peasant more cheaply was imported; to pay for it, the peasant devoted more of his energies in the cultivation of groundnuts. Indeed, it favored the colonial economic system, for French rice exporters in Indochina could find a market in Senegal. Only when Indochina became independent of France did France make efforts to develop Senegal's own rice potential. Similarly, Cardinall, commenting on the imports of foodstuffs in the Gold Coast in 1930, noted that the country could have produced itself half "the fresh fish, rice, maize and other meal, beans, salted and fresh meat, edible oils, spices and fresh vegetables (imported), or in other words would have saved 200,000 pounds."

The only crops that did radically alter the standard of living of their producers were cocoa and coffee in the Gold Coast, Ivory Coast, and Western Nigeria. The price for both these crops the price was consistently sufficiently high for the farmer safely to depend on imported goods in substitution for domestically produced goods. Under the stimulus of a crop whose value increased in the Gold Coast from £4,764,067 in 1921 to £11,229,000 in 1928 on the eve of the Depression, great tracts of new land were opened to cocoa cultivation by immigrant "rural capitalists" who used the profits from their first crops to purchase further farm land. It has often been thought that the revolutionary aspect of the Gold Coast cocoa industry was the fact that Africans sold land that was supposed to have been communally owned. But . . . the sale of land had been common in some areas for fifty years or so before the introduction of cocoa into the Akwapim and Akim-Abuakwa area. What was an innovation was not the idea of sale of land itself, but the intensity of its application.

In the Ivory Coast, the Abe found no difficulty in selling land, but the Agni strongly resisted it. The cocoa boom in the Gold Coast and later in the Ivory Coast stimulated migrations of farmers into new lands. Those who could not buy land worked for the owners. In the case of the Gold Coast, two systems of tenant-farmer relation have been [documented.] The first was that of *abusa*, whereby the labourer was paid one third of the cocoa he plucked for his employing farmer, the second that of *ntotokano*, whereby the labourer was paid a fixed sum per load for the cocoa he plucked for his employing farmer.

The cocoa industry in Ghana created a rich class of farmers who were able to undertake social innovations at their own initiative and who showed that the African peasant, if prices were good, did not have to be forced into production. . . . The same was true of the Ivory Coast cocoa industry, which grew from a mere 1,000 tons in 1920 to 52,714 tons in 1938, and the coffee industry, which grew from 248 tons in 1928 to 14,076 tons in 1938.

Of the peasant-farmers in West Africa, only those producing cocoa and coffee were significantly involved in the money economy and experienced substantial social change as a result. In Larteh, Akwapim, in Ghana, cocoa-farming and the wealth it brought had far-reaching effects on all aspects of economic and social life. The farmers of Larteh, on their own initiative, built roads and bridges to link their farms with the government road and the main cocoa-collecting centers. In 1914 they even employed a Swiss engineer to build a wooden bridge, still standing today, for which nine of them and one other subscribed £2,000. Between 1914 and 1930, the people of Akwapim spent at least £30,000 on roads to connect with the government-built road. One such road, built entirely without government assistance, was actually opened in 1926 by the acting governor, to whom the chief responsible addressed a request for government assistance with the debt of £2,600 still outstanding to the contractor. The chief, the Benkumhene, also asked that government "appoint a town engineer to lay and carry out the construction of streets and other works of public utility" in Larteh. These demands for development were refused and a warning given against the construction of further roads. As it was, apart from the railway the communications system of the area was built by the local people with little or no government assistance and encouragement.

Over half of Larteh's completed houses in 1963—some 1,000—were built with profits from the cocoa trade before 1910. Apart from investment in communications, housing, education, and funerals became the main items of expenditure of the cocoa farmers. Unfortunately, . . . the acquisition of wealth did not mean a necessary improvement in basic standards of living and nutrition, for far too much money was spent on luxuries, and at the same time, concentration on cocoa farming led to neglect of subsistence farming. No other group was brought into the money economy in the way the cocoa and coffee farmers were. The migrant labourer depended on currency, but he earned very little, and most of it was taken in taxes and by his family on his return.

The African Labourer

Those employed on the European plantations of the Ivory Coast or Guinea were little affected by their experience. Their terms of labor were seasonal for the most part, and they were not only underpaid, but not given, as we have seen in Ivory Coast, all that they earned in cash. No rural proletariat arose from among the workers on the European plantations. Before 1940 only the railways employed a large number of regular workers, among whom many were, or were trained as, skilled artisans. The only comparable industries to the railways as employers of labor were the mines. But much of the labor in the mines was irregular. In Jos, the tin mines employed for the most part daily-paid unskilled and illiterate labor to dig at the faces of the open mines. In the gold mines of Ashanti, the main problems were the shortage of labor and its irregularity. And most of those employed were immigrants who intended on returning home eventually. In Enugu, labourers were press-ganged by unscrupulous chiefs into work on the coal mines in the early years from 1915 until 1922. After that, labor flowed freely into the mines so that by 1930 the management, which was a government agency, was able to be selective in the employment policy. The peoples of the area in which the mines were situated tended to be less educated than those from neighboring divisions, and management deliberately pursued a policy of recruiting illiterate locals rather than their neighbors, who were relatively more educated and could voice their grievances and were therefore regarded as troublemakers.

The mines, then, employed a labor force which was either of temporary immigrant nature, as in the case of the Gold Coast gold mines, or, where locally recruited, as in the case of the Jos and Enugu mines, largely illiterate. Wages in all three mines were low for the ordinary labourer: in the coal mines in 1929 they were about 7d.-1s. 6d. per day; in 1930 in the gold mines they were 1s. a day for unskilled surface labourers and between 1s. 3d. and 1s. 9d. for unskilled underground labourers; in the tin mines, 1s. 6d. per day for unskilled labourers.

The wages for these labourers were too low to alter their standard of living significantly. Before 1940, none of the mine workers had organized themselves into effective trade unions, though wildcat strikes had taken place before that time. For instance, in 1925, pit boys in the Enugu mines downed tools in protest against the failure of management to raise their pay to 1922 levels. They were dismissed. In 1937, after the recovery of the colliery from the Depression, workers undertook considerable but uncoordinated agitation for an increase in their rates of pay. In September of that year, the tub boys struck when a European overman assaulted one of their fellows. In 1924, there was a strike at Obuasi on the Ashanti goldfields against the introduction of time clocks. None of these strikes were organized by a union. Indeed, until the Second World War trade unions were of no real significance in either British or French West Africa. In the latter they were illegal until the advent of the Popular Front Government in 1937. In the former they were tolerated but not recognized until about the same time. Trade Union Ordinances were passed for Gambia in 1932, Sierra Leone in 1939, Nigeria in 1939, and Gold Coast in 1941. The attitude of the Sierra Leone government to Trade Unions was not much different from that of the Southern Nigerian government with respect to employment on the Enugu mines. In 1921 it refused to recognize a union on the grounds that:

> A tribal ruler is elected for each tribe in Freetown by the members of the tribe themselves. These tribal rulers are recognized by law and form the intermediaries between the members of the tribe and the government, and it is not possible for the government to deal with or recognize any rival authority introduced by strangers to the colony.

Only some ten trade unions of any importance seem to have been formed and to have survived any length of time in West Africa before 1940. Significantly of these five were African Civil Servants unions, and two were railway workers unions.

Civil servants and railway employees formed the only two major coherent groups of workers among whom there was an educated elite in any way capable of organizing workers against government. Thus in 1919 daily-paid workers on the Sierra Leone railway went on strike from 15 to 22 July because they had not been paid their "war bonus." The railway was brought to a standstill, and work was only resumed when they were promised payment of their war bonus as soon as possible.

Daily-paid staff of the Public Works Department also went on strike at the same time. In 1926 the unrecognized Sierra Leone Railway Workers' Union led a strike for improved conditions of service, which led to a slowdown of service. Government took a very tough line against the strikers, who returned to work on its terms. The 1926 strike, in contrast to those in 1919, had the active support of the Sierra Leone members of the National Congress of British West Africa.

In French West Africa, the railways too were the main focus of strikes. In 1925 railway workers on the Dakar-St. Louis line went on strike, and in the same year Bambara conscripted for work on the Thies-Kayes line provoked a general strike after three of their leaders were arrested as a result of discontent among them. The troops, many of whom were Bambara, refused to be involved in any action against the strikers and the administration had to release the Bambara leaders to bring an end to the strike.

From a social point of view, then, the impact of the colonial economy was much less than has usually been supposed. Perhaps the most important effect was the ousting and consequent frustration of the African businessman from a share in the profits from the expansion of the economy that took place under colonial rule.

How Europe Underdeveloped Africa

WALTER RODNEY[4]

The ... benefits from colonialism were small and they were not gifts from the colonialists, but rather fruits of African labor and resources for the most part. Indeed, what was called "the development of Africa" by the colonialists was a cynical shorthand expression for "the intensification of colonial exploitation in Africa to develop capitalist Europe." The analysis has gone beyond that to demonstrate that numerous false claims are made purporting to show that Europe developed Africa in the sense of bringing about social order, nationalism, and economic modernization. However, all of that would still not permit the conclusion that colonialism had a negative impact on Africa's development. In offering the view that colonialism was negative, the aim is to draw attention to the way that previous African development was blunted, halted, and turned back. In place of that interruption and blockade, nothing of compensatory value was introduced.

The decisiveness of the short period of colonialism and its negative consequences for Africa spring mainly from the fact that Africa lost power. Power is the ultimate determinant in human society, being basic to the relations within any group and between groups. It implies the ability to defend one's interests and, if necessary, to impose one's will by any means available. In relations between peoples, the question of power determines maneuverability in bargaining, the extent to which one people respect the interests of another, and eventually the extent to which a people survive as a physical and cultural entity. When one society finds itself forced to relinquish power entirely to another society, that in itself is a form of underdevelopment.

During the centuries of precolonial trade, some control over social, political, and economic life was retained in Africa, in spite of the disadvantageous com-

---

[4] This excerpt is taken from Walter Rodney, *How Europe Underdeveloped Africa* (Washington, D.C.: Howard University Press, 1982), pages 223-38. Originally published in 1972 by Bogle-L'Overture Publications, London, and Tanzanian Publishing House. Walter Rodney (1942-1980) was a Guyanese scholar and political activist. He was assassinated in 1980.

merce with Europeans that little control over internal matters disappeared under colonialism. Colonialism went much further than trade. It meant a tendency towards direct appropriation by Europeans of the social institutions within Africa. Africans ceased to set indigenous cultural goals and standards and lost full command of training young members of the society. Those were undoubtedly major steps backward. The Tunisian, Albert Memmi, puts forward the following proposition:

> The most serious blow suffered by the colonized is being removed from history and from the community. Colonization usurps any free role in either war or peace, every decision contributing to his destiny and that of the world, and all cultural and social responsibility.

Sweeping as that statement may initially appear, it is entirely true. The removal from history follows logically from the loss of power, which colonialism represented. The power to act independently is the guarantee to participate actively and *consciously* in history. To be colonized is to be removed from history, except in the most passive sense. A striking illustration of the fact that colonial Africa was a passive object is seen in its attraction for white anthropologists, who came to study "primitive society." Colonialism determined that Africans were no more makers of history than were beetles—objects to be looked at under a microscope and examined for unusual features.

The negative impact of colonialism in political terms was quite dramatic. Overnight, African political states lost their power, independence, and meaning—irrespective of whether they were big empires or small polities. Certain traditional rulers were kept in office, and the formal structure of some kingdoms was partially retained, but the substance of political life was quite different. Political power had passed into the hands of foreign overlords. Of course, numerous African states in previous centuries had passed through the cycle of growth and decline. But colonial rule was different. So long as it lasted, not a single African state could flourish.

To be specific, it must be noted that colonialism crushed by force the surviving feudal states of North Africa; that the French wiped out the large Moslem states of the Western Sudan, as well as Dahomey and kingdoms in Madagascar; that the British eliminated Egypt, the Mahdist Sudan, Asante, Benin, the Yoruba kingdoms, Swaziland, Matabeleland, the Lozi, and the East African lake kingdoms as great states. It should further be noted that a multiplicity of smaller and growing states were removed from the face of Africa by the Belgians, Portuguese, British, French, Germans, Spaniards, and Italians. Finally, those that appeared to survive were nothing but puppet creations. For instance, the Sultan of Morocco retained nominal existence under colonial rule that started in 1912; and the same applied to the Bey of Tunis; but Morocco and Tunisia were just as much under the power of French colonial administrators as neighboring Algeria, where the feudal rulers were removed altogether.

Sometimes, the African rulers who were chosen to serve as agents of foreign colonial rule were quite obviously nothing but puppets. The French and the Portuguese were in the habit of choosing their own African "chiefs"; the British went to Iboland and invented "warrant chiefs"; and all the colonial powers found it convenient to create "superior" or "paramount" rulers. Very often, the local population hated and despised such colonial stooges. There were traditional rulers such as the Sultan of Sokoto, the Kabaka of Buganda, and the Asantehene of Asante, who retained a great deal of prestige in the eyes of Africans, but they had no power to act outside the narrow boundaries laid down by colonialism lest they find themselves in the Seychelles Islands as "guests of His Majesty's Government."

One can go so far as to say that colonial rule meant the effective eradication of African political power throughout the continent, since Liberia and Ethiopia could no longer function as independent states within the context of continent-wide colonialism. Liberia in particular had to bow before foreign political, economic, and military pressures in a way that no genuinely independent state could have accepted; and although Ethiopia held firm until 1936, most European capitalist nations were not inclined to treat Ethiopia as a sovereign state, primarily because it was African, and Africans were supposed to be colonial subjects.

The pattern of arrest of African political development has some features which can only be appreciated after careful scrutiny and the taking away of the blinkers the colonizers put on the eyes of their subjects. An interesting case in point is that of women's role in society. Until today, capitalist society has failed to resolve the inequality between man and woman, which was entrenched in all modes of production prior to localism. The colonialists in Africa occasionally paid lip service to women's education and emancipation, but objectively there was deterioration in the status of women owing to colonial rule.

A realistic assessment of the role of women in independent precolonial Africa shows two contrasting but combined tendencies. In the first place, women were exploited by men through polygamous arrangements designed to capture the labor power of women. As always, exploitation was accompanied by oppression; and there is evidence to the effect that women were sometimes treated like beasts of burden, as for instance in Moslem African societies. Nevertheless, there was a countertendency to insure the dignity of women to greater or lesser degree in all African societies. Mother-right was a prevalent feature of African societies, and particular women held a variety of privileges based on the fact that they were the keys to inheritance.

More important still, some women had real power in the political sense, exercised either through religion or directly within the politico-constitutional apparatus. In Mozambique, the widow of an Nguni king became the priestess in charge of the shrine set up in the burial place of her deceased husband, and the reigning king had to consult her on all important matters. In a few instances, women were actually heads of state. Among the Lovedu of Transvaal, the key figure was the Rain-Queen, combining political and religious functions. The most frequently encountered role of importance played by women was that of "Queen Mother" or "Queen Sister." In practice, that post was filled by a female of royal blood, who might be mother, sister, or aunt of the reigning king in places such as Mali, Asante, and Buganda. Her influence was considerable, and there were occasions when the "Queen Mother" was the real power and the male king a mere puppet.

What happened to African women under colonialism is that the social, religious, constitutional, and political privileges and rights disappeared, while the economic exploitation continued and was often intensified. It was intensified because the division of labor according to sex was frequently disrupted. Traditionally, African men did the heavy labor of felling trees, clearing land and building houses, apart from conducting warfare and hunting. When they were required to leave their farms to seek employment, women remained behind, burdened with every task necessary for the survival of themselves, the children, and even the men as far as foodstuffs were concerned. Moreover, since men entered the money sector more easily and in greater numbers than women, women's work became greatly inferior to that of men within the new value system of colonialism: men's work was "modern" and women's was "traditional" and "backward." Therefore, the deterioration in the status of African women was bound up with the consequent loss of the right to set indigenous standards of what work had merit and what did not.

One of the most important manifestations of historical arrest and stagnation in colonial Africa is that which commonly goes under the title of "tribalism." That term, in its common journalistic setting, is understood to mean that Africans have a basic loyalty to tribe rather than nation and that each tribe still retains a fundamental hostility towards its neighboring tribes. The examples favored by the capitalist press and bourgeois scholarship are those of Congo and Nigeria. Their accounts suggest that Europeans tried to make a nation out of the Congolese and Nigerian peoples, but failed because the various tribes had their age-long hatreds; and, as soon as the colonial power left, the natives returned to killing each other. To this phenomenon, Europeans often attach the word "atavism," to carry the notion that Africans were returning to their primitive savagery. Even a cursory survey of the African past shows that such assertions are the exact opposite of the truth.

All of the large states of nineteenth-century Africa were multi-ethnic, and their expansion was continually making anything like "tribal" loyalty a thing of the past by substituting in its place national and class ties. However, in all parts of the world, that substitution of national and class ties for purely ethnic ones is a lengthy historical process; and, invariably, there remains for long periods certain regional pockets of individuals who have their own narrow, regional loyalties, springing from ties of kinship, language, and culture. In Asia, the feudal states of Vietnam and Burma both achieved a considerable degree of national homogeneity over the centuries before colonial rule. But there were pockets of "tribes" or "minorities" who remained outside the effective sphere of the nation-state and the national economy and culture.

Colonialism blocked the further evolution of national solidarity, because it destroyed the particular Asian or African states which were the principal agents for achieving the liquidation of fragmented loyalties. Because ethnic and regional loyalties that go under the name of "tribalism" could not be effectively resolved by the colonial state, they tended to fester and grow in unhealthy forms. Indeed, the colonial powers sometimes saw the value of stimulating the internal tribal jealousies so as to keep the colonized from dealing with their principal contradiction with the European overlords—i.e., the classic technique of divide and rule. Certainly, the Belgians consciously fostered that; and the racist whites in South Africa had by the 1950s worked out a careful plan to "develop" the oppressed African population as Zulu, as Xhosa, and as Sotho so that the march towards broader African national and class solidarities could be stopped and turned back.

The civil war in Nigeria is generally regarded as having been a tribal affair. To accept such a contention would mean extending the definition of tribe to cover Shell Oil and Gulf Oil! . . . What came to be called tribalism at the beginning of the new epoch of political independence in Nigeria was itself a product of the way that people were brought together under colonialism so as to be exploited. It was a product of administrative devices, of entrenched regional separations, and of differential access by particular ethnic groups into the colonial economy and culture.

Precolonial trade had started the trend of the disintegration of African economies and their technological impoverishment. Colonial rule speeded up that trend. The story is often told that in order to make a telephone call from Accra in the British colony of the Gold Coast to Abidjan in the adjacent French colony of Ivory Coast, it was necessary to be connected first with an operator in London and then with an operator in Paris who could offer a line to Abidjan. That was one reflection of the fact that the Gold Coast economy was integrated into the British economy, and the Ivory Coast economy was integrated into the French economy, while the neighboring African colonies had little or no effective economic relations. The following conclusion reached by the United Nations Economic Commission for Africa in 1959 goes directly to the point:

The most outstanding characteristic of the transportation systems of Africa is the comparative isolation in which they have developed within the confines of individual countries and territories. This is reflected in the lack of links between countries and territories within the same geographical sub-region.

Africa was denied the opportunity of developing healthy trade links with parts of the world other than Europe and North America. Some trade persisted across the Indian Ocean, but on the whole it is fair to say that the roads in Africa led to the seaports and the sea lanes led to Western Europe and North America. That kind of lopsidedness is today part of the pattern of underdevelopment and dependence.

The damaging impact of capitalism on African technology is even more clearly measurable in the colonial period than in the earlier centuries. In spite of the slave trade and of the import of European goods, most African handicraft industries still had vitality at the start of the colonial period. They had undergone no technological advance and they had not expanded, but they had survived. The mass production of the more recent phase of capitalism virtually obliterated African industries such as cloth, salt, soap, iron, and even potterymaking.

In North Africa, handicraft industries had made the greatest advances before colonialism, in spheres ranging from brasswork to woolens. As in the towns of feudal Europe, craft workshops flourished in Algerian towns like Oran, Constantine, Algiers, and Tlemcen. But French colonialism destroyed the handicraft industries and threw thousands out of work. The same thing had happened in Europe itself when new machines had thrown artisans out of employment in places like Lancashire and Lyons, but in that instance the new machines became the basis of the prevailing mode of production, and formerly independent artisans returned to factories as proletarians to master different skills and expand the productive capacity of their society. In Africa, it was simply destruction without redress. By the time political independence was achieved, surviving craftsmanship had been turned towards attracting tourists rather than meeting the real needs of African people.

Besides, as was true of the European slave trade, the destruction of technology under colonialism must be related to the barriers raised in the path of African initiative. The vast majority of Africans drawn into the colonial money economy were simply providing manual labor, which stimulated perspiration rather than scientific initiative. Africans connected to the trading sector were sometimes successful in a limited way. The resourcefulness of West African market women is well known, but it was put to petty purposes. The problem posed to capitalists and workers in Europe while making insecticide from African pyrethrum was one requiring that resourcefulness be expressed in a technical direction. But the problem posed to an African market woman by the necessity to make a penny more profit on every tin of imported sardines was resolved sometimes by a little more vigor, sometimes by a touch of dishonesty, and sometimes by resort to *juju*.

Colonialism induced the African ironworker to abandon the process of extracting iron from the soil and to concentrate instead on working scraps of metal imported from Europe. The only compensation for that interruption would have been the provision of modern techniques in the extraction and processing of iron. However, those techniques were debarred from Africa, on the basis of the international division of labor under imperialism. As was seen earlier, the non-industrialization of Africa was not left to chance. It was deliberately enforced by stopping the transference to Africa of machinery and skills which would have given competition to European industry in that epoch.

In the period of African development preceding colonialism, some areas moved faster than others and provided the nuclei for growth on a wide regional basis. Northern Nigeria was one of those, but virtually went to sleep during the colonial period. The British cut it off from the rest of the Moslem world and fossilized social relations, so that the serfs could not achieve any change at the expense of the ruling aristocracy.

Instead of speeding up growth, colonial activities such as mining and cash-crop farming speeded up the decay of "traditional" African life. In many parts of the continent, vital aspects of culture were adversely affected, nothing better was substituted, and only a lifeless shell was left. The capitalist forces behind colonialism were interested in little more than the exploitation of labor. Even areas that were not directly involved in the money economy exploited labor. In extracting that labor, they tampered with the factor that was the very buttress of the society, for African "traditional" life when deprived of its customary labor force and patterns of work was no longer "traditional."

During the colonial era, many thinly populated villages appeared in Central and Southern Africa, comprising women, children, and old men. They practiced subsistence agriculture, which was not productive enough, and colonialists contrasted them with cash-crop areas, which in comparison were flourishing. However, it was precisely the impact of colonialism that left so many villages deserted and starving, because the able-bodied males had gone off to labor elsewhere. Any district deprived of its effective laboring population could not be expected to develop.

There were several spots within different colonies which were sufficiently far removed from towns and colonial administration that they neither grew cash crops nor supplied labor. In southern Sudan, for instance, there were populations who continued to live a life not dissimilar to that which they had followed in previous centuries. Yet, even for such traditional African societies, the scope for development no longer existed. They were isolated by the hold that the colonialists had on the rest of the continent. They could not interact with other parts of Africa. They were subject to increasing encroachment by the money economy and were more and more to be regarded as historical relics. The classic example of this type of obstructed historical development is to be found in the U.S.A., where the indigenous population of Indians who survived slaughter by the whites were placed in reservations and condemned to stagnation. Indian reservations in North America are living museums, visited by white tourists who purchase curios.

In South Africa and Rhodesia, the policy of establishing "native reserves" was openly followed. Inside a reserve, the major means of production was the land. But the quantity and fertility of the land allocated was entirely inadequate to support the numbers of Africans who were driven in. The reserves were reservoirs of cheap labor and dumping grounds for those who could not be accommodated within the money economy of the racist southern section of Africa. Further north, there were no areas named as reserves except in colonial Kenya and to a very limited extent in Tanganyika. But the money economy was constantly transforming the traditional sector into one which was just as deprived as any reserve.

The money economy of colonialism was a growing sector. That is not to be denied. However, it has already been indicated how limited that growth was, viewed over the continent as a whole. The growth in the so-called modern sector exercised adverse effects on the non-monetary sector. What remains is to emphasize that the character of growth in Africa under colonialism was such that it did not constitute development—i.e., it did not enlarge the capacity of the society to deal with the natural environment, to adjudicate relations between members of the society, and to protect the population from external forces. Such a statement is already implicitly borne out in the inability of capitalism to stimulate skilled labor in colonial Africa. A system that must stand in the way of the accumulation of skills does not develop anything or anybody. It is implicit, too, in the manner in which Africa was cut into economic compartments having no relation one to another, so that, even though the volume of commercial activity within each compartmentalized colony may have increased, there was no development comparable to that which linked together the various states of the U.S.A.

In recent times, economists have been recognizing in colonial and postcolonial Africa a pattern that has been termed "growth without development." That phrase has now appeared as the title of books on Liberia and Ivory Coast. It means that goods and services of a certain type are on the increase. There may be more rubber and coffee exported, there may be more cars imported with the proceeds, and there may be more gasoline stations built to service the cars. But the profit goes abroad, and the economy becomes more and more a dependency of the metropoles. In no African colony was there economic integration, or any provision for making the economy self-sustained and geared to its own local goals. Therefore, there was growth of the so-called enclave import-export sector, but the only things that developed were dependency and underdevelopment.

A further revelation of growth without development under colonialism was the overdependence on one or two exports. The term "monoculture" is used to describe those colonial economies that were centered around a single crop. Liberia (in the agricultural sector) was a monoculture dependent on rubber, Gold Coast on cocoa, Dahomey and southeast Nigeria on palm produce, Sudan on cotton, Tanganyika on sisal, and Uganda on cotton. In Senegal and Gambia, groundnuts accounted for 85 to 90 percent of money earnings. In effect, two African colonies were told to grow nothing but peanuts!

Every farming people have a staple food, plus a variety of other supplements. Historians, agronomists, and botanists have all contributed to showing the great variety of such foods within the precolonial African economy. There were numerous crops which were domesticated within the African continent, there were several wild food species (notably fruits), and Africans had shown no conservatism in adopting useful food plants of Asian or American origin. Diversified agriculture was within the African tradition. Monoculture was a colonialist invention.

There was nothing "natural" about monoculture. It was a consequence of imperialist requirements and machinations, extending into areas that were politically independent in name. Monoculture was a characteristic of regions falling under imperialist domination. Certain countries in Latin America, such as Costa Rica and Guatemala, were forced by United States capitalist firms to concentrate so heavily on growing bananas that they were contemptuously known as "banana republics." In Africa, this concentration on one or two cash crops for sale abroad had many harmful effects. Sometimes, cash crops were grown to the exclusion of staple foods—thus causing famines. For instance, in Gambia rice farming was popular before the colonial era, but so much of the best land was transferred to groundnuts that rice had to be imported on a large scale to try to counter the fact that famine was becoming endemic. In Asante, concentration on cocoa raised fears of famine in a region previously famous for yams and other foodstuff.

Yet the threat of famine was a small disadvantage compared to the extreme vulnerability and insecurity of monoculture. When the crop was affected by internal factors such as disease, that amounted to an overwhelming disaster, as in the case of Gold Coast cocoa when it was hit by swollen-shoot disease in the 1940s. Besides, at all times, the price fluctuations (which were externally controlled) left the African producer helpless in the face of capitalist maneuvers.

From a capitalist viewpoint, monocultures commended themselves most because they made colonial economies entirely dependent on the metropolitan buyers of their produce. At the end of the European slave trade, only a minority of Africans were sufficiently committed to capitalist exchange and sufficiently dependent upon European imports to wish to continue the relationship with Europe at all costs. Colonialism increased the dependence of Africa on Europe in terms of the numbers of persons brought into the money economy and in terms of the number of aspects of socio-economic life in Africa which derived their existence from the connection with the metropole. The ridiculous situation arose by which European trading firms, mining companies, shipping lines, banks, insurance houses, and plantations all exploited Africa and at the same time caused Africans to feel that without those capitalist services no money or European goods would be forthcoming, and therefore Africa was in debt to its exploiters!

The factor of dependency made its impact felt in every aspect of the life of the colonies, and it can be regarded as the crowning vice among the negative social, political, and economic consequences of colonialism in Africa, being primarily responsible for the perpetuation of the colonial relationship into the epoch that is called neocolonialism.

In the light of the prevailing balance-sheet concept of what colonial rule was about, it still remains to take note of European innovations in Africa, such as modern medicine, clinical surgery, and immunization. It would be absurd to deny that these were objectively positive features, however limited they were quantitatively. However, they have to be weighed against the numerous setbacks received by Africa in all spheres due to colonialism, as well as against the contributions Africa made to Europe. European science met the needs of its own society, particularly those of the bourgeoisie. The bourgeoisie did not suffer from hunger and starvation. Bourgeois science therefore did not consider those things as needs that had to be met and overcome—not even among their own workers and least of all on behalf of Africans. This is just a specific application of the general principle that the exploitation of Africa was being used to create a greater gap between Africa and capitalist Europe. The exploitation and the comparative disadvantage are the ingredients of underdevelopment.

The Colonial Impact

A. ADU BOAHEN[5]

Nowhere in Africa did the colonial system last more than a hundred years—from the 1890s to the 1970s. In the history of a continent, a hundred years is a very brief span indeed, a mere episode or interlude in the life of the peoples. Yet, short and episodic as it was, there is no doubt that colonialism made an impact on the continent. . . . I would like to examine the nature of the legacies that colonialism has bequeathed to Africa, as well as assess the significance of colonialism for Africa and Africans.

The first obvious positive political legacy was undoubtedly the establishment of continuous peace and stability in Africa, especially after the First World War. Let me hasten to add, first, that Africa was certainly not in a Hobbesian state of nature at the dawn of the colonial era and [that colonialism] . . . introduced into Africa far more violence, instability, anarchy, and loss of African lives than probably any other period in its history. The population of the Belgian Congo fell by 50 percent, and that of the Herero by 80 percent, as a result of the oppressive and inhuman treatment of the Africans by the colonizers during the period. There is no doubt, however, that after the wars of occupation and the repression of African opposition and resistance, an era of continuous peace, order, and stability set in. This certainly facilitated and accelerated the economic and social changes that occurred on the continent during the colonial period.

The second positive political impact has been the very appearance of the independent African states of today. The partition of Africa by the imperial colonial powers led ultimately to the establishment of some forty-eight new states, most of them with clearly defined boundaries, in place of the existing innumerable lineage and clan groups, city-states, kingdoms, and empires with-

---

[5] This excerpt is taken from A. Adu Boahen, *African Perspectives on Colonialism* (Baltimore, MD: Johns Hopkins University Press, 1987), pages 94-112. A. Adu Boahen (1932-2006) was a professor of history and the former vice-chancellor at the University of Ghana. He was also President of the UNESCO International Scientific Committee for the drafting of a General History of Africa.

out any fixed boundaries. It is significant that the boundaries of these states have been maintained ever since independence.

However, the creation of the states has proved to be more of a liability than an asset to the present independent African nations. Had the boundaries of these states been laid down in accordance with any well-defined, rational criteria and in full cognizance of the ethnocultural, geographical, and ecological realities of Africa, the outcome would have been wholesome. Unfortunately, many of these boundaries were arbitrarily drawn on African maps in the chancelleries of the imperial powers in Europe. The result has been that most of these states are artificial creations, and this very artificiality has created very serious problems, many of which have still not been solved.

A second problem has been that of interstate boundary disputes. Not only did these artificial boundaries create multiethnic states, but worse still, they often run across preexisting nations, ethnicities, states, kingdoms, and empires. The Bakongo, for instance, are divided by the boundaries of the Congo, Zaire, Angola, and Gabon. Some of the Ewe live in Ghana, some in Togo, and others in Benin, while the Akan are found in the Ivory Coast and Ghana. The Somali are shared among Ethiopia, Kenya, and Somalia. The Senufo now live in Mali, the Ivory Coast, and Burkina Faso.

A third problem has been the uneven sizes and unequal natural resources and economic potentialities of these states. Some of the states that emerged from the partition were really giants; . . . others were midgets. Moreover, some states have miles and miles of coastline, while others are landlocked, with no access to the sea.

. . . Some have very fertile lands and several mineral resources, but others . . . are mere desert. Finally, while some states . . . have only a border or two to police, others have four or more, and Zaire has seven.

The third positive political impact of colonialism was its introduction of two new institutions—a new bureaucracy of civil servants and a new judicial system. On the first score, the contribution of the Europeans was uneven: the British bequeathed a far better-trained and numerically stronger civil service to its former colonies than the French, while the record of the Belgians and the Portuguese is the worst in this field. However, the judicial systems, bequeathed by the colonial administrations, have not undergone any fundamental changes in any of the independent African states.

Another positive colonial impact was the generation of a sense of nationalism as well as the intensification of the spirit of Pan-Africanism. The colonial system generated a sense of identity and consciousness among the different ethnic groups of each colonial state, while the anti-colonial literary activities of some of the educated Africans and, more especially, the Fascist attack on Ethiopia and the connivance of the other European imperial powers, diffused and strengthened the spirit of Pan-Africanism throughout the black world.

But it should be immediately pointed out that African nationalism was one of the accidental by-products of colonialism. No colonial power ever deliberately set out to generate or promote that consciousness. Moreover, the nationalism that was generated by colonialism was not a positive but a negative one, arising out of the sense of anger, frustration, and humiliation produced by the oppressive, discriminatory, and exploitative measures and activities of the colonial administrators.

Another political legacy bequeathed to independent African states was the professional army.... These armies were among the most conspicuous legacies, apart from physical structures, bequeathed to independent African states. ... In retrospect, they have become nothing but a chronic source of instability, confusion, and anarchy as a result of their often unnecessary and unjustifiable interventions in the political processes of African countries. Indeed, African armies are the greatest millstones around the necks of African leaders.

The final political impact, and a very negative and regrettable one, is the delay that colonialism caused in the political development and maturity of African states. If colonialism meant anything at all politically, it was the loss of sovereignty and independence by the colonized peoples. This loss of sovereignty, in turn, implied the loss of the right of a state to control its own destiny; to plan its own development; to decide which outside nations to borrow from, associate with, or emulate; to conduct its own diplomacy and international relations; and above all, to manage or even mismanage its own affairs, derive pride and pleasure from its successes, and derive lessons, frustrations, and experience from its failures.

The impact of colonialism in the economic field, as in the political field, was clearly a mixed one. The most important economic benefit was the provision of an infrastructure of roads, railways, harbors, the telegraph, and the telephone. The basic infrastructure of every modern African state was completed during the colonial period, and in most countries, not even a mile of railroad has been constructed since independence. A second important economic impact was the development of the primary sector of Africa's economy. It was during this period that the mineral potential of many African countries was discovered and modern scientific mining introduced. Above all, it was during this period that the production of such cash crops as cotton, peanuts, palm oil, coffee, tobacco, rubber, and cocoa became the main feature of the political economy of many an African state.

These fundamental economic changes, in turn, had some far-reaching consequences. In the first place, land acquired great commercial value and assumed far greater importance than it had ever had before. Secondly, the spread of cash-crop agriculture enabled Africans of whatever social status, especially rural Africans in many regions, to acquire wealth and raise their standard of living. Another significant impact was the spread and consolidation of the money economy in Africa, and with it not only a change in the traditional standards of wealth and status but also a phenomenal increase in the class of wage earners and salaried persons. In the wake of the money economy came the banking activities which have become such a feature in the economies of independent African states. The sum total of all these colonial economic reforms was what has been described by economists as the completion of the integration of the African economy into the world economy in general and into the capitalist economy of the former colonial powers in particular.

But the economic changes introduced by colonialism had a negative side also. First, the transportation and communications infrastructure that was provided was not only inadequate but was also very unevenly distributed in nearly all the colonies. The roads and railways were by and large constructed to link areas with the potential for cash crops and with mineral deposits with the sea or the world commodity market. In other words, the infrastructures were meant to facilitate the exploitation of the natural resources but not to promote the accessibility and development of all regions of the colony. The outcome of this has been uneven regional economic development in most African countries, still a major stumbling block in the way of nation-building in Africa today.

Secondly, the colonial system led to the delay of industrial and technological developments in Africa. As has been pointed out already, one of the typical features of the colonial political economy was the total neglect of industrialization and of the processing of locally produced raw materials and agricultural products in the colonies. . . . Preexisting industries were almost completely eradicated by the importation of cheap and even better substitutes from Europe and India, while Africans were driven out of the mining industry as it became an exclusive preserve of Europeans. This neglect of industrialization, destruction of the existing industries and handicrafts in Africa, and elimination of Africans from the mining field further explain Africa's present technological backwardness.

Thirdly, colonialism saddled most colonies with monocrop economies. During the colonial period, as may be recalled, each colony was made to produce a single cash crop or two, and no attempts were made to diversify the agricultural economy. The habit of producing these single cash crops appears to have become so ingrained that it has not been changed to any appreciable degree since independence. The other consequence of this concentration on the production of cash crops for export was the neglect of the internal sector of the economy and, in particular, of the production of food for internal consumption, so that rice, maize, fish, and other foods had to be imported. Thus, during the colonial period, Africans were encouraged to produce what they did not consume and to consume what they did not produce, a clear proof of the exploitative nature of the colonial political economy.

Finally, the monetary policies pursued by all the colonial powers must be held partly responsible for the present underdeveloped state of the continent. Under these policies, all the colonial currencies were tied to those of the metropolitan countries, and all their foreign exchange earnings were kept in the metropolitan countries and not used for internal development. The expatriate commercial banks and companies were also allowed to repatriate their deposits, savings, and profits instead of reinvesting them in the colonies for further development. The consequence of all this was that at the time of independence, no African state apart from the Union of South Africa had the strong economic or industrial base needed for a real economic takeoff. And if this base could not be provided during the eighty-year period of colonial rule, should we expect it to have been done in twenty years of independence, especially in the light of the changing international economic order?

What about the impact in the social field? Here again, there are both credit and debit sides. In the first place, there is no doubt that after the initial decline, population growth resumed after the First World War. Caldwell has estimated that the population of Africa increased by 37 percent during the colonial period. The increase was undoubtedly due to some of the policies and activities of the colonial administrators—such as the provision of roads and railways, which made for mobility; the campaign launched against such epidemic diseases as sleeping sickness, bubonic plagues, yellow fever, and yaws; and the provision of some medical facilities.

A second important benefit was urbanization. Not only did preexisting towns expand, but completely new urban centers emerged following the establishment of the colonial system. . . . There is no doubt that the quality of life for Africa's population was relatively improved through the provision of piped water, hospitals and dispensaries, better housing, and sanitary facilities.

A third important social benefit of colonialism was the spread of Christianity and Islam and especially of Western education. During the colonial period, Christianity gained far more converts and penetrated farther, especially in East and Central Africa, than it had in all the previous three or four centuries put together. Islam also gained a lot of ground thanks to the patronage of the French and British colonial administrators in particular. It should be emphasized that traditional African religion maintained its position in the face of all the inroads by these foreign religions.

The spread of Western education was due mainly to the activities of the Christian missionaries. . . . Education . . . was mainly responsible for producing the educated African *elite*, which not only spearheaded the overthrow of the colonial system but also constitutes the backbone of the civil service of independent African states.

The other beneficial result of the spread of Western education was the provision of a lingua franca for each colony or cluster of colonies. In all the colonies, the mother tongue of the metropolitan country became the official language as well as the main medium of communication among the multi-ethnic populations of each colony.

The final social benefit was the new social order that emerged in Africa as a result of the operation of the colonial system. Though there was social mobility in the traditional African social order, undue weight was given to birth. The colonial system, on the other hand, emphasized individual merit and achievement rather than birth, and this greatly facilitated social mobility.

It would appear that the positive contribution of colonialism in the social field was quite considerable. Unfortunately, so also—and probably more so—was the negative impact. In the first place, it was the colonial system that initiated the gap that still exists between the urban and rural areas. All of the modern facilities—schools, hospitals, street lights, radio, postal services—and above all most of the employment opportunities were concentrated in the urban centers. The combination of modern life and employment pulled rural dwellers, especially the young ones and those with schooling, in the direction of the cities.

Secondly, the social services provided by colonialism were grossly inadequate and unevenly distributed. For instance, while in Nigeria by the 1930s twelve modern hospitals had been built for Europeans, who numbered only 4,000, there were only fifty-two for Africans, numbering 40 million. In Dar es Salaam, the ratio of beds to population by 1920 was approximately 1 to 10 for the European hospital and 1 to 400-500 for the African hospital.

There was even greater deficiency, uneven distribution, and in this case even misdirected orientation in the educational facilities that were provided in colonial Africa. University education was totally ignored in all the colonies until the 1940s, and only one university was subsequently established for each colony. In Portuguese Africa, there were no universities. Moreover, most of the secondary schools were in the major cities and the coastal areas of the colonies and seldom in the interior and rural regions. Thirdly, in no colony was the demand for education at all levels ever adequately met.

The effects of colonial education were really unfortunate. First, because of its inadequacy, large numbers of Africans remained illiterate and illiteracy is still widespread. Secondly, the *elite* produced by these colonial educational institutions were, with few exceptions, people who were alienated from their own society in terms of their dress, outlook, and tastes in food, music, and even dance. They were people who worshiped European culture, equating it with civilization, and looked down upon their own culture. Radical African scholars are now talking of colonial miseducation rather than education. Unfortunately, it is this very alienated and badly oriented *elite* that has dominated both the political and the social scene in Africa since independence. Above all, the neglect of technical education and the emphasis on liberal education created in educated Africans a contempt for manual work and an admiration for white-collar jobs, and this contempt and admiration have still not left them. Finally, the use of the metropolitan language as the lingua franca also had the most regrettable effect of preventing the development of an official African language as a lingua franca in each colony or even in a cluster of colonies.

Another negative social impact of colonialism was the downgrading of the status of women in Africa. During the colonial period, there were far fewer facilities for girls than for boys. Women could therefore not gain access into the professions—medicine, law, the civil service, and the bench. Very few women were ever appointed to any "European post," while there was never a female governor of a colony.

The colonial administrators and their allies, the European missionaries, condemned everything African in culture—African names, music, dance, art, religion, marriage, the system of inheritance—and completely discouraged the teaching of all these things in their schools and colleges. Even the wearing of African clothes to work or school was banned. All this could not but retard the cultural development of the continent.

But the last and the most serious negative impact of colonialism has been psychological. This is seen, first, in the creation of a colonial mentality among educated Africans in particular and also among the populace in general. This mentality manifests itself in the condemnation of anything traditional, in the preference for imported goods to locally manufactured goods (since independence), and in the style of dress—such as the wearing of three-piece suits in a climate where temperatures routinely exceed eighty degrees Fahrenheit.

The final and worst psychological impact has been the generation of a deep feeling of inferiority as well as the loss of a sense of human dignity among Africans. Both complexes were surely the outcome not only of the wholesale condemnation of everything African already referred to but, above all, of the practice of racial discrimination and the constant humiliation and oppression to which Africans were subjected throughout the colonial period. The sense of human dignity seems to have been regained, but the feeling of inferiority has not entirely disappeared, even after two decades of independence.

It should be obvious from the above, then, that all those historians who see colonialism as a "one-armed bandit" are totally wrong. Equally guilty of exaggeration are those colonial apologists who see colonialism as an unqualified blessing for Africa as well as those who see its record as a balanced one. Colonialism definitely did have its credit and debit sides, but quite clearly the debit side far outweighs the credit side. Indeed, my charge against colonialism is not that it did not do anything for Africa, but that it did so little and that little so accidentally and indirectly; not that the economy of Africa under colonialism did not grow, but that it grew more to the advantage of the colonial powers and the expatriate owners and shareholders of the companies operating in Africa than to the Africans; not that improvements did not take place in the lives of the African peoples, but that such improvements were so limited and largely confined to the urban areas; not that education was not provided, but that what was provided was so inadequate and so irrelevant to the needs and demands of the African themselves; not that there was no upward social mobility, but that such a relatively small number of Africans did get to the top. In short, given the opportunities, the resources, and the power and influence of the colonial rulers, they could and should have done far more than they did for Africa. And it is for this failure that the colonial era will go down in history as a period of wasted opportunities, of ruthless exploitation of the resources of Africa, and on balance of the underdevelopment and humiliation of the peoples of Africa.

African Economic Development and Colonial Legacies

GARETH AUSTIN[6]

This article asks how the legacies of European rule, both generally and in particular categories of colony, have affected post-colonial economic development in Sub-Saharan Africa. The year 1960 is conventionally used as the "stylised date" of independence, for the good reason that it saw the end of colonial rule in most of the French colonies south of the Sahara as well as in the most populous British and Belgian ones (Nigeria and Congo respectively). Half a century is a reasonable period over which to review the economic impact of legacies because it allows us to consider the issue in the context of different phases of post-colonial policy and performance.

The causal significance of legacies varies, in that they affect subsequent freedom of maneuver to different extents and in different directions. At its strongest, legacy takes the form of "path determination," implying that colonial choices determined post-colonial ones, or at least conditioned them, such that departure from the colonial pattern was, and perhaps remains, difficult and costly. Besides asking about the strength of the influence of the past on the future, we need to consider the nature of that influence. Did colonial rule put African countries on a higher or lower path of economic change? It will be argued here that the "path(s)" on which African economies were (to a greater or lesser extent) set by the time of independence are most usefully seen not as necessarily initiated in the colonial period, but often rather as continuations and adjustments from paths of change established before the European partition of the continent. . . .

A feature of the theoretical and ideological debate about the history of eco-

---

[6] This excerpt is taken from "African Economic Development and Colonial Legacies," web-published in "International Development Policy," January 2010, at www.poldev.revues.org/78. Gareth Austin is a professor of international history at the Graduate Institute of Inernational Studies in Geneva, Switzerland. The original version of this essay contains extensive citations that readers may consult online.

nomic development in Africa is that it is possible to reach rather similar conclusions from very different scholarly and political starting-points. Regarding the colonial impact, the case for the prosecution, which a generation ago was urged most strongly by dependency theorists and radical nationalists, is now championed by "rational choice" growth economists. Daron Acemoglu, Simon Johnson, and James A. Robinson have argued that Africa's relative poverty at the end of the 20th century was primarily the result of the form taken by European colonialism on the continent: Europeans settling for extraction rather than settling themselves in overwhelming numbers and thereby introducing the kinds of institution (private property rights and systems of government that would support them) that, according to Acemoglu, Johnson and Robinson, was responsible for economic development in Europe and the colonies of European settlement in North America and Australasia.

Colonial extraction in Africa could be seen most decisively in the appropriation of land for European settlers or plantations, a strategy used not only to provide European investors and settlers with cheap and secure control of land, but also to oblige Africans to sell their labour to European farmers, planters or mine-owners. Even in the "peasant" colonies, i.e., where the land remained overwhelmingly in African ownership, we will see that major parts of the services sector were effectively monopolised by Europeans. Then there was coercive recruitment of labour by colonial administrations, whether to work for the state or for European private enterprise. Of potentially great long-term importance was the unwillingness of colonial governments to accept, still less promote, the emergence of markets in land rights on land occupied by Africans, whether in "settler" or "peasant" colonies. From the perspectives of both dependency theory and "rational choice" institutionalism, the original sin of colonialism in Africa was that it did not introduce a full-blooded capitalist system, based upon private property and thereby generating the pressures towards competition and accumulation necessary to drive self-sustained economic growth.

A narrower but important argument was made by the then small group of liberal development economists between the 1950s and 1970s. At a time when development economists (especially but not exclusively those writing in French) tended to favour a leading role for the state in the search for development in mixed economies, P. T. Bauer attacked the late colonial state for introducing statutory marketing boards and thereby laying the foundation of what he considered to be deadening state interventionism.

Explicitly positive overviews of colonial rule in Africa are rare (but see Duignan and Gann 1975). Many studies, though, mention the suppression of intra-African warfare, the abolition of internal slave trading and slavery, the introduction of mechanised transport and investment in infrastructure, and the development of modern manufacturing in the "settler" economies and in the Belgian Congo. . . .

Besides optimism and pessimism, a third view of colonial rule, and by implication of its legacy, is that its importance has been overrated. There are different routes to this conclusion. Many historians are struck by the brevity of colonial rule south of the Sahara, i.e. about 60 years in most of tropical Africa, and by the weakness of the colonial state. In this setting it can plausibly be argued that whatever went well in the "peasant" economies (and cash crop economies expanded greatly) was mainly the responsibility of Africans, through their economic rationality and entrepreneurship. . . .

To evaluate the colonial legacy, we need to distinguish it from the situation and trends at the beginning of colonial rule, which in most of Sub-Saharan Africa occurred during the European "scramble," from 1879 to *circa* 1905. At that time the region was, as before, characterised generally (not everywhere all the time) by an abundance of cultivable land in relation to the labour available to till it. This did not mean "resource abundance" as much of Africa's mineral endowment was either unknown or inaccessible with pre-industrial technology or was not yet valuable even overseas. For example, many of the major discoveries (notably of oil in Nigeria and diamonds in Botswana) were to occur only during the period of decolonisation. Moreover, the fertility of much of the land was relatively low or at least fragile, making it costly or difficult to pursue intensive cultivation, especially in the absence of animal manure. Sleeping sickness prevented the use of large animals, whether for ploughing or transport, in the forest zones and much of the savannas. The extreme seasonality of the annual distribution of rainfall rendered much of the dry season effectively unavailable for farm work. The consequent low opportunity cost of dry-season labour reduced the incentive to raise labour productivity in craft production. Conversely, the characteristic choices of farming techniques were land-extensive and labour-saving; but the thinness of the soils constrained the returns on labour. All this helps to explain why the productivity of African labour was apparently higher outside Africa over several centuries: the underlying economic logic of the external slave trades which in turn, ironically, aggravated the scarcity of labour within Africa itself.

Within Africa, the structure of incentives encouraged a high degree of self-sufficiency, and by the middle of the 20th century it was widely assumed that pre-colonial economies had necessarily been overwhelmingly subsistence-oriented. The last half-century of research has progressively changed this assessment, especially for West Africa where a strong tendency towards extra-subsistence production was evident in the 16th and 17th centuries. While damaged by the aggravated "Dutch disease" effects of the Atlantic slave trade, this tendency was strongly resumed from the first decade of the 19th century when that trade began to be abolished, with West Africans producing on a wider and larger scale for internal as well as overseas markets. Given the relative scarcity of labour, and in the absence (generally) of significant economies of scale in production, it was rare for the reservation wage (the minimum wage rate sufficient to persuade people to sell their labour rather than work for themselves) to be low enough for a would-be employer to afford to pay it. Hence the labour markets of pre-colonial Africa mainly took the form of slave trading.

The same abundance of land made political centralisation difficult to achieve and sustain. Political fragmentation had facilitated the Atlantic slave trade, in that larger states would have had stronger incentives and capacities for rejecting participation in it. This fragmentation later facilitated the European conquest. Ethiopia was the exception that proved the rule, with its fertile central provinces and large agricultural surplus supporting a long-established and modernising state that, alone in Africa, had the economic base to resist the "scramble" successfully.

By no coincidence, most of Sub-Saharan Africa was colonised at a time when the industrialisation of Europe was creating or expanding markets for various commodities that could profitably be produced in Africa. The land-labour ratio, the environmental constraints on intensive agriculture and also the specific qualities of particular kinds of land in various parts of the continent gave Africa at least a potential comparative advantage in land-extensive primary production. By the time of colonisation, especially in West Africa, the indigenous populations were increasingly taking advantage of the combination of these supply-side features and of access to expanding overseas markets. From Senegal to Cameroon thousands of tonnes of groundnuts and palm oil, and from the 1880s rubber, were being produced for sale to European merchants. . . .

The particular identity of the colonial power made some difference to the lives of those subjected to European rule. Contrasts between the two largest empires in Africa are traditionally made with reference to greater British reliance on African chiefs as intermediaries ("indirect rule") and the French doctrine of assimilating a small minority of Africans into French culture and citizenship. On the whole it is arguable that, in economic terms, the similarities were much greater than the differences, except when the latter arose from the composition of their respective African empires. French rule, like British, relied on African intermediaries, including chiefs, even though France was much more insistent on abolishing African monarchies (as in Dahomey, in contrast to the British treatment of the structures and dynasties of the states of Buganda, Botswana, Lesotho and, after an abortive attempt at abolition, Ashanti). In West Africa the French made much greater use of forced labour, but that was primarily because the French territories were, from the start, relatively lacking in cash-earning and therefore wage-paying potential. That specific policy—*corvée* and its use to benefit white planters rather than African farmers—made a difference to the colonial legacy in Ghana and Côte d'Ivoire. It meant that

African cocoa farming took off much more quickly and dramatically in the former, so that Ghana was much wealthier at independence, when Côte d'Ivoire was in the process of catching up (and overtaking) after a late start, which it proceeded to do by the 1980s. . . .

The "extraversion" and "monoculture" of African economies is widely lamented and condemned as a victory of colonial over African interests. The risks entailed in extreme specialisation, however, need to be set against the long-run income gain to be expected from the exploitation of comparative advantage. But again, although the location of a colonial economy's comparative advantage could be identified, sooner or later the task of capitalising on it raised the question of what investments might profitably deepen that advantage and, above all, of how the costs and benefits would be distributed. Conflicts of ideology, and especially the balance of power between different interest groups, worked out variously across the range of African colonies. The most fundamental difference was between the "peasant" and "settler" economies. Let us consider the contrasting cases of export agriculture in the former, notably in West Africa, and mining in the latter, most obviously in South Africa.

We have noted that, by the eve of the European partition of the continent, Africa had already revealed an emerging comparative advantage in export agriculture. In West Africa in particular it was in the joint interests of the population, European merchants, and the colonial administrations to further this. In Ghana British planters were initially allowed to enter to grow cocoa beans. But lacking the discriminatory support from the government that their counterparts enjoyed in Kenya and southern Africa, they failed in commercial competition with African producers, just as French planters were later to be eclipsed by African ones in Côte d'Ivoire following the abolition of *corvée*. Colonial reliance on the efforts of African small capitalists and peasants in the growing and local marketing of export crops paid off in what became Ghana and Nigeria, with more than 20-fold increases in the real value of foreign trade between 1897 and 1960 benefiting British commercial interests as well as (via customs duties) the colonial treasury. The efforts of W. H. Lever, the soap manufacturer, to win government permission, along with the necessary coercive support, to establish huge oil palm plantations in Nigeria continued from 1906 to 1925, but they were always rebuffed in favour of continued African occupation of virtually all agricultural land. Ultimately this was because African producers literally delivered the goods through land-extensive methods well adapted to the factor endowment. They rejected the advice of colonial agricultural officers when it conflicted with the requirements of efficient adaptation. The positive contribution of the administrations was to reinforce and permit the exploitation of these economies' comparative advantage in export agriculture. They did this partly by investment in transport infrastructure, investment to which African entrepreneurs also contributed. Equally important, although the colonial administration never really established a system of land titling, in Ghana (for example) it upheld the indigenous customary right of farmers to ownership of trees they had planted, irrespective of the outcome of any later litigation about the ownership of the land the trees stood upon. Thus, African producers enjoyed sufficient security of tenure to feel safe in investing in tree crops on a scale sufficient to create, in the case of Ghana, what became for nearly 70 years the world's largest cocoa economy.

South Africa had gold and diamonds, but their profitable exploitation required that the cost of labour be reduced far below what the physical labour-land ratio implied. C. H. Feinstein's quantitative exercise indicates that without such coercive intervention in the labour market, most of South Africa's mines would have been unprofitable until the end of the gold standard era in 1932. If South Africa eventually obtained a "free market" comparative advantage in mining, it was only after several decades of using extra-market means to repress black wages, notably through land appropriation and measures to stop Africans from working on European-owned land except as labourers rather than tenants.

Comparison of the economic legacies of European rule for poverty in "settler" and "peasant" economies is complicated by the many variations between individual colonies. However, some generalisations are possible. It is clear that the distribution of wealth and income was, and has remained, much more unequal in the "settler" economies than in the "peasant" ones. Preliminary findings by Sue Bowden, Blessing Chiripanhura, and Paul Mosley support the proposition that possession of land put a floor under real wages in the "peasant" colonies, enabling labourers migrating into export-crop growing areas to share in the gains from exports that were otherwise divided between European firms, African and Asian middlemen and African farm-owners. Bowden, Chiripanhura, and Mosley find real wages beginning to rise from the 1920s and 1930s in the "peasant" colonies of Ghana and Uganda respectively and not falling back afterwards to the 1914 floor. In contrast, it was only in the 1970s that the real wages of black gold-miners in South Africa began a sustained rise above their early 20th century level. In the sample taken by Bowden, Chiripanhura, and Mosley it was only in the "pure settler" economies, South Africa and Zimbabwe (Southern Rhodesia), not in the "peasant" colonies of Ghana or Uganda nor even in the intermediate case of Kenya, that there were declines in rural African living standards over periods of longer than 15 years within the 20th century. This pattern in real wages, together with the long-term expansion of African export agriculture which underpinned the growth of real wages in the "peasant" colonies, was reflected in the earlier onset of falling infant mortality in Ghana and Uganda compared to Southern Rhodesia and South Africa.

It should be added that many African colonies were short of both known mineral deposits and the kinds of land suitable for profitable export agriculture.

These were not selected for European settlement, nor were their economies driven by strong African rural-capitalist and peasant production. They had to rely on seasonal exports of male wage labourers, and on growing the less lucrative cash crops such as cotton, the timing of whose labour requirements conflicted with those of food crops, thereby creating risks to food security. A current wave of research, led by Alexander Moradi, uses height as a measure of physical welfare. The average height of African populations rose during the colonial period in Ghana and even in the "semi-settler" economy of Kenya. When this research is extended to poorer colonies such as southern Sudan, Tanganyika (mainland Tanzania), or those in the West African Sahel, it would be no surprise if welfare improvements there are found to have been smaller than in the better-endowed economies studied so far. It was particularly in (selected areas of) the less favourably-endowed economies that colonial governments sought to raise productivity through very large-scale, capital-intensive and authoritarian projects, notably the massive irrigation scheme of the Office du Niger in Mali and the mechanisation campaign of the East African Groundnut Project in Tanganyika. Both were spectacular failures in their own output and productivity terms, not least because they were inefficient in relation to the prevailing factor ratios and physical environments.

Poor as was the record of "settler" colonialism for the living standards of the indigenous population, it was in colonies where Europeans appropriated land on a large scale, for settlers or for companies, that the earlier and larger beginnings were made in modern manufacturing. Where industrialisation has occurred in Asia, it has tended to follow a more labour-intensive route than in Europe and North America, substituting longer working hours for additional machinery where possible and generally having a higher proportion of labour to capital at any given level of output. A region in which labour as well as capital was scarce in relation to land, such as Sub-Saharan Africa, was not well suited to follow either route in the early 20th century.

Yet, South Africa, followed on a smaller scale by Southern Rhodesia, acquired a substantial manufacturing sector by the time most of the rest of Africa achieved independence. The "artificially" low cost of black labour helped, but only in unskilled jobs because the skilled ones were anyway reserved for whites and the choice of technique was generally capital-intensive. Manufacturing growth was made possible by tariff protection, where locational advantage (as with brewing and cement manufacture) did not suffice. Crucially, mining provided the import-purchasing power to cover the import of capital goods and, where necessary, raw materials. It was also the direct or indirect source of much of the revenue used by governments to invest in manufacturing, whether directly or through the provision of infrastructure. The large European populations were a source of both educated workers and capital, but arguably their most important contribution to industrialisation was the political commitment to support it even at the cost of consumer prices that were often above world market levels.... Besides these "settler" colonies, there was a third case of precocious growth of modern manufacturing, the Belgian Congo. This was absolutely not a case of settler independence or autonomy. As in southern Africa, however, mines provided a favourable context for import-substituting industry, providing infrastructure, import-purchasing power and part of the market. South Africa remained the flagship of manufacturing in the region, but the scope for further expansion was increasingly restricted by the high price of skilled labour in an economy where only a minority of the population had access to secondary education and by the limited market for mass-produced goods that resulted from the low level of black wages. If the radical school was right about the contribution of repressive racial policies to economic growth in the early 20th century, the liberals were right about the period preceding the fall of apartheid: the system was now a brake, not a booster, on the development of the economy.

In 1960 modern manufacturing in South Africa was large but not very competitive internationally. In the rest of Sub-Saharan Africa it was much smaller. There were only two countries in which manufacturing accounted for more than 10% of recorded or officially-estimated GDP: Southern Rhodesia (16%) and the Belgian Congo (14%).... Given the relative scarcity of labour and the small markets, together with the comparative advantage in land-extensive primary production, it is not surprising that there was not much more manufacturing by the end of the colonial period. Where there were opportunities, colonial governments were rarely interested in upsetting the status quo in which colonial markets for manufactured goods were supplied largely by monopsonistic European merchants, selling goods disproportionately produced in the European metropolitan economy concerned. But given that, despite rising population, the factor endowments of even the larger African economies were not suited to industrialisation in 1960, the more important question is perhaps whether colonial rule, directly or indirectly, laid foundations on which Africa might later develop the conditions for a much larger growth of manufacturing.

Asian experience suggests that this would most plausibly take a labour-intensive form. In the long term the most fundamental change of the colonial period was probably the start of sustained population growth, which in aggregate can be dated from the end of the 1918 influenza pandemic, although local timing varied. How far the demographic breakthrough was the result of colonial actions, such as the suppression of slave raiding, the post-1918 peace within Africa and public health measures that reduced crisis mortality, is difficult to determine. The Sub-Saharan population is estimated to have doubled to about 200 million between 1900 and 1960. So the demographic conditions for cheaper labour were beginning, but only beginning, to be established. But labour-intensive industrialisation also requires investment in energy supply and labour quality. It needs workers who are disciplined and perhaps have specific skills or are trained to facilitate the acquisition of new ones. School enrolment rates rose during the colonial era from low or non-existent levels and in many countries doubled or tripled between 1950 and 1960. This was especially helped by African politicians gaining control of domestic budgets during the transition to independence, such as in Nigeria where primary enrolment was raised from 971,000 to 2,913,000 and secondary enrolment was raised from 28,000 to 135,000. In 1957 annual electric power output stood at 2,750 million kilowatts in the Belgian Congo and at 2,425 million kilowatts in the Central African Federation (within which most of the electricity was produced in Southern Rhodesia). In contrast, according to figures for the previous year, French West Africa produced a combined total of 138 million kilowatts, Nigeria 273 million kilowatts, and the rest of British West Africa 84 million kilowatts. Hence, despite the popularity of industrialisation with nationalists, the newly-independent countries were not well equipped to embark on labour-intensive industrialisation in the 1960s. Those that sought to industrialise opted for capital-intensive methods (subsidising capital, protective tariffs) and the factories tended to became creators of economic rents rather than of profits from competitive success.

African entrepreneurship has driven changes in the choice of products and in the means and organisation of production in various contexts before, during, and since colonial rule. This has been particularly conspicuous in West Africa, whose 19th century pre-colonial economies tended to be regarded as more market-oriented than those of the other major regions of Sub-Saharan Africa. The colonial impact on African entrepreneurship and on the markets in which they operated again turned to a large extent on whether there were large-scale appropriations of land for the use of Europeans, be they individual settlers or corporations.

This familiar division between "settler" and "plantation" colonies, on one hand, and "peasant" (and rural capitalist) colonies, on the other, was far from purely exogenous to African economic history. Where African producers were able to enter export markets early and on a wide scale, before European exporters really got going, their success was sufficient to tip the balance of the argument among colonial policy-makers in favour of those who thought it economically as well as politically wisest to leave agricultural production in African hands.... British West Africa was the major example of this. In South Africa, Southern Rhodesia, and Kenya African farmers responded quickly to opportunities to grow additional grain to supply internal markets. But the governments reacted by trying to drive Africans out of the produce market and into the labour market by reserving land for Europeans, while either prohibiting Africans from leasing it back or (as in inter-war Kenya) limiting the time that

African "squatters" could work for themselves rather than for their European landlords. African production for the market proved resilient, however, and the governments eventually accepted this and shifted to imposing controls on agricultural marketing that favoured European producers rather than trying to displace African ones. In Kenya it was only in the mid-1950s, during the Mau Mau revolt, that the government lifted restrictions on African production of high-value cash crops. Thus, to the extent that African production for the market in the late 19th century was greater in what became the "peasant" agricultural-export economies than in what became the "settler" economies, that contrast was reinforced by government actions in the latter over the following decades.

Not that the maintenance of African ownership of land necessarily entailed support for African capitalism. Admittedly, we have seen that the colonial state in Ghana protected the property of agricultural investors, in the sense of preserving the ownership of a farmer over trees or crops that he or she had planted, irrespective of the outcome of legal disputes about the ownership of the land on which they stood. But in "settler" and "peasant" colonies alike colonial governments were hesitant and usually hostile to the emergence of land markets in areas controlled by Africans. This policy eventually changed in Southern Rhodesia and Kenya, with selective promotion of land registration, in response to the *de facto* emergence of land sales and individual proprietorship (cultivable land having become increasingly scarce in the areas left to Africans) and with African land-owners being seen as a politically conservative force in the context of Mau Mau. In West Africa, without the settler pressure on African access to land, and given the expansion of cash crops that occurred early in the colonial period and again in the 1950s, neither the political case nor the economic case for compulsory land titling was as yet compelling. . . .

Colonial rule facilitated the import of capital into this capital-scarce continent. But only in mining, and to some extent in "settler" and "plantation" agriculture, did this happen on a large scale. The survey by Herbert S. Frankel (1938) of external capital investment in white-ruled Africa remains the only comprehensive study for the colonial period. According to Frankel, in gross and nominal terms, during 1870-1936 such investment totaled £1,221 million, of which 42.8% was in South Africa. This meant £55.8 per head in South Africa, but only £3.3 in the French colonies and £4.8 in British West Africa. Public investment constituted 44.7% of the grand total and almost 46% of the non-South Africa total. Governments, and to some extent mining and plantation companies, invested in the transport infrastructure required for the development of, mainly, the export-import trade. In Nigeria and Ghana, Africans also took a leading role in building motor roads and pioneering lorry services. In institutional terms the colonial period saw the eventual abolition of human pawning, with its replacement by promissory notes and, in those areas of West

Africa where it was possible, by loans on the security of cocoa farms. It also saw the introduction of modern banking, but the banks were much more willing to accept Africans' savings than to offer them loans, partly because of the colonial governments' non-introduction of compulsory land titling. . . .

Until the advent of independence it remained the case in the "peasant" colonies that the markets dominated by Europeans (shipping, banking, the export-import trade, banking) were cartelistic, whereas the markets populated by Africans were characterised by extreme competition. Despite this, the more economically successful "peasant" colonies saw the continuation of a tradition of entrepreneurship and mostly (but not always) small-scale accumulation in agriculture, crafts and trade. The result, as John Iliffe noted, was "a strong contrast between West Africa, with its long-established capitalistic sector and its entrepreneurs from artisanship and trade, and eastern and southern Africa, where entrepreneurs had emerged chiefly through . . . Western education and modern sector employment." Early post-colonial policy did not always build on this, for example in the case of Ghana, with high taxation of export agriculture and the creation of state monopolies in certain sectors.

It is widely accepted that states have a critical role in economic development, at least in enforcing the rules of economic activity and providing physical public goods. Therefore, we should ask how colonial rule affected the historic constraint on political centralisation in Africa, namely the difficulty of raising revenue. Beyond this we need to consider the size of the state and the nature of authority and legitimacy; whether colonisation was responsible for fragmenting Africa, as is often said, or whether, as the colonial rulers themselves claimed, they were a modernising force, bringing the state to the "stateless" and replacing patrimonial authority with bureaucratic authority. [*Editors' note: This debate is examined in Chapter II of this volume.*]

Colonial administrations themselves suffered acute budgetary constraints. Although European empires introduced to Africa the possibility of raising loan finance (at least in an impersonal, law-governed though undemocratic way), the colonial administrations were restricted in their resort to money markets by the metropolitan insistence that each colony be fiscally self-sufficient and balance its budget. The introduction in each colony of a single currency as legal tender probably reduced net transaction costs (although in some cases the demonetisation of existing currencies hurt Africans holding them). But the metropolitan treasuries denied their colonial subordinates the autonomy to print money. . . .

Given that they faced much the same practical constraints as the African states that had preceded them, colonial governments generally continued the reliance of pre-colonial kingdoms upon taxes on trade and people, rather than on land or agriculture. It was the above-mentioned discovery, during the Second World War, that the export marketing board could be a major revenue-raiser, which was the major fiscal innovation of colonial rule. As independence approached, this unintended consequence of a wartime expedient offered African politicians unprecedented opportunities to, for example, transform educational opportunities for their populations. The marketing board as a fiscal instrument was an important colonial legacy, and its possibilities and implications were only beginning to be understood. By the 1980s the limits of the device had become clear, as ordinary traders and producers could evade it by trading on parallel markets. . . .

Amidst the varying and/or poor growth records of post-colonial African economies, Botswana has stood out. Acemoglu, Johnson and Robinson argue that it is an exception that proves the rule, i.e., that while Botswana did not have the beneficial institutional legacy characteristic of the "full settler" colonies like Australia, it was exceptionally lightly ruled by Britain and as a result escaped the worst of the extractive propensities that they see as generally characteristic of non-"settler" colonialism. In my view two considerations point to a different conclusion. First, without the discovery of diamonds, it is hard to see how post-colonial Botswana could have grown dramatically faster than colonial Bechuanaland. Indeed, during the first three decades of independence the non-diamond mining sector of Botswana did no better than Zambia. Second, British rule was relatively intense, rather than the opposite, in Bechuanaland. By the criterion of the number of Africans per administrator, *circa* 1937 it was fifth out of 33 African colonies.

The limited revenue-generating potential of African colonies (especially before some of the more spectacular mineral discoveries) helps to explain the decisions of the French and British governments, faced with rising popular expectations channeled into growing nationalist movements, to accept early decolonisation. Simultaneously French firms were apparently becoming less interested in colonial economies. If so, it is ironic that the French government remained closely involved with its former colonies after their independence, not least through the franc zone. Again, in the 1950s British firms on the spot expressed concern about their future under independent African governments, but they failed to attract much notice from the decolonising authorities. The irony of the latter case is that a few years later the British government's attitude to the Biafran secession was influenced by the interests of British oil companies. . . .

Colonial governments and European firms invested in both infrastructure and (especially in southern Africa) in institutions designed to develop African economies as primary-product exporters. In both cases the old economic logic for coercing labour continued to operate: the continued existence of slavery in early colonial tropical Africa and the use of large-scale land grabs to promote migrant labour flows in "settler" economies. But there were changes and variations. While we have noted differences between French and British policy, for example in West Africa, the bigger contrasts were between "peasant" and "settler" colonies.

In British West Africa in particular, there was a genuine coincidence of interest between African farmers, European merchants, and colonial governments in enlarging and exploiting West Africa's comparative advantage in land-extensive agriculture. The resultant income at least enabled many of the slave-owners to become employers instead. In these cases the British government (and the French in Côte d'Ivoire after 1945) correctly recognised where their own self-interest lay when they supported African investment in export agriculture. It was in those "peasant" colonies that were best endowed with lands suitable for producing the more lucrative crops that African populations experienced significant improvements in purchasing power and had the most improvement in physical welfare. In the same countries, however, colonial rulers, partly because of fiscal constraints as well as a probably realistic assessment of the short-term economic prospects, did little directly to prepare the economies to move "up the value chain." Thus, the first generation of postcolonial rulers presided over economies which were as yet too short of educated (and cheap) labour and sufficient (and sufficiently cheap) electricity to embark successfully on industrialisation. It has taken post-colonial investment in education and other public goods to move West African economies, and tropical Africa generally, closer to the prospect of a substantial growth of labour-intensive manufacturing, if international competition permits it.

"Settler" colonies had a worse record for poverty reduction, especially considering the mineral resources of South Africa and Southern Rhodesia, but they had a better one for structural change. The large-scale use of coercion was the basis for the construction of white-ruled economies that, especially in South Africa, eventually became profitable enough for a partly politically-impelled policy of import-substituting industrialisation to achieve some success. Thus, the rents extracted from African labourers were channeled into structural change, although the process became self-defeating as it progressed, contributing to the fall of apartheid.

As promoters of market institutions, the colonial regimes had a very mixed record; but probably in all Sub-Saharan countries there was far more wage labour, and a lot more land sales, and a lot more people more deeply dependent on markets, by 1960 than there had been in 1890 or 1900. A final legacy of the colonial period has a rather unclear relationship to colonial policy: the sustained growth of (total) population since 1918 has progressively transformed the factor ratios and, on the whole, increased the long-term economic potential of the continent.

Suggested Readings

Austen, Ralph, *African Economic History: Internal Development and External Dependency* (London: J. Currey, 1987).
Brett, E. A., *Colonialism and Underdevelopment in East Africa: The Politics of Economic Change, 1919-1939* (London: Heinemann, 1973).
Daryll Forde, Cyril, and Margery Freda Bower, *The Economics of a Tropical Dependency* (London: Faber and Faber, 1946).
Davidson, Basil, *Which Way Africa? The Search for a New Society* (Baltimore, MD: Penguin Books, 1964).
_____, *Modern Africa: A Social and Political History* (London: Longmans, 1989).
Falola, Toyin, ed., *Britain and Nigeria: Exploitation or Development?* (London: Zed Press, 1987).
Heldring, Leander, and James A. Robinson, "Colonialism and Economic Development in Africa," web-published at http://www.nber.org/papers/w18566.
Howard, Rhoda, *Colonialism and Underdevelopment in Ghana* (London: Groom Helm, 1978).
Huttenback, Robert, *Mammon and the Pursuit of Empire: The Economics of British Imperialism* (New York: Cambridge University Press, 1988).
Kitching, Gavin, *Development and Underdevelopment in Historical Perspective* (London: Routledge, 1989).
Memmi, Albert, *The Colonizer and the Colonized* (Boston: Beacon Press, 1967).
Offiong, Daniel, *Imperialism and Dependency: Obstacles to African Development* (Washington, D.C.: Howard University Press, 1982).
Suret-Canale, Jean, *French Colonialism in Tropical Africa, 1900-1945* (New York: Pica Press, 1971).
Williams, Eric, *Capitalism and Slavery* (Chapel Hill: University of North Carolina Press, 1944).
Woolf, Leonard, *Empire and Commerce in Africa: A Study of Economic Imperialism* (New York: H. Fertig, 1968).

Acknowledgments

The editor gratefully acknowledges the following authors and publishers: The Humanities Press International, Inc., Atlantic Highlands, NJ, for permission to reprint from *Africa and the Victorians: The Official Mind of Imperialism* (1961) by Ronald Robinson and John Gallagher, pp. 163, 166, 168-74, 274, 281-89, 376-78; Gareth Austin for permission to print an edited version of his essay "African Economic Development and Colonial Legacies" web-published in "International Development Policy," January 2010, at www.poldev.revues.org/78; Cambridge University Press for permission to reprint "Connections between Primary Resistance Movements and Modern Mass Nationalism in East and Central Africa: Part 1," and "Connections between Primary Resistance Movements and Modern Mass Nationalism in East and Central Africa: Part 2," by Terence Ranger, originally published in *The Journal of African History* 9, no. 3 (1968), pp. 437-53, and *The Journal of African History* 9, no. 4 (1968), pp. 631-41, "The Invention of Tradition in Colonial Africa" from Eric Hobsbawm and Terence Ranger, eds., *The Invention of Tradition* (2nd edition, 2012), pp. 211-63, and from Melissa Leach and James Fairhead *Misreading the African Landscape: Society and Ecology in a Forest-Savanna Mosaic* (1996), pp. 1-21; Frank Cass Publishers for permission to reprint from *The Dual Mandate in British Tropical Africa* by John Frederick Lugard (1965), pp. 94-97, 102-5, 199-218; The International African Institute, London School of Economics, for permission to reprint "Et Maintenant, Lord Lugard" by Hubert Jules Deschamps, which appeared in the journal *Africa* 33, no. 4 (1963), pp. 293-305; Howard University Press for permission to reprint an excerpt from *How Europe Underdeveloped Africa* by Walter Rodney (1982), pp. 223-38, 240-41, 243, 245-47, 249-53; L. H. Gann and Peter Duignan for permission to reprint from *Burden of Empire: An Appraisal of Western Colonialism in Africa South of the Sahara* (1967), pp. v-vii, 229-31, 234, 236-52; George Weidenfeld & Nicholson for permission to reprint from *The Colonial Empires: A Comparative Survey from the Eighteenth Century* by D. K. Fieldhouse (1967), pp. 380-87, 389-94; Northwestern University Press for permission to reprint from *West Africa under Colonial Rule* by Michael Crowder (1986), pp. 345-53.

Grateful appreciation is also expressed to Johns Hopkins University Press for permission to reprint from *African Perspectives on Colonialism* by A. Boahen (1987), pp. 94-112; *The English Historical Review* for permission to reprint "Imperialism and the Victorians: The Dynamics of Territorial Expansion" by John Darwin, 112, no. 447 (June 1997), pp. 614-42; Oxford University Press for permission to reprint from *Tools of Empire: Technology and European Im-*

perialism in the 19th Century by Daniel Headrick (1981), pp. 58-76; Michael Adas for permission to reprint from *Machines as the Measure of Men: Science, Technology, and Ideologies of Western Dominance* (Ithaca, NY: Cornell University Press, 1989) pp. 153-66; The University of Wisconsin Press for permission to reprint from *No Condition Is Permanent: The Social Dynamics of Agrarian Change in Sub-Saharan Africa* by Sara Berry (1993), pp. 24-35; Princeton University Press for permission to reprint from Mahmood Mamdani, *Citizen and Subject: Contemporary Africa and the Legacy of Late Colonialism* (1996), pp. 72-90; *The International Journal of African Historical Studies* for permission to reprint David Gordon's "Owners of the Land and Lunda Lords: Colonial Chiefs in the Borderlands of Northern Rhodesia and the Belgian Congo" 34, no. 2 (2001), pp. 315-38; Brill Publishing for permission to reprint Aidan Southall's "The Illusion of Tribe," published in *The Journal of Asian and African Studies* 5, 1-2 (January 1970), pp. 28-50; The University of California Press and James Currey/Boydell for permission to reprint "Ethnicity in Southern African History" by Leroy Vail, originally published in *The Creation of Tribalism in Southern Africa* (1991), pp. 1-20; Indiana University Press for permission to reprint from *Religious Encounter and the Making of the Yoruba* by J.D.Y Peel (2003), pp. 278-309; Harvard University Press for permission to reprint from *Terrific Majesty: Shaka Zulu and the Limits of Historical Invention* by Carolyn Hamilton (1998), pp. 25-35, and from *Political Change in a West African State: A Study of the Modernization Process in Sierra Leone* by Martin Kilson (1966), pp. 53-54, 60-67, 68-72, 89-93.

Also to Grove/Atlantic for permission to reprint excerpts from *The Wretched of the Earth* by Frantz Fanon (1963), pp. 208-35; *Canadian Journal of African Studies/Revue Canadienne des Études Africaines* for permission to reprint from Bruce Berman's "Nationalism, Ethnicity, and Modernity: The Paradox of Mau Mau," 25, no. 2 (1991), pp. 181-206; Random House for permission to reprint from *The Black Man's Burden: Africa and the Curse of the Nation-State* by Basil Davidson (1992), pp. 162-67, 173, 180, 182, 185 (used by permission of Times Books, an imprint of Random House LLC); William Beinart for permission to reprint his address "African History and Environmental History"; Taylor & Francis for permission to reprint "Ecology and History: The Example of Eastern Zambia" by Leroy Vail from *The Journal of Southern African Studies* 3, no. 2 (April 1977), pp. 129-55, and from P. J. Cain and A. G. Hopkins, *British Imperialism, 1688-2000* (2nd edition, 2003); JoAnn McGregor for permission to reprint "Conservation, Control and Ecological Change: The Politics and Ecology of Colonial Conservation in Shurugwi, Zimbabwe," originally published in *Environment and History* 1, no. 3, Zimbabwe (October 1995), pp. 257-79; The University of Chicago Press for permission to reprint from *Africa as a Living Laboratory: Empire, Development, and the Problem of Scientific Knowledge, 1870-1950* by Helen Tilley (2011), pp. 117-34.